SEVEN SEAS ENTERTAI

Spirit

story and art by **SATOSHI MIZUKAMI**

TRANSLATION
Jocelyne Allen

ADAPTATION
Ysabet Reinhardt MacFarlane

LETTERING AND LAYOUT
Lys Blakeslee

COVER DESIGN
Nicky Lim

PROOFREADER
Shanti Whitesides
Danielle King

ASSISTANT EDITOR
Jenn Grunigen

PRODUCTION ASSISTANT
CK Russell

PRODUCTION MANAGER
Lissa Pattillo

EDITOR-IN-CHIEF
Adam Arnold

PUBLISHER
Jason DeAngelis

Originally published in Japan in 2015 by SHONENGAHOSHA Co., Ltd., Tokyo.
English translation rights arranged through TOHAN CORPORATION, Tokyo.

ISBN: 978-1-626927-29-2

Printed in Canada

First Printing: April 2018

10 9 8 7 6 5 4 3 2 1

FOLLOW US ONLINE: ***www.sevenseasentertainment.com***

READING DIRECTIONS

This book reads from ***right to left***, Japanese style. If this is your first time reading manga, you start reading from the top right panel on each page and take it from there. If you get lost, just follow the numbered diagram here. It may seem backwards at first, but you'll get the hang of it! Have fun!!

1
2
3
4
5
6
7
8
9

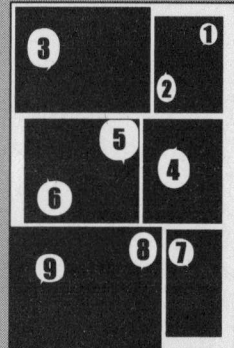

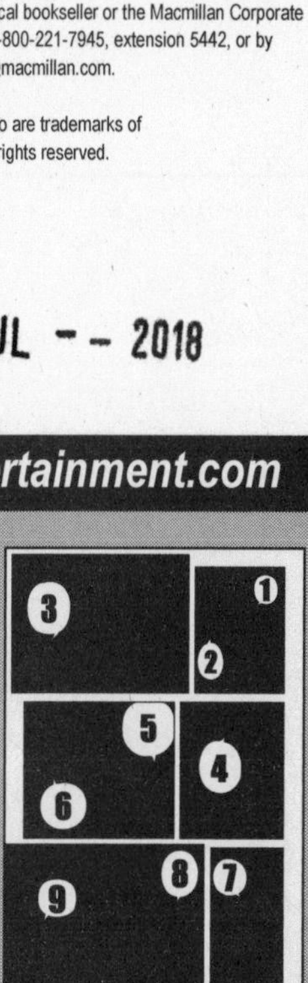

Volume 3

Production staff
Jueru Choden
Hitoshi Usui
Akira Sagami

Title logo/Cover design
Eiichi Hagiwara (bigbody)

Supervising editor
Takehiro Sumi

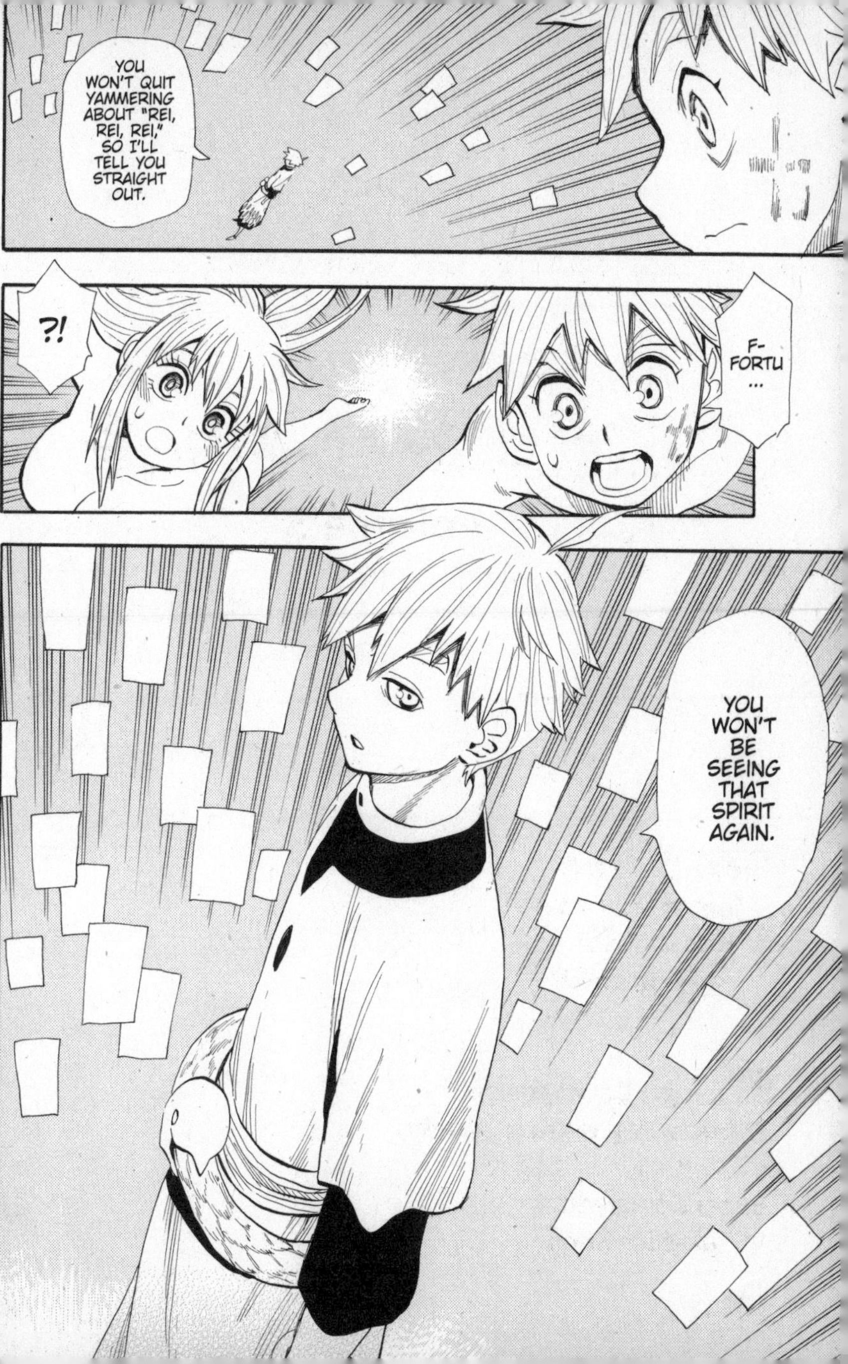
YOU WON'T QUIT YAMMERING ABOUT "REI, REI, REI," SO I'LL TELL YOU STRAIGHT OUT.
F-FORTU...
?!
YOU WON'T BE SEEING THAT SPIRIT AGAIN.
Circle.21/END

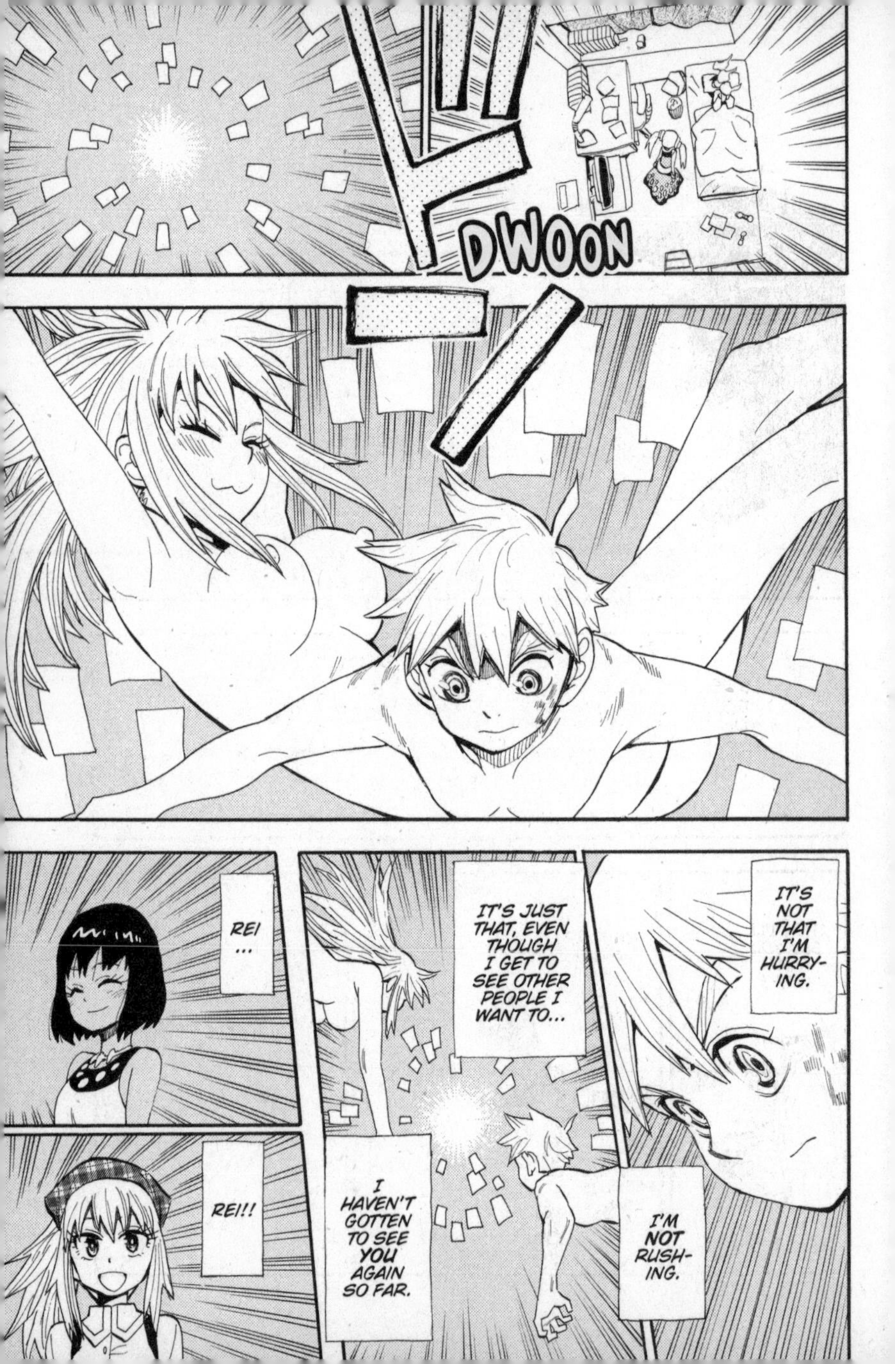
DWOON
IT'S NOT THAT I'M HURRY-ING.
I'M NOT RUSH-ING.
IT'S JUST THAT, EVEN THOUGH I GET TO SEE OTHER PEOPLE I WANT TO...
I HAVEN'T GOTTEN TO SEE YOU AGAIN SO FAR.
REI...
REI!!

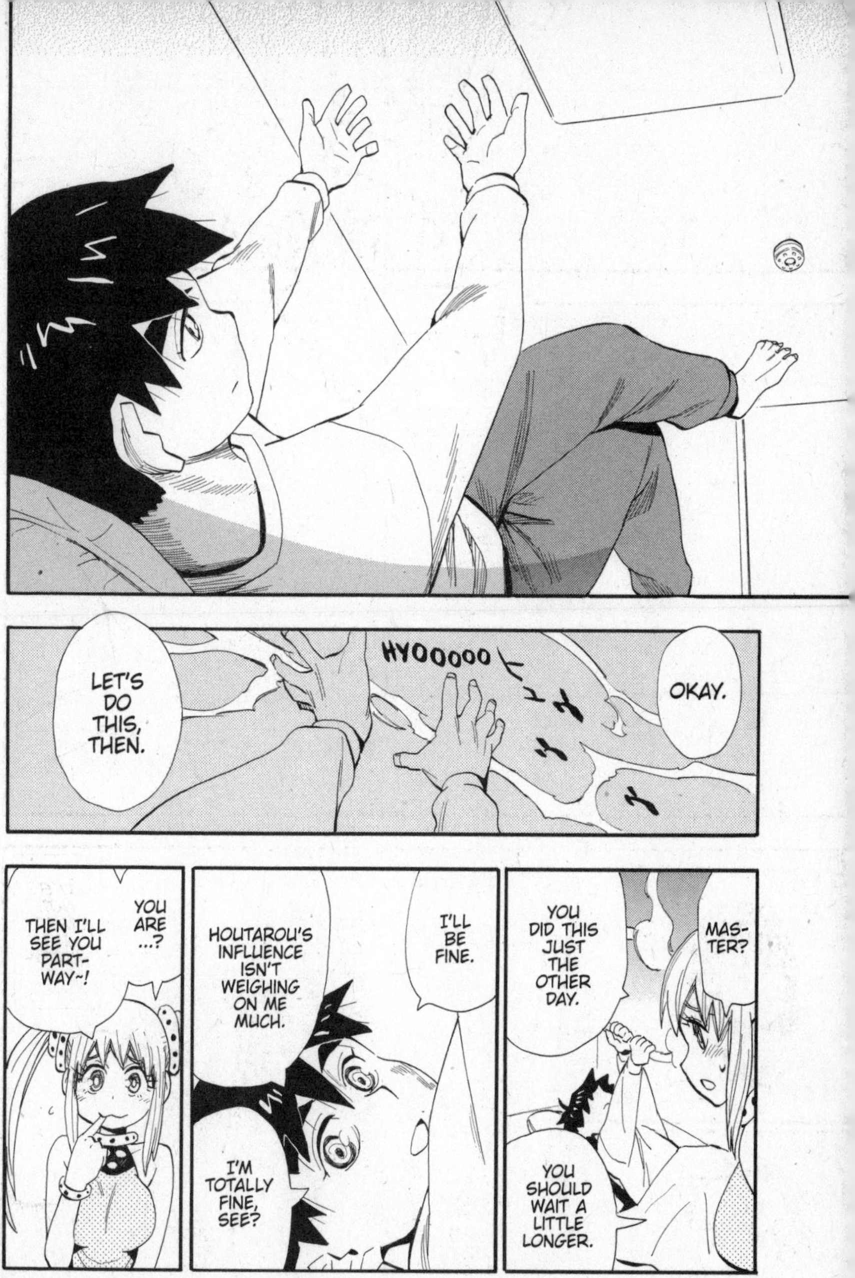
OKAY.
HYOOOOO
LET'S DO THIS, THEN.
MAS-TER?
YOU DID THIS JUST THE OTHER DAY.
YOU SHOULD WAIT A LITTLE LONGER.
I'LL BE FINE.
HOUTAROU'S INFLUENCE ISN'T WEIGHING ON ME MUCH.
I'M TOTALLY FINE, SEE?
YOU ARE ...?
THEN I'LL SEE YOU PART-WAY~!

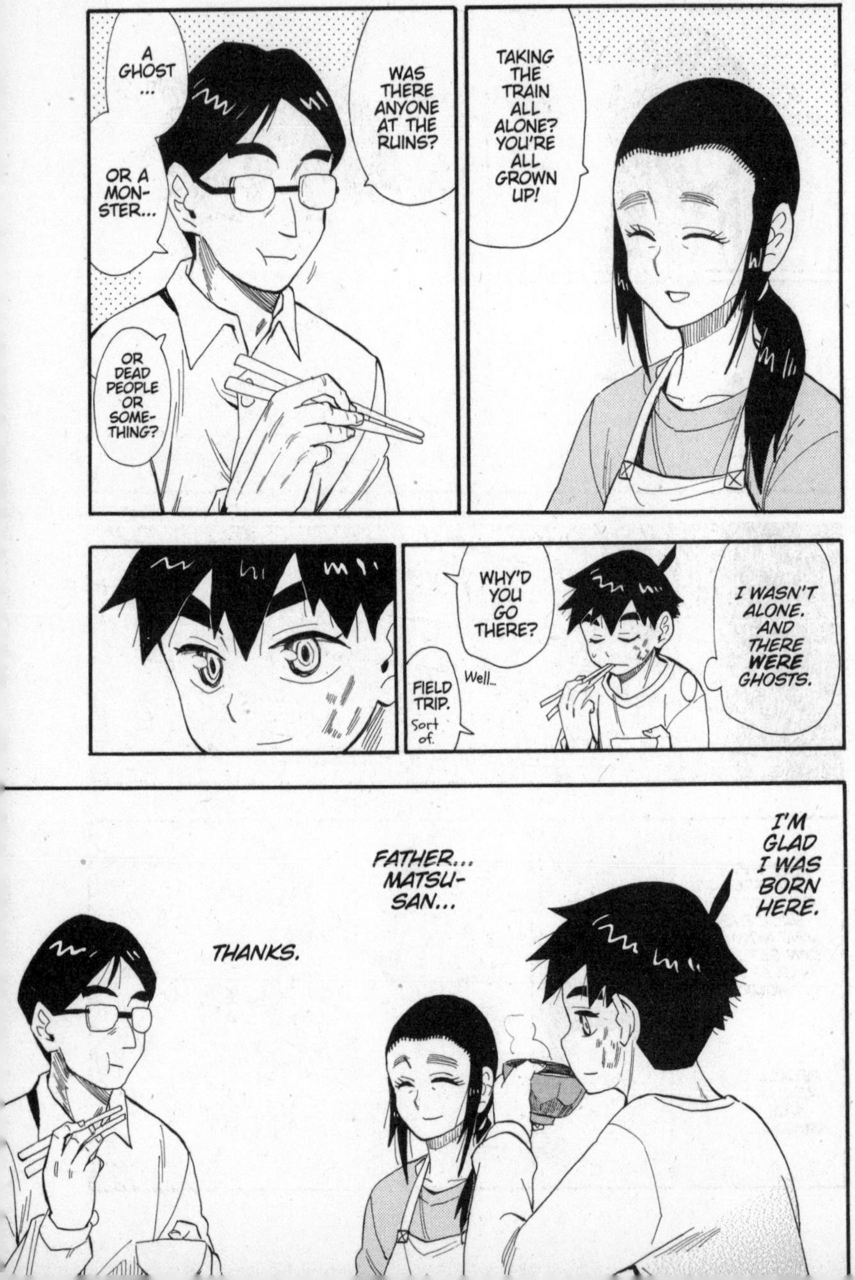
TAKING THE TRAIN ALL ALONE? YOU'RE ALL GROWN UP!
WAS THERE ANYONE AT THE RUINS?
A GHOST ...
OR A MON-STER...
OR DEAD PEOPLE OR SOME-THING?
I WASN'T ALONE. AND THERE WERE GHOSTS.
WHY'D YOU GO THERE?
Well...
FIELD TRIP.
Sort of.
I'M GLAD I WAS BORN HERE.
FATHER... MATSU-SAN...
THANKS.

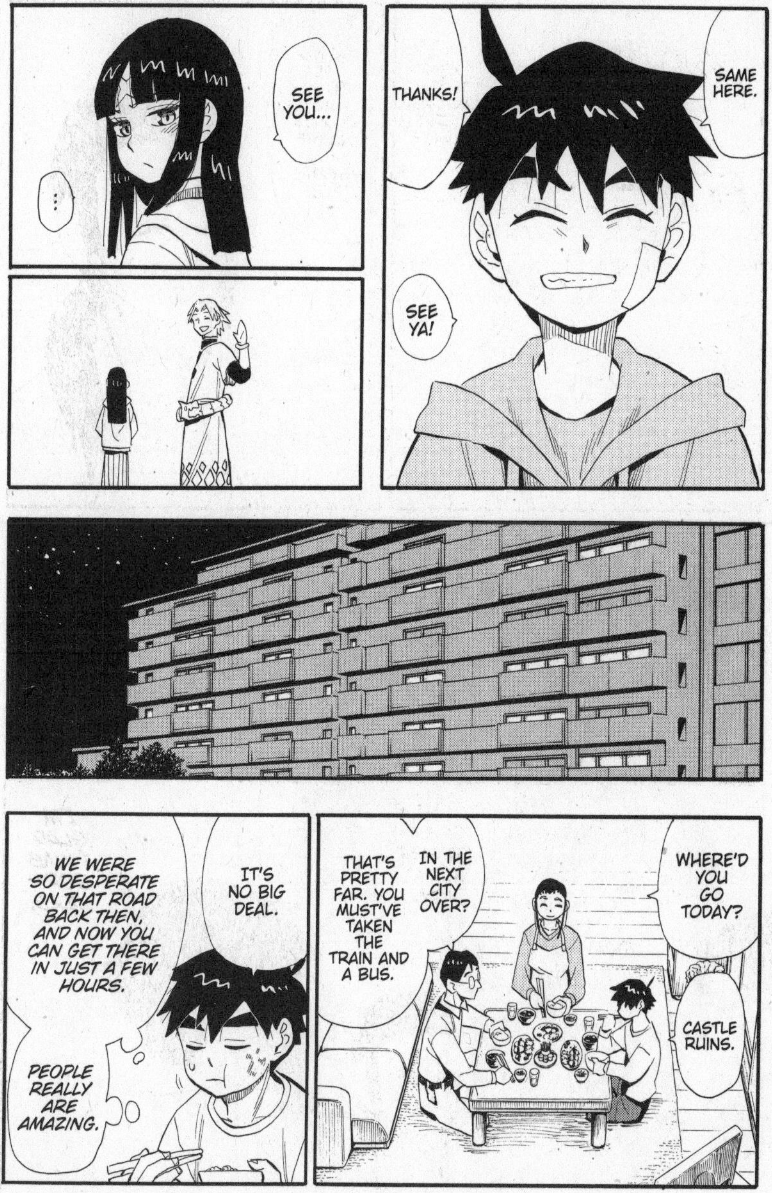
SAME HERE.
THANKS!
SEE YA!
SEE YOU...
...
WHERE'D YOU GO TODAY?
CASTLE RUINS.
IN THE NEXT CITY OVER?
THAT'S PRETTY FAR. YOU MUST'VE TAKEN THE TRAIN AND A BUS.
IT'S NO BIG DEAL.
WE WERE SO DESPERATE ON THAT ROAD BACK THEN, AND NOW YOU CAN GET THERE IN JUST A FEW HOURS.
PEOPLE REALLY ARE AMAZING.

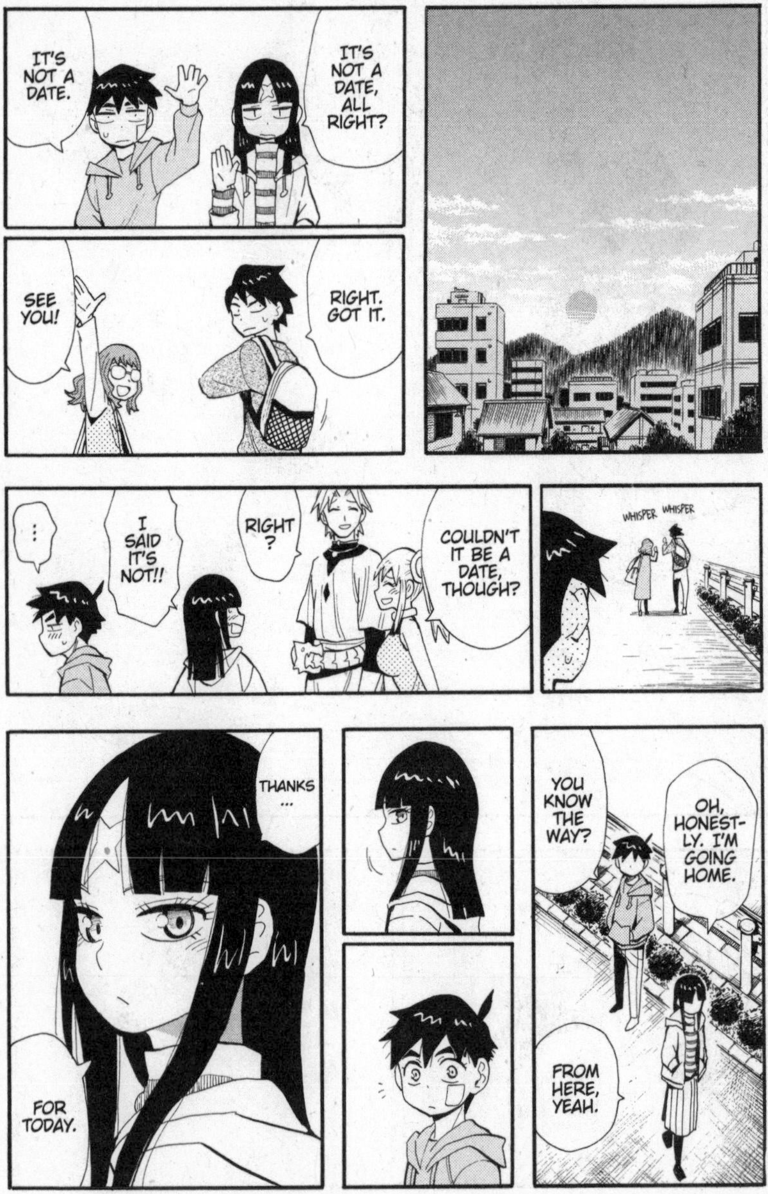
IT'S NOT A DATE, ALL RIGHT?
IT'S NOT A DATE.
RIGHT. GOT IT.
SEE YOU!
WHISPER WHISPER
COULDN'T IT BE A DATE, THOUGH?
RIGHT?
I SAID IT'S NOT!!
...
OH, HONESTLY. I'M GOING HOME.
YOU KNOW THE WAY?
FROM HERE, YEAH.
THANKS...
FOR TODAY.

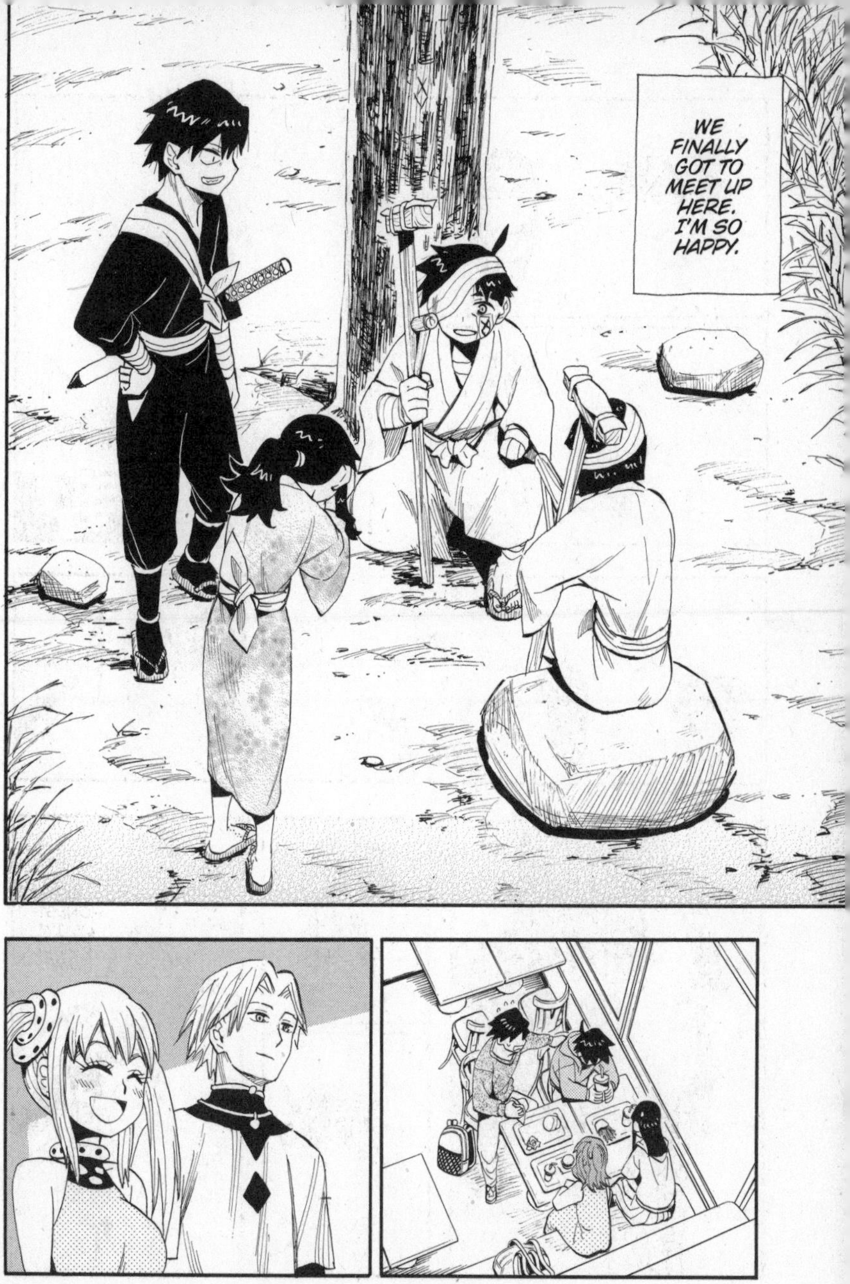
WE FINALLY GOT TO MEET UP HERE. I'M SO HAPPY.

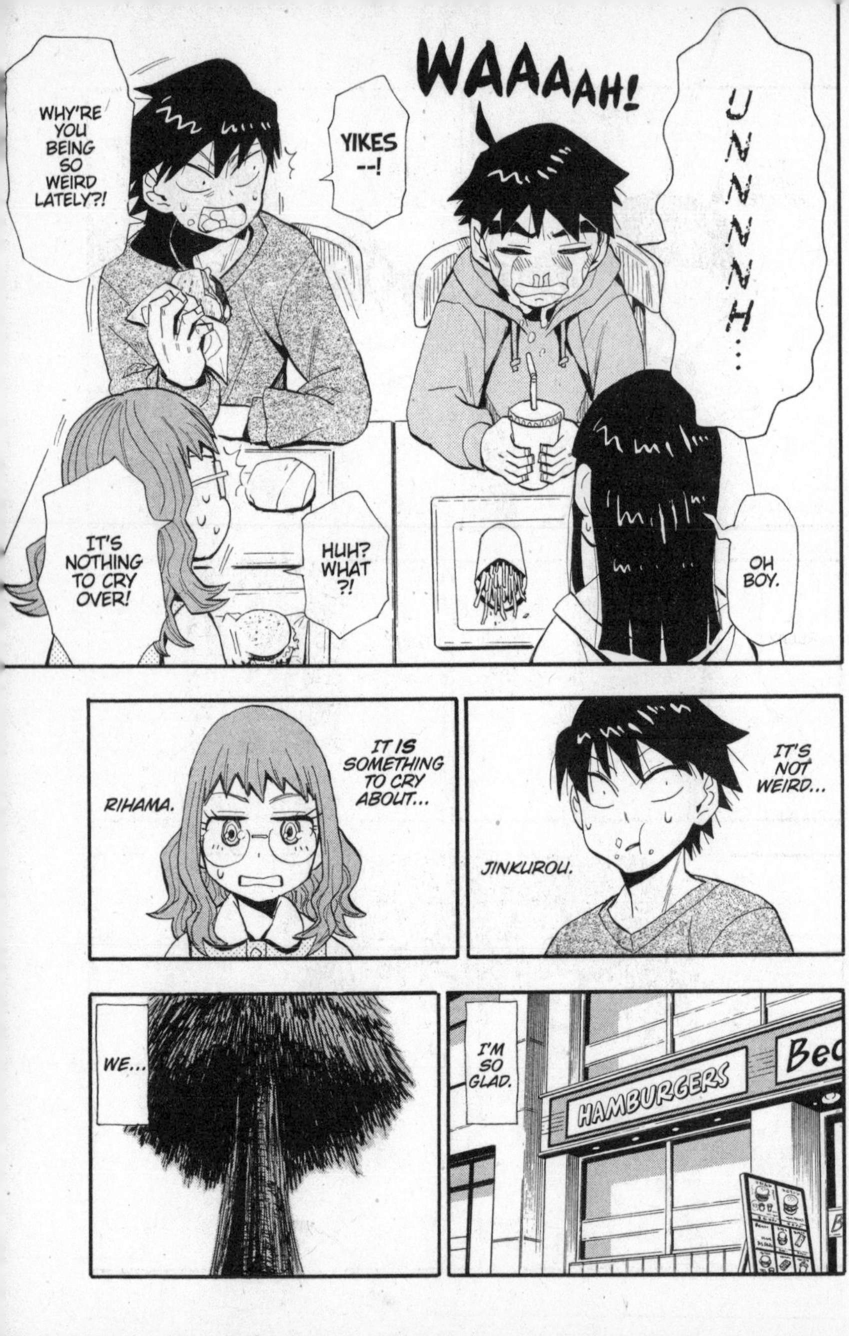
UNNNNH...
WAAAAAH!
YIKES --!
WHY'RE YOU BEING SO WEIRD LATELY?!
OH BOY.
HUH? WHAT?!
IT'S NOTHING TO CRY OVER!
IT'S NOT WEIRD...
JINKUROU.
IT IS SOMETHING TO CRY ABOUT...
RIHAMA.
I'M SO GLAD.
HAMBURGERS
WE...

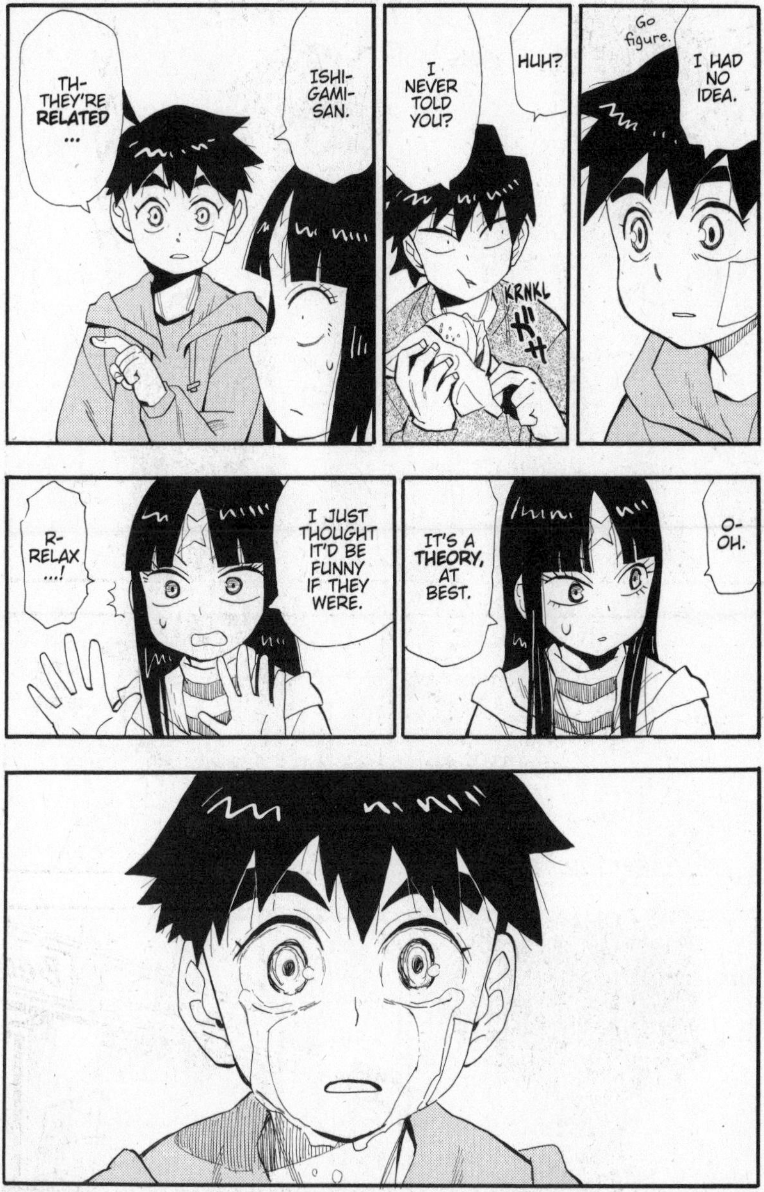
I HAD NO IDEA.
Go figure.
HUH?
I NEVER TOLD YOU?
KRNKL
ISHI-GAMI-SAN.
TH-THEY'RE RELATED...
O-OH.
IT'S A THEORY, AT BEST.
I JUST THOUGHT IT'D BE FUNNY IF THEY WERE.
R-RELAX...!

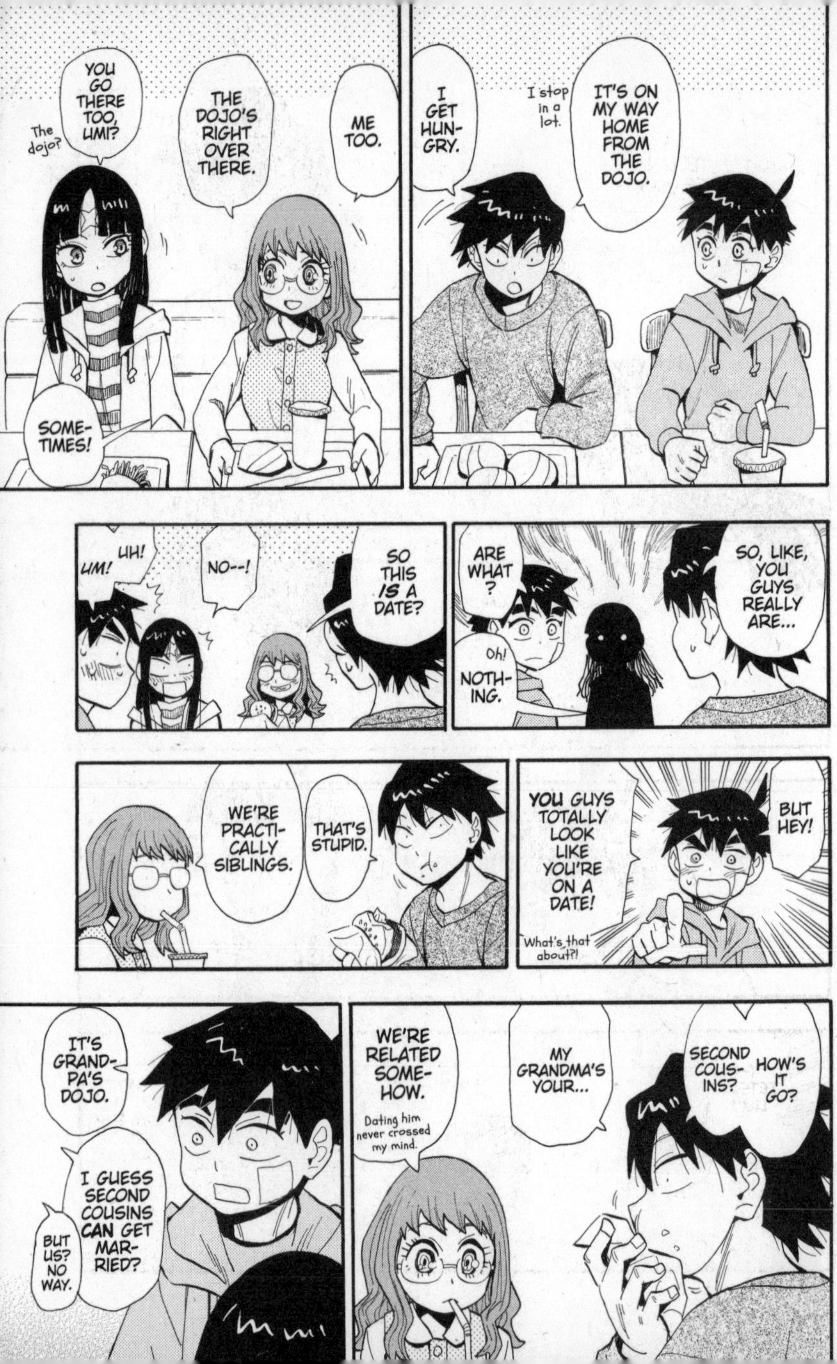
IT'S ON MY WAY HOME FROM THE DOJO.
I stop in a lot.
I GET HUNGRY.
ME TOO.
THE DOJO'S RIGHT OVER THERE.
YOU GO THERE TOO, UMI?
The dojo?
SOMETIMES!
SO, LIKE, YOU GUYS REALLY ARE...
ARE WHAT?
Oh! NOTHING.
SO THIS IS A DATE?
NO--!
UH!
UM!
BUT HEY!
YOU GUYS TOTALLY LOOK LIKE YOU'RE ON A DATE!
What's that about?!
THAT'S STUPID.
WE'RE PRACTICALLY SIBLINGS.
HOW'S IT GO?
SECOND COUSINS?
MY GRANDMA'S YOUR...
WE'RE RELATED SOMEHOW.
Dating him never crossed my mind.
IT'S GRANDPA'S DOJO.
I GUESS SECOND COUSINS CAN GET MARRIED?
BUT US? NO WAY.

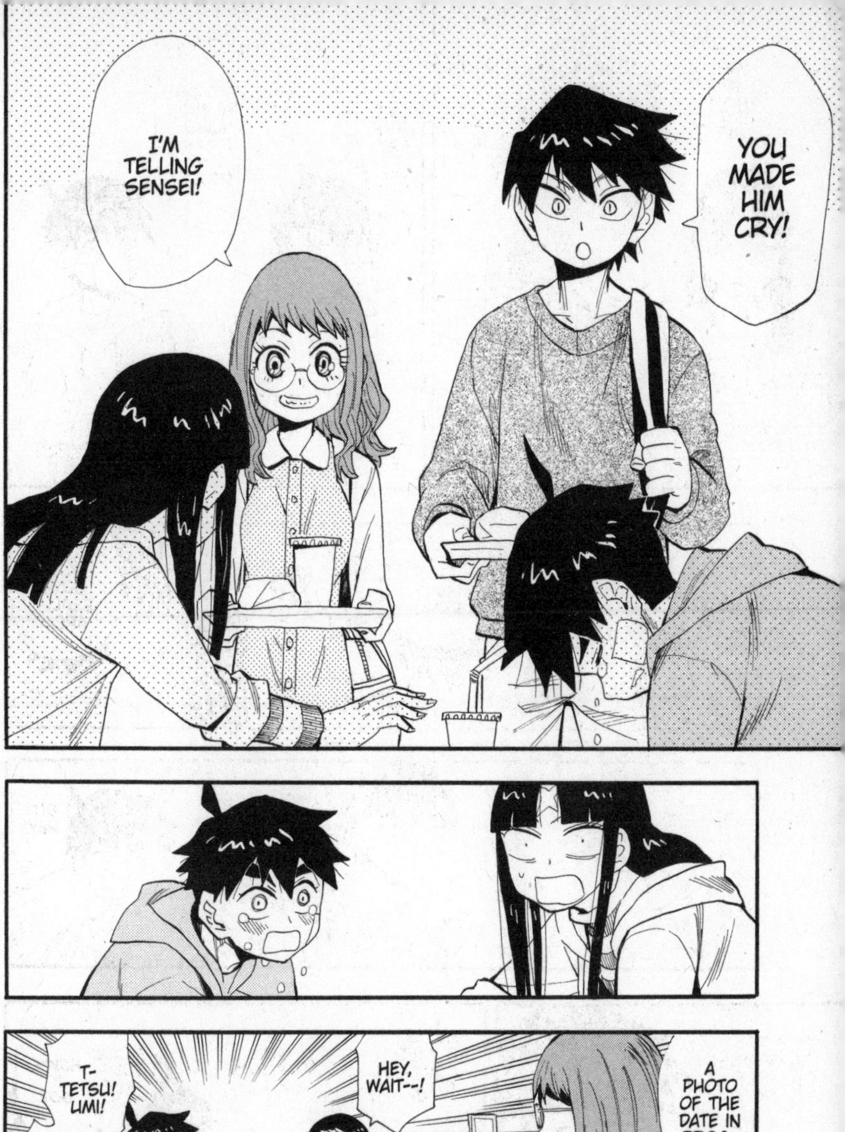
YOU MADE HIM CRY!
I'M TELLING SENSEI!
A PHOTO OF THE DATE IN PROGRESS!
KA-SNAP
HEY, WAIT--!
T-TETSU! UMI!
WHAT'RE YOU DOING HERE?!

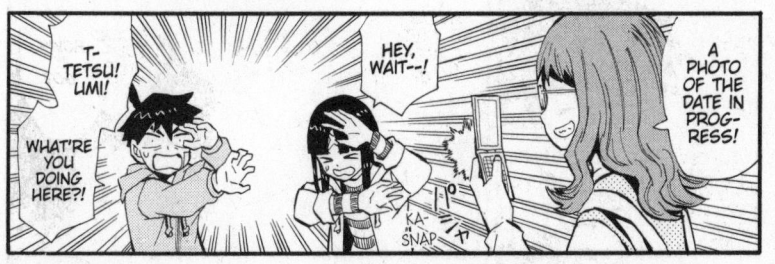

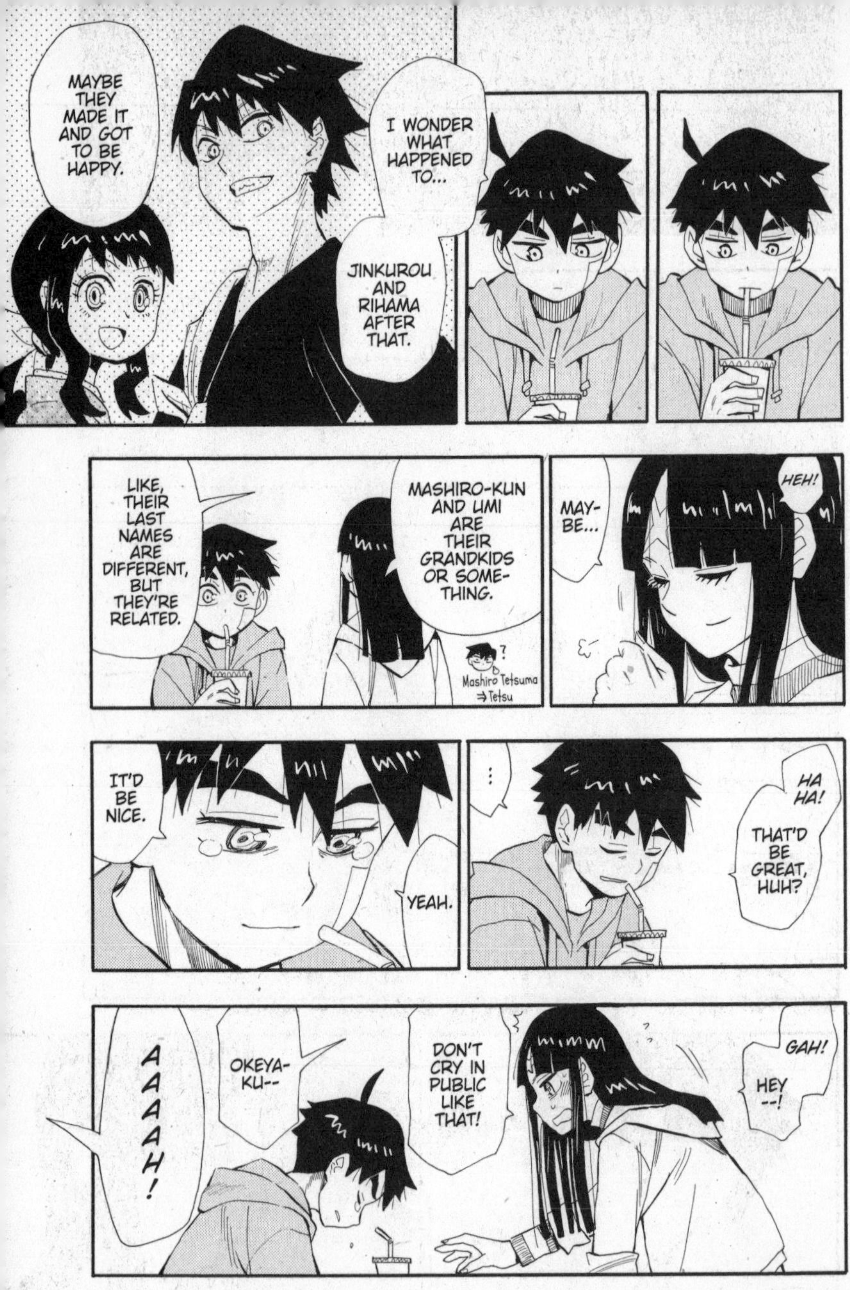
I WONDER WHAT HAPPENED TO...
JINKUROU AND RIHAMA AFTER THAT.
MAYBE THEY MADE IT AND GOT TO BE HAPPY.
HEH!
MAY-BE...
MASHIRO-KUN AND UMI ARE THEIR GRANDKIDS OR SOME-THING.
Mashiro Tetsuma ⇒ Tetsu
LIKE, THEIR LAST NAMES ARE DIFFERENT, BUT THEY'RE RELATED.
HA HA!
THAT'D BE GREAT, HUH?
...
YEAH.
IT'D BE NICE.
GAH!
HEY --!
DON'T CRY IN PUBLIC LIKE THAT!
OKEYA-KU--
AAAAAH!

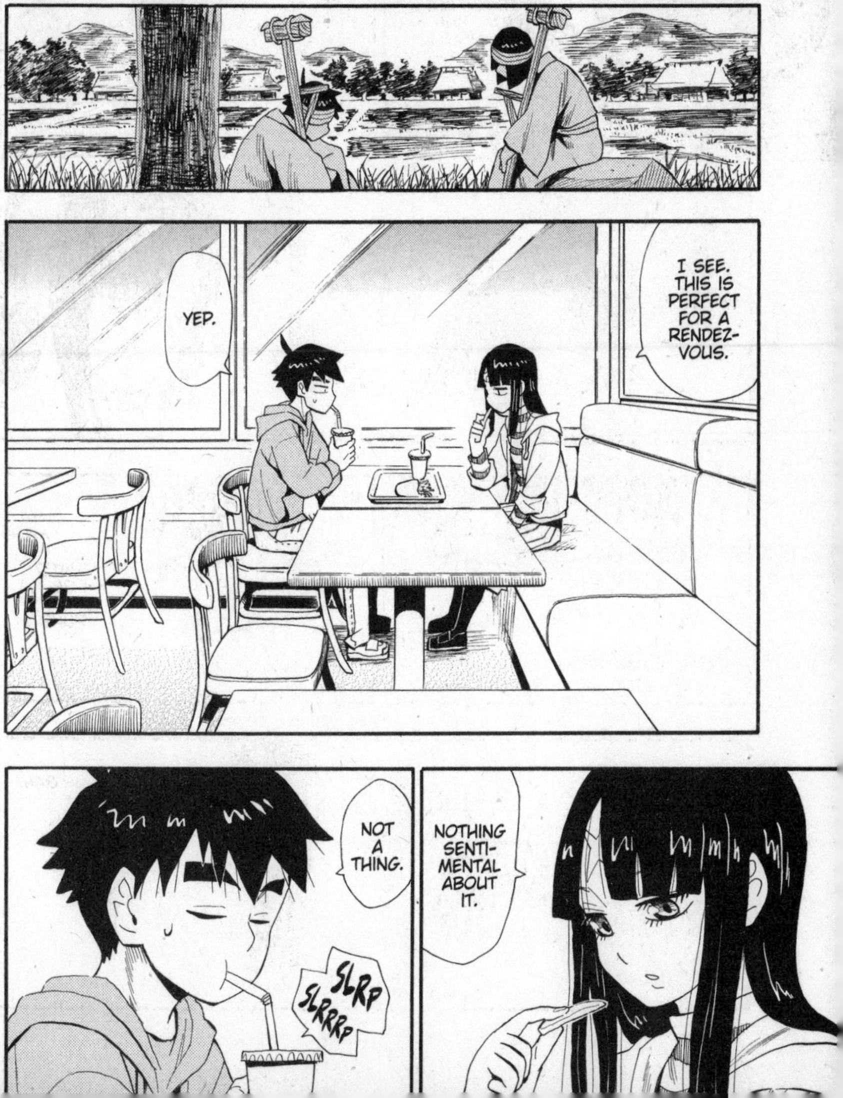
I SEE. THIS IS PERFECT FOR A RENDEZ-VOUS.
YEP.
NOTHING SENTI-MENTAL ABOUT IT.
NOT A THING.
SLRP
SLRRRP

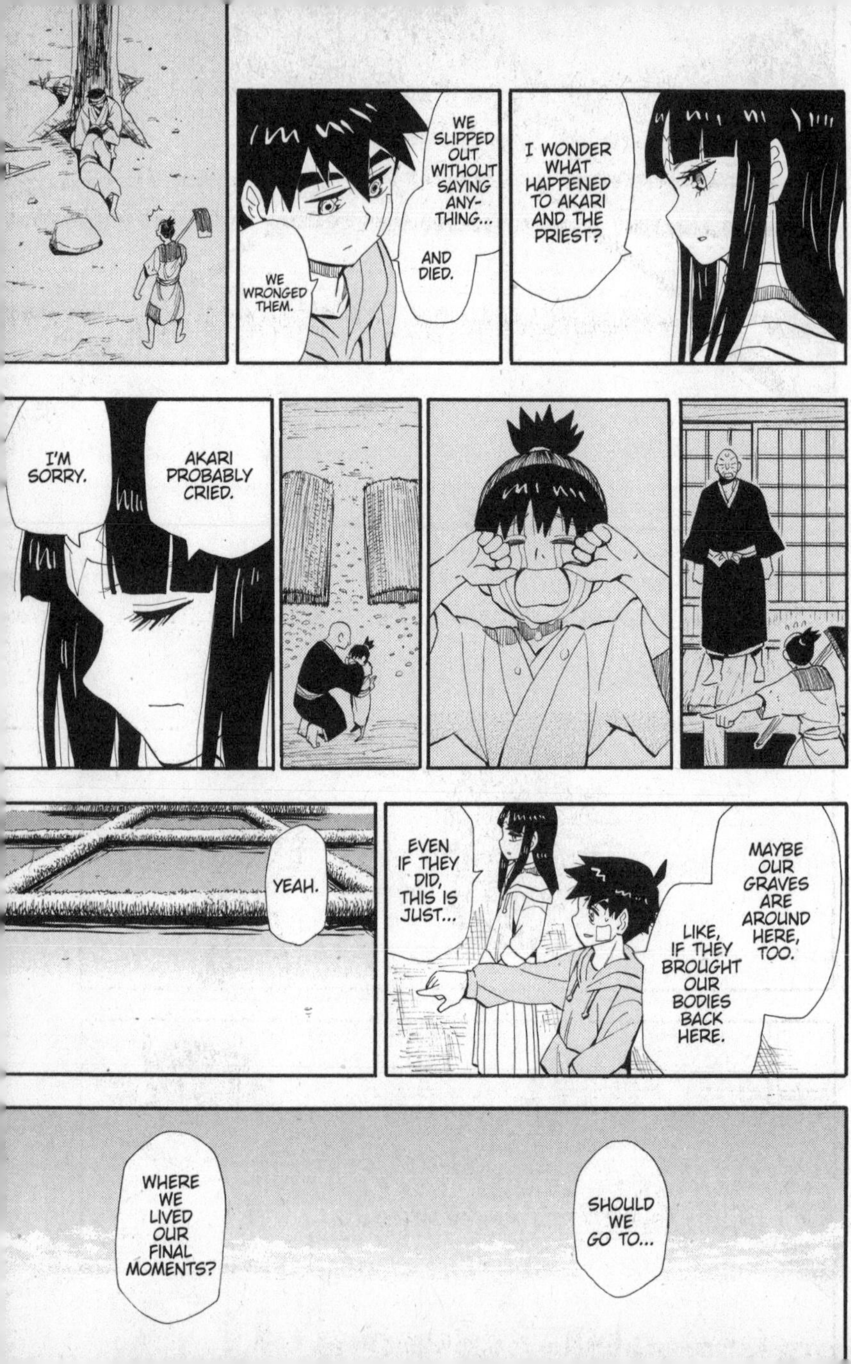
I WONDER WHAT HAPPENED TO AKARI AND THE PRIEST?
WE SLIPPED OUT WITHOUT SAYING ANY-THING...
AND DIED.
WE WRONGED THEM.
AKARI PROBABLY CRIED.
I'M SORRY.
MAYBE OUR GRAVES ARE AROUND HERE, TOO.
LIKE, IF THEY BROUGHT OUR BODIES BACK HERE.
EVEN IF THEY DID, THIS IS JUST...
YEAH.
SHOULD WE GO TO...
WHERE WE LIVED OUR FINAL MOMENTS?

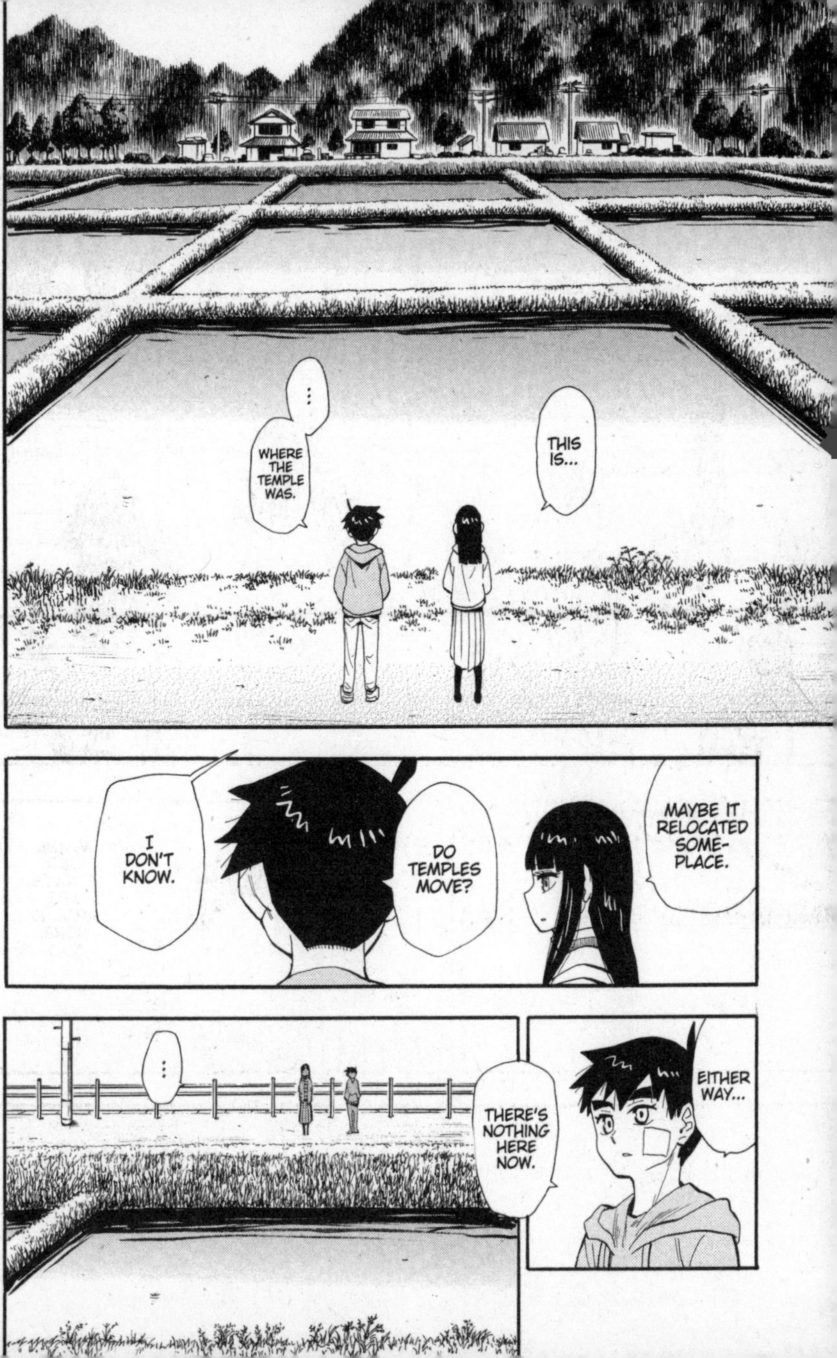
THIS IS...
...
WHERE THE TEMPLE WAS.
MAYBE IT RELOCATED SOME-PLACE.
DO TEMPLES MOVE?
I DON'T KNOW.
EITHER WAY...
THERE'S NOTHING HERE NOW.
...

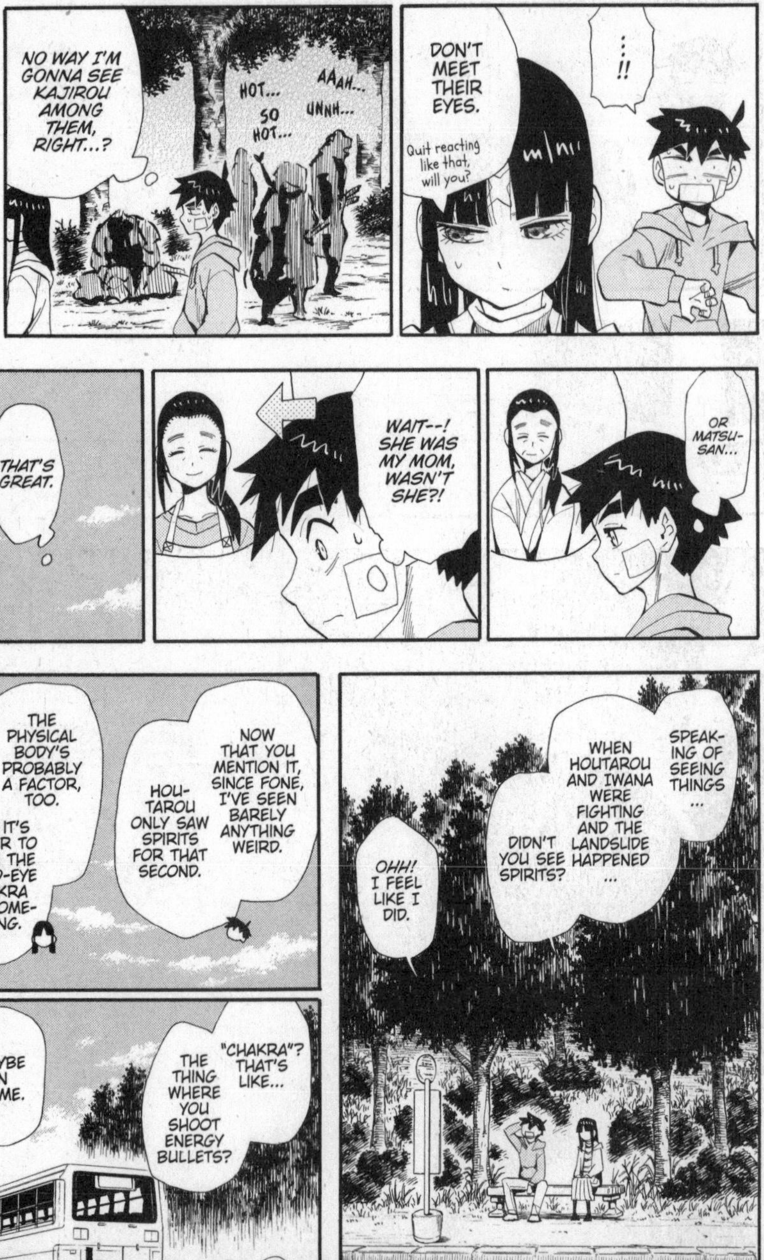
...!!
DON'T MEET THEIR EYES.
Quit reacting like that, will you?
NO WAY I'M GONNA SEE KAJIROU AMONG THEM, RIGHT...?
AAAH...
HOT...
UNNH...
SO HOT...
OR MATSU-SAN...
WAIT--! SHE WAS MY MOM, WASN'T SHE?!
THAT'S GREAT.
SPEAKING OF SEEING THINGS...
WHEN HOUTAROU AND IWANA WERE FIGHTING AND THE LANDSLIDE HAPPENED...
DIDN'T YOU SEE SPIRITS?
OHH! I FEEL LIKE I DID.
NOW THAT YOU MENTION IT, SINCE FONE, I'VE SEEN BARELY ANYTHING WEIRD.
HOUTAROU ONLY SAW SPIRITS FOR THAT SECOND.
THE PHYSICAL BODY'S PROBABLY A FACTOR, TOO.
LIKE IT'S EASIER TO OPEN THE THIRD-EYE CHAKRA OR SOMETHING.
"CHAKRA"? THAT'S LIKE...
THE THING WHERE YOU SHOOT ENERGY BULLETS?
MAYBE IN ANIME.

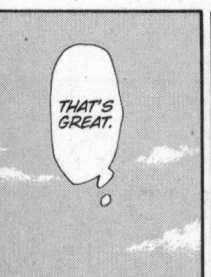

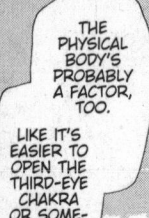

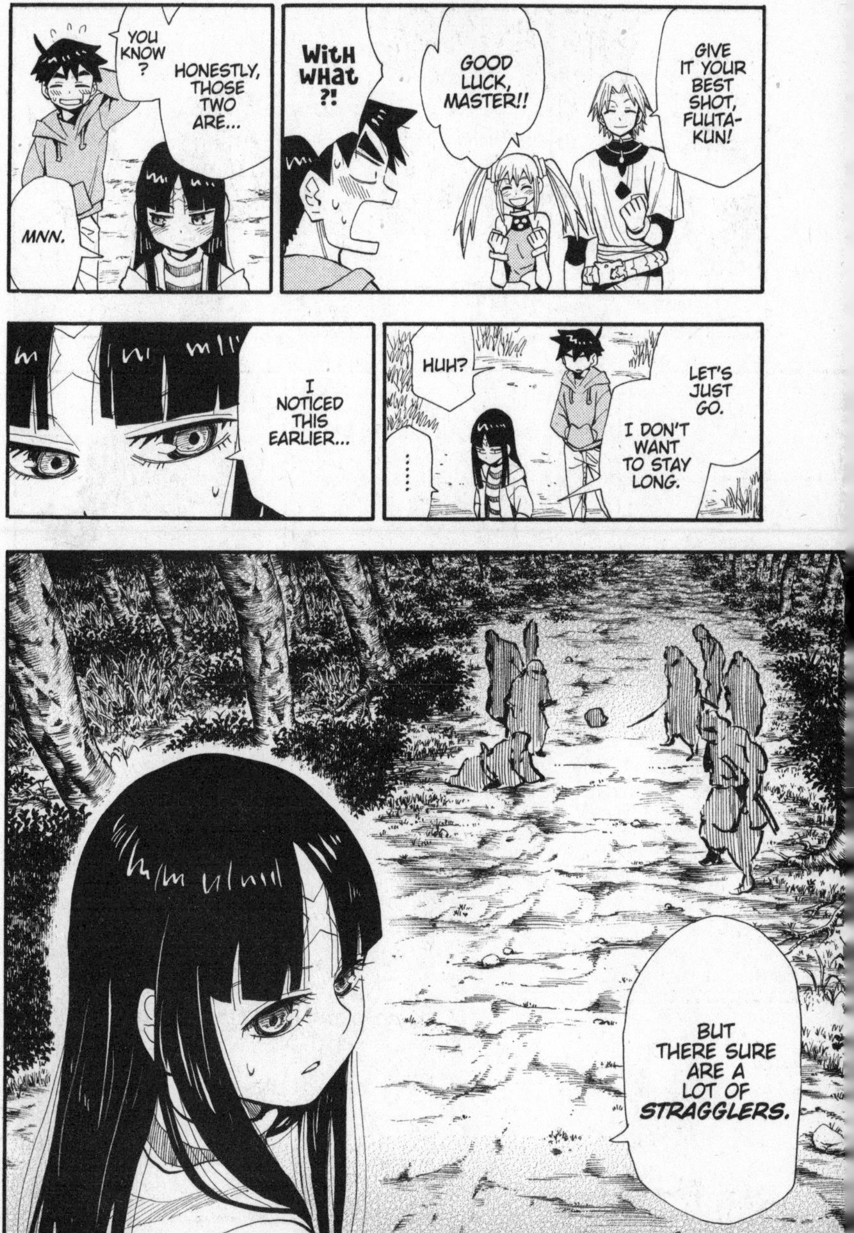
GIVE IT YOUR BEST SHOT, FUUTA-KUN!
GOOD LUCK, MASTER!!
WITH WHAT ?!
HONESTLY, THOSE TWO ARE...
YOU KNOW ?
MNN.
LET'S JUST GO.
I DON'T WANT TO STAY LONG.
HUH?
......
I NOTICED THIS EARLIER...
BUT THERE SURE ARE A LOT OF STRAGGLERS.

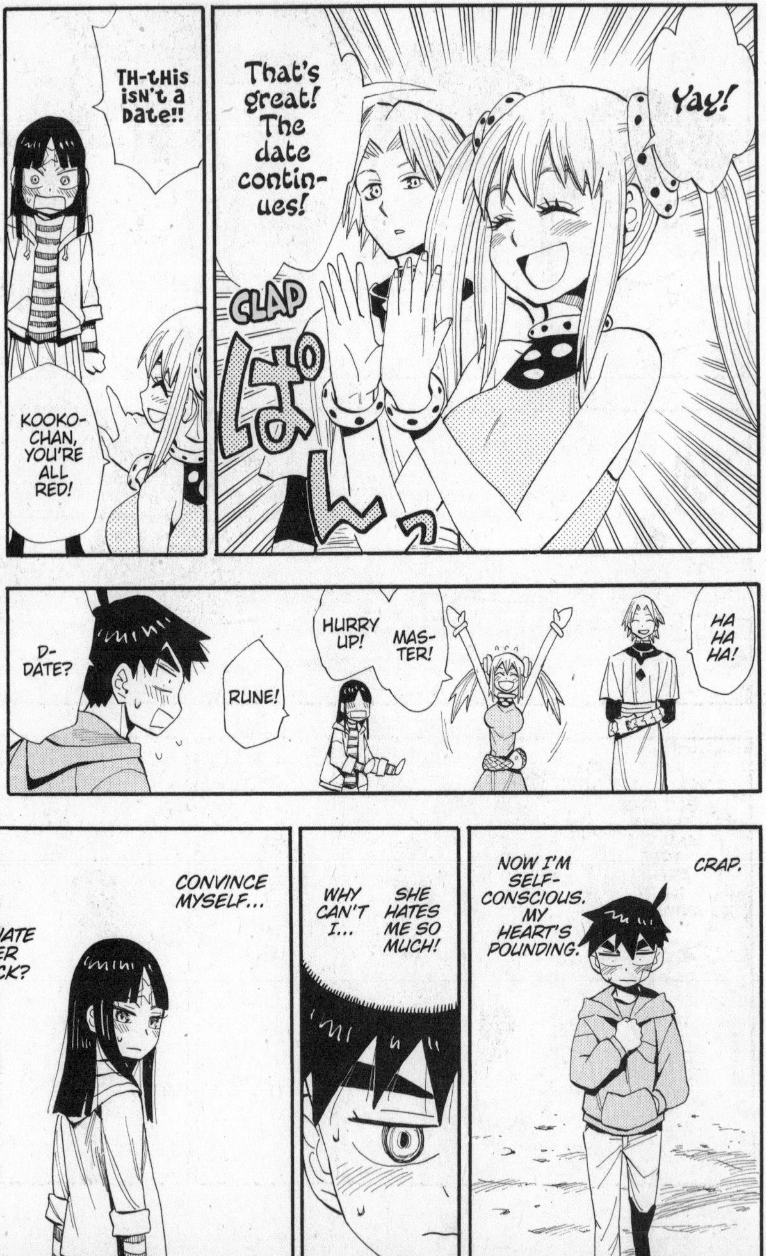
Yay!
That's great! The date contin-ues!
CLAP
ぱんっ
TH-tHis isn't a Date!!
KOOKO-CHAN, YOU'RE ALL RED!
HA HA HA!
HURRY UP! MAS-TER!
RUNE!
D-DATE?
CRAP.
NOW I'M SELF-CONSCIOUS. MY HEART'S POUNDING.
SHE HATES ME SO MUCH!
WHY CAN'T I...
CONVINCE MYSELF...
TO HATE HER BACK?

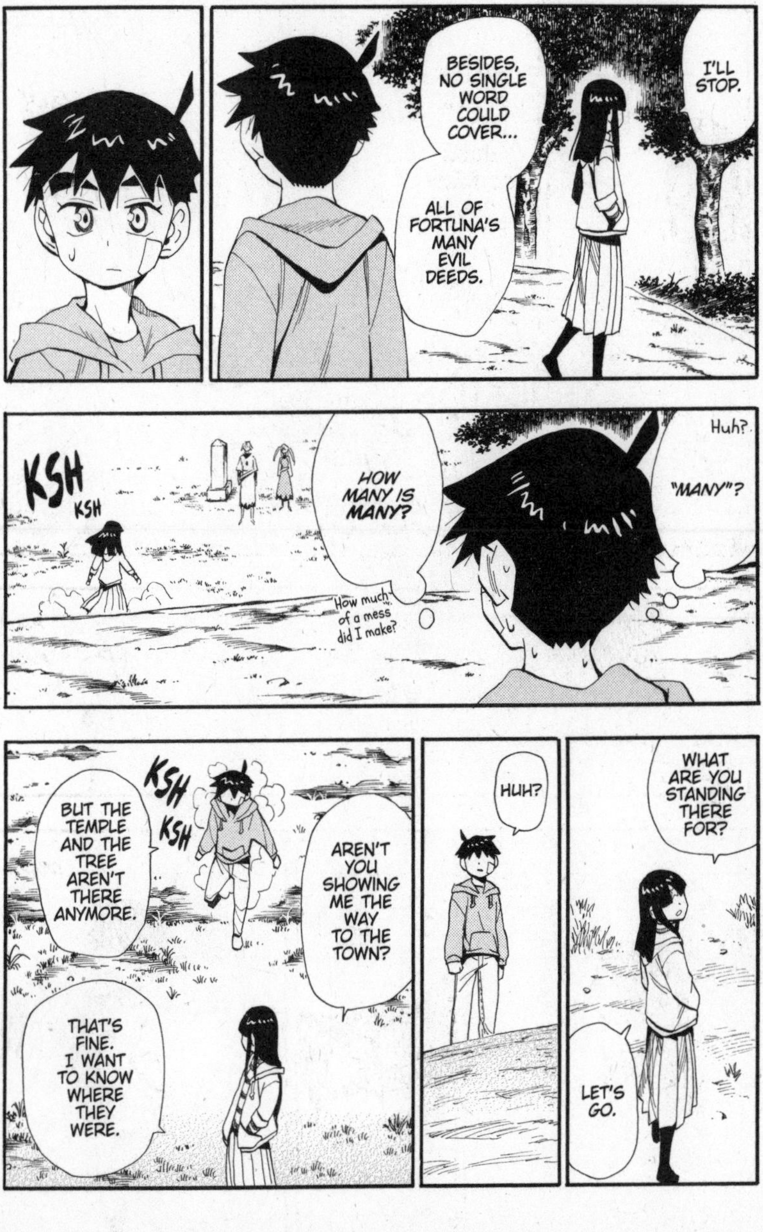
I'LL STOP.
BESIDES, NO SINGLE WORD COULD COVER...
ALL OF FORTUNA'S MANY EVIL DEEDS.
Huh?
"MANY"?
HOW MANY IS MANY?
How much of a mess did I make?
KSH KSH
WHAT ARE YOU STANDING THERE FOR?
LET'S GO.
HUH?
KSH KSH
AREN'T YOU SHOWING ME THE WAY TO THE TOWN?
BUT THE TEMPLE AND THE TREE AREN'T THERE ANYMORE.
THAT'S FINE. I WANT TO KNOW WHERE THEY WERE.

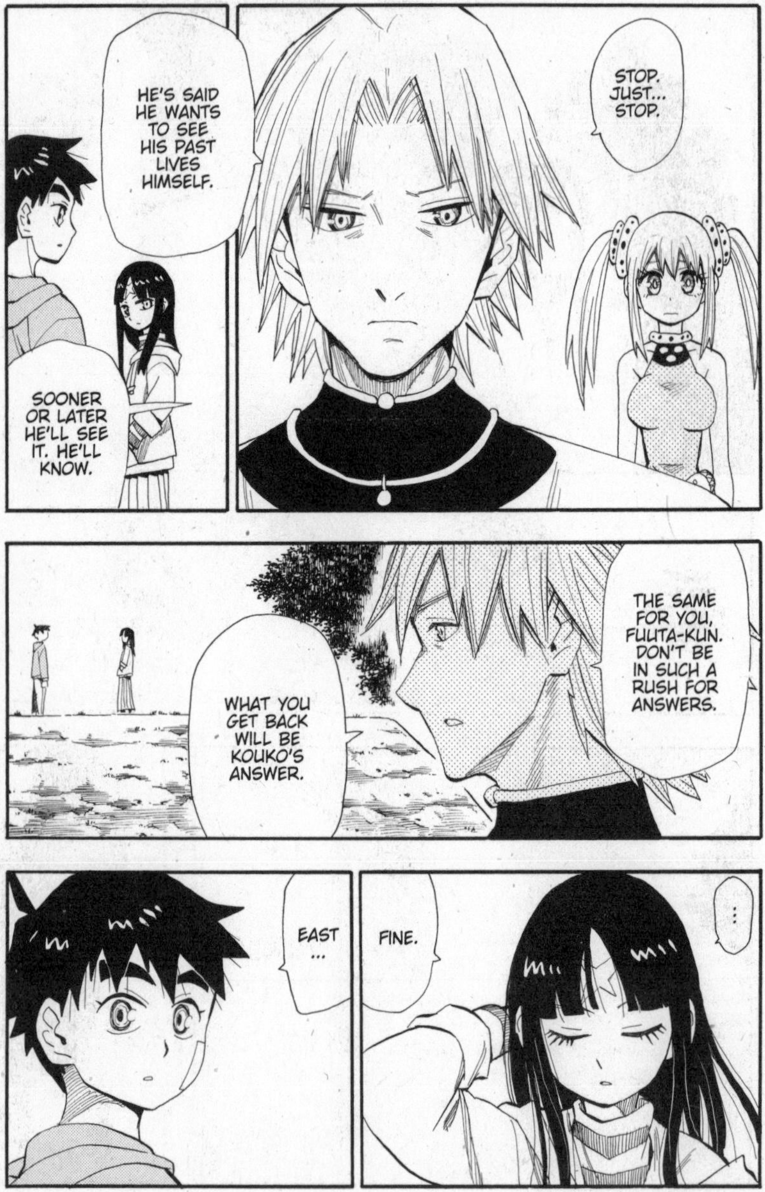
STOP. JUST... STOP.
HE'S SAID HE WANTS TO SEE HIS PAST LIVES HIMSELF.
SOONER OR LATER HE'LL SEE IT. HE'LL KNOW.
THE SAME FOR YOU, FUUTA-KUN. DON'T BE IN SUCH A RUSH FOR ANSWERS.
WHAT YOU GET BACK WILL BE KOUKO'S ANSWER.
...
FINE.
EAST ...

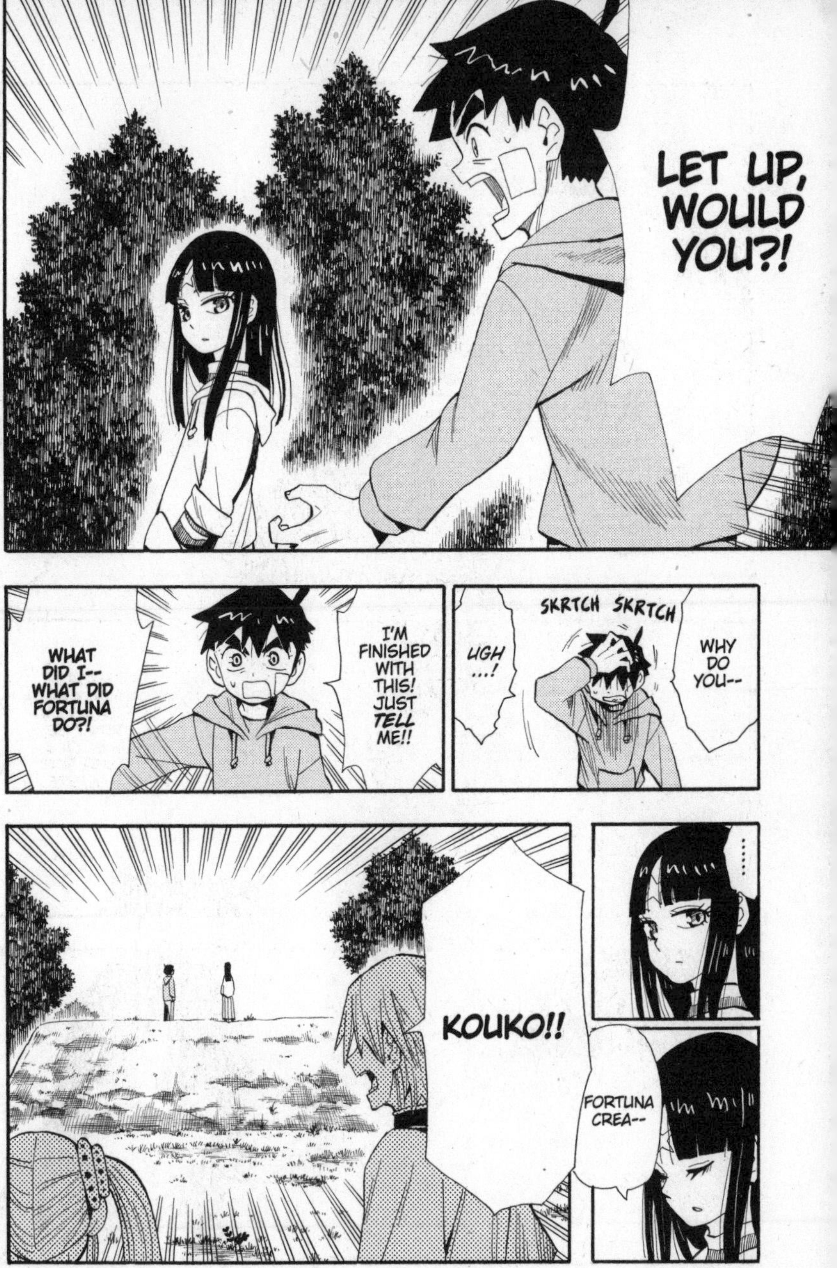
LET UP, WOULD YOU?!
WHY DO YOU--
SKRTCH SKRTCH
UGH ...!
I'M FINISHED WITH THIS! JUST TELL ME!!
WHAT DID I-- WHAT DID FORTUNA DO?!
......
FORTUNA CREA--
KOUKO!!

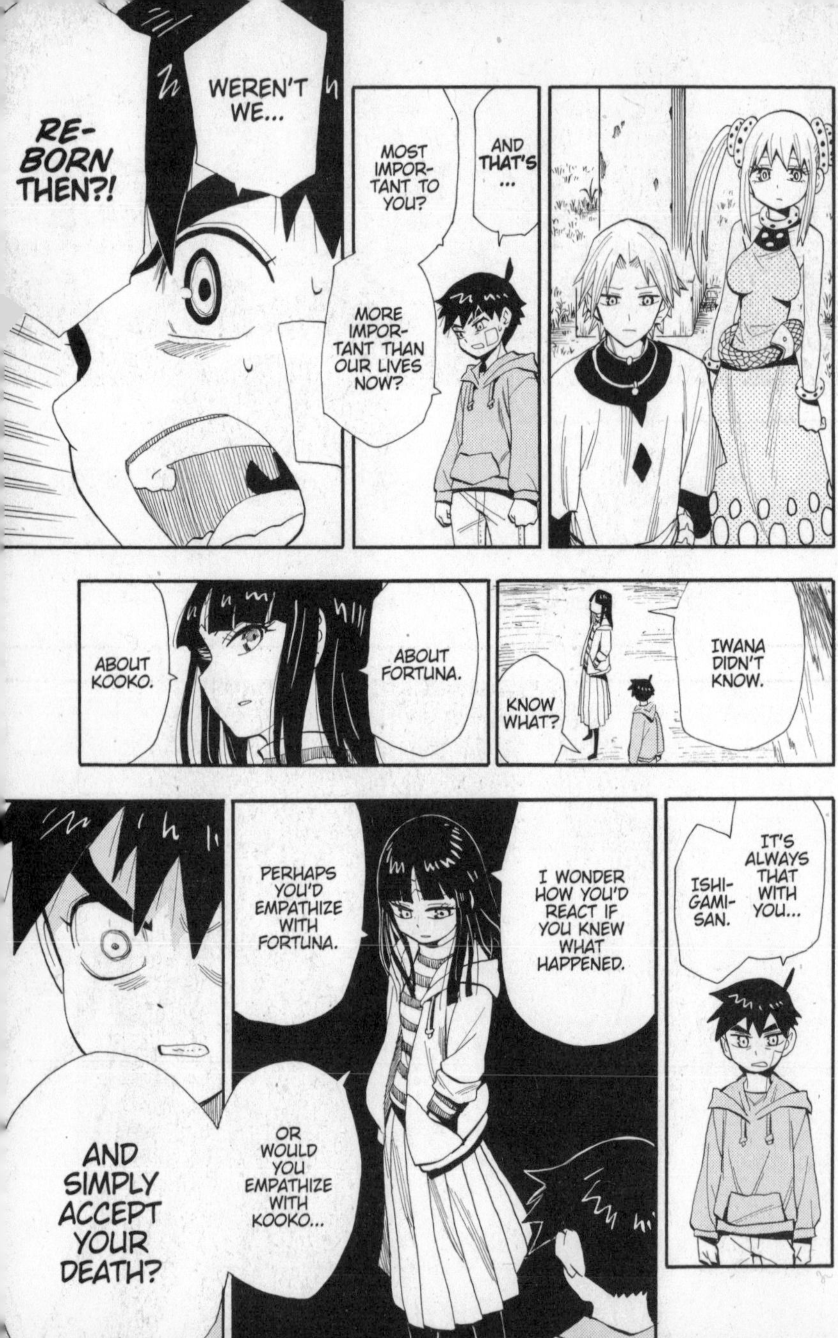
AND THAT'S...
MOST IMPORTANT TO YOU?
MORE IMPORTANT THAN OUR LIVES NOW?
WEREN'T WE...
REBORN THEN?!
IWANA DIDN'T KNOW.
KNOW WHAT?
ABOUT FORTUNA.
ABOUT KOOKO.
IT'S ALWAYS THAT WITH YOU...
ISHIGAMI-SAN.
I WONDER HOW YOU'D REACT IF YOU KNEW WHAT HAPPENED.
PERHAPS YOU'D EMPATHIZE WITH FORTUNA.
OR WOULD YOU EMPATHIZE WITH KOOKO...
AND SIMPLY ACCEPT YOUR DEATH?

WE BOTH WERE.

ISHI-GAMI-SAN...

BACK THEN, YOU WERE SATISFIED.

WHY WOULD IT?

HA!

SHOULDN'T IT HAVE ENDED THEN?

THE CHAIN OF HATRED...

THE THING THAT CONNECTS US...

I'M STILL KOOKO.

AND YOU'RE STILL FORTUNA.

Circle 21
Town 2

Fortuna

Spirit Circle

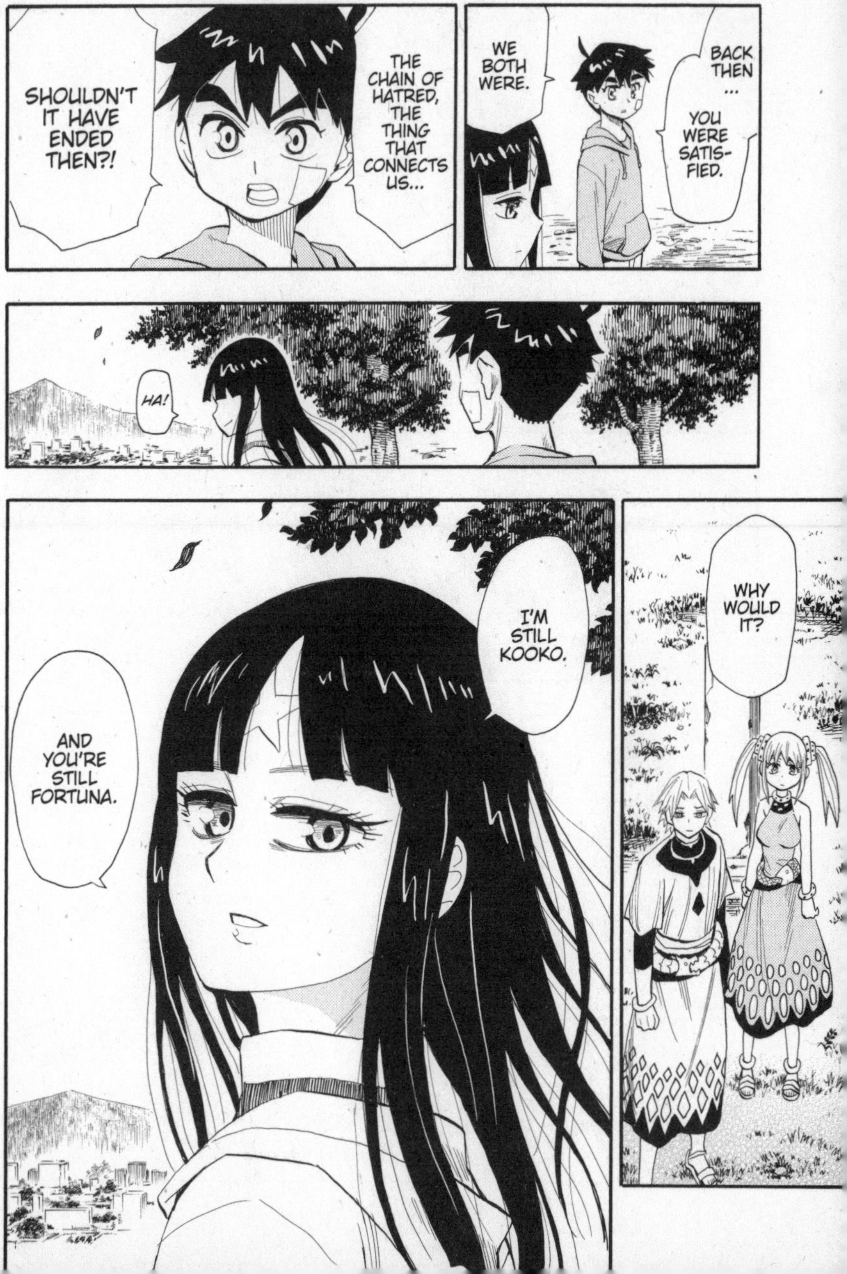
BACK THEN... YOU WERE SATIS-FIED.
WE BOTH WERE.
THE CHAIN OF HATRED, THE THING THAT CONNECTS US...
SHOULDN'T IT HAVE ENDED THEN?!
HA!
WHY WOULD IT?
I'M STILL KOOKO.
AND YOU'RE STILL FORTUNA.

Circle 20/END

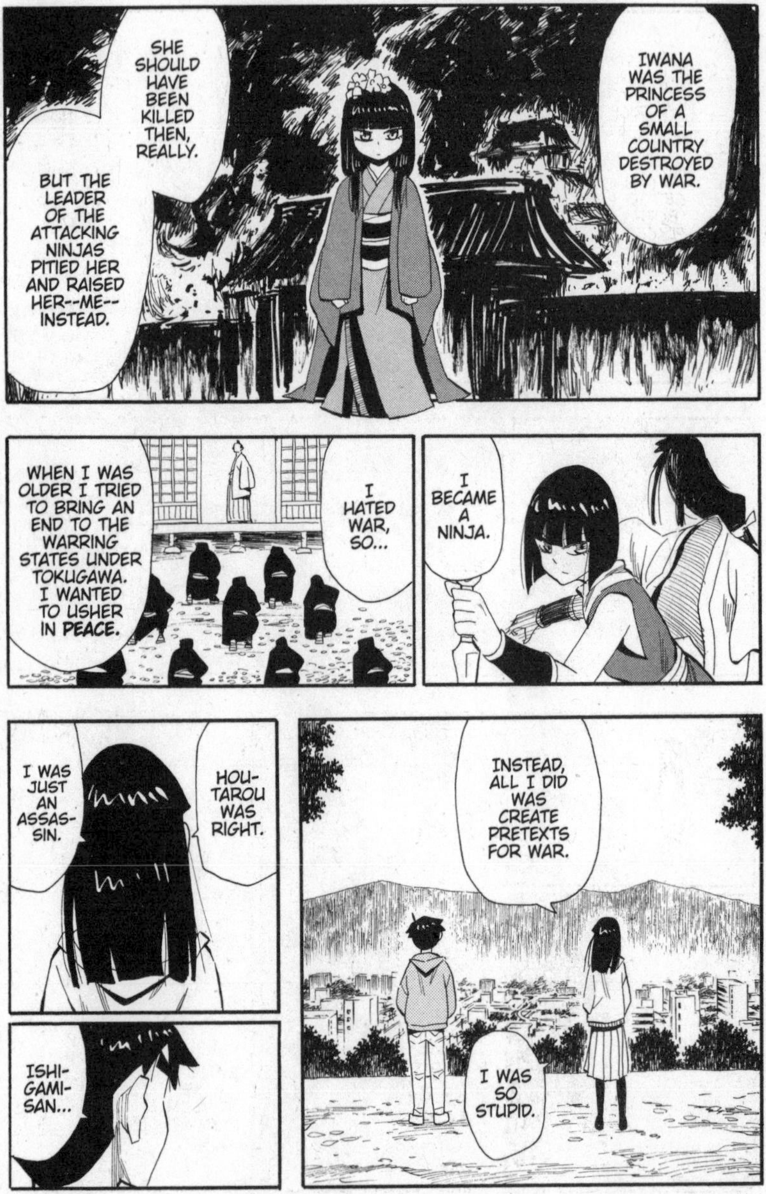
IWANA WAS THE PRINCESS OF A SMALL COUNTRY DESTROYED BY WAR.
SHE SHOULD HAVE BEEN KILLED THEN, REALLY.
BUT THE LEADER OF THE ATTACKING NINJAS PITIED HER AND RAISED HER--ME--INSTEAD.
I BECAME A NINJA.
I HATED WAR, SO...
WHEN I WAS OLDER I TRIED TO BRING AN END TO THE WARRING STATES UNDER TOKUGAWA. I WANTED TO USHER IN **PEACE.**
INSTEAD, ALL I DID WAS CREATE PRETEXTS FOR WAR.
I WAS SO STUPID.
HOU-TAROU WAS RIGHT.
I WAS JUST AN ASSAS-SIN.
ISHI-GAMI-SAN...

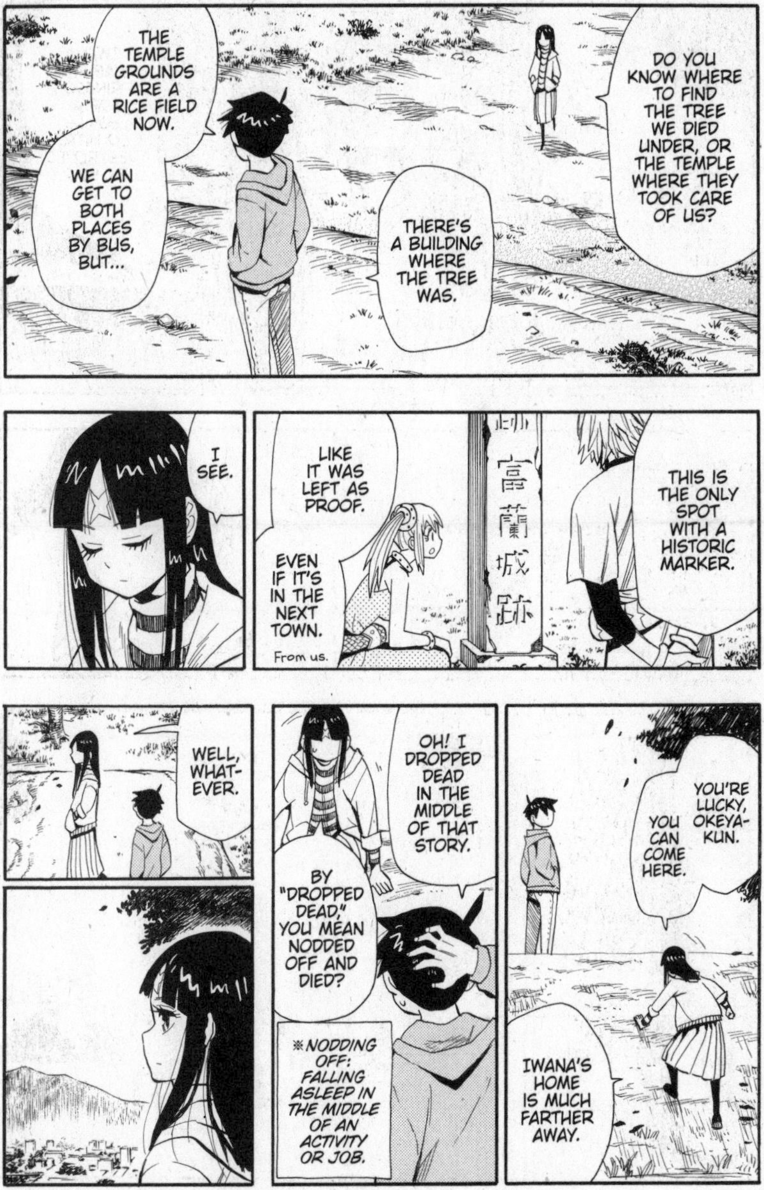
DO YOU KNOW WHERE TO FIND THE TREE WE DIED UNDER, OR THE TEMPLE WHERE THEY TOOK CARE OF US?
THERE'S A BUILDING WHERE THE TREE WAS.
THE TEMPLE GROUNDS ARE A RICE FIELD NOW.
WE CAN GET TO BOTH PLACES BY BUS, BUT...
THIS IS THE ONLY SPOT WITH A HISTORIC MARKER.
富蘭城跡
LIKE IT WAS LEFT AS PROOF.
EVEN IF IT'S IN THE NEXT TOWN.
From us.
I SEE.
YOU'RE LUCKY, OKEYA-KUN.
YOU CAN COME HERE.
IWANA'S HOME IS MUCH FARTHER AWAY.
OH! I DROPPED DEAD IN THE MIDDLE OF THAT STORY.
BY "DROPPED DEAD," YOU MEAN NODDED OFF AND DIED?
※NODDING OFF: FALLING ASLEEP IN THE MIDDLE OF AN ACTIVITY OR JOB.
WELL, WHATEVER.

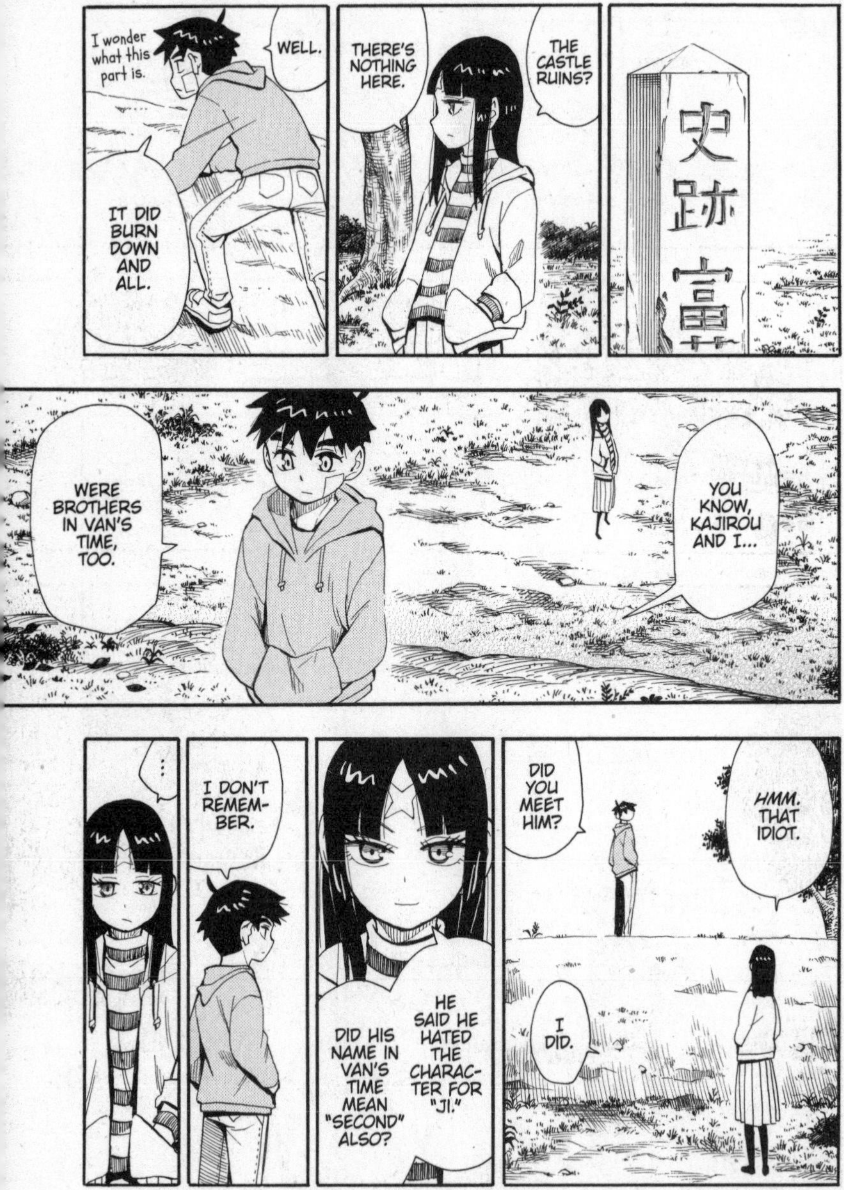
THE CASTLE RUINS?
史跡富
THERE'S NOTHING HERE.
WELL.
I wonder what this part is.
IT DID BURN DOWN AND ALL.
YOU KNOW, KAJIROU AND I...
WERE BROTHERS IN VAN'S TIME, TOO.
HMM. THAT IDIOT.
DID YOU MEET HIM?
I DID.
HE SAID HE HATED THE CHARAC-TER FOR "JI."
DID HIS NAME IN VAN'S TIME MEAN "SECOND" ALSO?
I DON'T REMEM-BER.
...

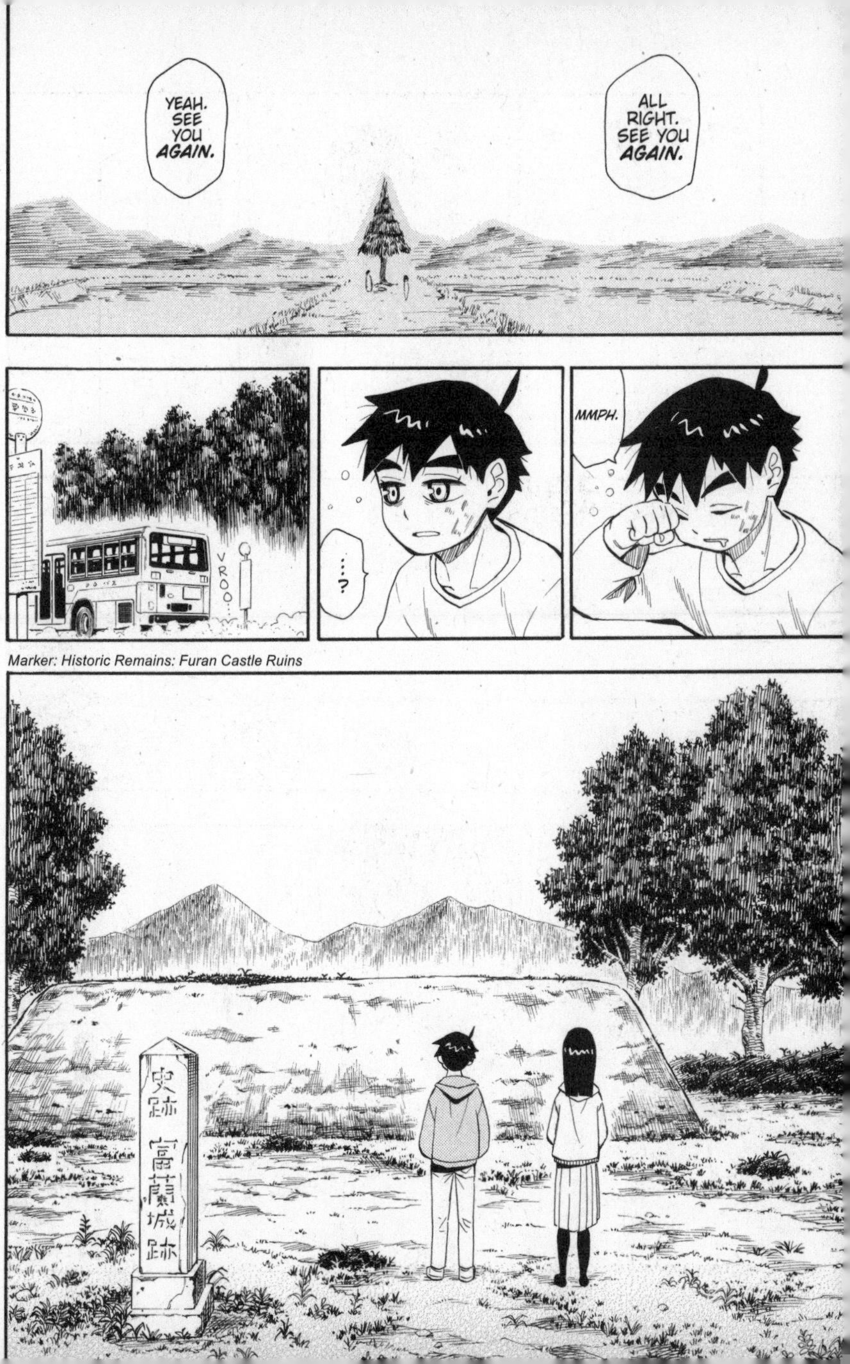
ALL RIGHT. SEE YOU AGAIN.
YEAH. SEE YOU AGAIN.
MMPH.
...?
VROOO...
Marker: Historic Remains: Furan Castle Ruins
史跡 富蘭城跡

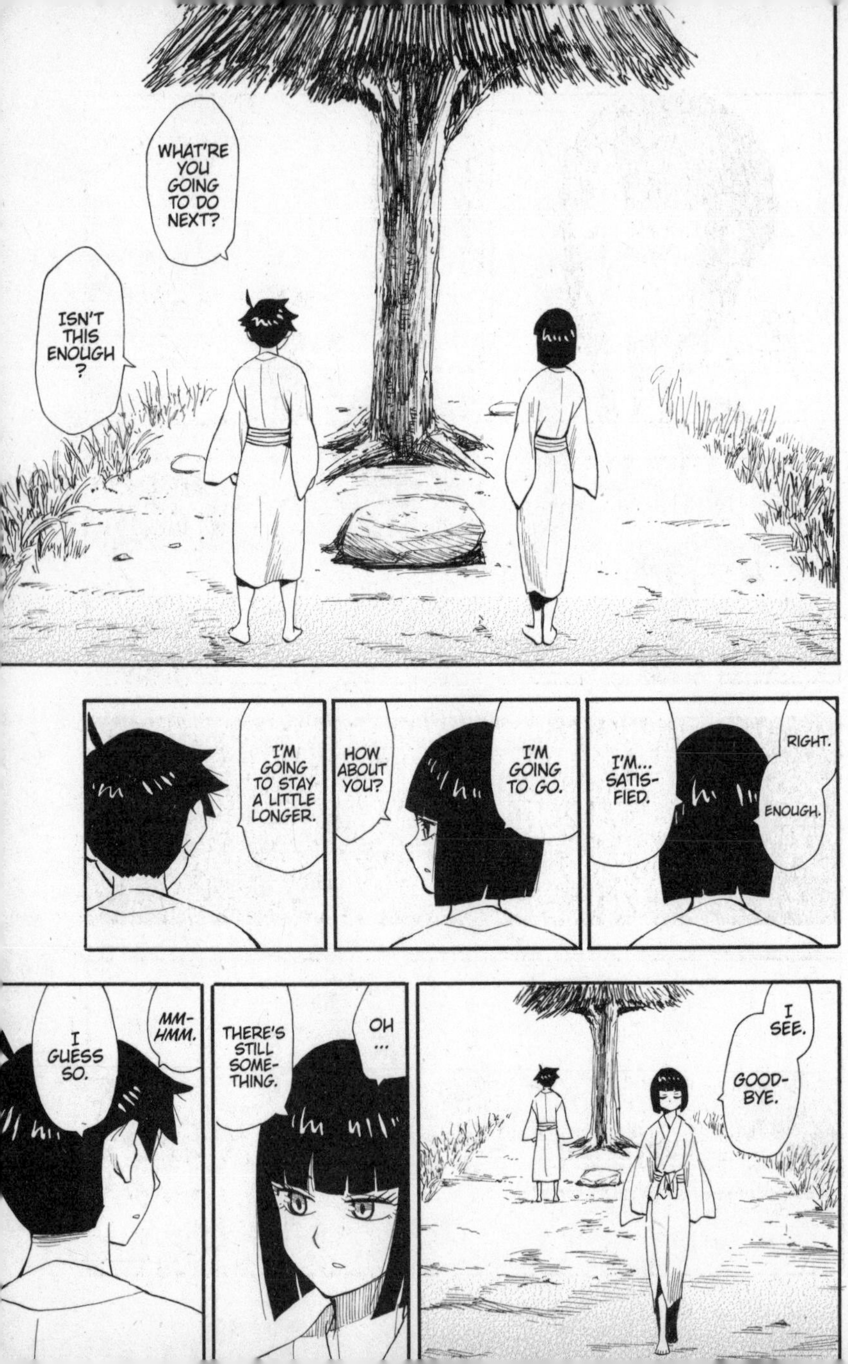
WHAT'RE YOU GOING TO DO NEXT?
ISN'T THIS ENOUGH?
RIGHT.
ENOUGH.
I'M... SATISFIED.
I'M GOING TO GO.
HOW ABOUT YOU?
I'M GOING TO STAY A LITTLE LONGER.
I SEE.
GOOD-BYE.
OH...
THERE'S STILL SOMETHING.
MM-HMM.
I GUESS SO.

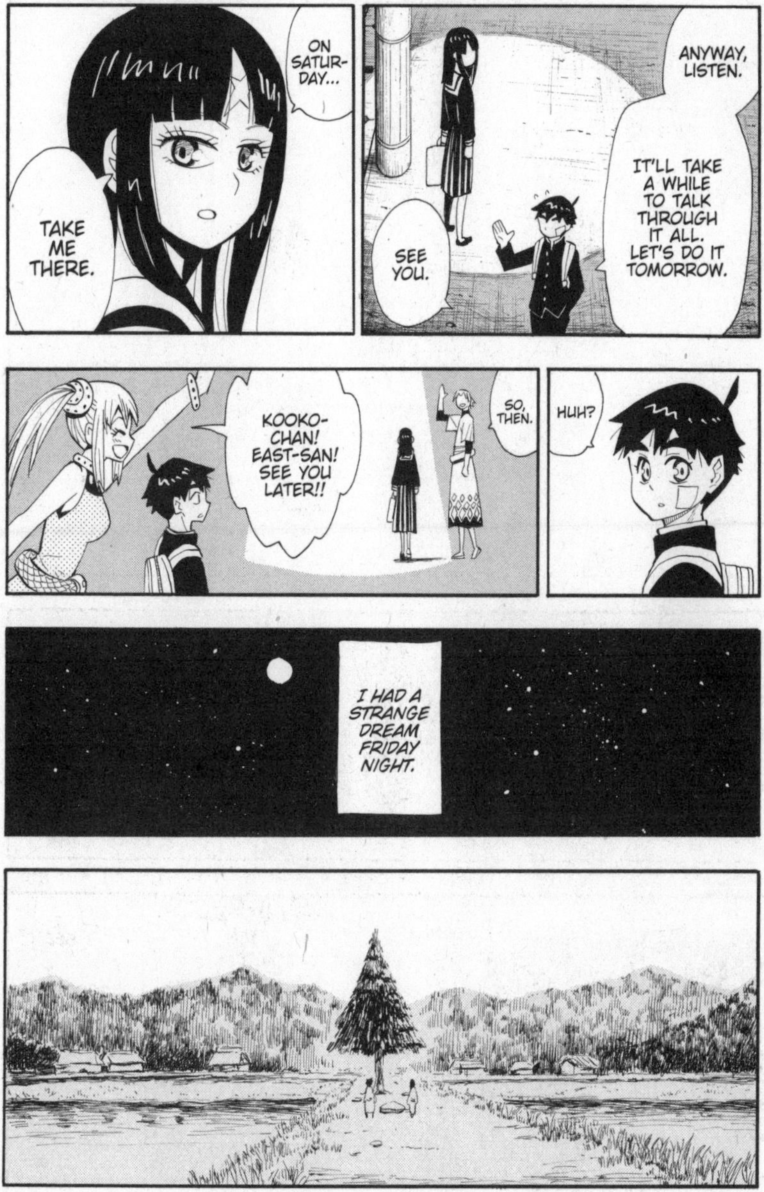
ANYWAY, LISTEN.
IT'LL TAKE A WHILE TO TALK THROUGH IT ALL. LET'S DO IT TOMORROW.
SEE YOU.
ON SATUR-DAY...
TAKE ME THERE.
HUH?
SO, THEN.
KOOKO-CHAN! EAST-SAN! SEE YOU LATER!!
I HAD A STRANGE DREAM FRIDAY NIGHT.

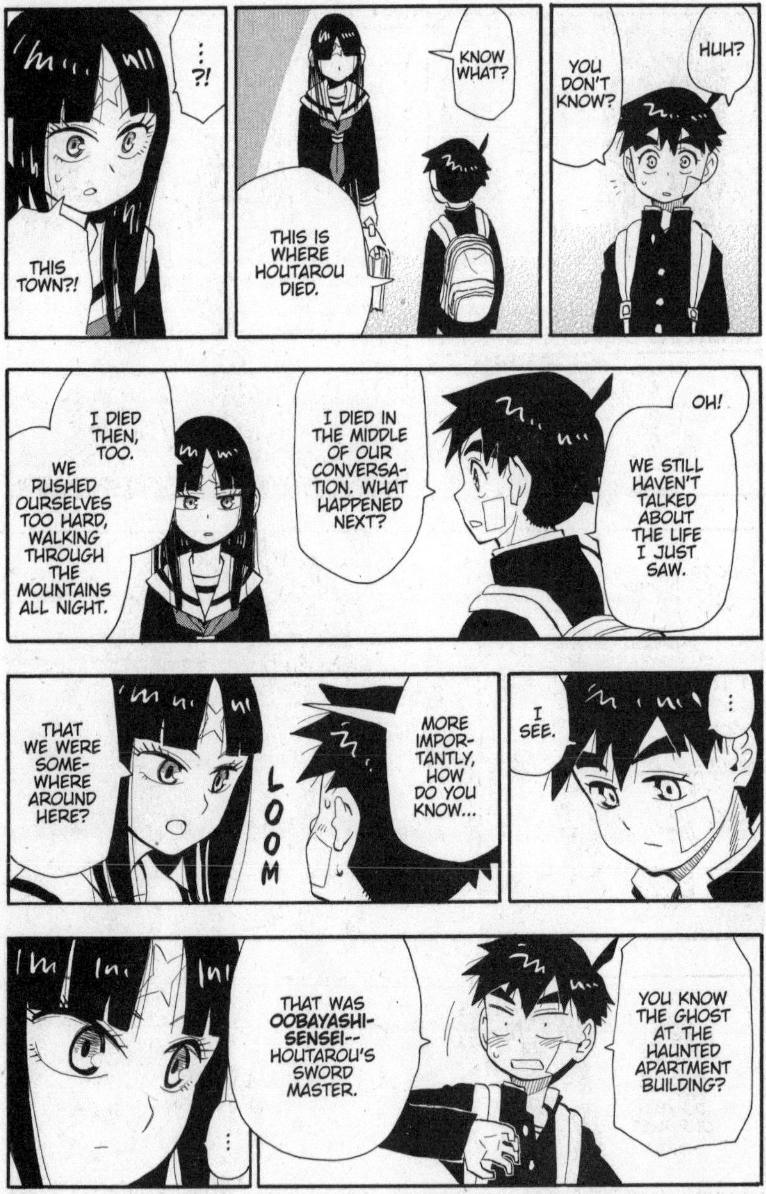
HUH?
YOU DON'T KNOW?
KNOW WHAT?
THIS IS WHERE HOUTAROU DIED.
...?!
THIS TOWN?!
OH!
WE STILL HAVEN'T TALKED ABOUT THE LIFE I JUST SAW.
I DIED IN THE MIDDLE OF OUR CONVERSATION. WHAT HAPPENED NEXT?
I DIED THEN, TOO.
WE PUSHED OURSELVES TOO HARD, WALKING THROUGH THE MOUNTAINS ALL NIGHT.
...
I SEE.
MORE IMPORTANTLY, HOW DO YOU KNOW...
LOOM
THAT WE WERE SOMEWHERE AROUND HERE?
YOU KNOW THE GHOST AT THE HAUNTED APARTMENT BUILDING?
THAT WAS OOBAYASHI-SENSEI--HOUTAROU'S SWORD MASTER.
...

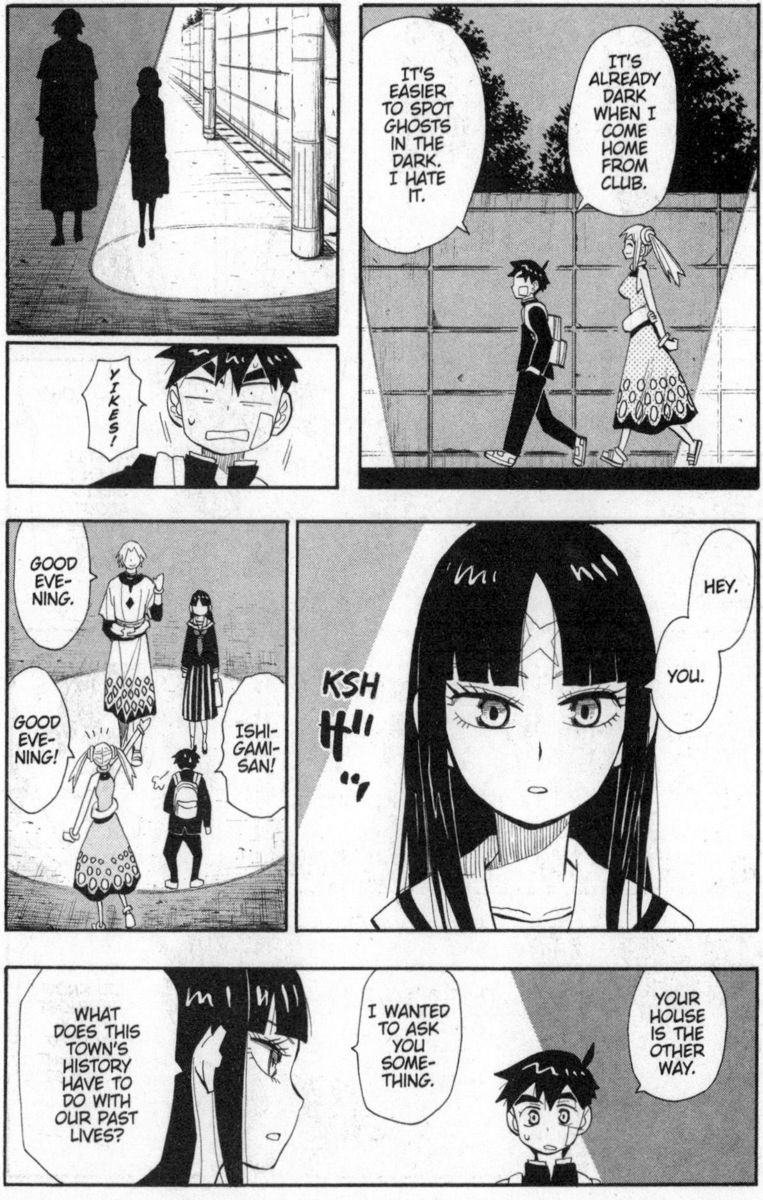
IT'S ALREADY DARK WHEN I COME HOME FROM CLUB.
IT'S EASIER TO SPOT GHOSTS IN THE DARK. I HATE IT.
YIKES!
HEY.
YOU.
KSH
GOOD EVENING.
ISHIGAMI-SAN!
GOOD EVENING!
YOUR HOUSE IS THE OTHER WAY.
I WANTED TO ASK YOU SOMETHING.
WHAT DOES THIS TOWN'S HISTORY HAVE TO DO WITH OUR PAST LIVES?

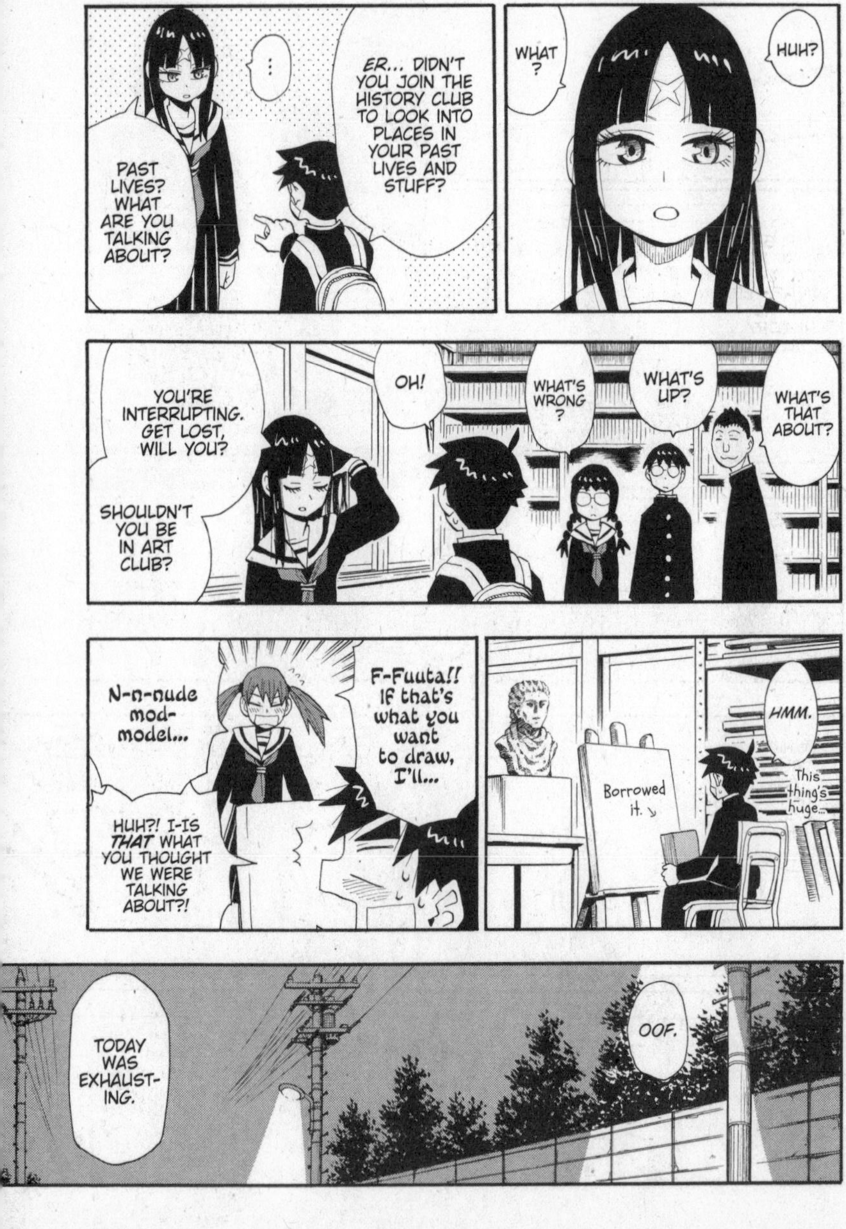
HUH?
WHAT?
ER... DIDN'T YOU JOIN THE HISTORY CLUB TO LOOK INTO PLACES IN YOUR PAST LIVES AND STUFF?
...
PAST LIVES? WHAT ARE YOU TALKING ABOUT?
WHAT'S THAT ABOUT?
WHAT'S UP?
WHAT'S WRONG?
OH!
YOU'RE INTERRUPTING. GET LOST, WILL YOU?
SHOULDN'T YOU BE IN ART CLUB?
HMM.
This thing's huge...
Borrowed it.
F-Fuuta!! If that's what you want to draw, I'll...
N-n-nude mod-model...
HUH?! I-IS THAT WHAT YOU THOUGHT WE WERE TALKING ABOUT?!
OOF.
TODAY WAS EXHAUST-ING.

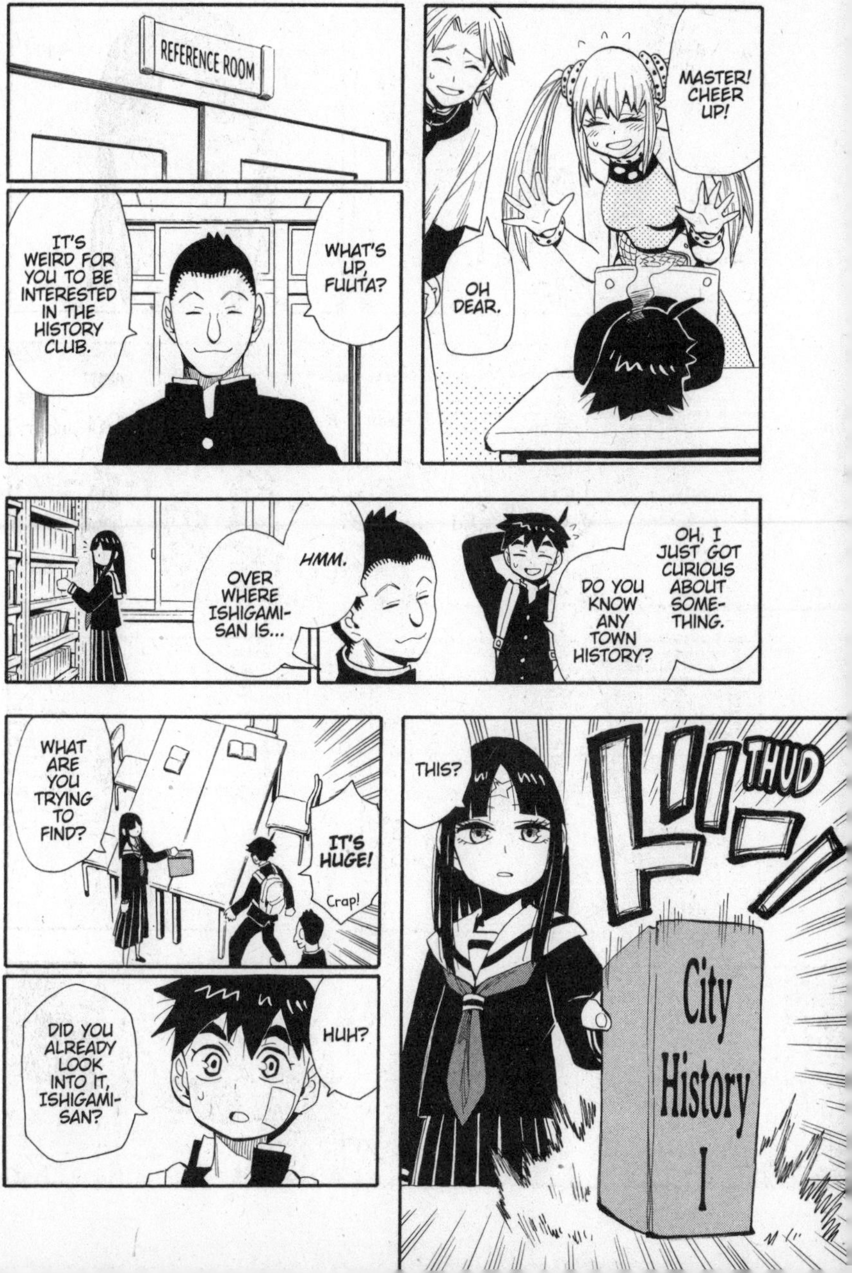
MASTER! CHEER UP!
OH DEAR.
REFERENCE ROOM
WHAT'S UP, FUUTA?
IT'S WEIRD FOR YOU TO BE INTERESTED IN THE HISTORY CLUB.
OH, I JUST GOT CURIOUS ABOUT SOMETHING.
DO YOU KNOW ANY TOWN HISTORY?
HMM.
OVER WHERE ISHIGAMI-SAN IS...
THIS?
THUD
City History I
WHAT ARE YOU TRYING TO FIND?
IT'S HUGE!
Crap!
HUH?
DID YOU ALREADY LOOK INTO IT, ISHIGAMI-SAN?

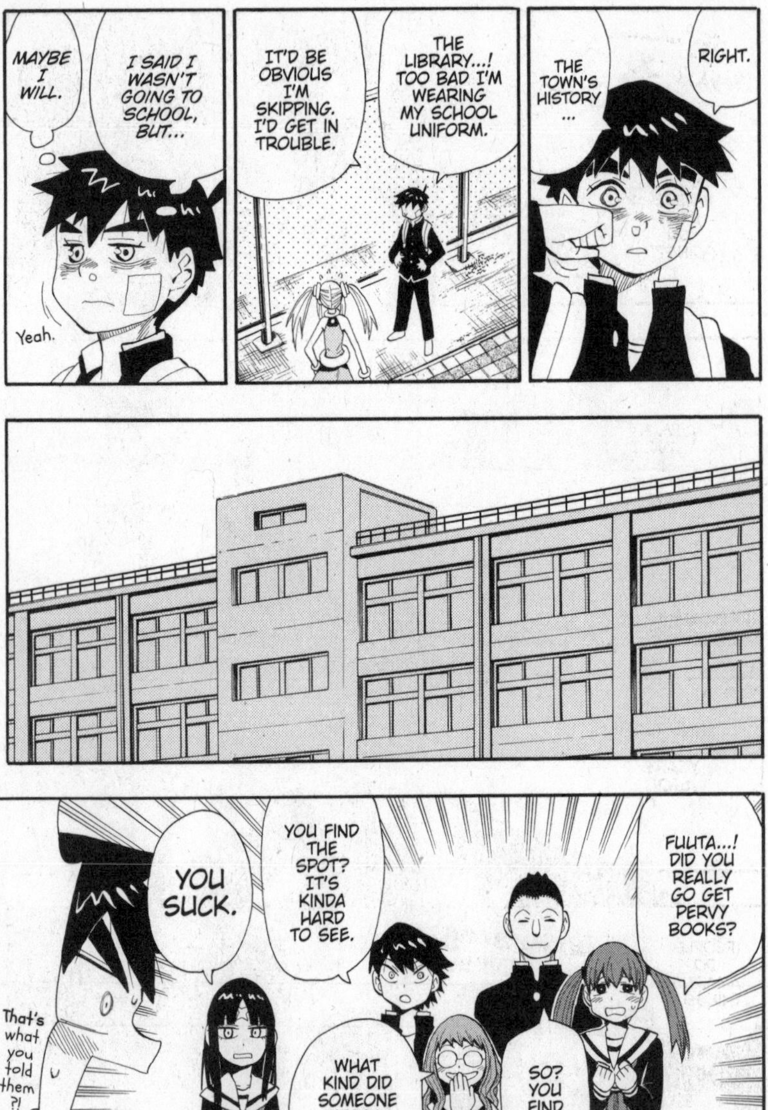
RIGHT.
THE TOWN'S HISTORY ...
THE LIBRARY...! TOO BAD I'M WEARING MY SCHOOL UNIFORM.
IT'D BE OBVIOUS I'M SKIPPING. I'D GET IN TROUBLE.
I SAID I WASN'T GOING TO SCHOOL, BUT...
MAYBE I WILL.
Yeah.
FUUTA...! DID YOU REALLY GO GET PERVY BOOKS?
YOU FIND THE SPOT? IT'S KINDA HARD TO SEE.
YOU SUCK.
SO? YOU FIND THEM?
WHAT KIND DID SOMEONE DITCH IN A PLACE LIKE THAT?
AAAAAH!!
That's what you told them?!

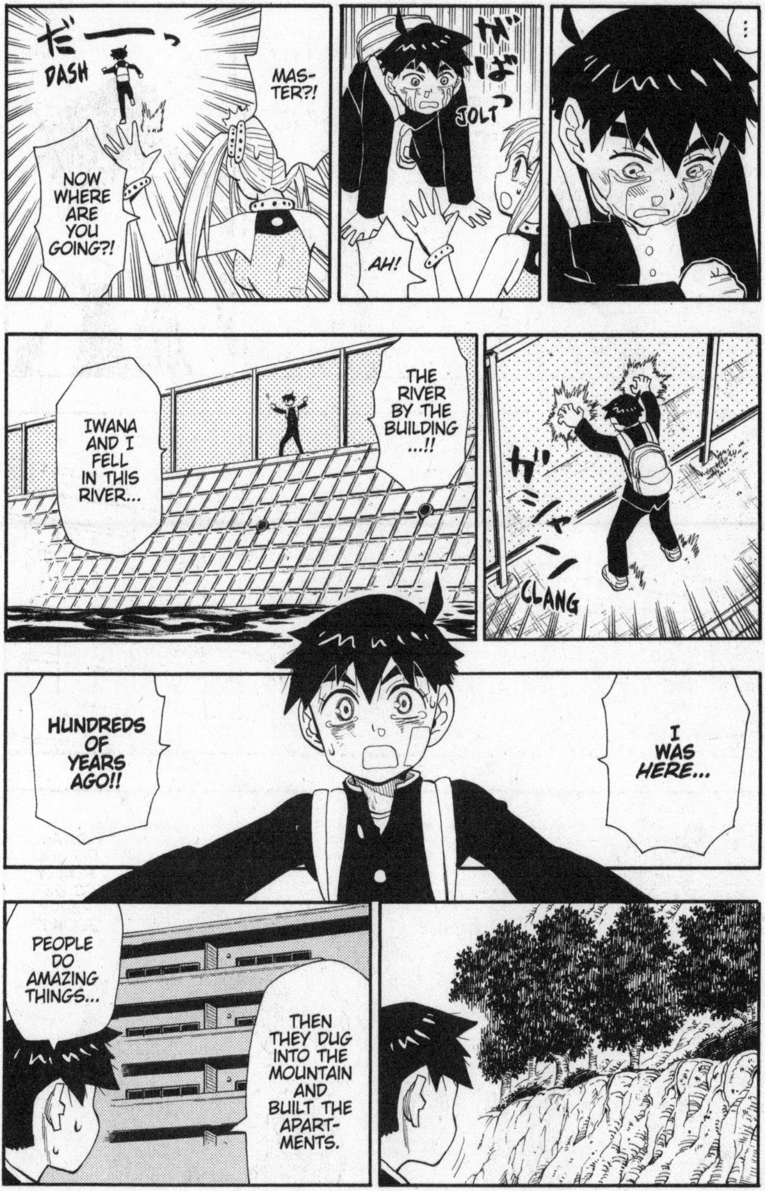

...
がばっ
JOLT
AH!
MAS-TER?!
だーっ
DASH
NOW WHERE ARE YOU GOING?!
ガシャーン
CLANG
THE RIVER BY THE BUILDING ...!!
IWANA AND I FELL IN THIS RIVER...
I WAS HERE...
HUNDREDS OF YEARS AGO!!
THEN THEY DUG INTO THE MOUNTAIN AND BUILT THE APART-MENTS.
PEOPLE DO AMAZING THINGS...

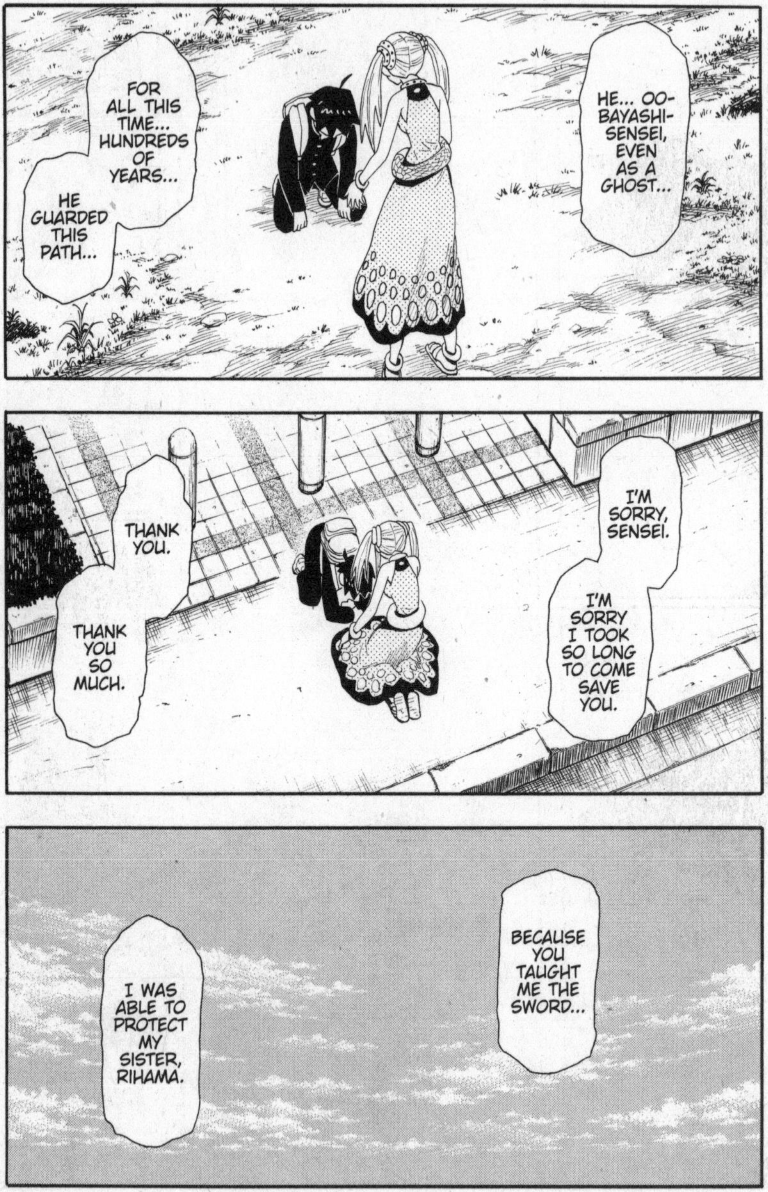
HE... OO-BAYASHI-SENSEI, EVEN AS A GHOST...
FOR ALL THIS TIME... HUNDREDS OF YEARS...
HE GUARDED THIS PATH...
I'M SORRY, SENSEI.
I'M SORRY I TOOK SO LONG TO COME SAVE YOU.
THANK YOU.
THANK YOU SO MUCH.
BECAUSE YOU TAUGHT ME THE SWORD...
I WAS ABLE TO PROTECT MY SISTER, RIHAMA.

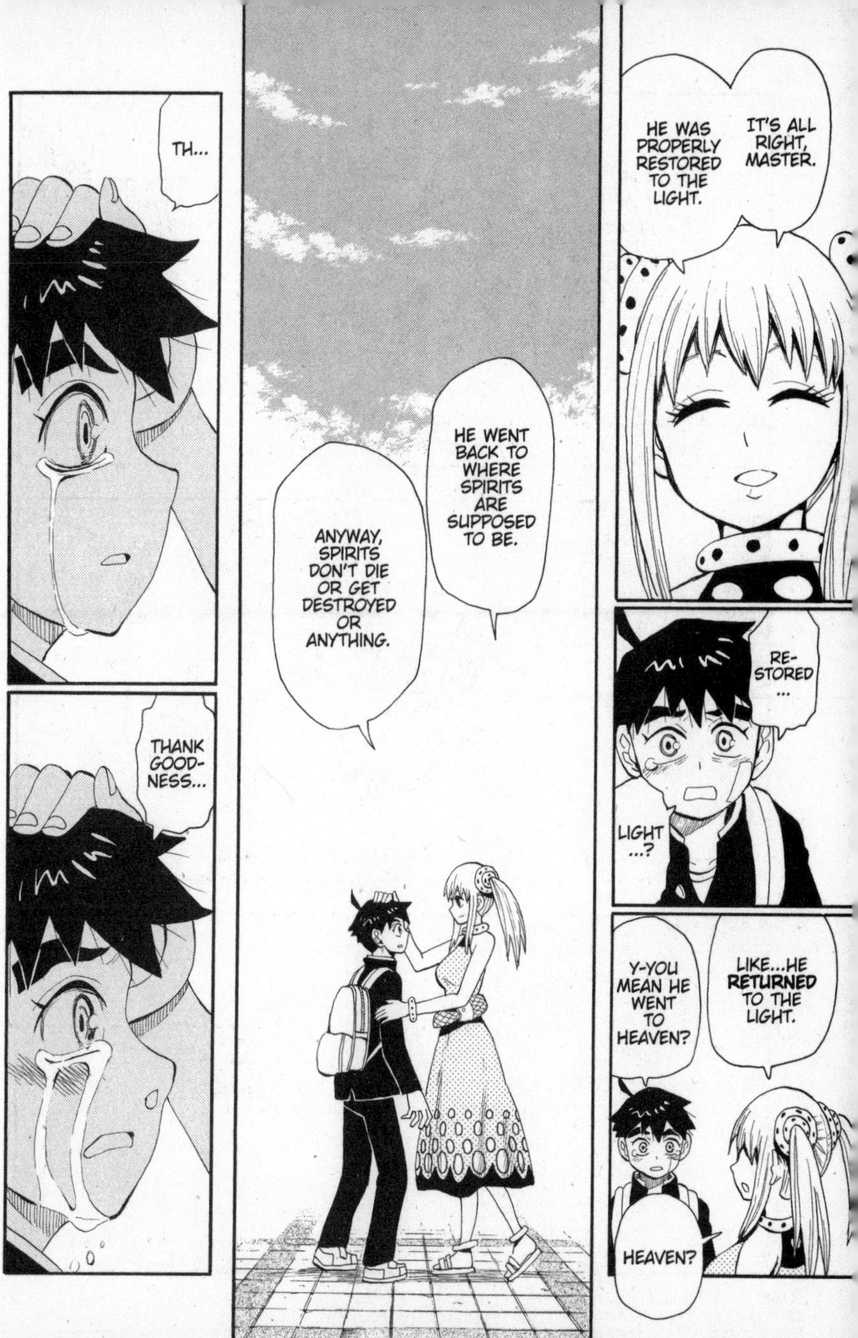
IT'S ALL RIGHT, MASTER.
HE WAS PROPERLY RESTORED TO THE LIGHT.
RE-STORED...
LIGHT...?
LIKE...HE **RETURNED** TO THE LIGHT.
Y-YOU MEAN HE WENT TO HEAVEN?
HEAVEN?
HE WENT BACK TO WHERE SPIRITS ARE SUPPOSED TO BE.
ANYWAY, SPIRITS DON'T DIE OR GET DESTROYED OR ANYTHING.
TH...
THANK GOODNESS...

AND THE LANCE HE TOOK FROM THE ENEMY, AND...

A SWORD...!

HE WAS SHOT FULL OF ARROWS!

MUTTER MUTTER

HE WAS WAVING HIS SWORD AND HIS FISTS.

FALLEN WARRIOR?

THAT PERSON WHO WAS STABBED ALL OVER?

WAS OOBAYASHI-SENSEI!!

THAT GHOST...

THAT PERSON...

WHAT HAPPENED TO OOBAYASHI-SENSEI!?!

RUNE!

OH! YOU KNEW HIM, HUH, MASTER?

THIS IS A WEAPON TO *KILL SPIRITS*, RIGHT?!

D-DID I--?!

I...I USED THE SPIRIT CIRCLE...

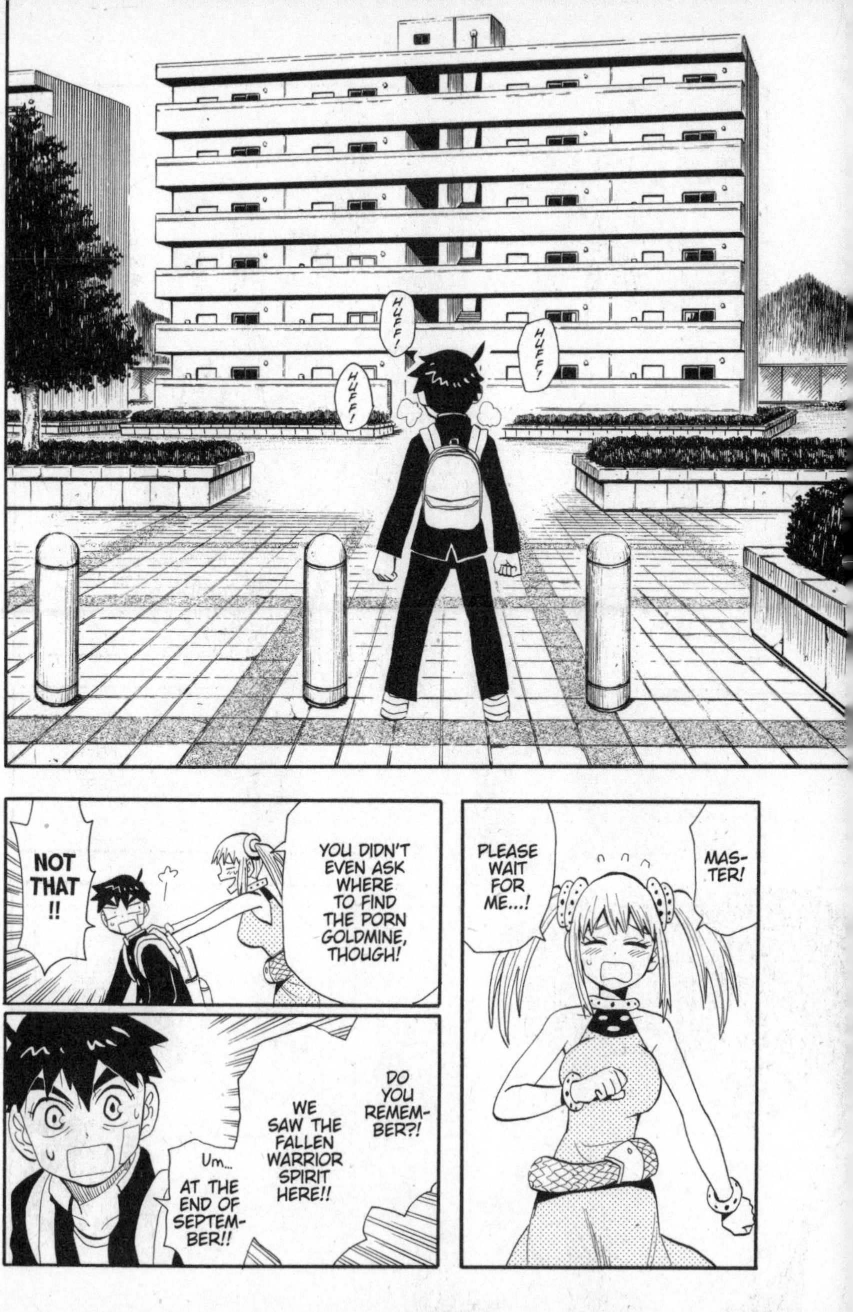
HUFF!
HUFF!
HUFF!
MAS-TER!
PLEASE WAIT FOR ME...!
YOU DIDN'T EVEN ASK WHERE TO FIND THE PORN GOLDMINE, THOUGH!
NOT THAT!!
DO YOU REMEM-BER?!
WE SAW THE FALLEN WARRIOR SPIRIT HERE!!
Um... AT THE END OF SEPTEM-BER!!

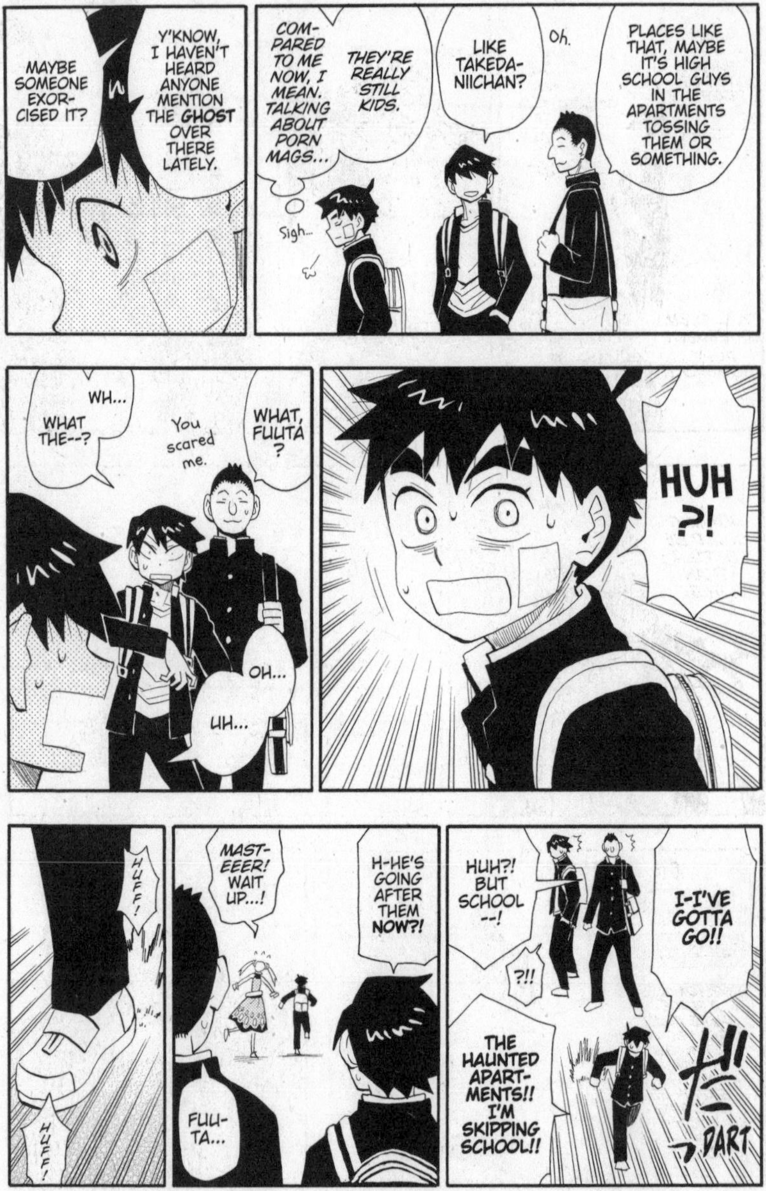
PLACES LIKE THAT, MAYBE IT'S HIGH SCHOOL GUYS IN THE APARTMENTS TOSSING THEM OR SOMETHING.
Oh.
LIKE TAKEDA-NIICHAN?
THEY'RE REALLY STILL KIDS.
COMPARED TO ME NOW, I MEAN. TALKING ABOUT PORN MAGS...
Sigh...
Y'KNOW, I HAVEN'T HEARD ANYONE MENTION THE GHOST OVER THERE LATELY.
MAYBE SOMEONE EXORCISED IT?
HUH ?!
WHAT, FUUTA ?
You scared me.
WH... WHAT THE--?
OH...
UH...
I-I'VE GOTTA GO!!
HUH?! BUT SCHOOL --!
?!!
THE HAUNTED APARTMENTS!! I'M SKIPPING SCHOOL!!
DART
H-HE'S GOING AFTER THEM NOW?!
MASTEEER! WAIT UP...!
FUUTA...
HUFF!
HUFF!

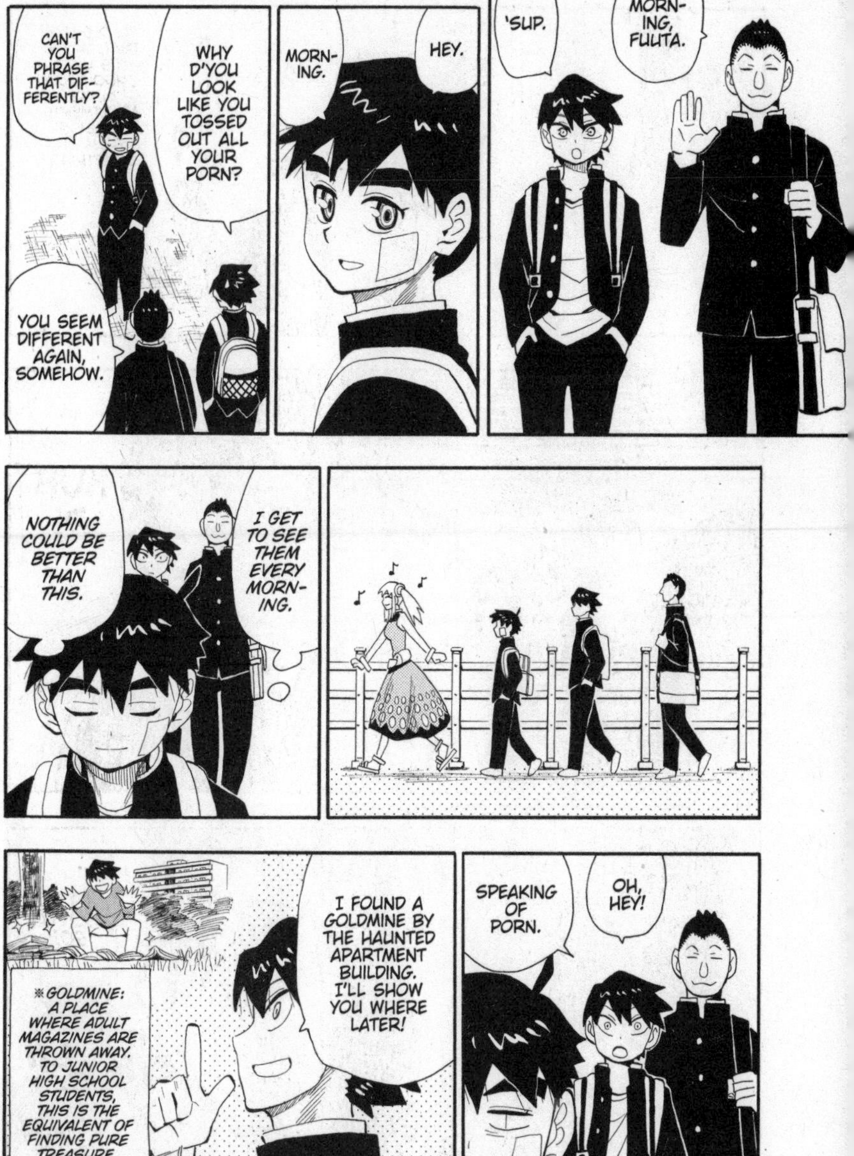
MORNING, FUUTA.
'SUP.
HEY.
MORNING.
WHY D'YOU LOOK LIKE YOU TOSSED OUT ALL YOUR PORN?
CAN'T YOU PHRASE THAT DIFFERENTLY?
YOU SEEM DIFFERENT AGAIN, SOMEHOW.
I GET TO SEE THEM EVERY MORNING.
NOTHING COULD BE BETTER THAN THIS.
OH, HEY!
SPEAKING OF PORN.
I FOUND A GOLDMINE BY THE HAUNTED APARTMENT BUILDING. I'LL SHOW YOU WHERE LATER!
※GOLDMINE: A PLACE WHERE ADULT MAGAZINES ARE THROWN AWAY. TO JUNIOR HIGH SCHOOL STUDENTS, THIS IS THE EQUIVALENT OF FINDING PURE TREASURE.

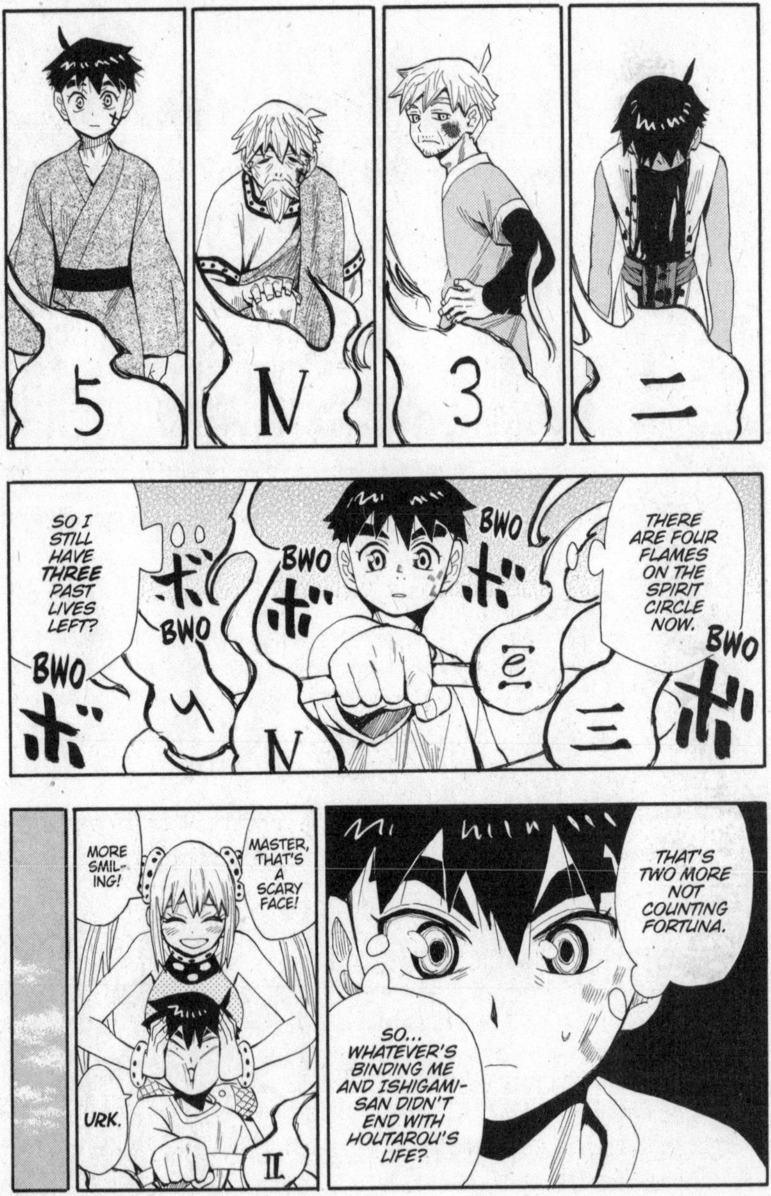

二
3
N
5
THERE ARE FOUR FLAMES ON THE SPIRIT CIRCLE NOW.
BWO ボ
BWO ボ
BWO ボ
BWO ボ
BWO ボ
SO I STILL HAVE THREE PAST LIVES LEFT?
THAT'S TWO MORE NOT COUNTING FORTUNA.
SO... WHATEVER'S BINDING ME AND ISHIGAMI-SAN DIDN'T END WITH HOUTAROU'S LIFE?
MASTER, THAT'S A SCARY FACE!
MORE SMILING!
URK.

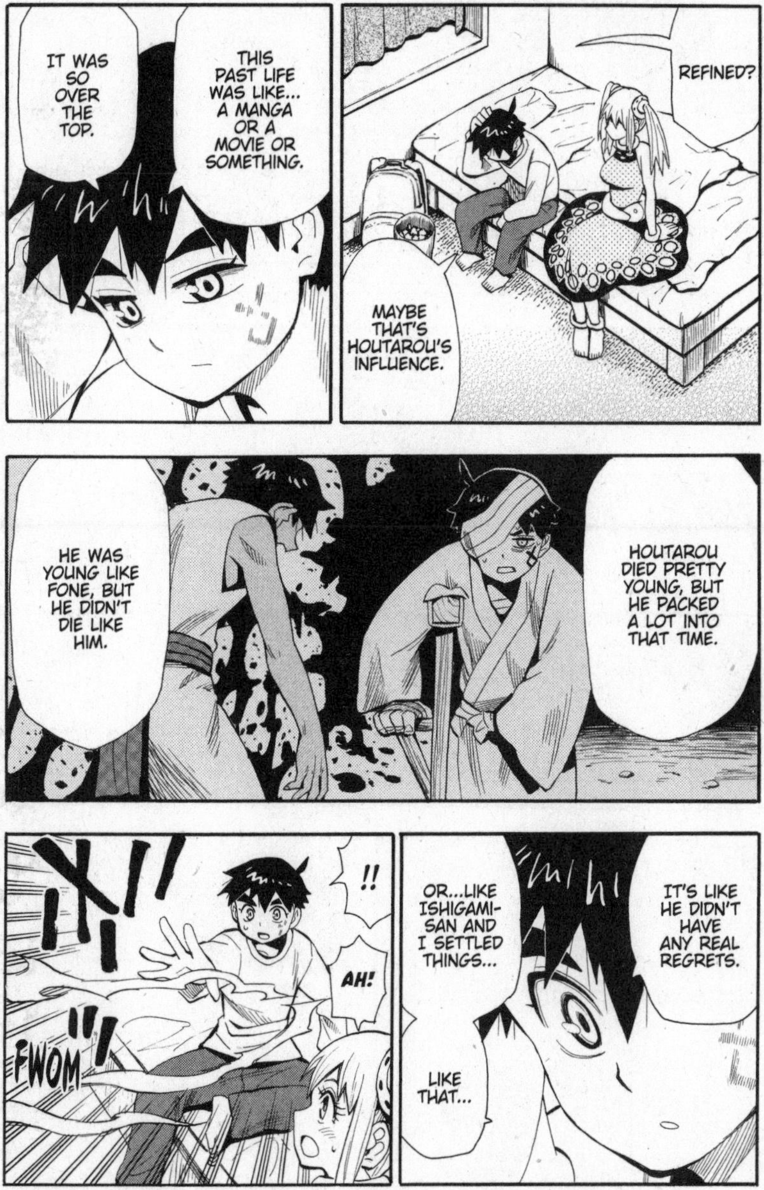
REFINED?
MAYBE THAT'S HOUTAROU'S INFLUENCE.
THIS PAST LIFE WAS LIKE... A MANGA OR A MOVIE OR SOMETHING.
IT WAS SO OVER THE TOP.
HOUTAROU DIED PRETTY YOUNG, BUT HE PACKED A LOT INTO THAT TIME.
HE WAS YOUNG LIKE FONE, BUT HE DIDN'T DIE LIKE HIM.
IT'S LIKE HE DIDN'T HAVE ANY REAL REGRETS.
OR...LIKE ISHIGAMI-SAN AND I SETTLED THINGS...
LIKE THAT...
!!
AH!
FWOM

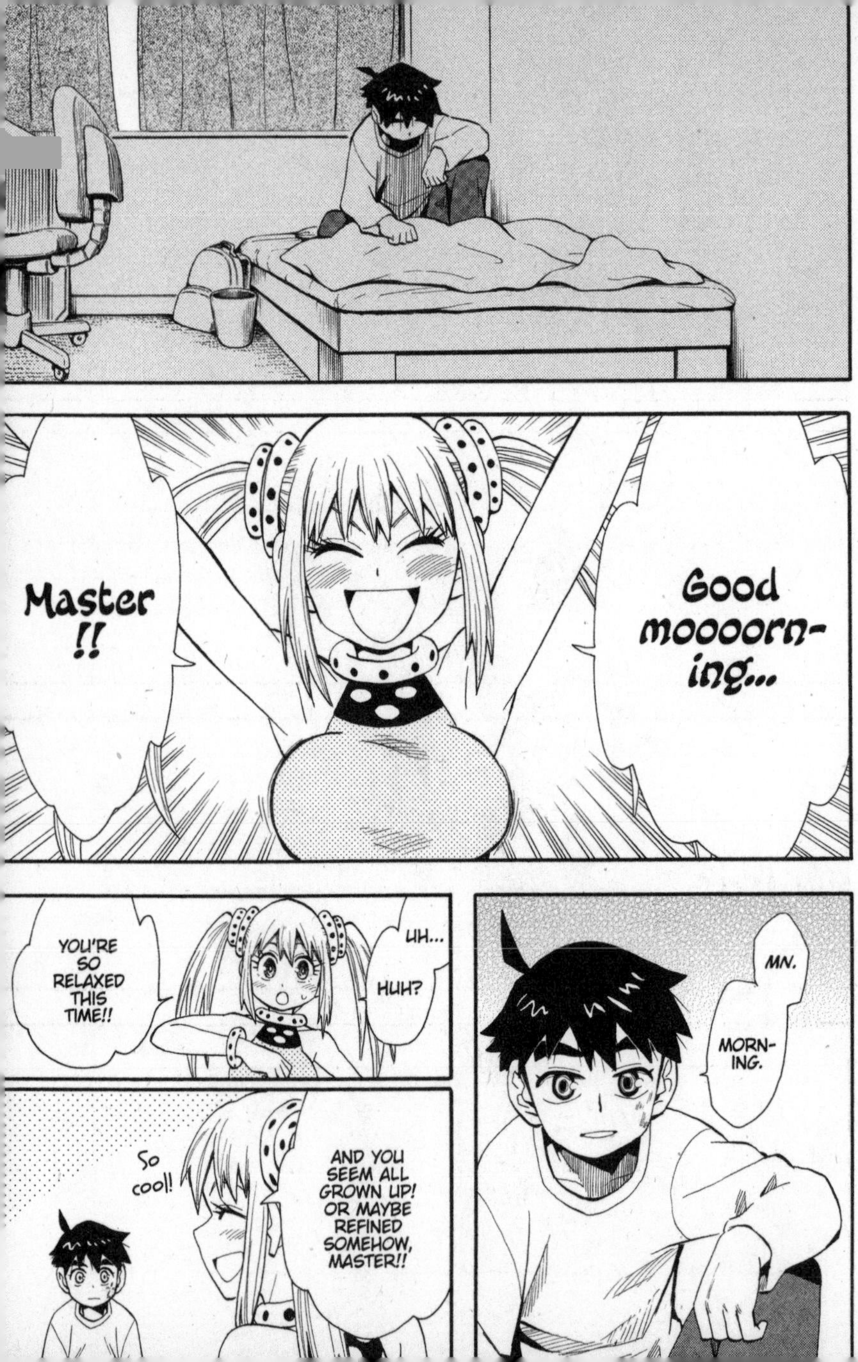
Good moooorn-ing...
Master!!
MN.
MORN-ING.
UH...
HUH?
YOU'RE SO RELAXED THIS TIME!!
AND YOU SEEM ALL GROWN UP! OR MAYBE REFINED SOMEHOW, MASTER!!
So cool!

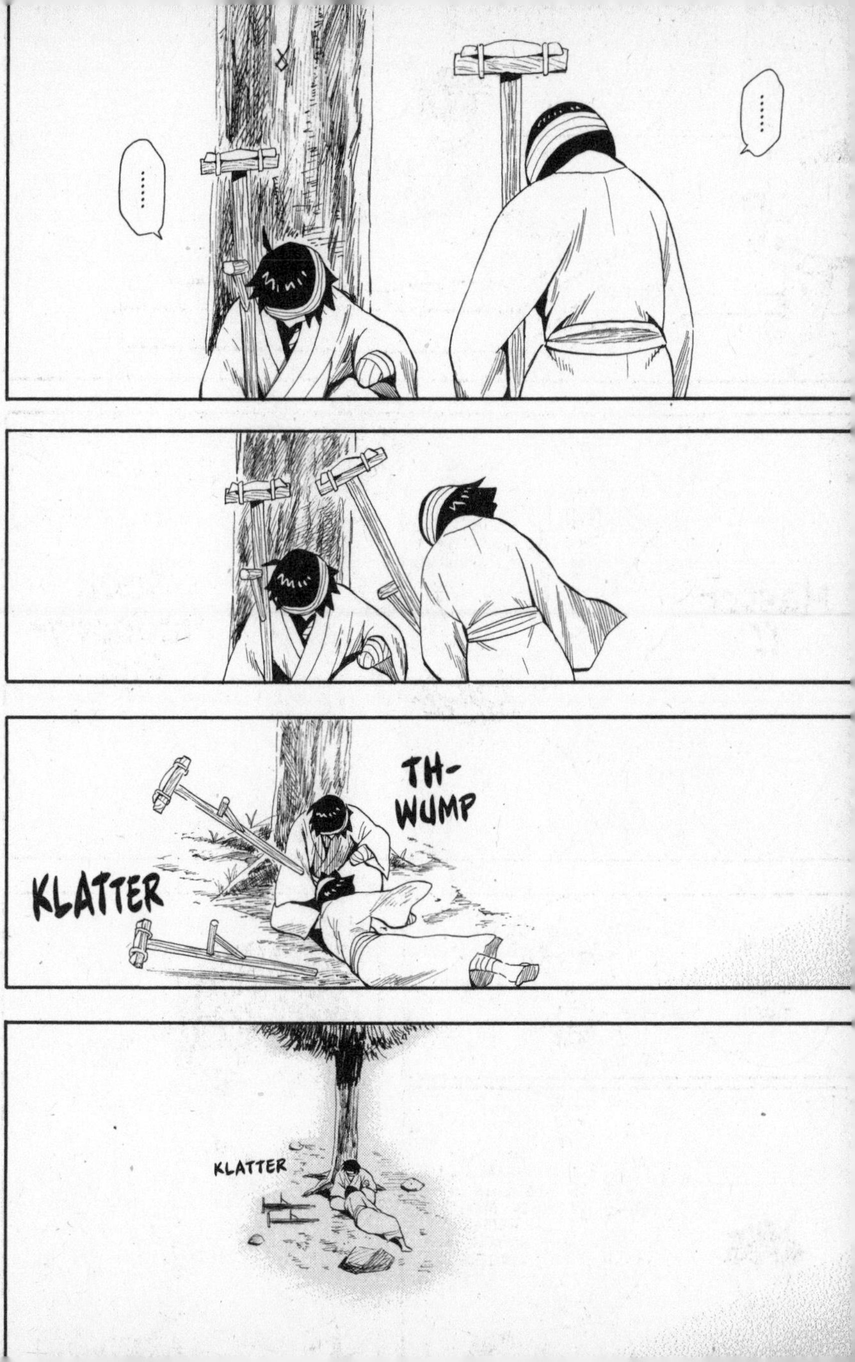
……
……
TH-WUMP
KLATTER
KLATTER

Circle 20
Town 1

Spacifica

Spirit Circle

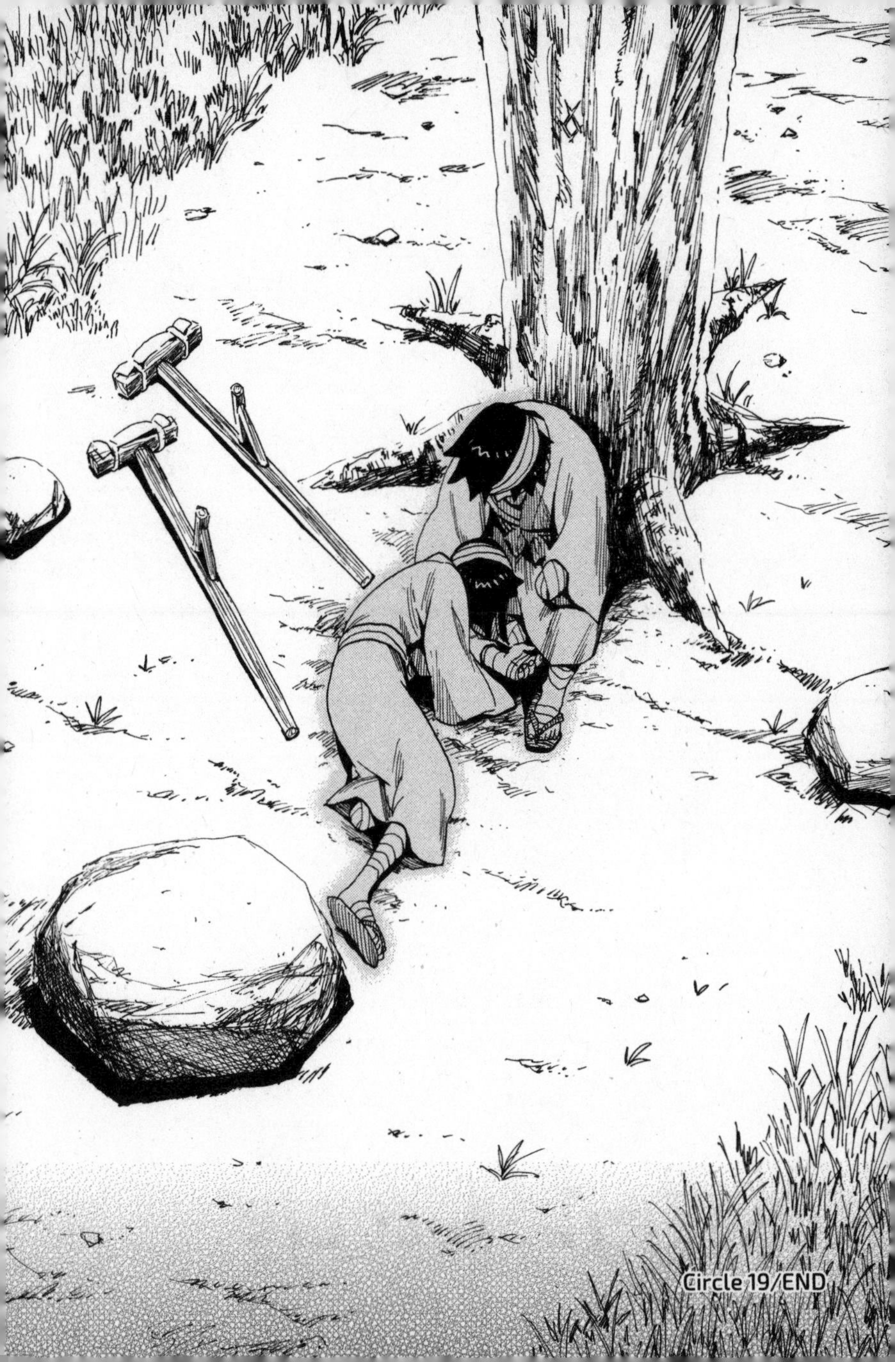
Circle 19/END

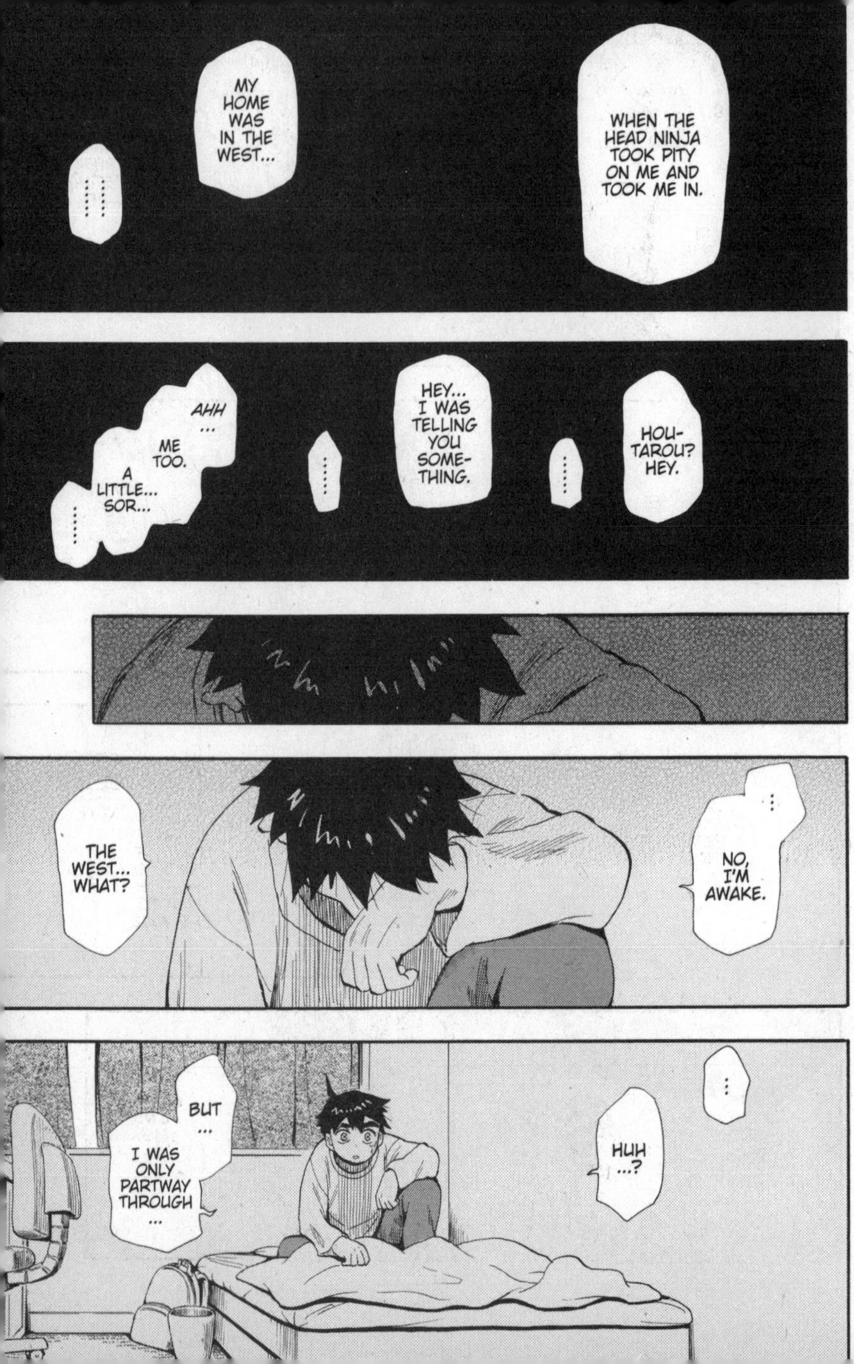
WHEN THE HEAD NINJA TOOK PITY ON ME AND TOOK ME IN.
MY HOME WAS IN THE WEST...
......
HOU-TAROU? HEY.
......
HEY... I WAS TELLING YOU SOMETHING.
......
AHH... ME TOO. A LITTLE... SOR...
......
...
NO, I'M AWAKE.
THE WEST... WHAT?
...
HUH...?
BUT... I WAS ONLY PARTWAY THROUGH...

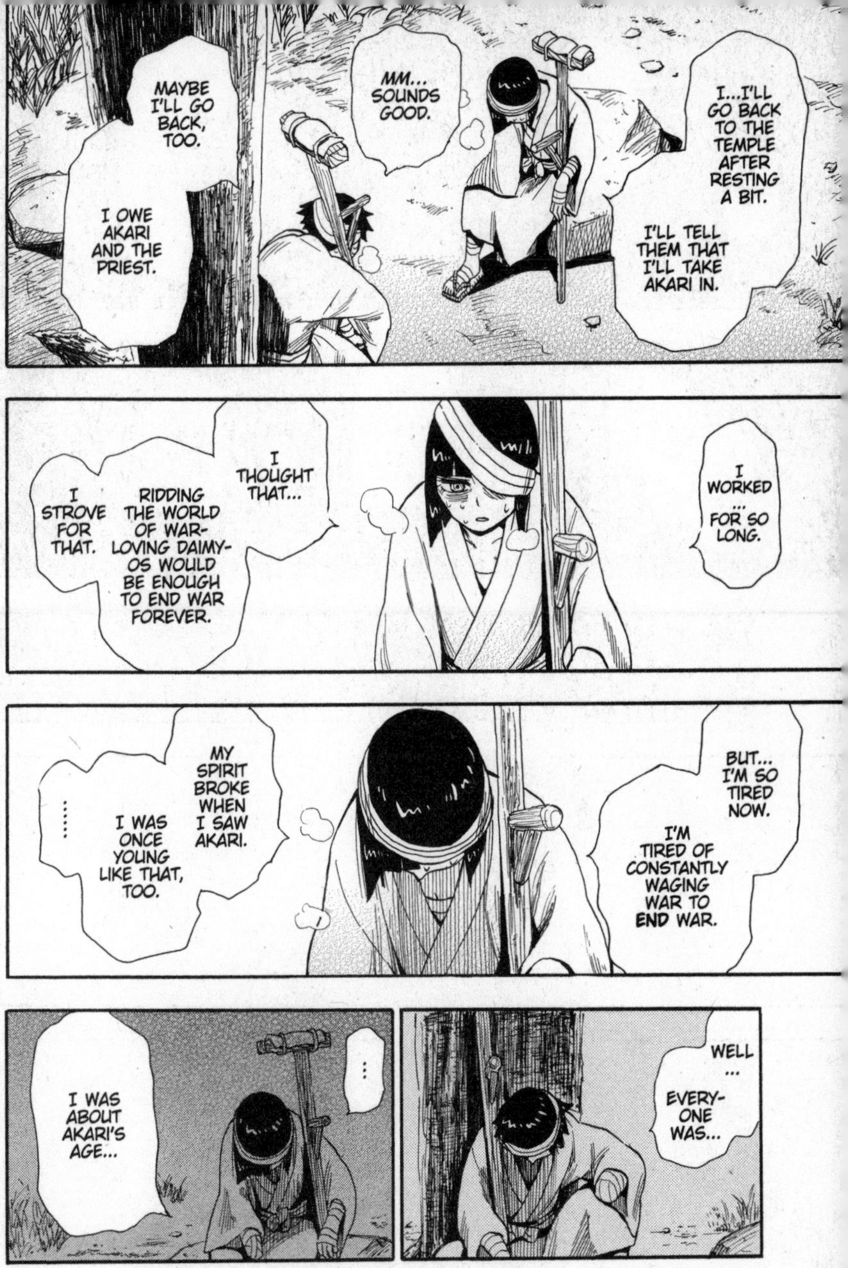
I...I'LL GO BACK TO THE TEMPLE AFTER RESTING A BIT.
I'LL TELL THEM THAT I'LL TAKE AKARI IN.
MM... SOUNDS GOOD.
MAYBE I'LL GO BACK, TOO.
I OWE AKARI AND THE PRIEST.
I WORKED... FOR SO LONG.
I THOUGHT THAT...
RIDDING THE WORLD OF WAR-LOVING DAIMY-OS WOULD BE ENOUGH TO END WAR FOREVER.
I STROVE FOR THAT.
BUT... I'M SO TIRED NOW.
I'M TIRED OF CONSTANTLY WAGING WAR TO END WAR.
MY SPIRIT BROKE WHEN I SAW AKARI.
I WAS ONCE YOUNG LIKE THAT, TOO.
......
WELL... EVERY-ONE WAS...
...
I WAS ABOUT AKARI'S AGE...

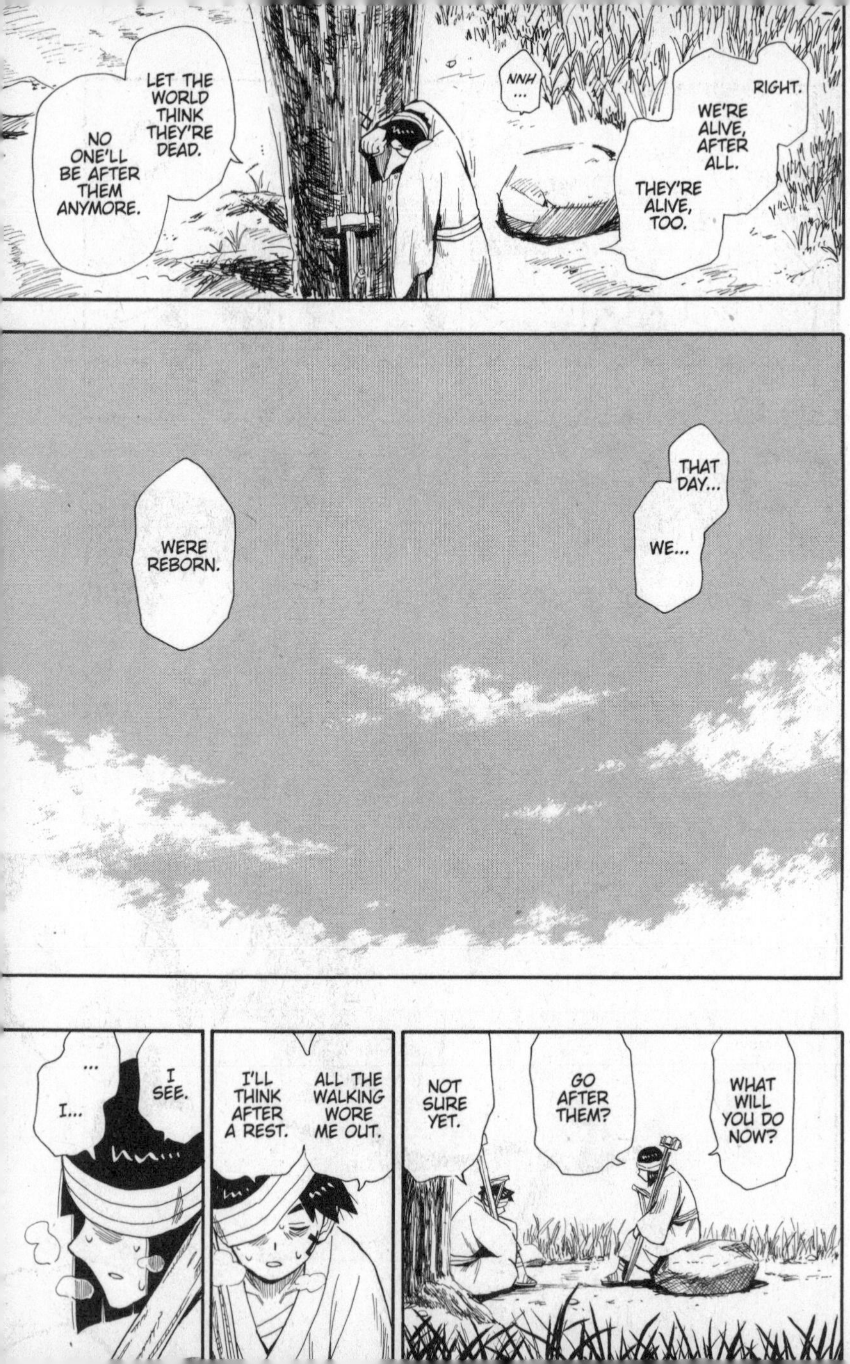
RIGHT. WE'RE ALIVE, AFTER ALL. THEY'RE ALIVE, TOO.
NNH ...
LET THE WORLD THINK THEY'RE DEAD. NO ONE'LL BE AFTER THEM ANYMORE.
THAT DAY... WE...
WERE REBORN.
WHAT WILL YOU DO NOW?
GO AFTER THEM?
NOT SURE YET.
ALL THE WALKING WORE ME OUT.
I'LL THINK AFTER A REST.
I SEE.
... I...

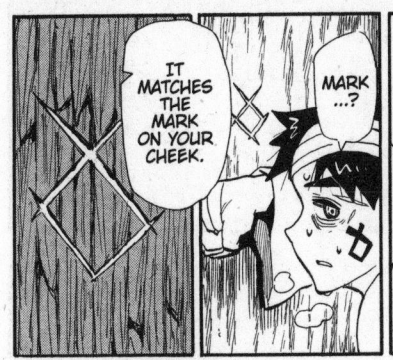

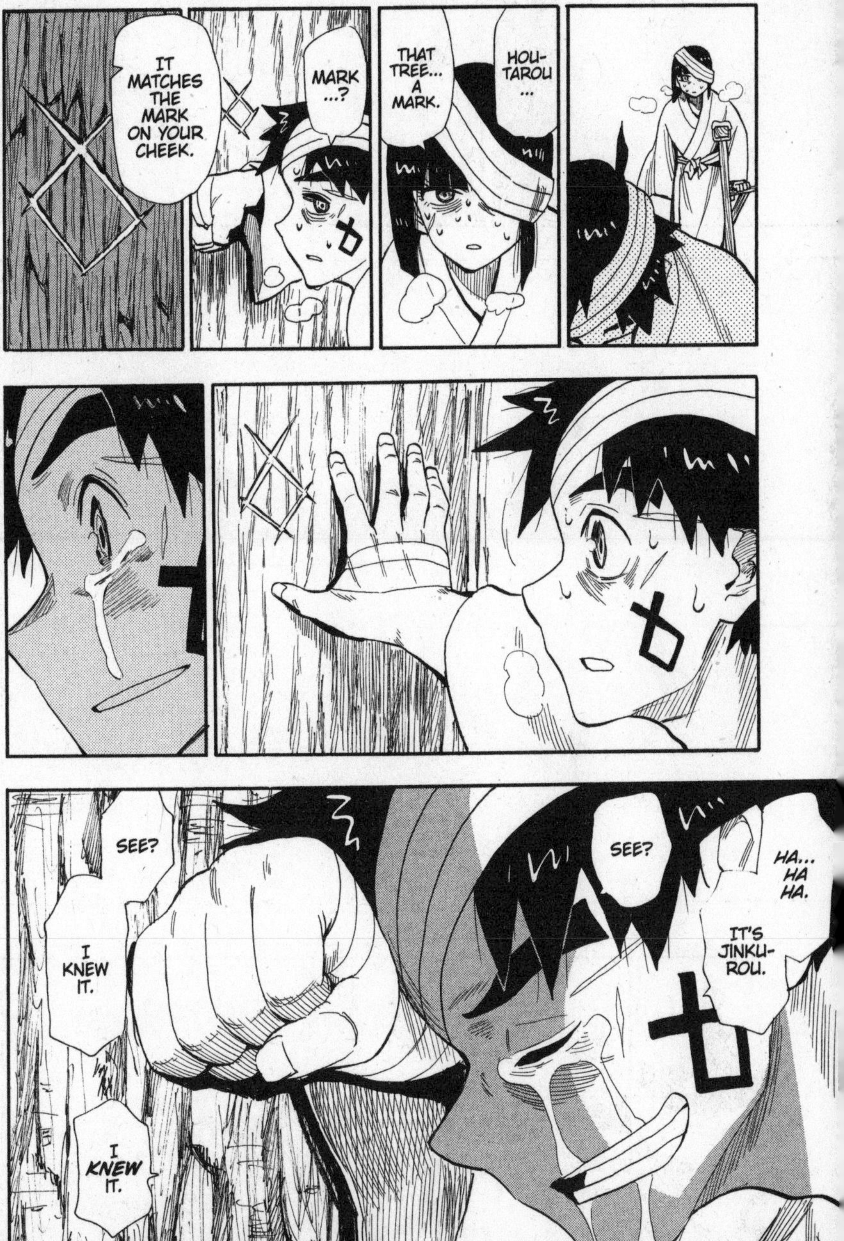

HOU-TAROU ...
THAT TREE... A MARK.
MARK ...?
IT MATCHES THE MARK ON YOUR CHEEK.
HA... HA HA.
SEE?
IT'S JINKU-ROU.
SEE?
I KNEW IT.
I *KNEW* IT.

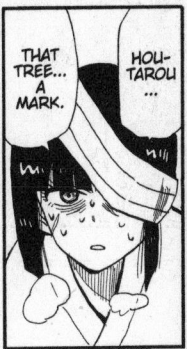

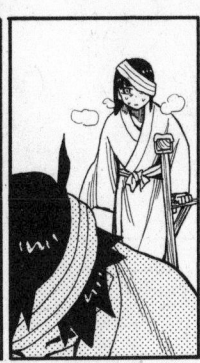

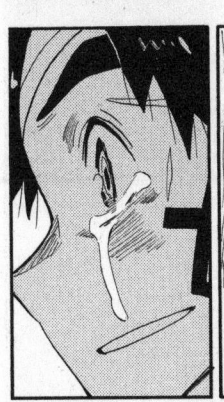

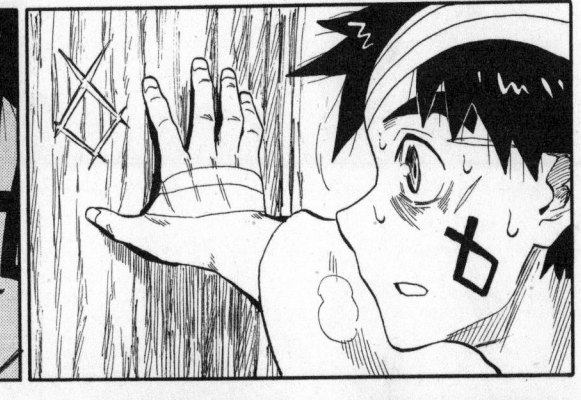

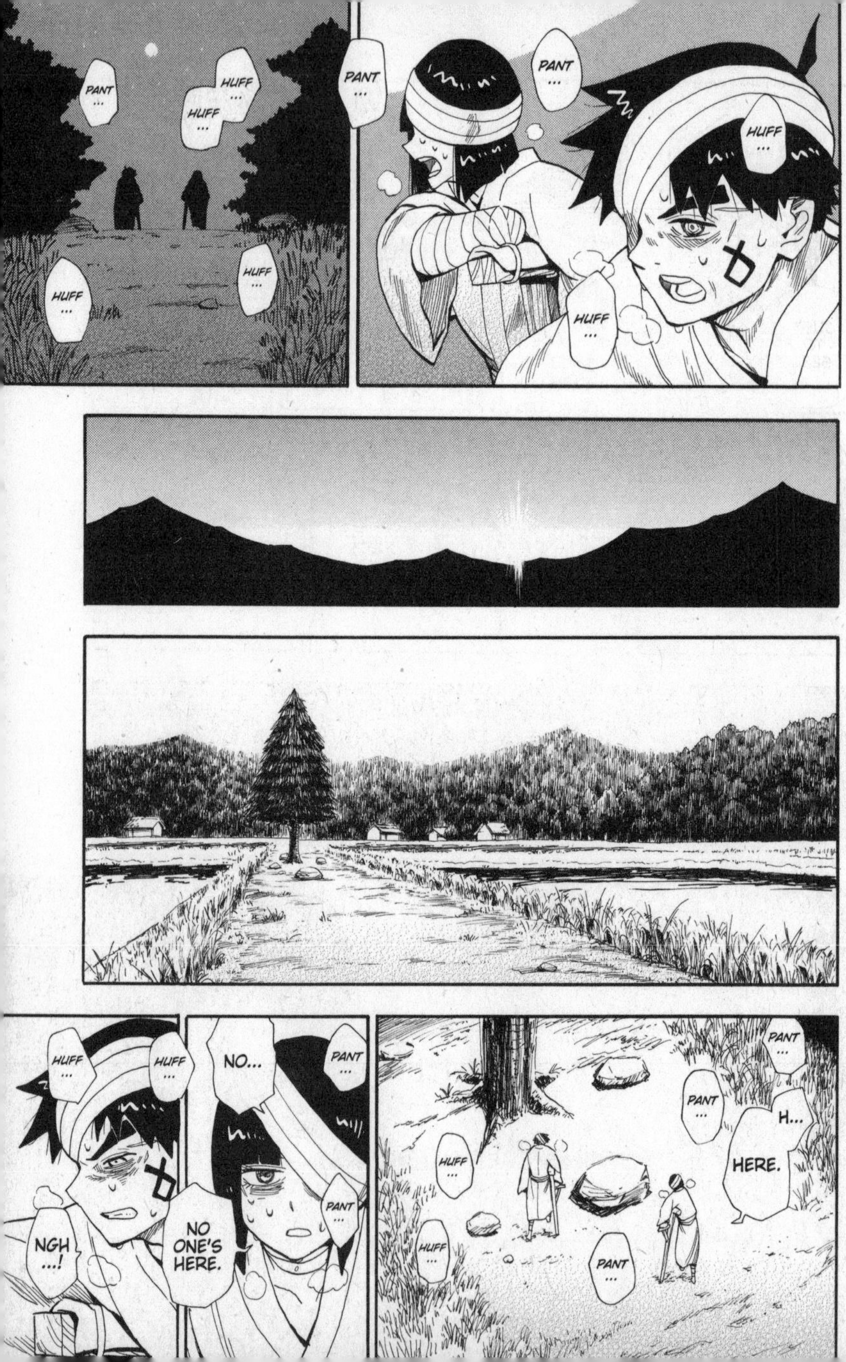
PANT ...
HUFF ...
PANT ...
HUFF ...
HUFF ...
HUFF ...
PANT ...
HUFF ...
HUFF ...
PANT ...
H... HERE.
PANT ...
HUFF ...
PANT ...
HUFF ...
PANT ...
NO...
PANT ...
NO ONE'S HERE.
HUFF ...
HUFF ...
NGH ...!

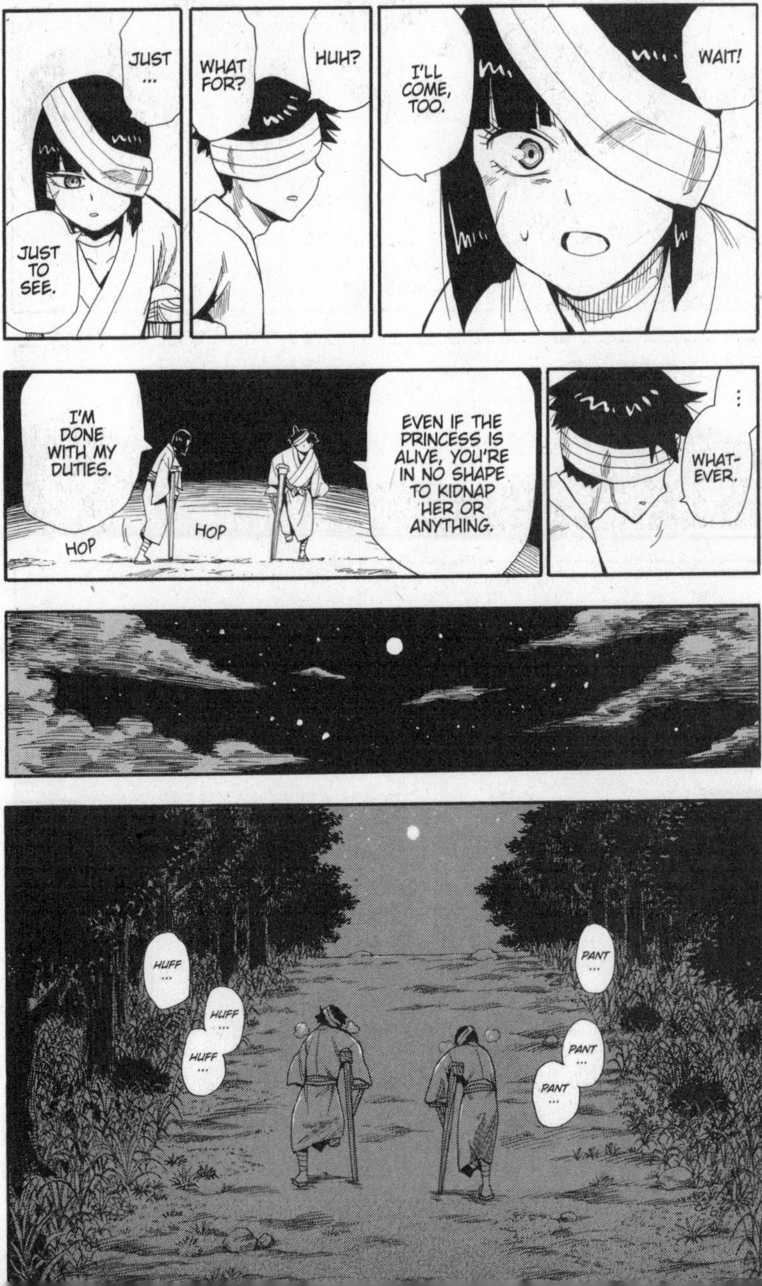
WAIT!
I'LL COME, TOO.
HUH?
WHAT FOR?
JUST ...
JUST TO SEE.
... WHAT-EVER.
EVEN IF THE PRINCESS IS ALIVE, YOU'RE IN NO SHAPE TO KIDNAP HER OR ANYTHING.
I'M DONE WITH MY DUTIES.
HOP
HOP
PANT ...
PANT ...
PANT ...
HUFF ...
HUFF ...
HUFF ...

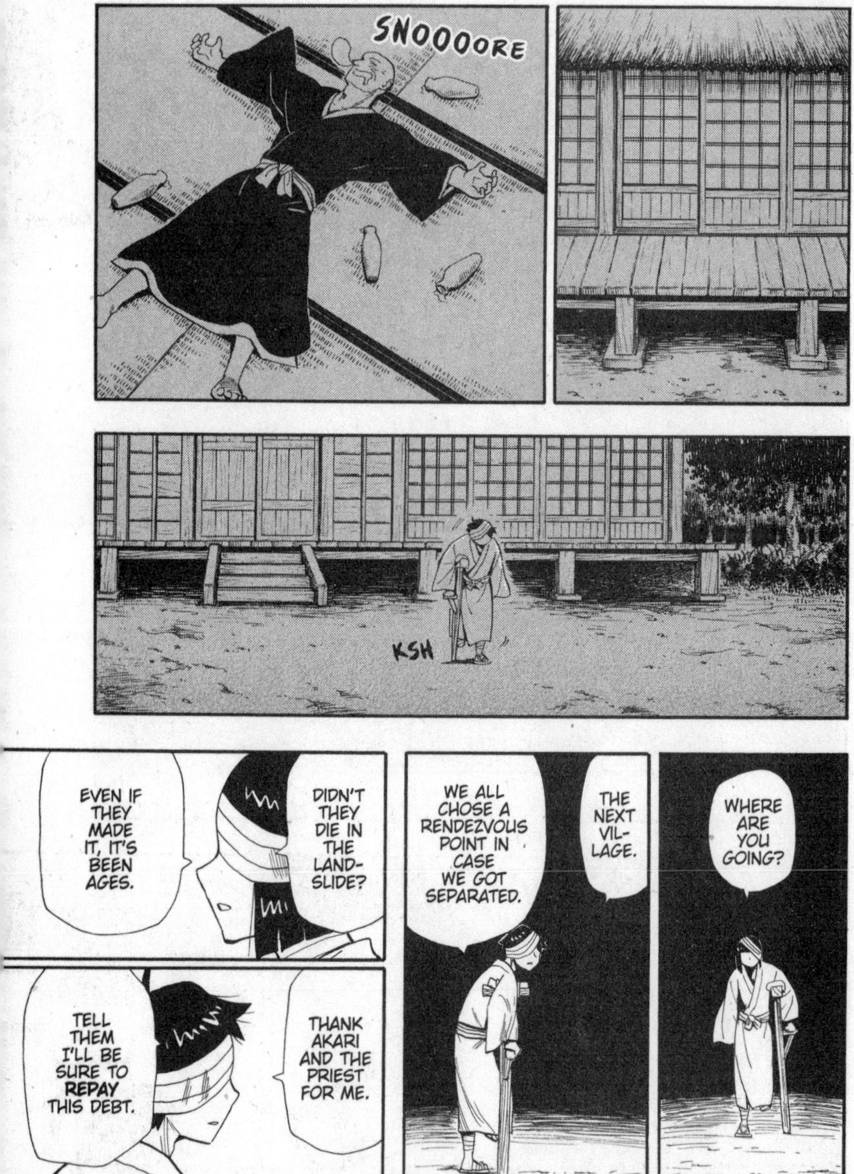
SNOOOORE
KSH
WHERE ARE YOU GOING?
THE NEXT VILLAGE.
WE ALL CHOSE A RENDEZVOUS POINT IN CASE WE GOT SEPARATED.
DIDN'T THEY DIE IN THE LANDSLIDE?
EVEN IF THEY MADE IT, IT'S BEEN AGES.
THANK AKARI AND THE PRIEST FOR ME.
TELL THEM I'LL BE SURE TO **REPAY** THIS DEBT.

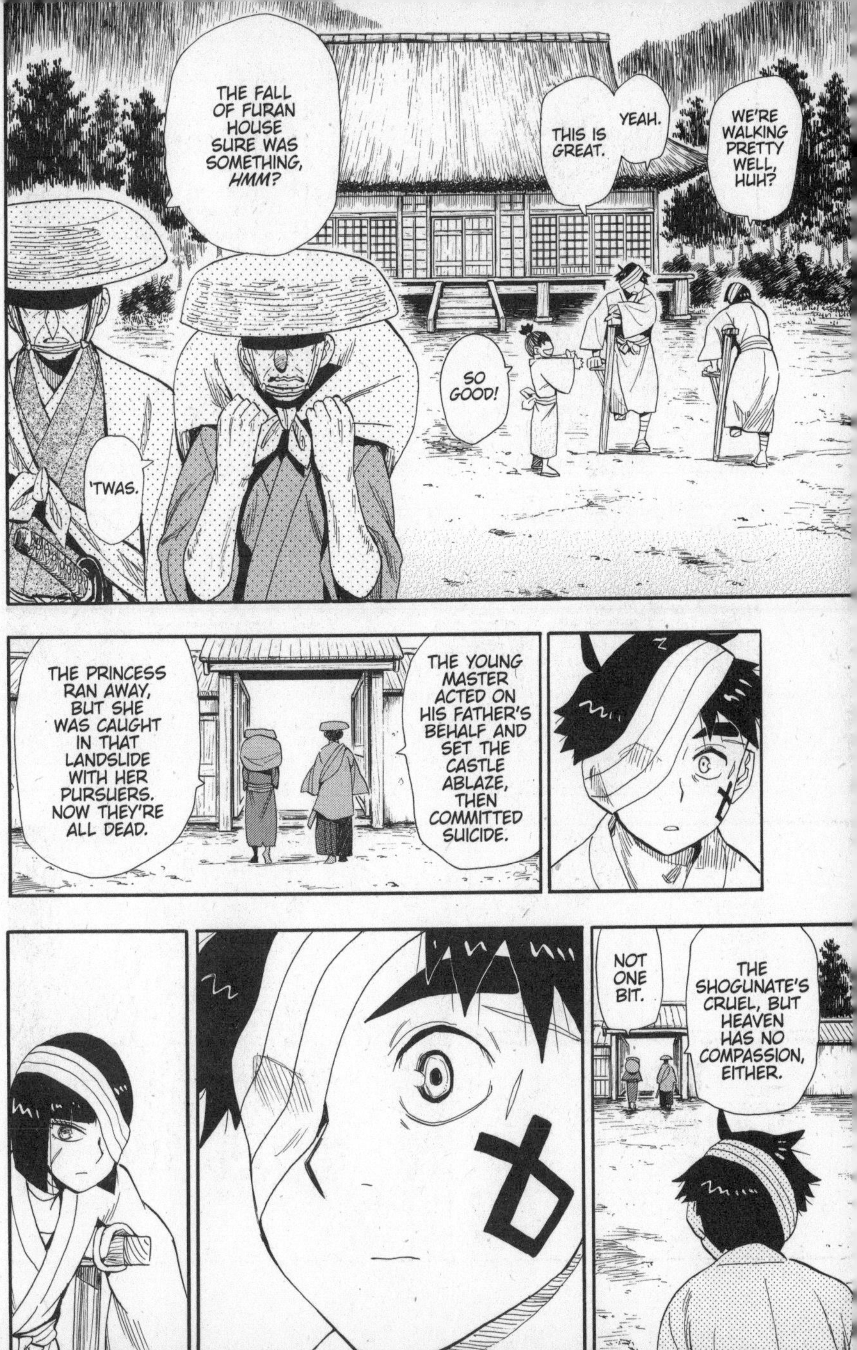
WE'RE WALKING PRETTY WELL, HUH?
YEAH.
THIS IS GREAT.
SO GOOD!
THE FALL OF FURAN HOUSE SURE WAS SOMETHING, *HMM?*
'TWAS.
THE YOUNG MASTER ACTED ON HIS FATHER'S BEHALF AND SET THE CASTLE ABLAZE, THEN COMMITTED SUICIDE.
THE PRINCESS RAN AWAY, BUT SHE WAS CAUGHT IN THAT LANDSLIDE WITH HER PURSUERS. NOW THEY'RE ALL DEAD.
THE SHOGUNATE'S CRUEL, BUT HEAVEN HAS NO COMPASSION, EITHER.
NOT ONE BIT.

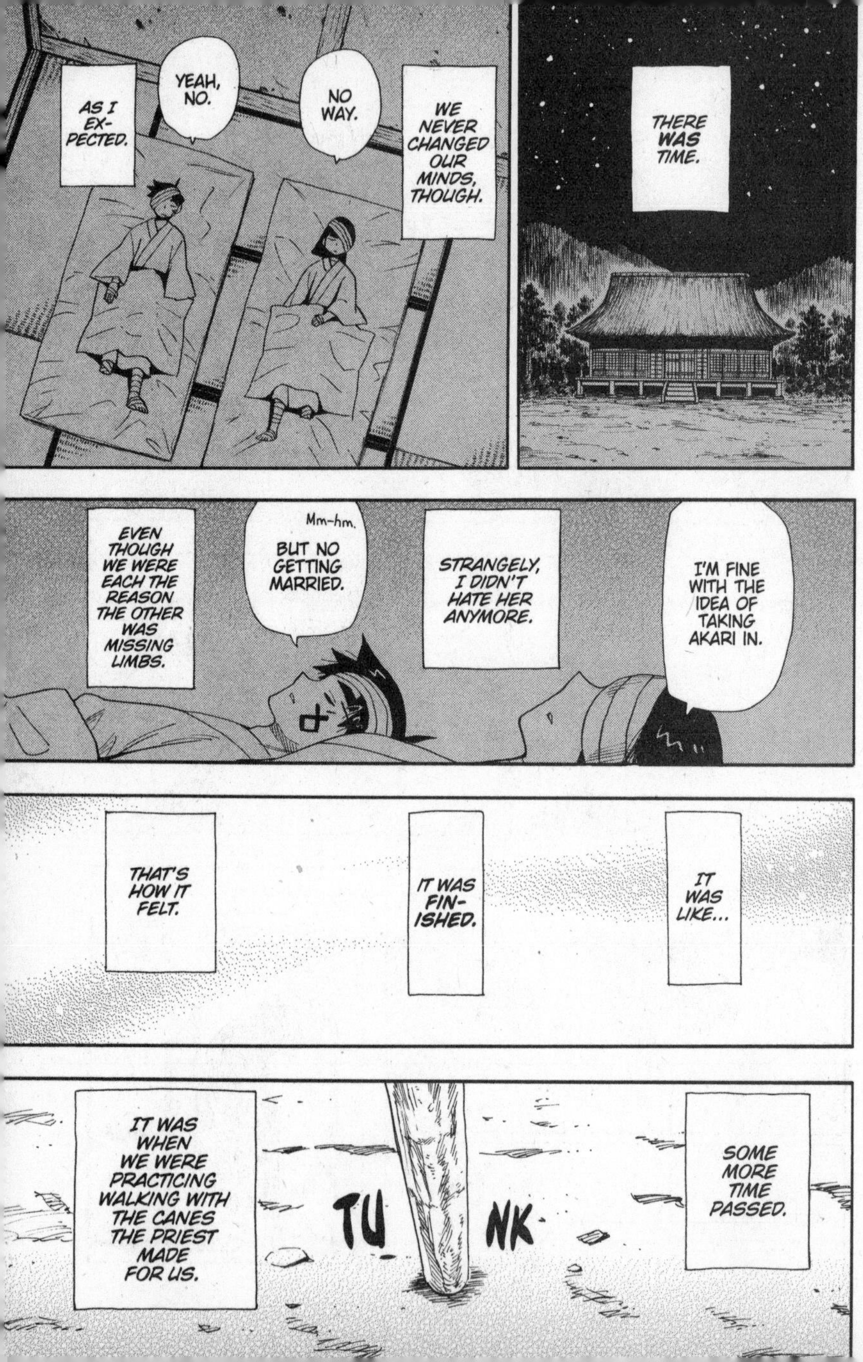
THERE WAS TIME.
WE NEVER CHANGED OUR MINDS, THOUGH.
NO WAY.
YEAH, NO.
AS I EX-PECTED.
I'M FINE WITH THE IDEA OF TAKING AKARI IN.
STRANGELY, I DIDN'T HATE HER ANYMORE.
Mm-hm.
BUT NO GETTING MARRIED.
EVEN THOUGH WE WERE EACH THE REASON THE OTHER WAS MISSING LIMBS.
IT WAS LIKE...
IT WAS FIN-ISHED.
THAT'S HOW IT FELT.
SOME MORE TIME PASSED.
TUNK
IT WAS WHEN WE WERE PRACTICING WALKING WITH THE CANES THE PRIEST MADE FOR US.

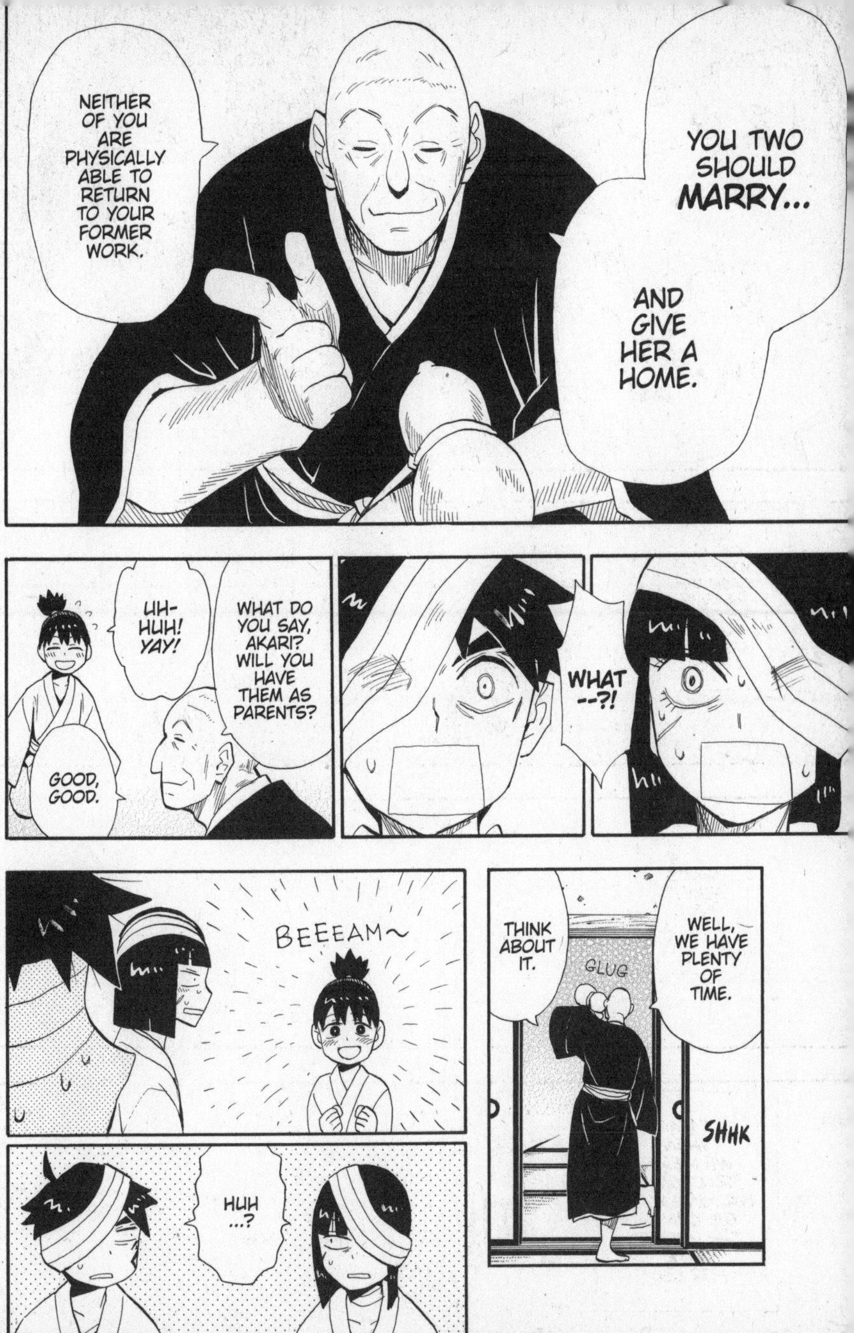
YOU TWO SHOULD MARRY...
AND GIVE HER A HOME.
NEITHER OF YOU ARE PHYSICALLY ABLE TO RETURN TO YOUR FORMER WORK.
WHAT --?!
WHAT DO YOU SAY, AKARI? WILL YOU HAVE THEM AS PARENTS?
UH-HUH! YAY!
GOOD, GOOD.
WELL, WE HAVE PLENTY OF TIME.
THINK ABOUT IT.
GLUG
SHHK
BEEEAM~
HUH ...?

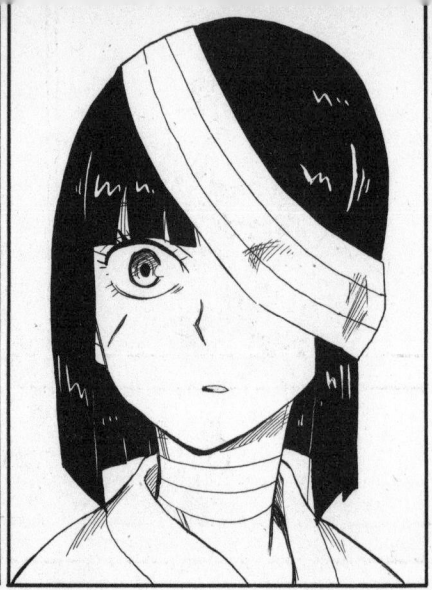

MY HEART JUST LIGHTENED?

WHAT?

SOMEHOW...

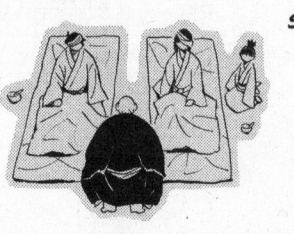

THIS, CHILD, AKARI...

SHE LOST HER PARENTS IN WAR. SHE'S AN ORPHAN.

HEH HEH HEH!

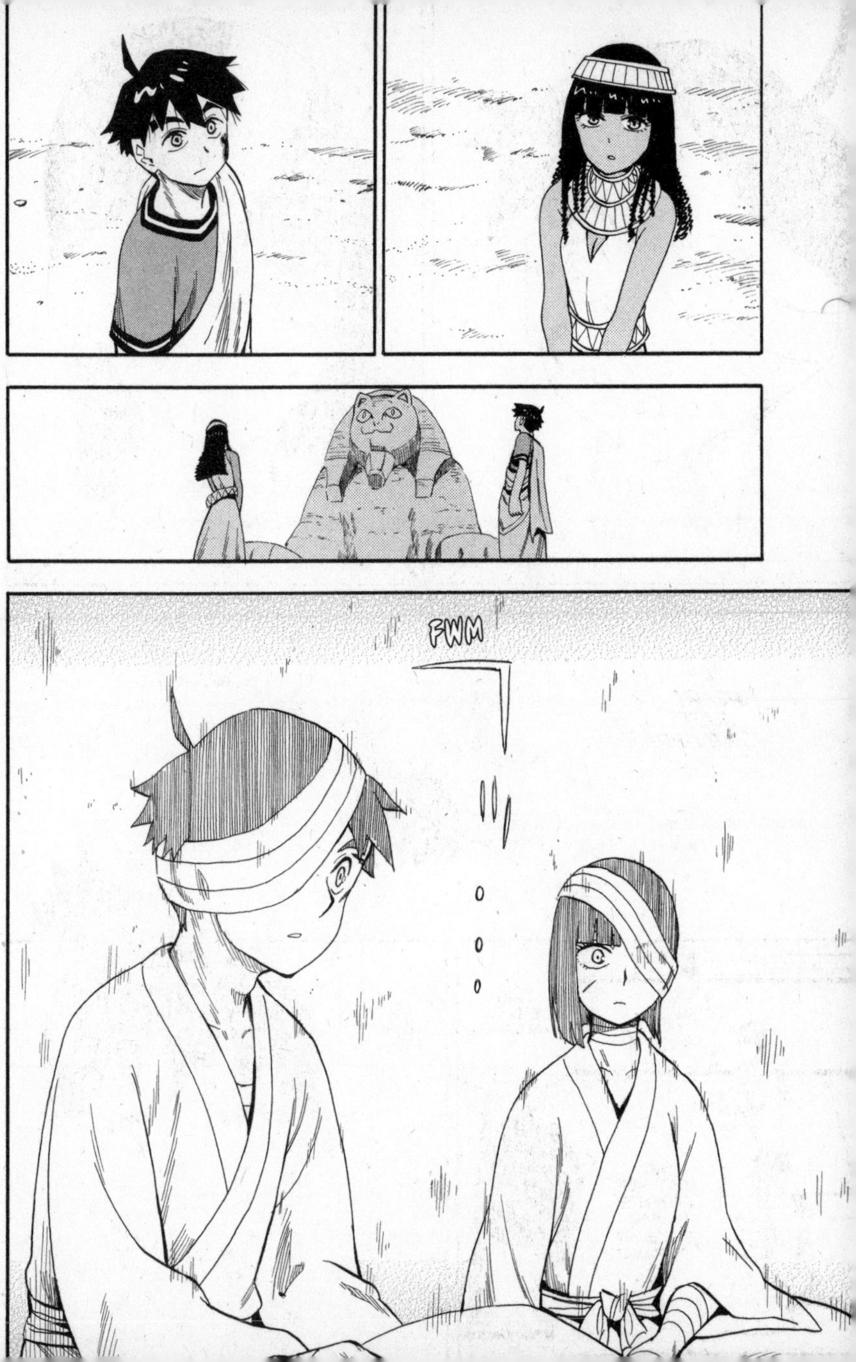
FWM

STOP?

ENOUGH ...?

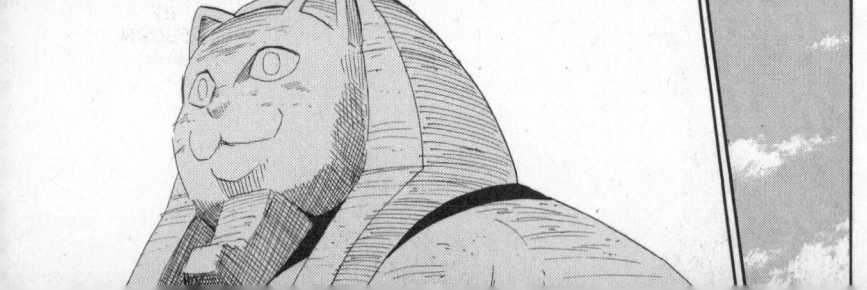

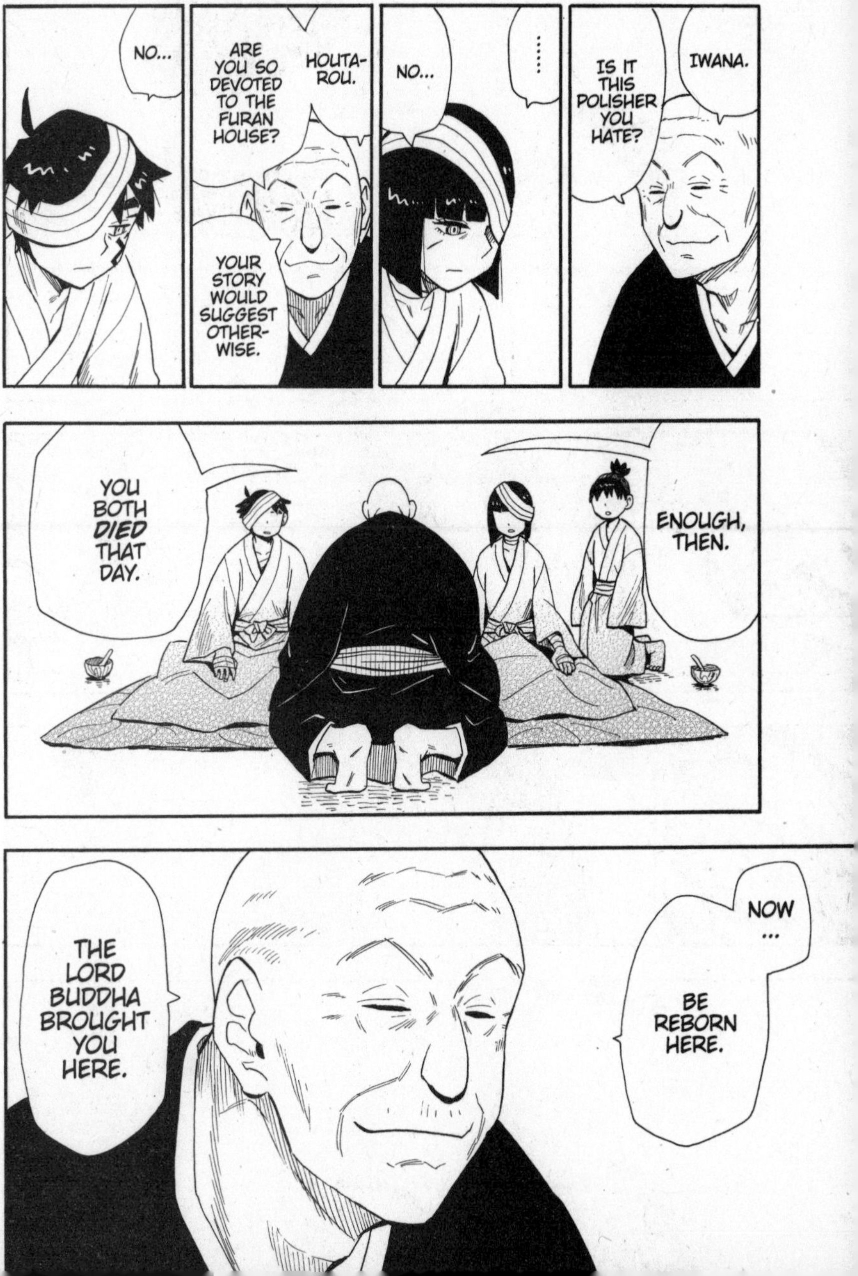
IWANA.
IS IT THIS POLISHER YOU HATE?
......
NO...
HOUTA-ROU.
ARE YOU SO DEVOTED TO THE FURAN HOUSE?
YOUR STORY WOULD SUGGEST OTHER-WISE.
NO...
ENOUGH, THEN.
YOU BOTH DIED THAT DAY.
NOW ...
BE REBORN HERE.
THE LORD BUDDHA BROUGHT YOU HERE.

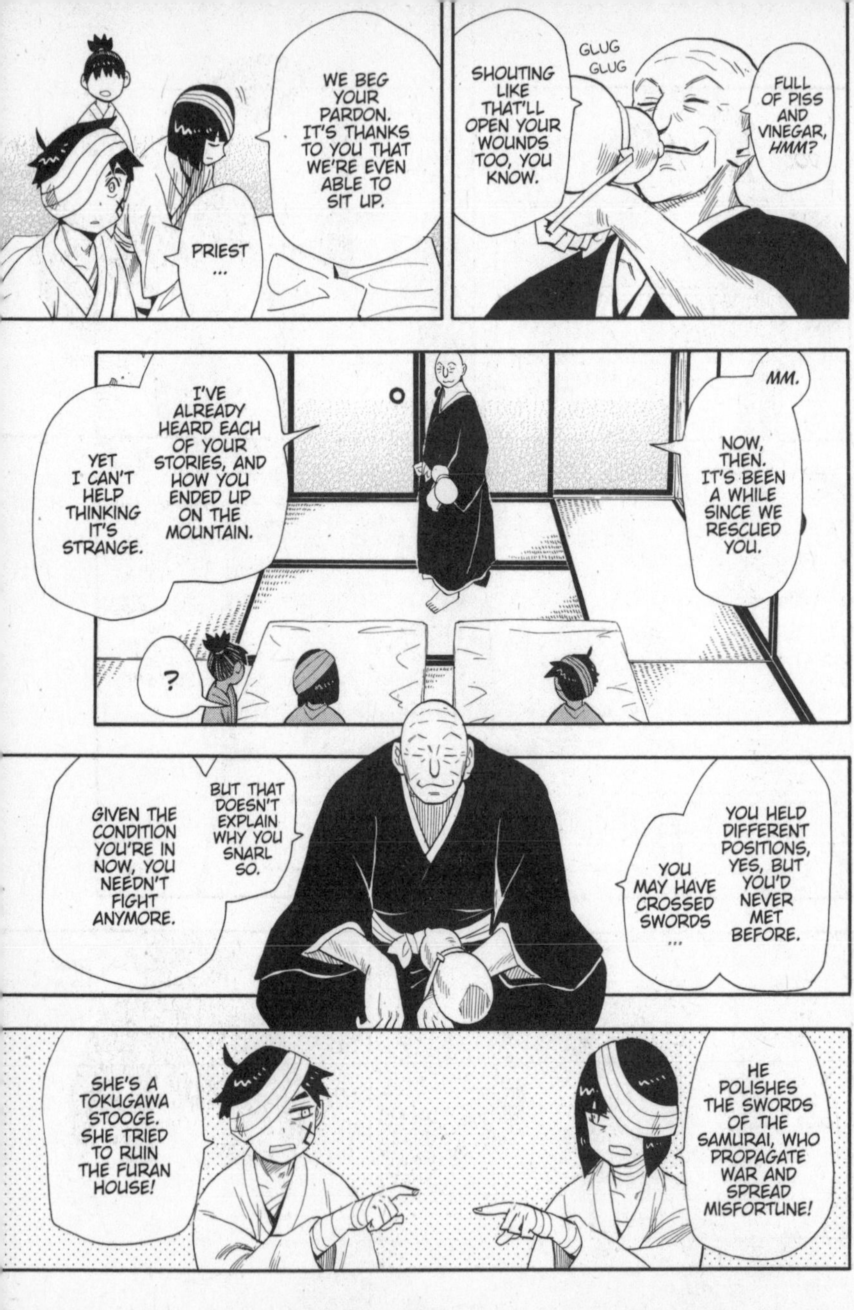
FULL OF PISS AND VINEGAR, *HMM?*
GLUG GLUG
SHOUTING LIKE THAT'LL OPEN YOUR WOUNDS TOO, YOU KNOW.
WE BEG YOUR PARDON. IT'S THANKS TO YOU THAT WE'RE EVEN ABLE TO SIT UP.
PRIEST ...
MM.
NOW, THEN. IT'S BEEN A WHILE SINCE WE RESCUED YOU.
I'VE ALREADY HEARD EACH OF YOUR STORIES, AND HOW YOU ENDED UP ON THE MOUNTAIN.
YET I CAN'T HELP THINKING IT'S STRANGE.
?
YOU HELD DIFFERENT POSITIONS, YES, BUT YOU'D NEVER MET BEFORE.
YOU MAY HAVE CROSSED SWORDS ...
BUT THAT DOESN'T EXPLAIN WHY YOU SNARL SO.
GIVEN THE CONDITION YOU'RE IN NOW, YOU NEEDN'T FIGHT ANYMORE.
HE POLISHES THE SWORDS OF THE SAMURAI, WHO PROPAGATE WAR AND SPREAD MISFORTUNE!
SHE'S A TOKUGAWA STOOGE. SHE TRIED TO RUIN THE FURAN HOUSE!

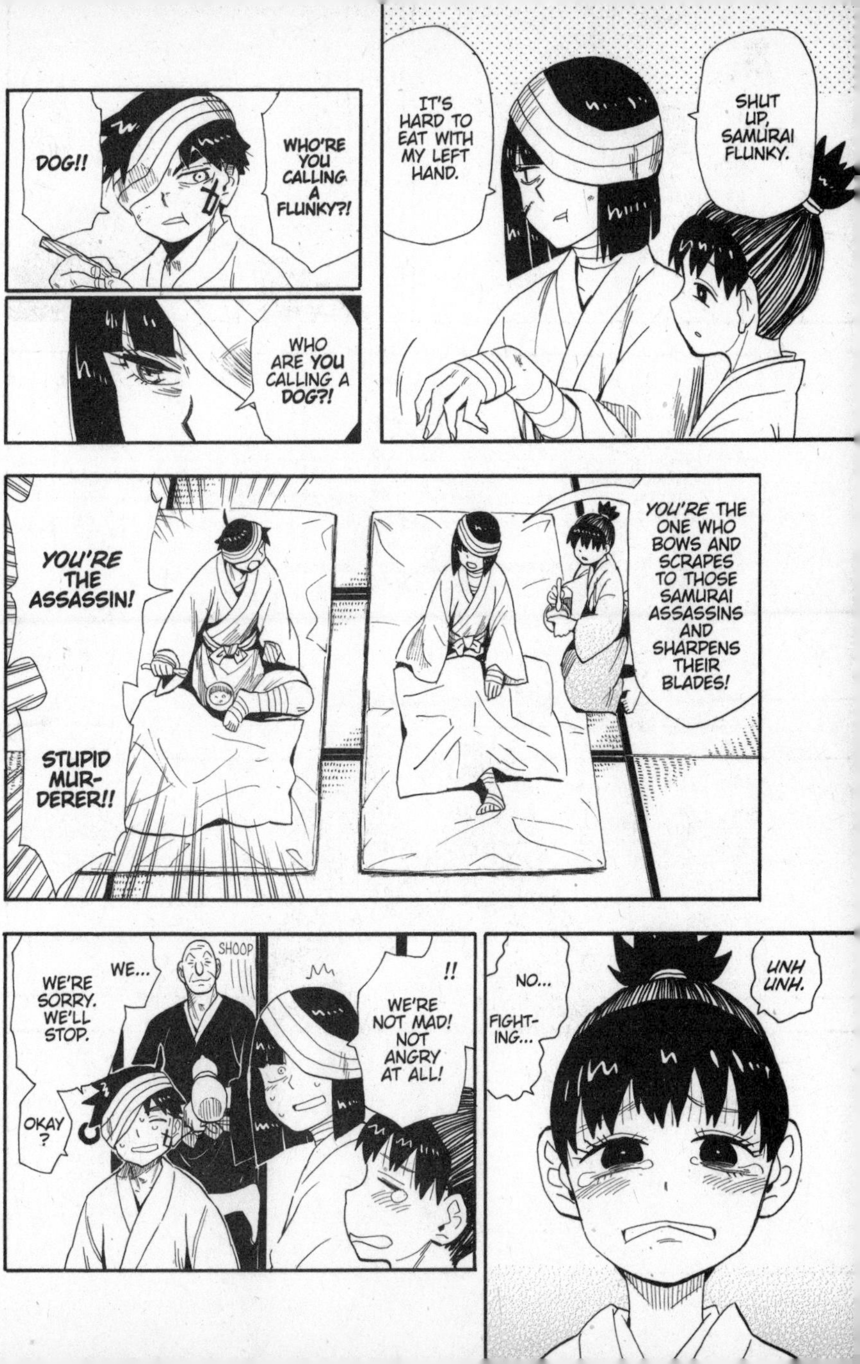

IT'S HARD TO EAT WITH MY LEFT HAND.
SHUT UP, SAMURAI FLUNKY.
WHO'RE YOU CALLING A FLUNKY?!
DOG!!
WHO ARE YOU CALLING A DOG?!
YOU'RE THE ONE WHO BOWS AND SCRAPES TO THOSE SAMURAI ASSASSINS AND SHARPENS THEIR BLADES!
YOU'RE THE ASSASSIN!
STUPID MUR-DERER!!
UNH UNH.
NO... FIGHT-ING...
!!
WE'RE NOT MAD! NOT ANGRY AT ALL!
SHOOP
WE...
WE'RE SORRY. WE'LL STOP.
OKAY?

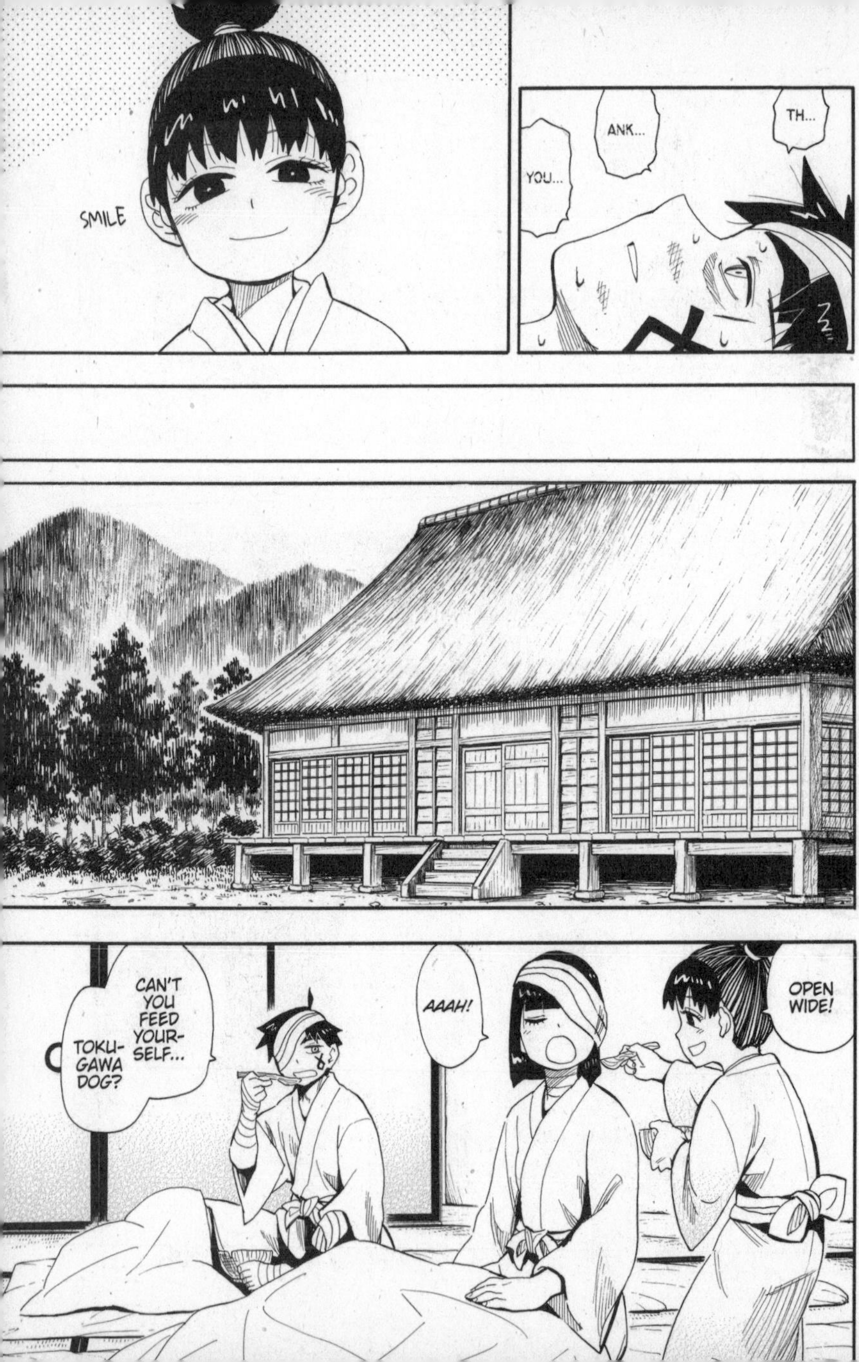
TH...
ANK...
YOU...
SMILE
OPEN WIDE!
AAAH!
CAN'T YOU FEED YOURSELF...
TOKUGAWA DOG?

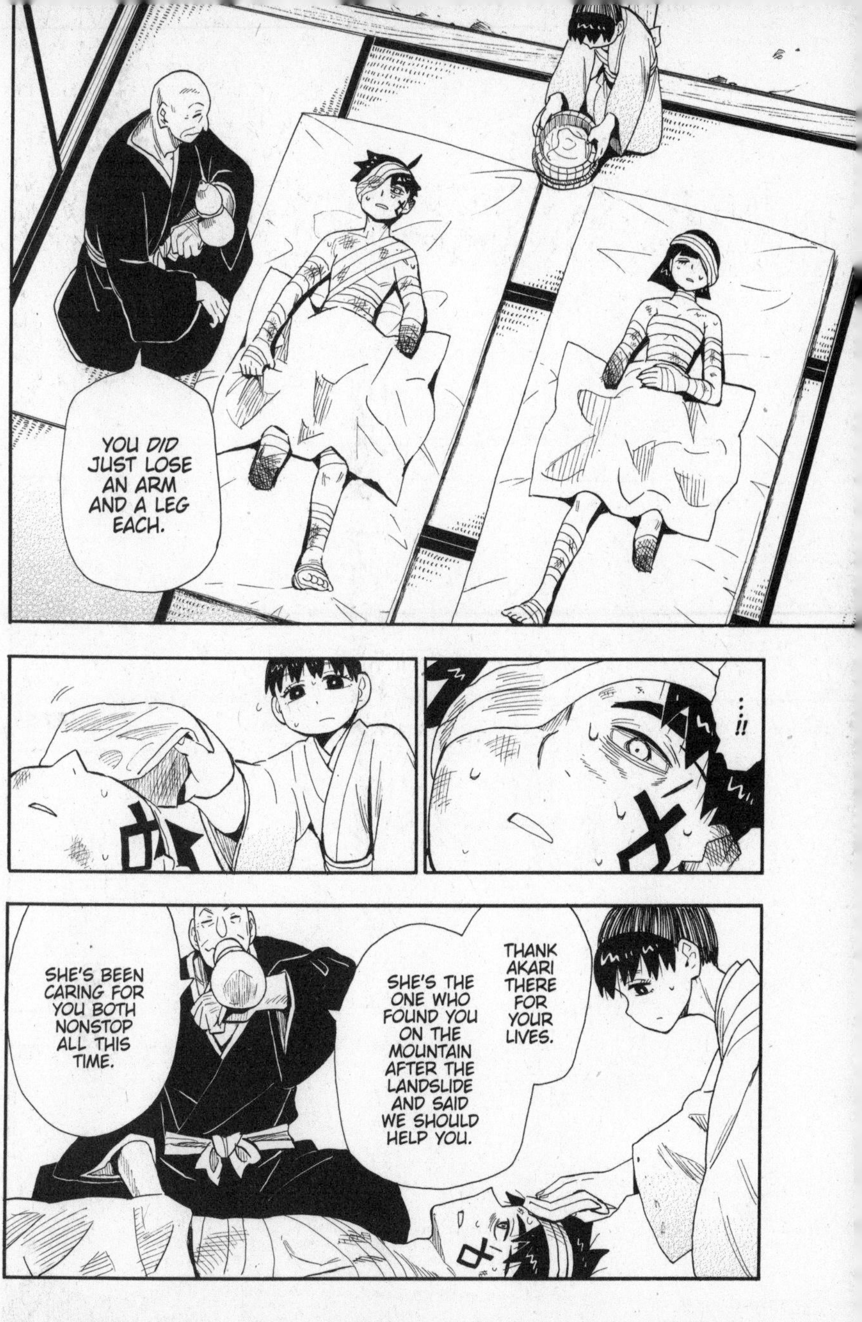
YOU *DID* JUST LOSE AN ARM AND A LEG EACH.
...!!
THANK AKARI THERE FOR YOUR LIVES.
SHE'S THE ONE WHO FOUND YOU ON THE MOUNTAIN AFTER THE LANDSLIDE AND SAID WE SHOULD HELP YOU.
SHE'S BEEN CARING FOR YOU BOTH NONSTOP ALL THIS TIME.

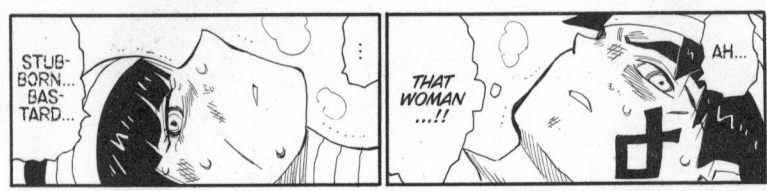

STUB-
BORN...
BAS-
TARD...

: : :

*THAT
WOMAN
...!!*

AH...

YOU'LL
OPEN
YOUR
WOUNDS.

STOP.

HNGH!

NGH
...
UNH!

AL-
THOUGH,
I SUP-
POSE...

YOU
CAN'T
ACTUALLY
MOVE.

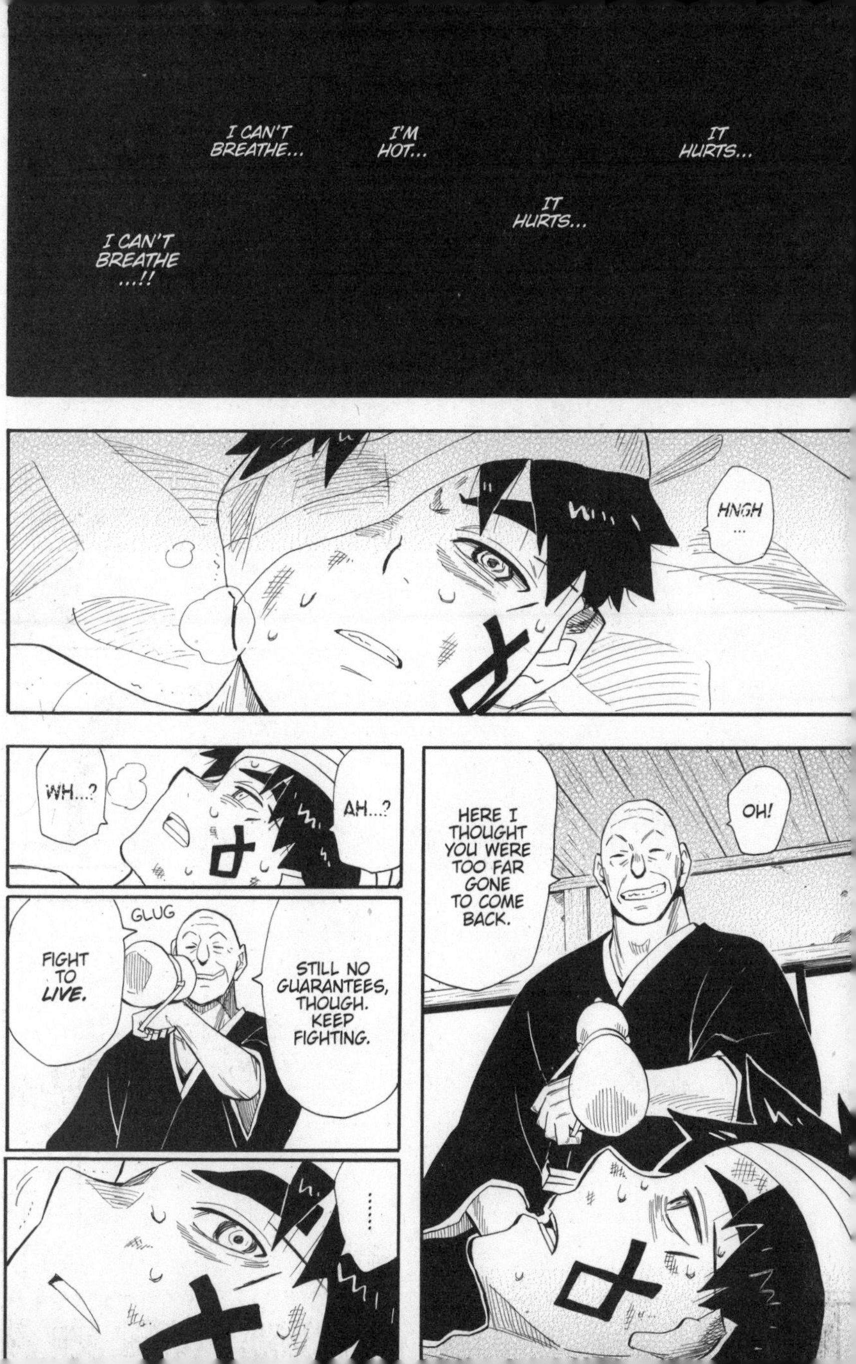
IT HURTS...
I'M HOT...
I CAN'T BREATHE...
IT HURTS...
I CAN'T BREATHE ...!!
HNGH ...
OH!
HERE I THOUGHT YOU WERE TOO FAR GONE TO COME BACK.
AH...?
WH...?
STILL NO GUARANTEES, THOUGH. KEEP FIGHTING.
GLUG
FIGHT TO *LIVE.*
......

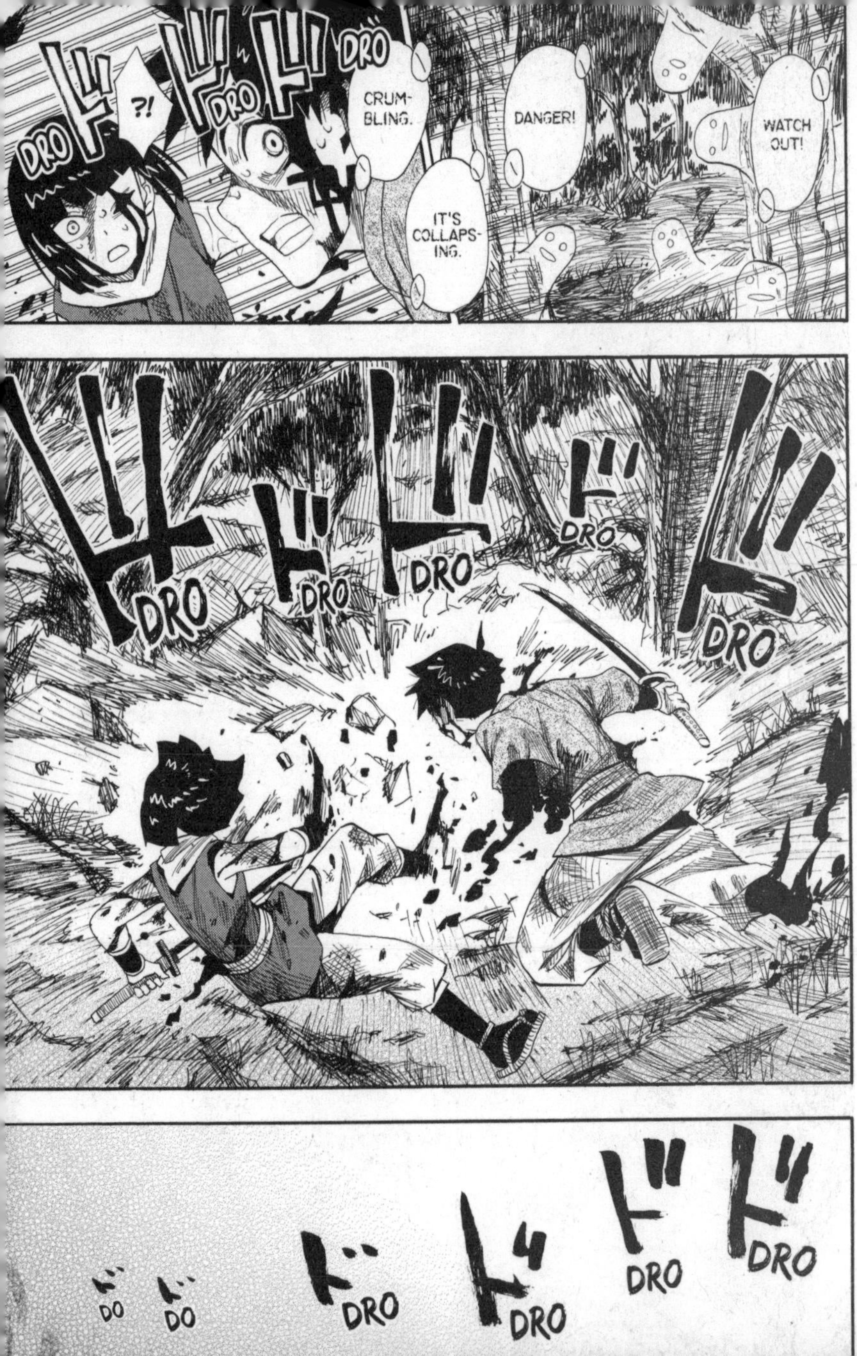
WATCH OUT!
DANGER!
IT'S COLLAPSING.
CRUMBLING.
DRO
DRO
?!
DRO
DRO
DRO
DRO
DRO
DRO
DRO
DRO
DRO
DRO
DRO
DO
DO

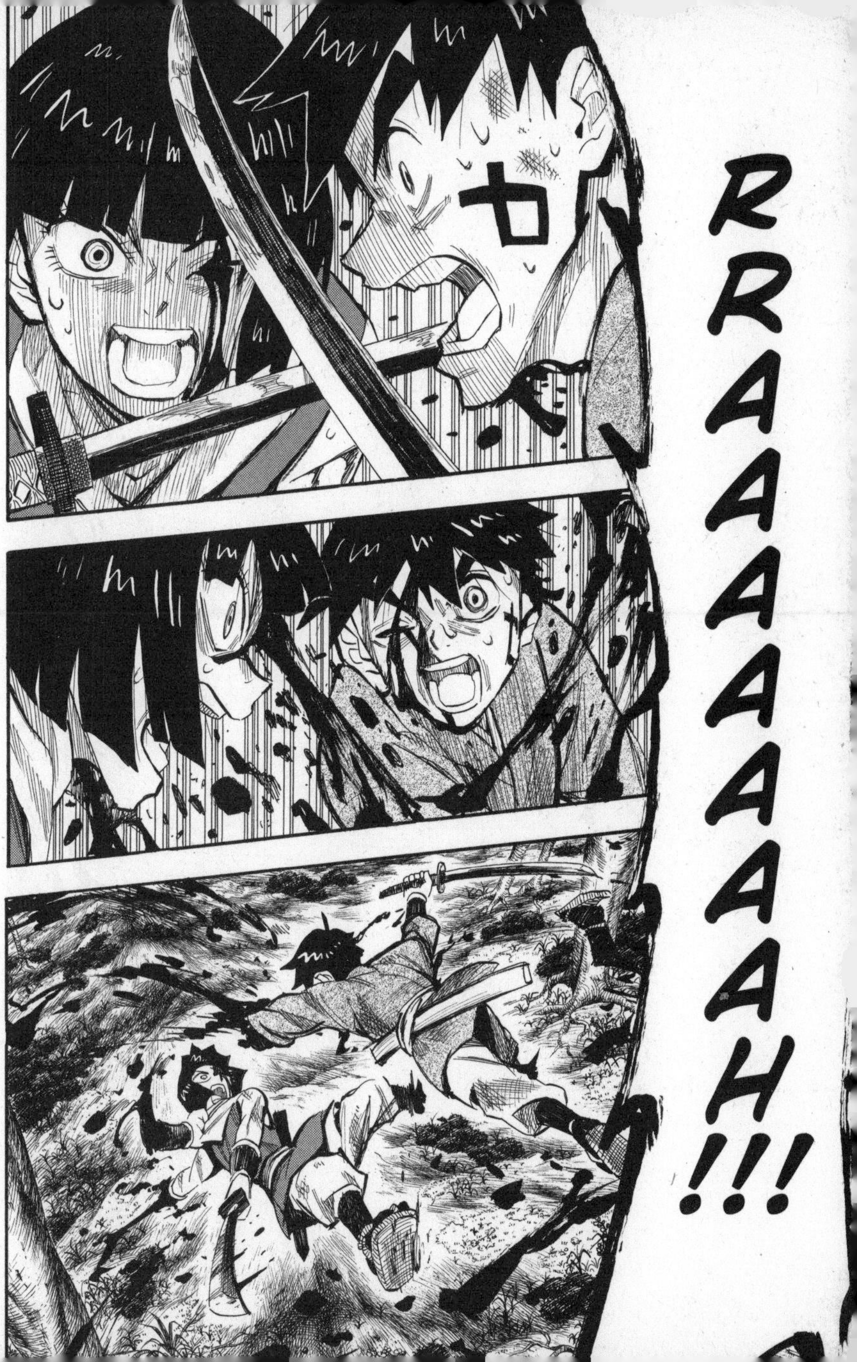
RRAAAAAAAAH!!!

Circle 19
Houtarou
5

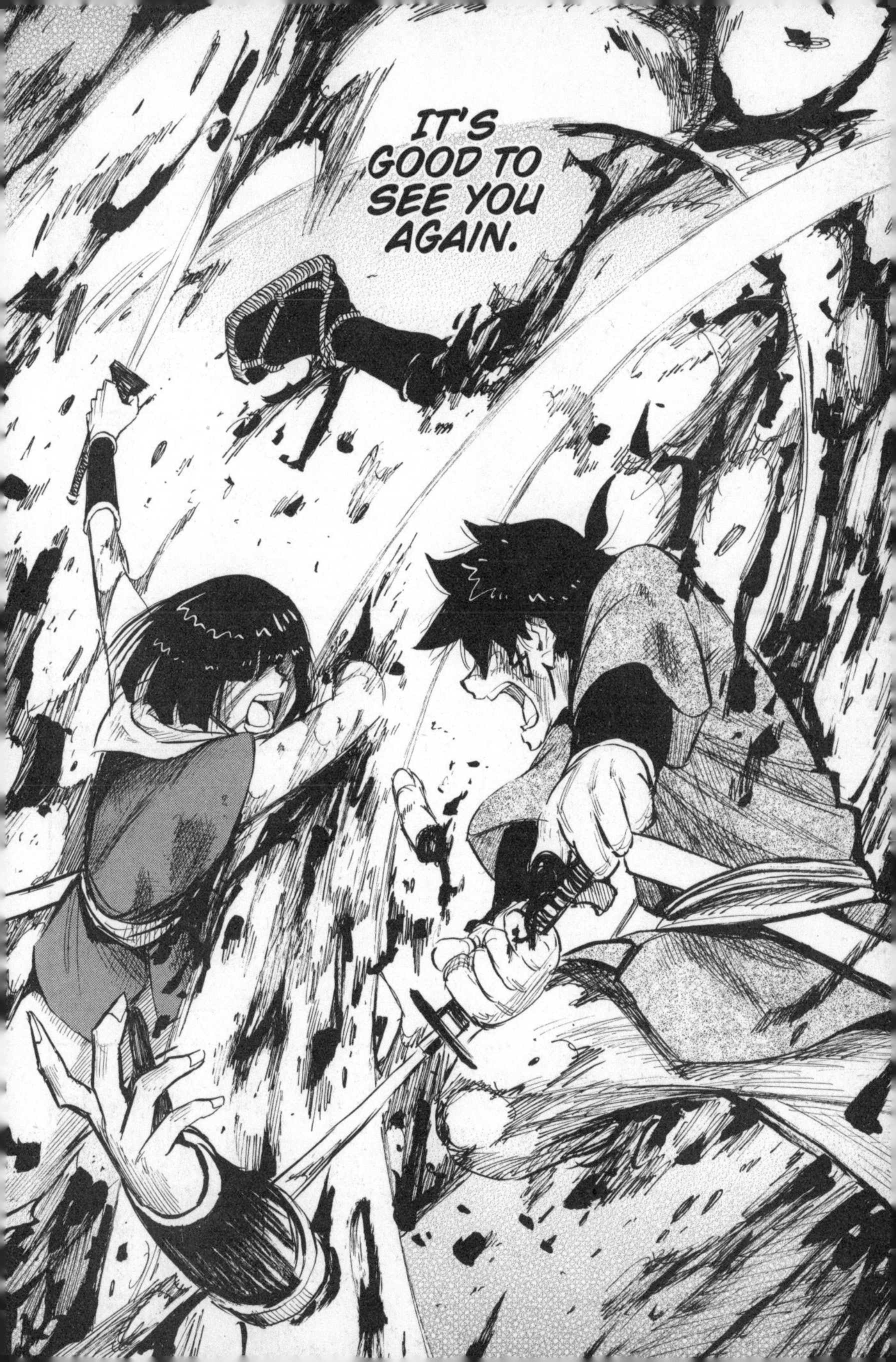
IT'S GOOD TO SEE YOU AGAIN.

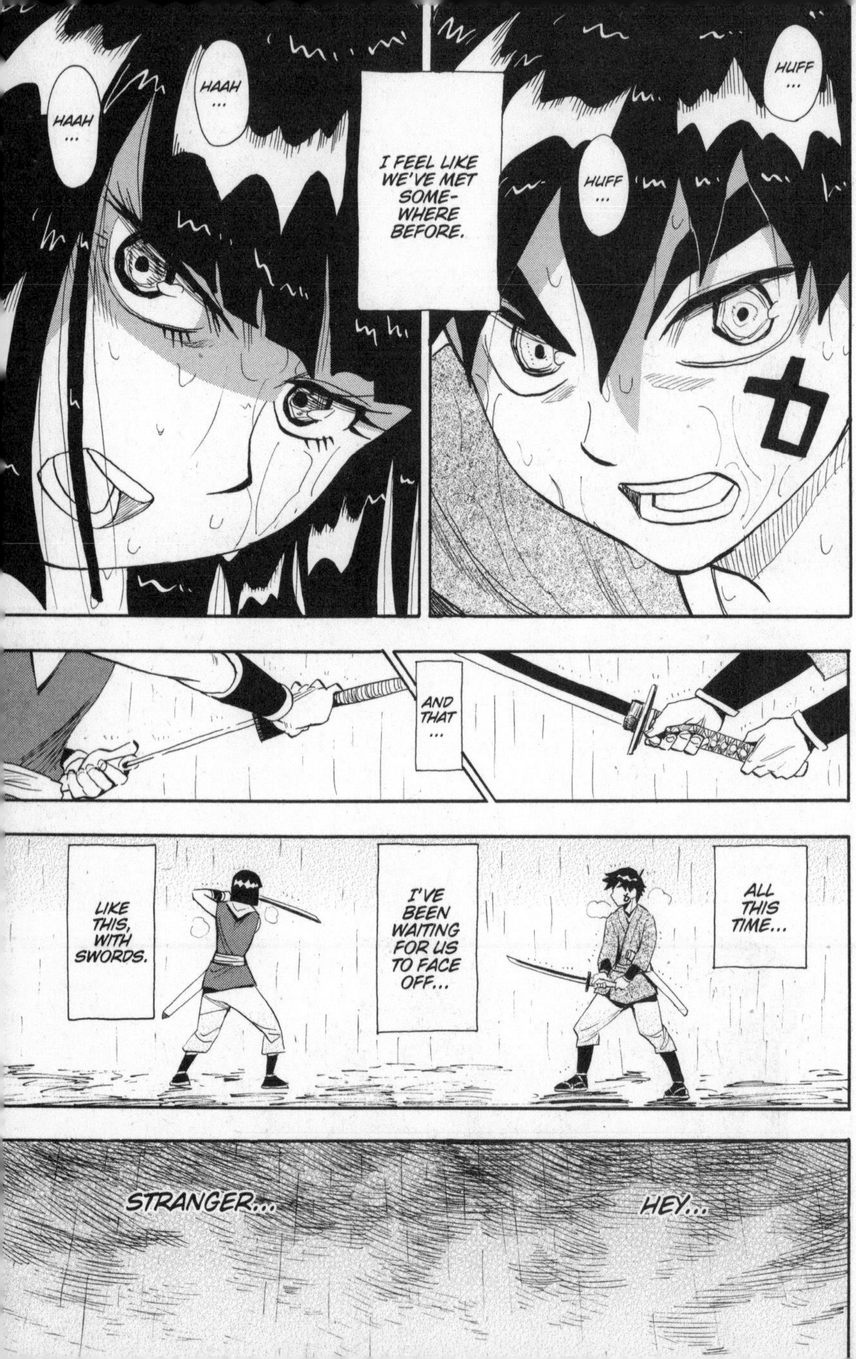

HUFF...
HUFF...
I FEEL LIKE WE'VE MET SOME-WHERE BEFORE.
HAAH...
HAAH...
AND THAT...
ALL THIS TIME...
I'VE BEEN WAITING FOR US TO FACE OFF...
LIKE THIS, WITH SWORDS.
HEY...
STRANGER...

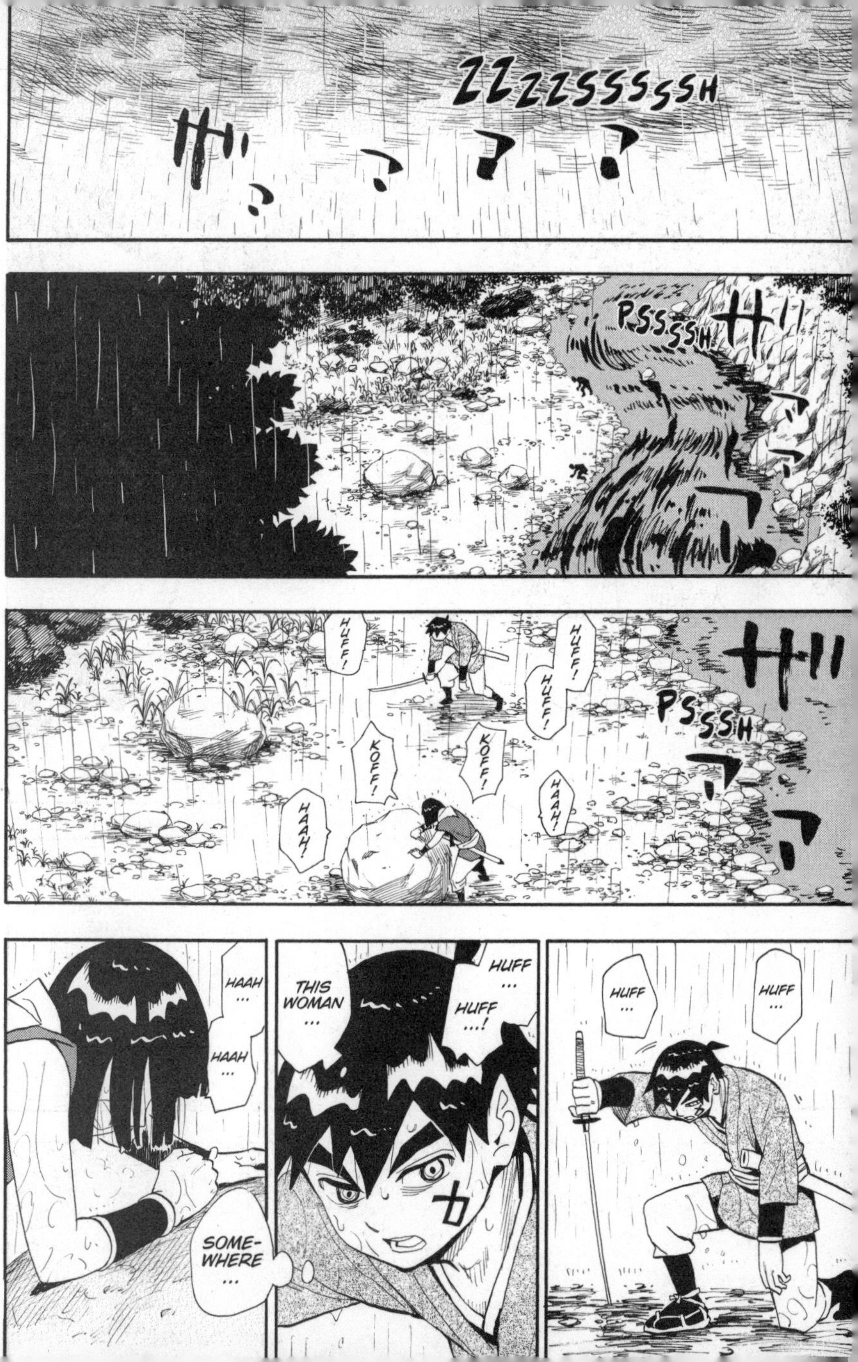
ZZZZSSSSSH
PSSSSSH
PSSSH
HAAAH!
HUFF! HUFF!
KOFF!
HUFF!
KOFF!
HAAAH!
HUFF ...
HUFF ...
HUFF ...
HUFF ...!
THIS WOMAN ...
SOME-WHERE ...
HAAH ...
HAAH ...

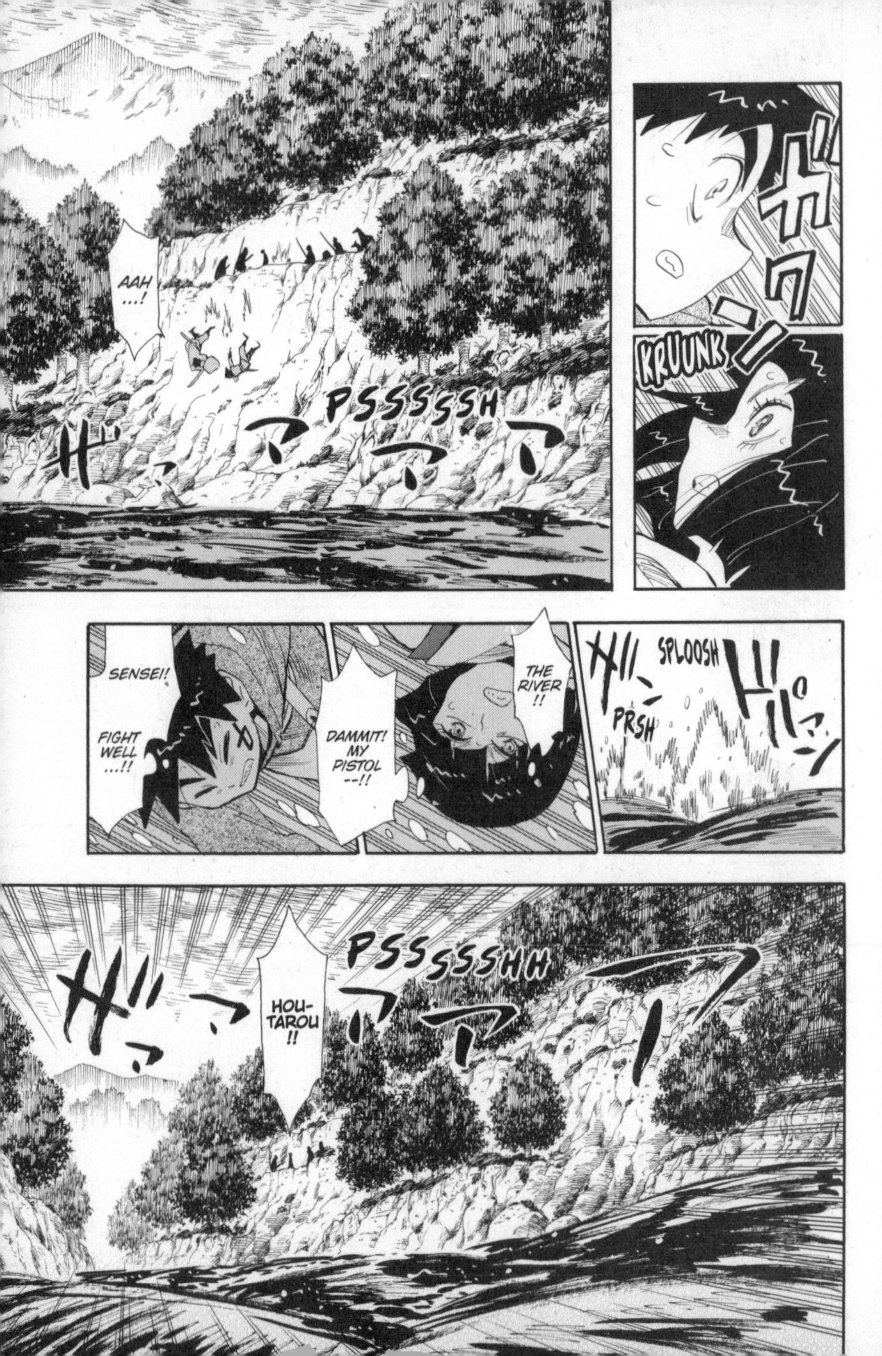
KRUUNK
AAH ...!
PSSSSSH
SPLOOSH
PRSH
THE RIVER !!
DAMMIT! MY PISTOL --!!
SENSEI!
FIGHT WELL ...!!
PSSSSSHH
HOU-TAROU !!

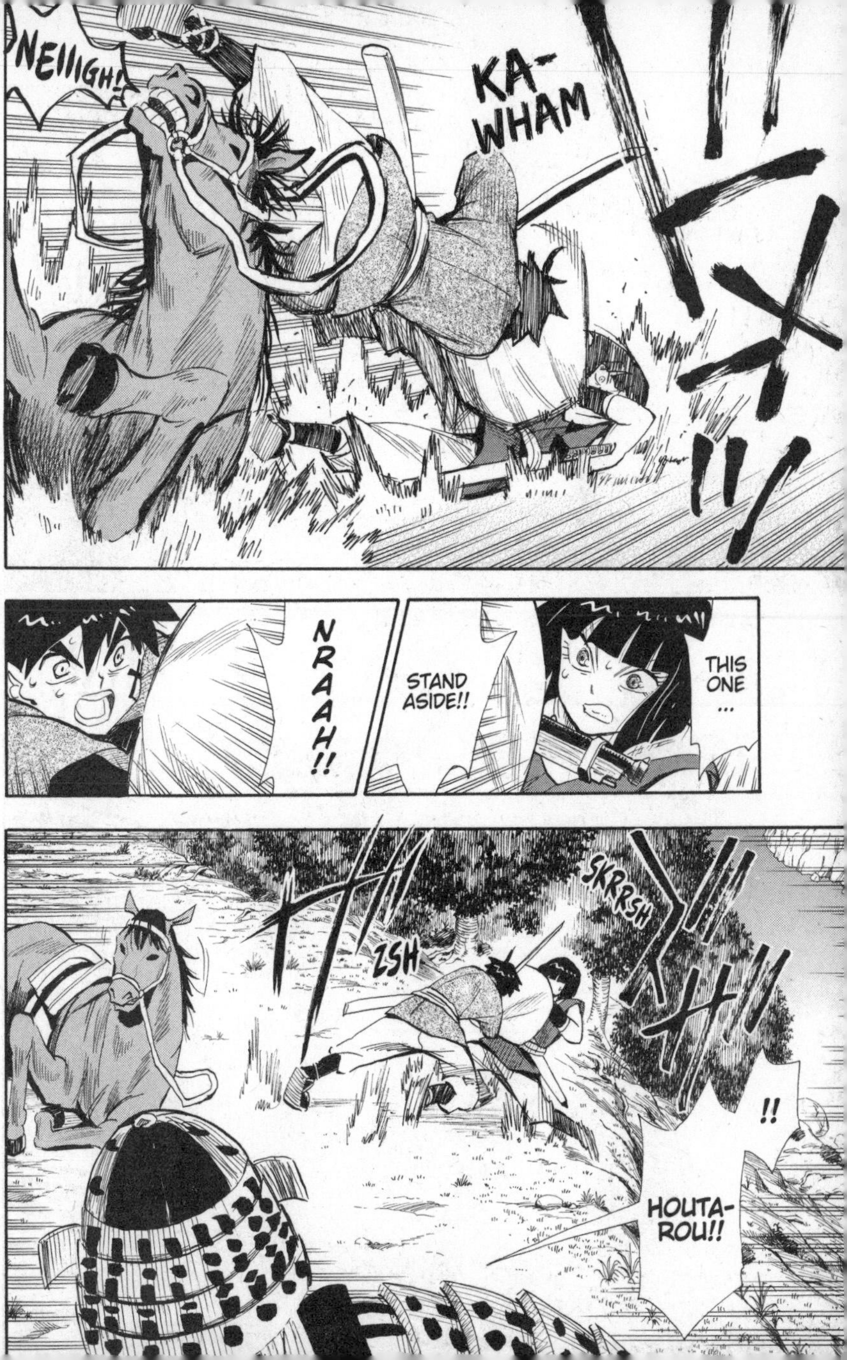

KA-
WHAM
NEIIIGH!
THIS ONE ...
STAND ASIDE!!
NRAAAH!!
SKRRSH
ZSH
!!
HOUTA-
ROU!!

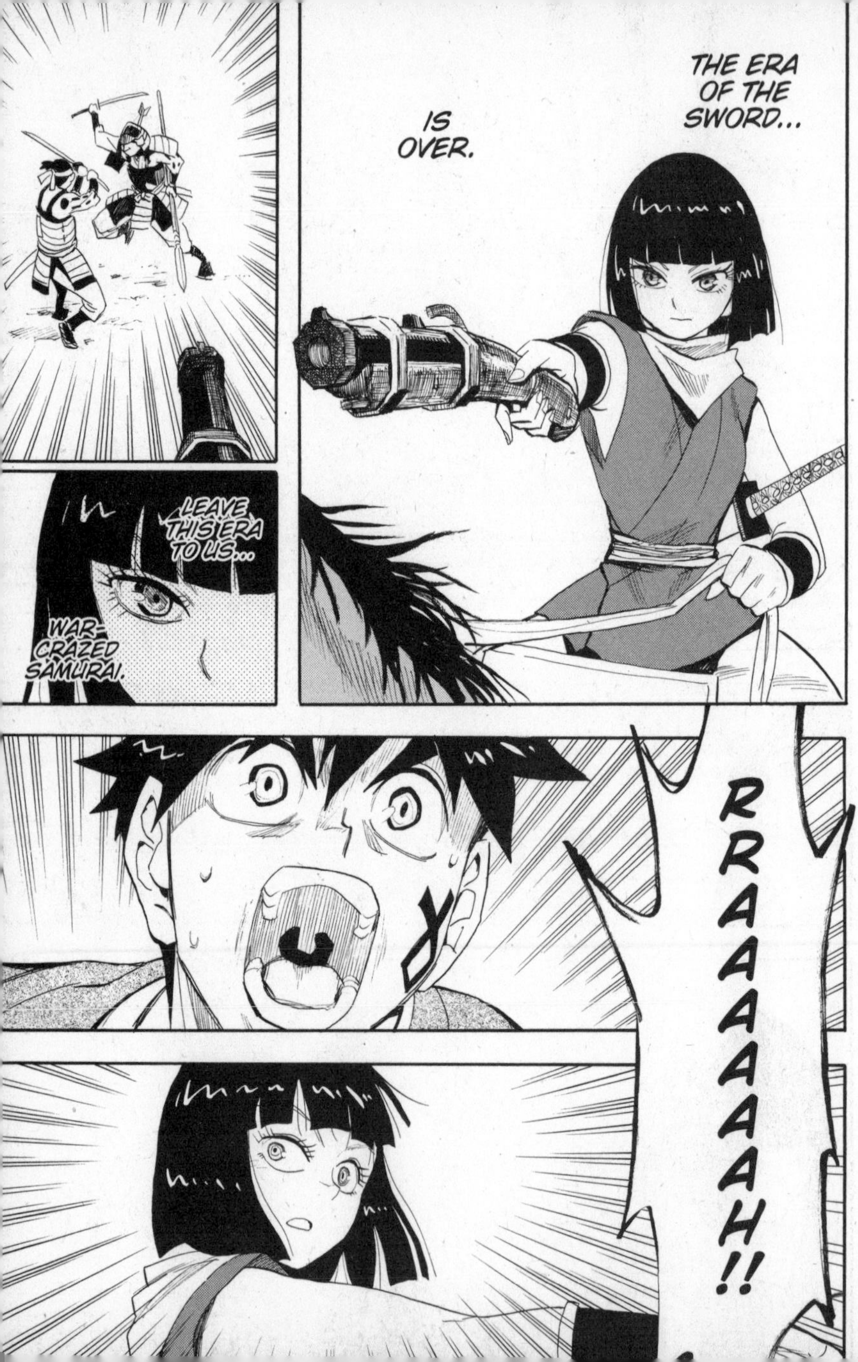
THE ERA OF THE SWORD...
IS OVER.
LEAVE THIS ERA TO US...
WAR-CRAZED SAMURAI.
RRAAAAAAH!!

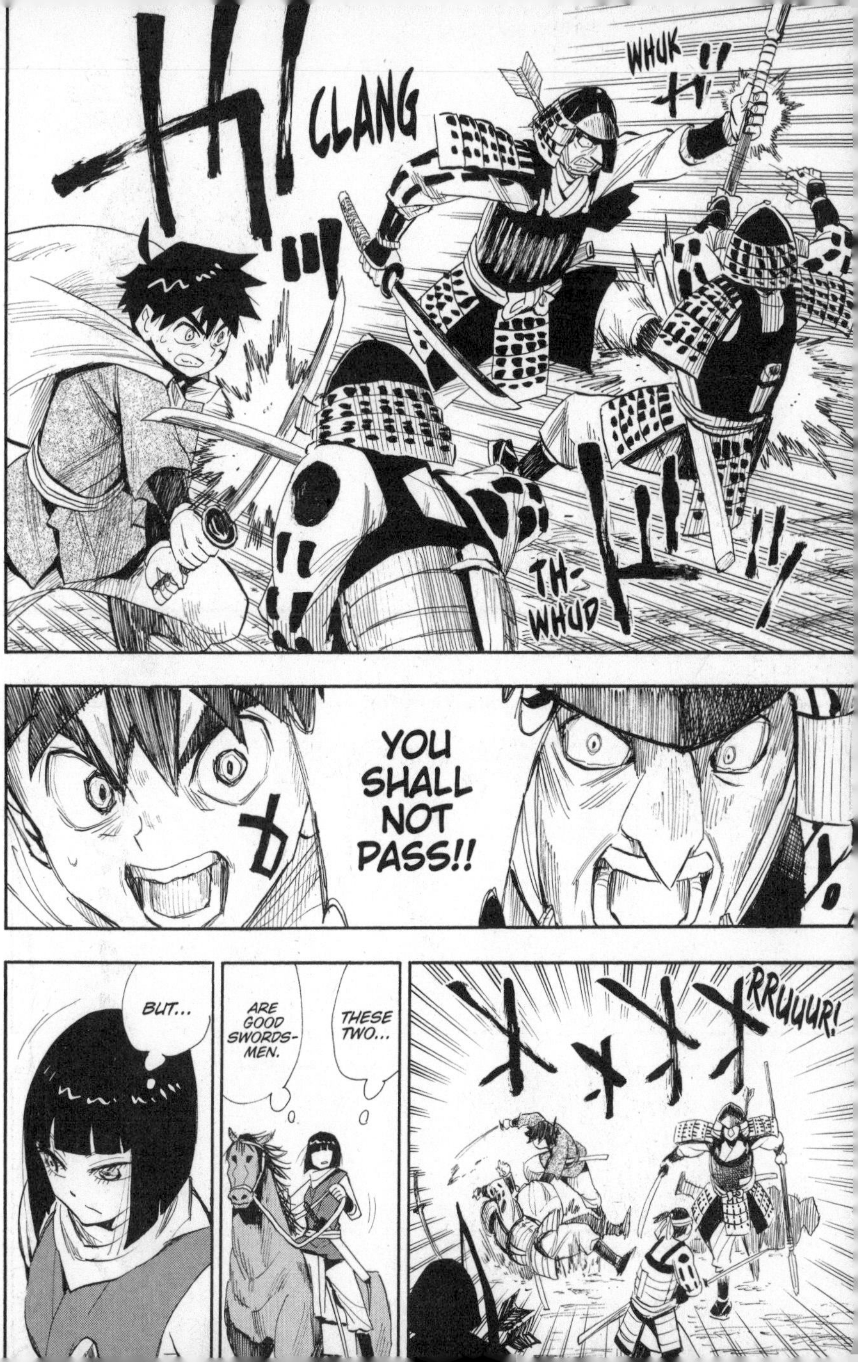
WHUK
CLANG
TH-WHUD
YOU SHALL NOT PASS!!
RRUUUR!
THESE TWO...
ARE GOOD SWORDS-MEN.
BUT...

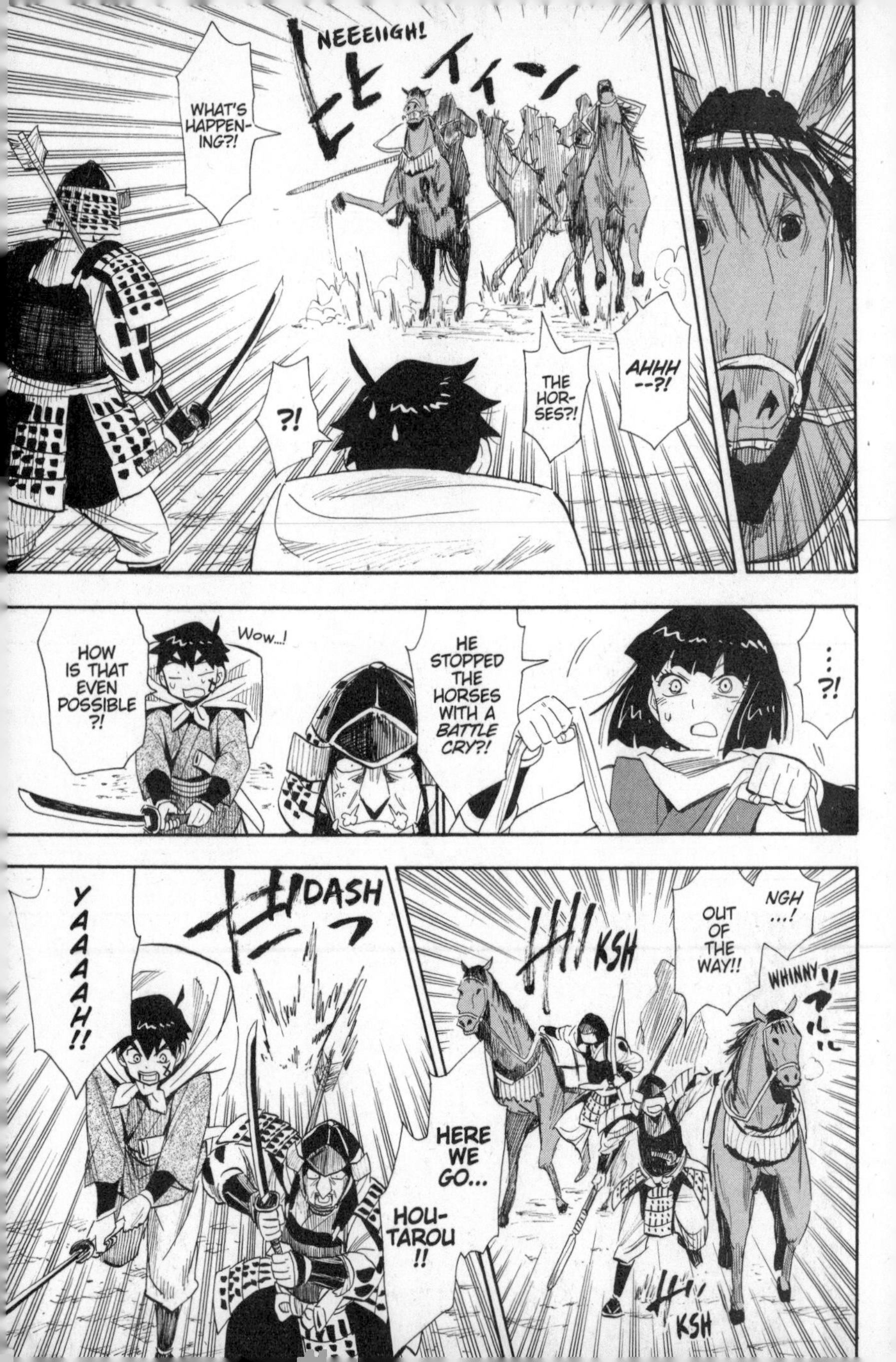
NEEEIIGH!
ヒヒイーン
AHHH--?!
THE HORSES?!
WHAT'S HAPPENING?!
?!
...?!
HE STOPPED THE HORSES WITH A BATTLE CRY?!
Wow...!
HOW IS THAT EVEN POSSIBLE?!
NGH...!
OUT OF THE WAY!!
WHINNY!!
KSH
HERE WE GO... HOUTAROU!!
KSH
DASH
YAAAAAH!!

IT'S
UP
TO
YOU!!

HOUTA-
ROU!!

JIN--

YANK

!

DART

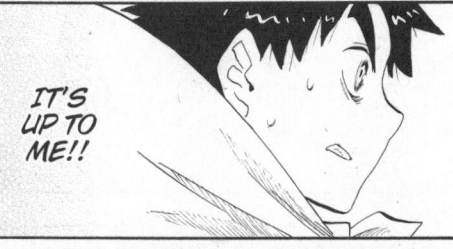

IT'S
UP TO
ME!!

YES...!!

KEEEEEE!!

CLOP CLOP CLOP

FWOO
...

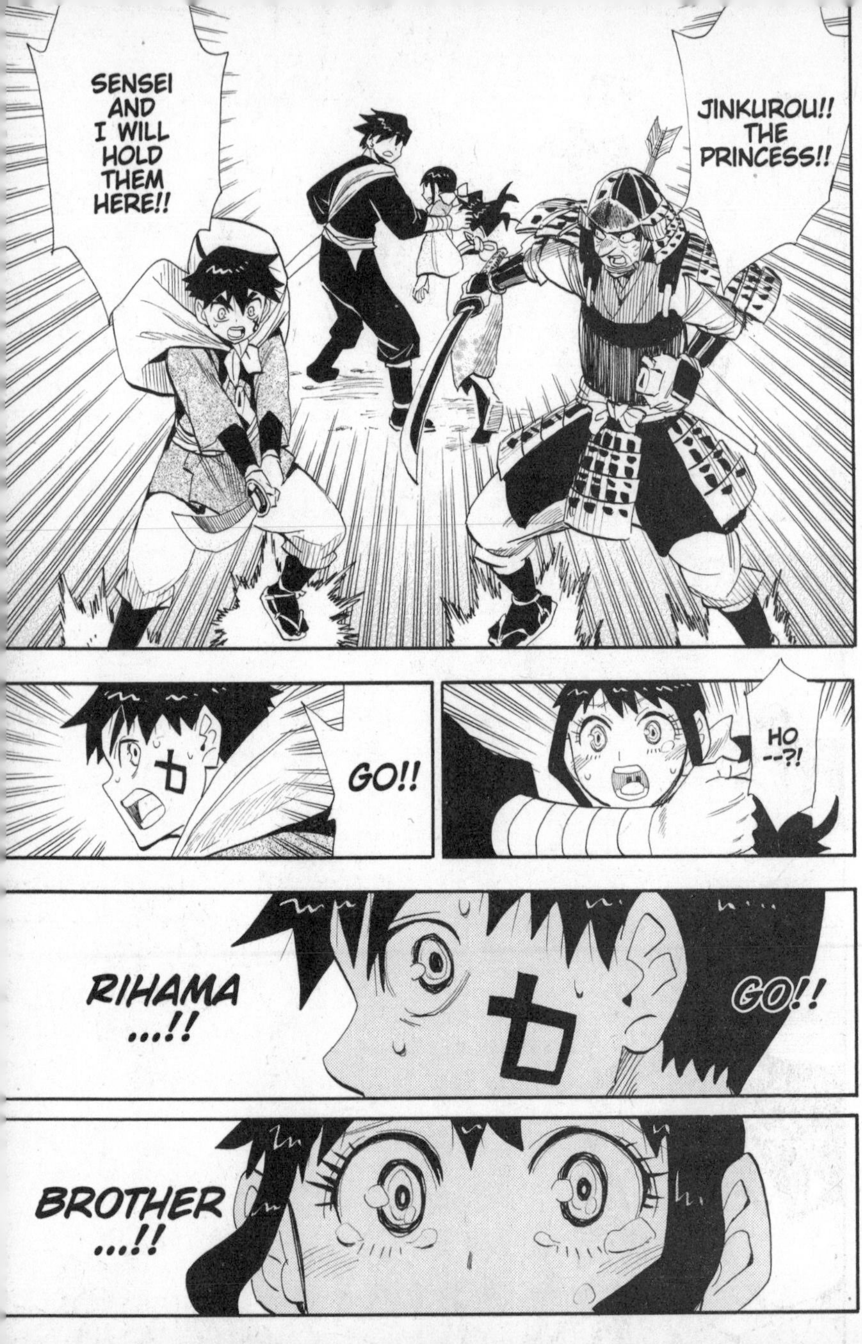
JINKUROU!! THE PRINCESS!!
SENSEI AND I WILL HOLD THEM HERE!!
HO --?!
GO!!
GO!!
RIHAMA ...!!
BROTHER ...!!

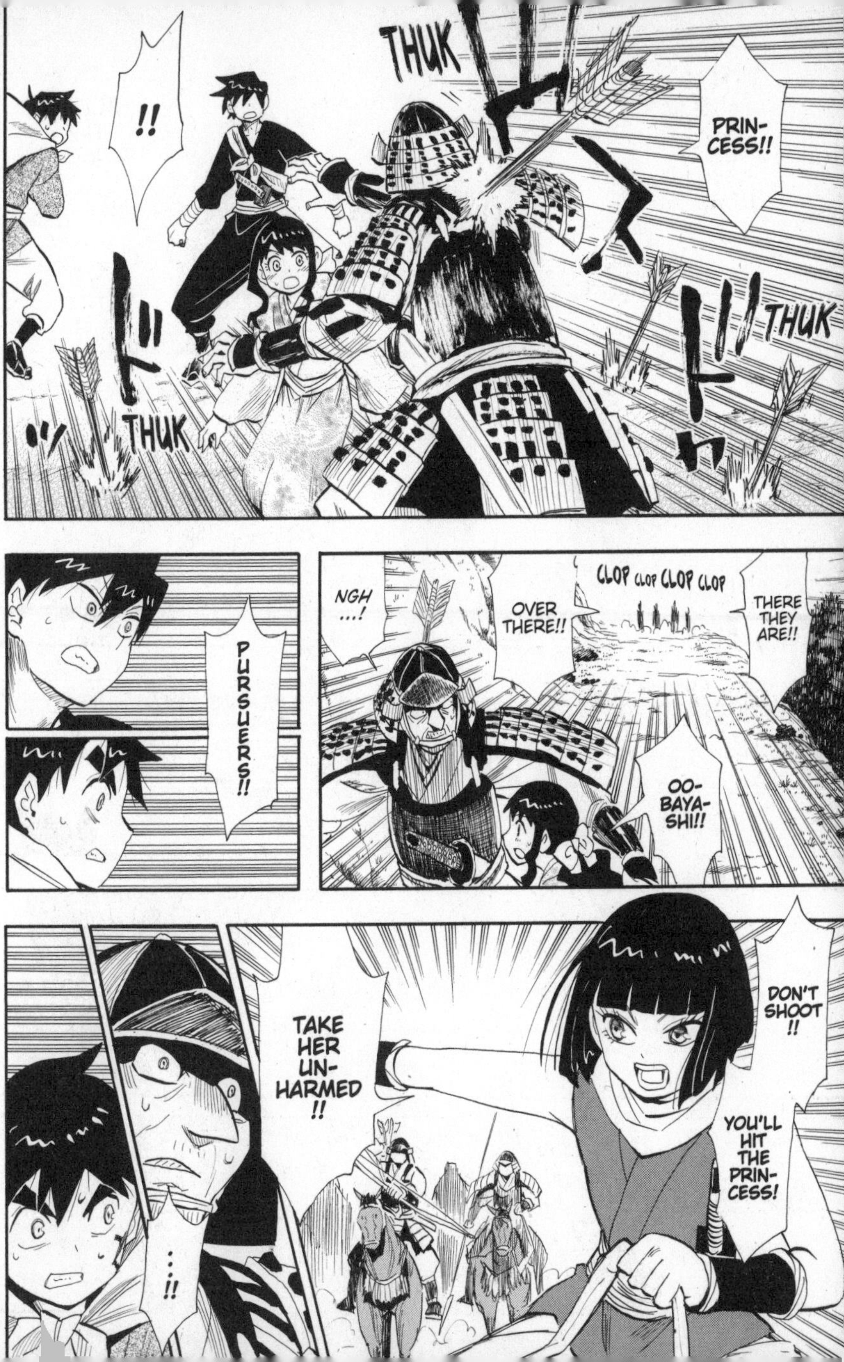
THUK
PRINCESS!!
THUK
!!
THUK
THERE THEY ARE!!
CLOP clop CLOP clop
OVER THERE!!
NGH...!
OO-BAYASHI!!
PURSUERS!!
DON'T SHOOT!!
YOU'LL HIT THE PRINCESS!
TAKE HER UNHARMED!!
...!!

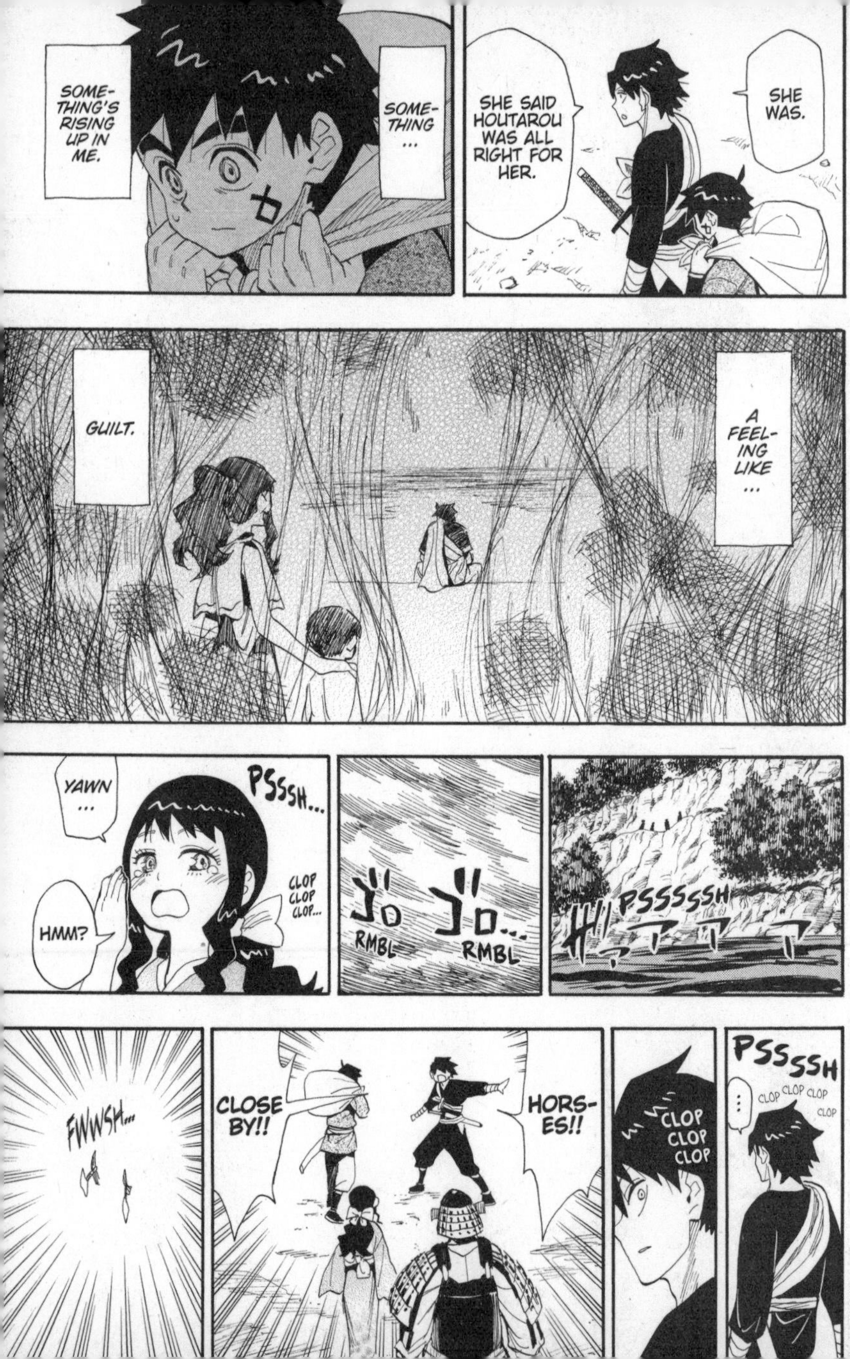

SHE WAS.
SHE SAID HOUTAROU WAS ALL RIGHT FOR HER.
SOME-THING...
SOME-THING'S RISING UP IN ME.
A FEEL-ING LIKE...
GUILT.
PSSSSSH
ゴロ
RMBL
ゴロ...
RMBL
YAWN...
PSSSH...
CLOP CLOP CLOP...
HMM?
PSSSSSH
...
CLOP CLOP CLOP CLOP
CLOP CLOP CLOP
HORS-ES!!
CLOSE BY!!
FWWSH...

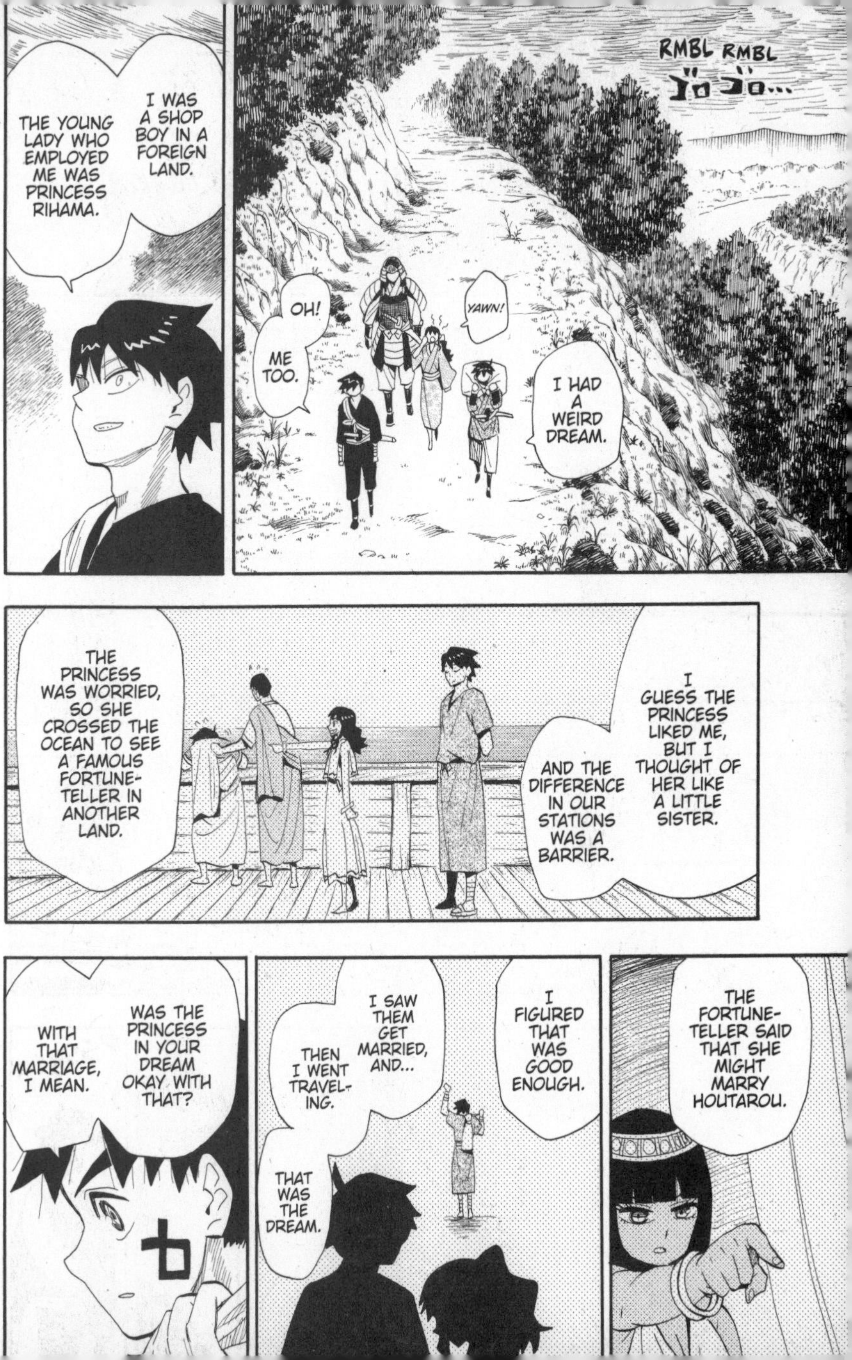
RMBL RMBL
ゴロゴロ...
YAWN!
I HAD A WEIRD DREAM.
OH!
ME TOO.
I WAS A SHOP BOY IN A FOREIGN LAND.
THE YOUNG LADY WHO EMPLOYED ME WAS PRINCESS RIHAMA.
I GUESS THE PRINCESS LIKED ME, BUT I THOUGHT OF HER LIKE A LITTLE SISTER.
AND THE DIFFERENCE IN OUR STATIONS WAS A BARRIER.
THE PRINCESS WAS WORRIED, SO SHE CROSSED THE OCEAN TO SEE A FAMOUS FORTUNE-TELLER IN ANOTHER LAND.
THE FORTUNE-TELLER SAID THAT SHE MIGHT MARRY HOUTAROU.
I FIGURED THAT WAS GOOD ENOUGH.
I SAW THEM GET MARRIED, AND...
THEN I WENT TRAVEL-ING.
THAT WAS THE DREAM.
WAS THE PRINCESS IN YOUR DREAM OKAY WITH THAT?
WITH THAT MARRIAGE, I MEAN.

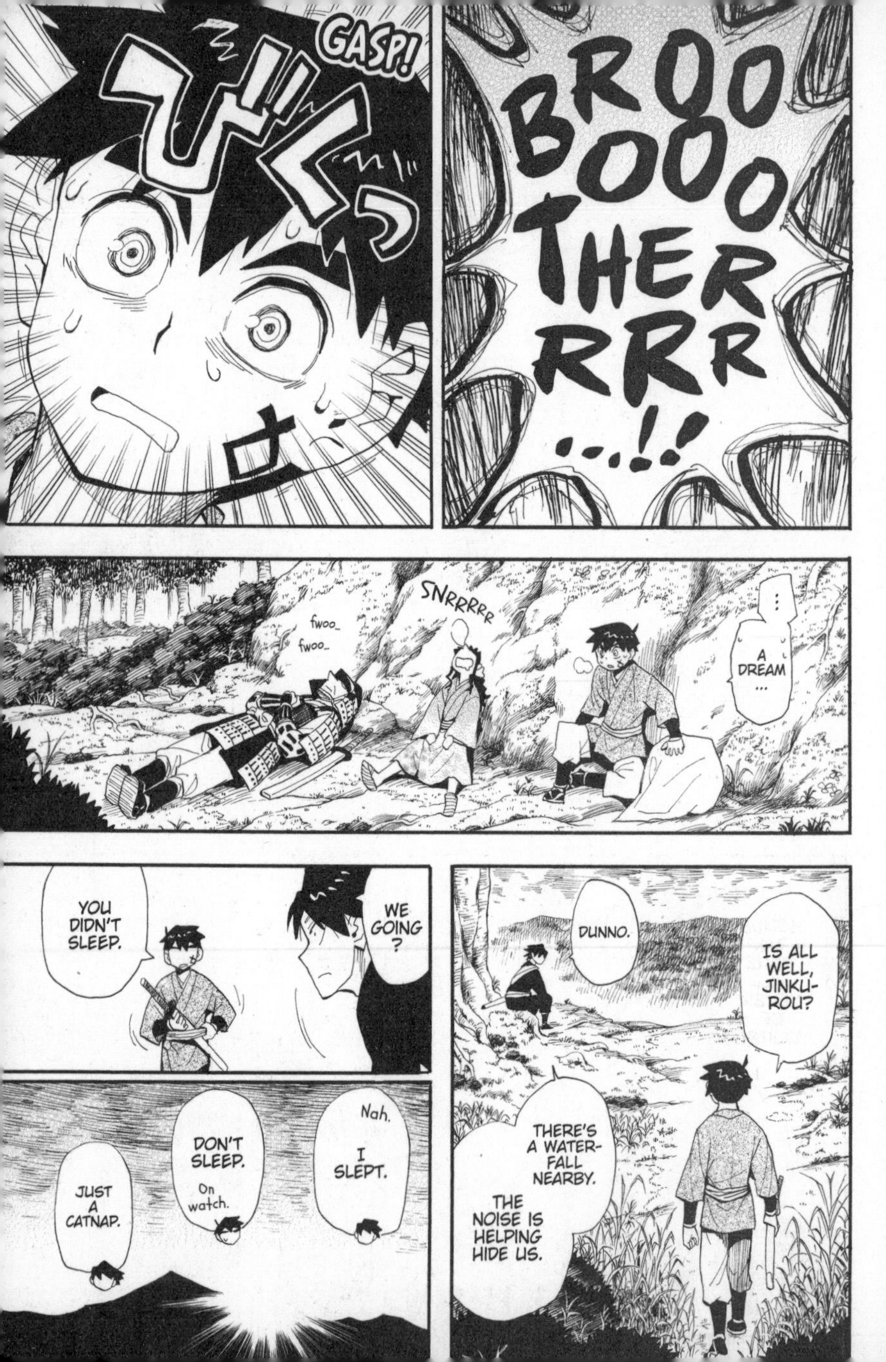

BROOOOOTHERRRR...!!
GASP!
...
A DREAM...
SNRRRRR
fwoo.. fwoo..
IS ALL WELL, JINKU-ROU?
DUNNO.
THERE'S A WATER-FALL NEARBY.
THE NOISE IS HELPING HIDE US.
WE GOING?
YOU DIDN'T SLEEP.
Nah.
I SLEPT.
DON'T SLEEP.
On watch.
JUST A CATNAP.

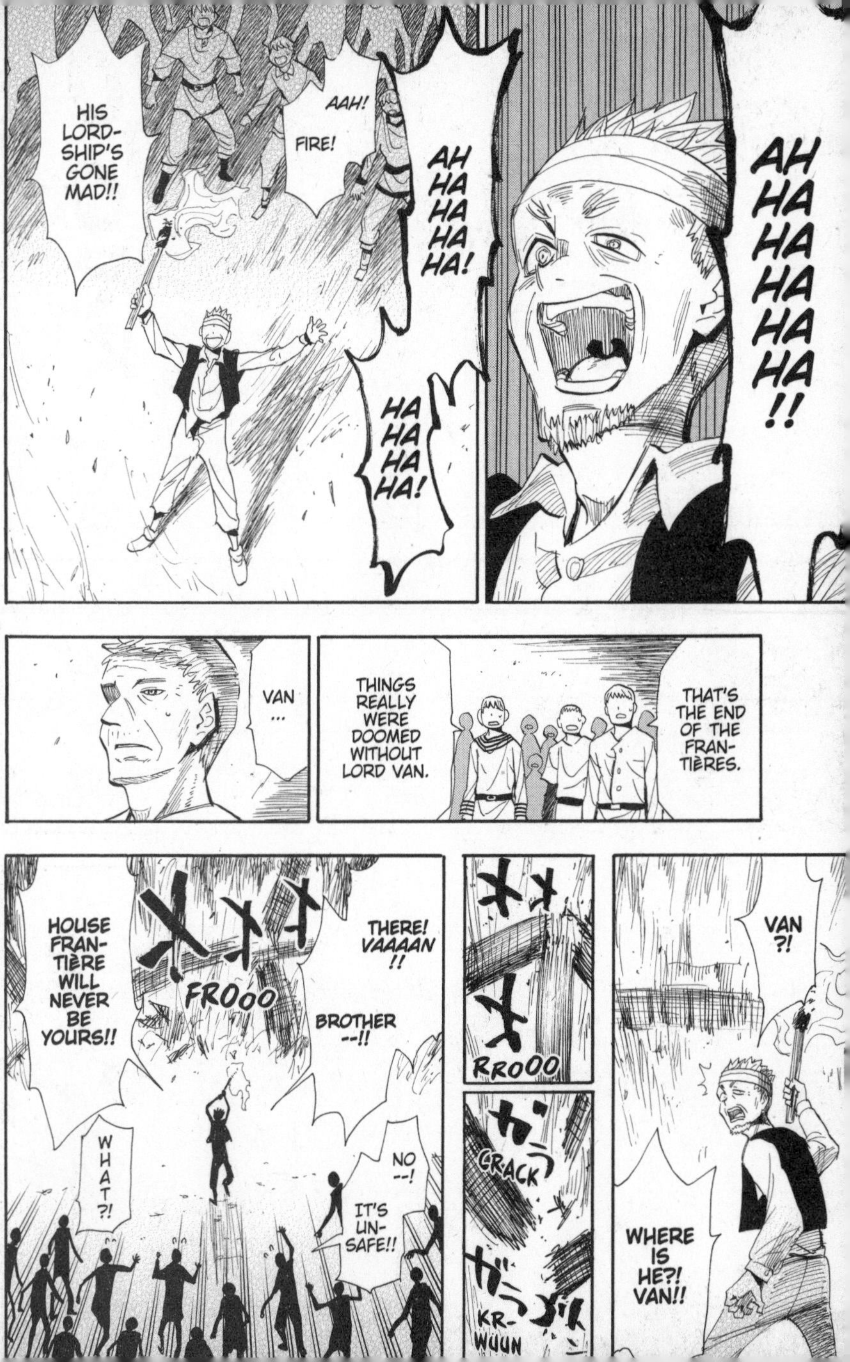
AH HA HA HA HA HA HA!!
AH HA HA HA HA!
AAH!
FIRE!
HIS LORDSHIP'S GONE MAD!!
HA HA HA HA!
THAT'S THE END OF THE FRANTIÈRES.
THINGS REALLY WERE DOOMED WITHOUT LORD VAN.
VAN...
VAN?!
WHERE IS HE?! VAN!!
RROOO
CRACK
KR-WUUN
THERE! VAAAAN!!
FROOO
HOUSE FRANTIÈRE WILL NEVER BE YOURS!!
BROTHER--!!
NO--!
IT'S UNSAFE!!
WHAT?!

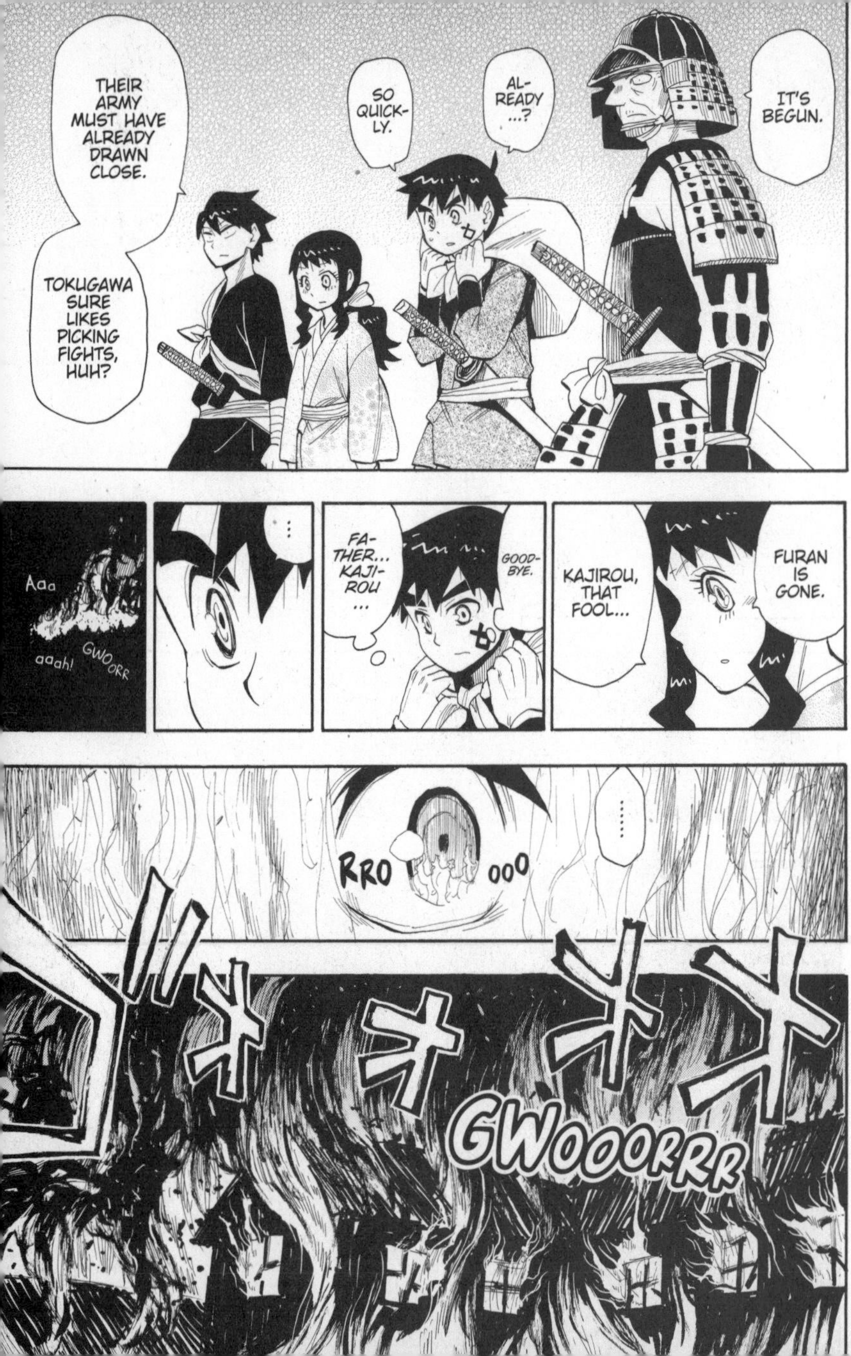
IT'S BEGUN.
AL-READY...?
SO QUICK-LY.
THEIR ARMY MUST HAVE ALREADY DRAWN CLOSE.
TOKUGAWA SURE LIKES PICKING FIGHTS, HUH?
FURAN IS GONE.
KAJIROU, THAT FOOL...
GOOD-BYE.
FA-THER... KAJI-ROU...
...
Aaa aaah!
GWOORR
......
RRO OOO
GWOOORRR

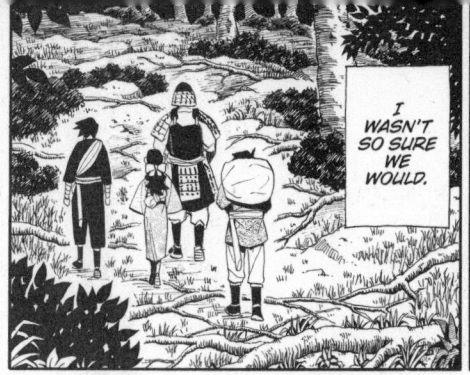

YES...
PRIN-CESS.
I WASN'T SO SURE WE WOULD.
OLD MAN, WEREN'T YOU THROWING YOUR LOT IN WITH FURAN?
...
AS I WAS GOING ABOUT THE CASTLE PREPARING FOR WAR, O-MATSU-DONO TOOK ME ASIDE AND ENTRUSTED THE PRINCESS TO ME.
PROTECTING HER WILL ALLOW THE FAMILY'S REBIRTH.
TO THINK THERE WAS A SECRET PASSAGE IN SUCH A PLACE...!
WHAT WAS THE SECRET PASSAGE LIKE, THOUGH...?
ROOO
Yaah!
Aaaah!

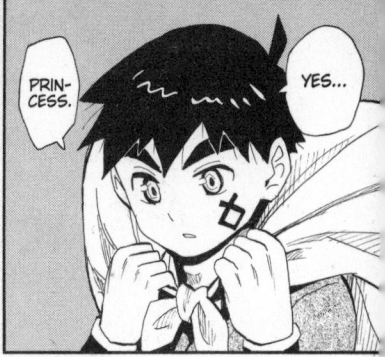

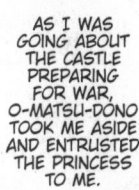

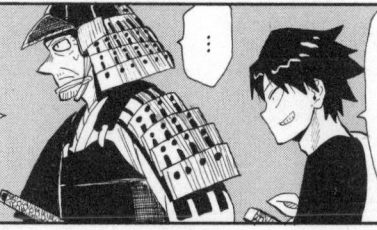

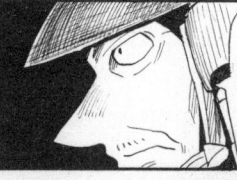

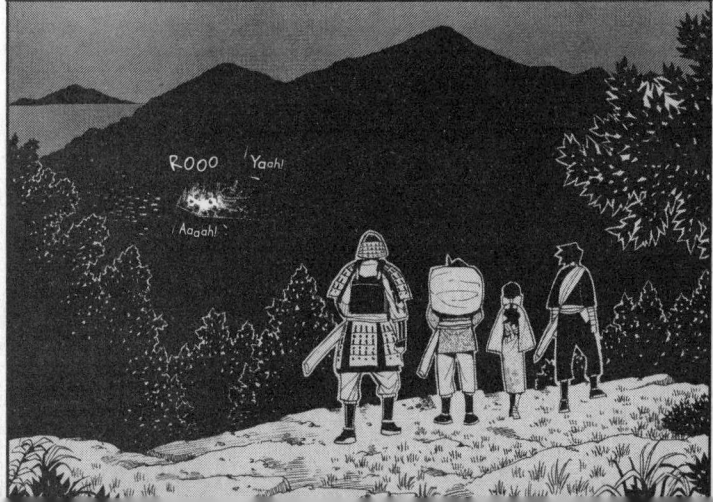

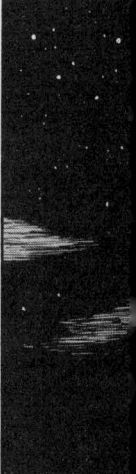

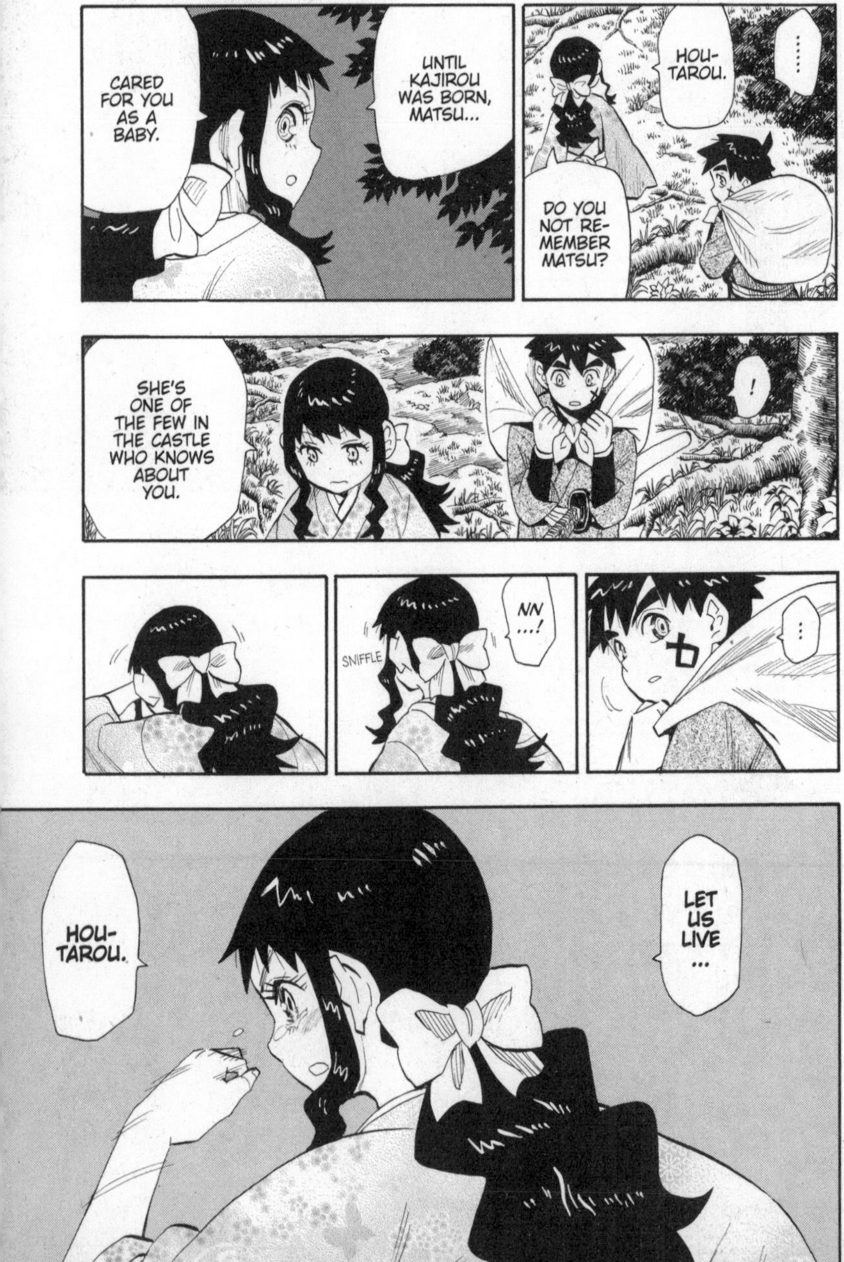
......
HOU-TAROU.
DO YOU NOT RE-MEMBER MATSU?
UNTIL KAJIROU WAS BORN, MATSU...
CARED FOR YOU AS A BABY.
!
SHE'S ONE OF THE FEW IN THE CASTLE WHO KNOWS ABOUT YOU.
...
NN ...!
SNIFFLE
LET US LIVE ...
HOU-TAROU.

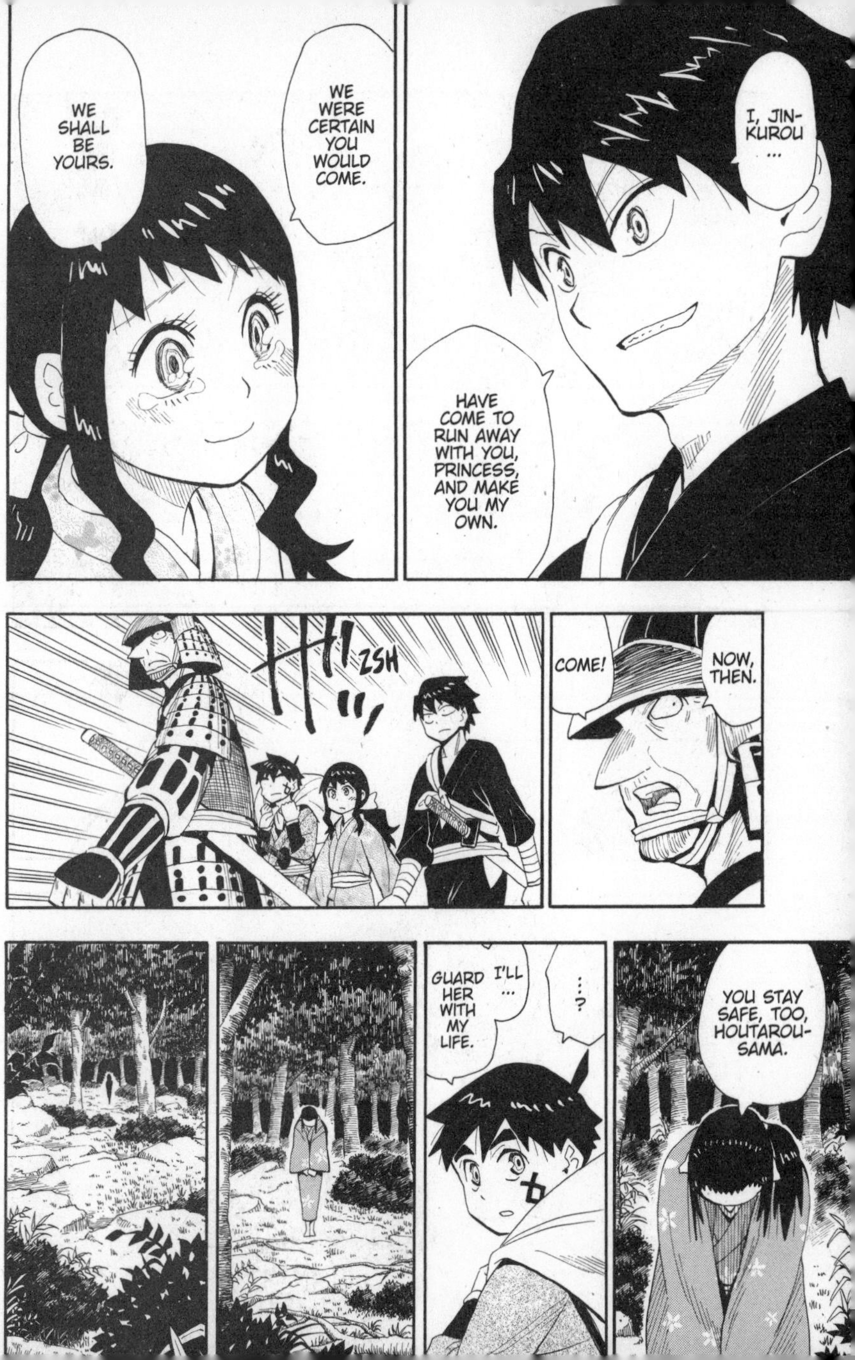
I, JIN-KUROU ...
HAVE COME TO RUN AWAY WITH YOU, PRINCESS, AND MAKE YOU MY OWN.
WE WERE CERTAIN YOU WOULD COME.
WE SHALL BE YOURS.
NOW, THEN.
COME!
ZSH
YOU STAY SAFE, TOO, HOUTAROU-SAMA.
...?
I'LL ...
GUARD HER WITH MY LIFE.

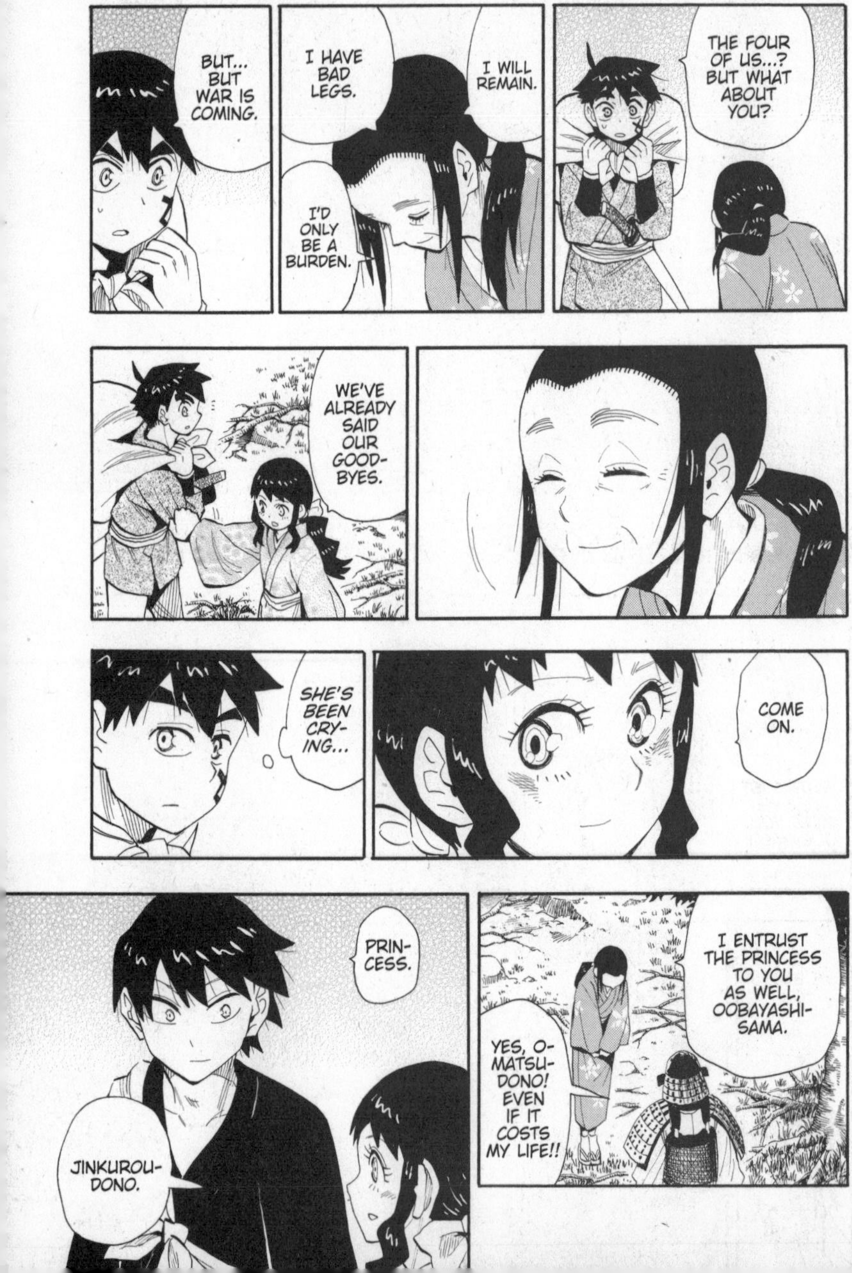
THE FOUR OF US...? BUT WHAT ABOUT YOU?
I WILL REMAIN.
I HAVE BAD LEGS.
I'D ONLY BE A BURDEN.
BUT... BUT WAR IS COMING.
WE'VE ALREADY SAID OUR GOOD-BYES.
COME ON.
SHE'S BEEN CRY-ING...
I ENTRUST THE PRINCESS TO YOU AS WELL, OOBAYASHI-SAMA.
YES, O-MATSU-DONO! EVEN IF IT COSTS MY LIFE!!
PRIN-CESS.
JINKUROU-DONO.

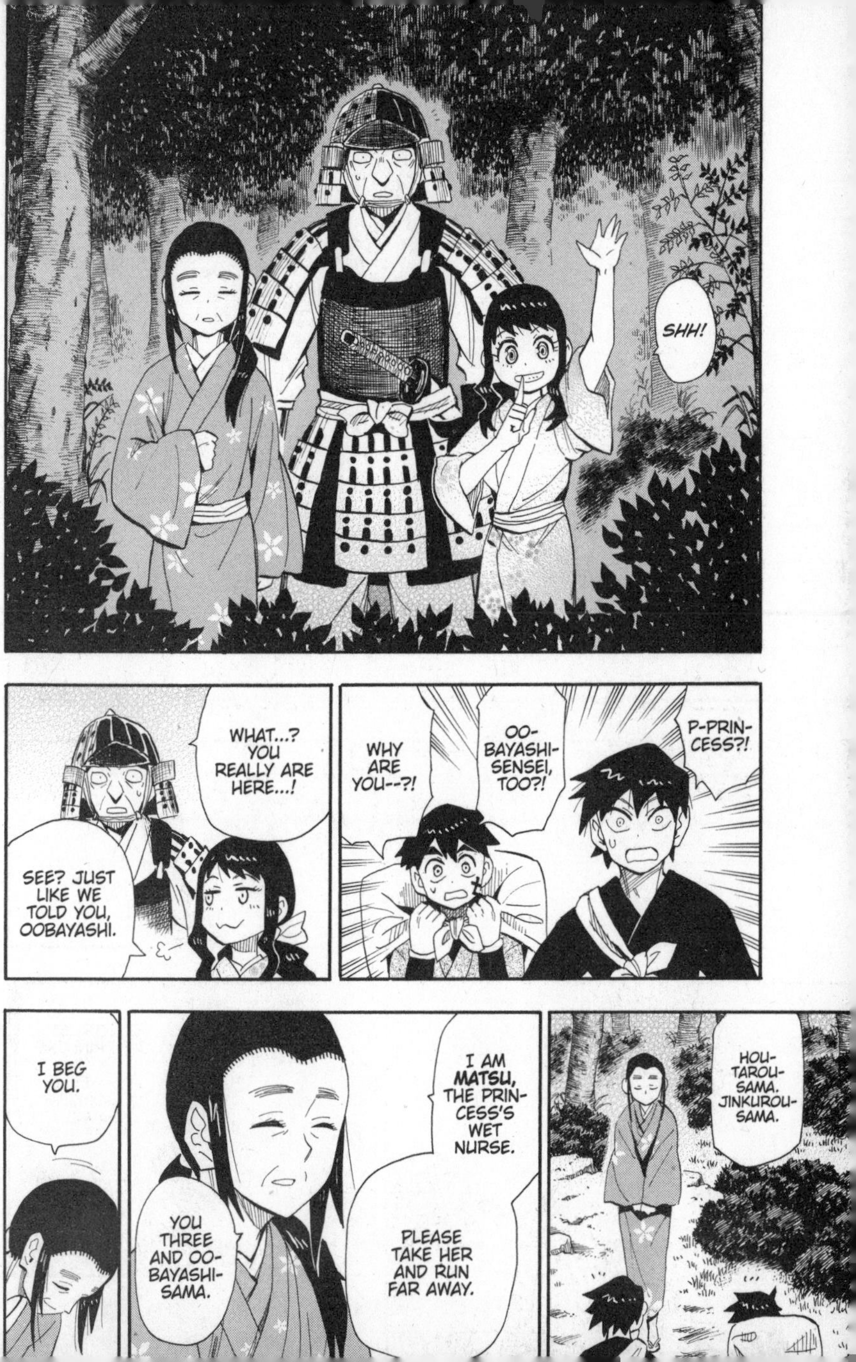
SHH!
P-PRIN-CESS?!
OO-BAYASHI-SENSEI, TOO?!
WHY ARE YOU--?!
WHAT...? YOU REALLY ARE HERE...!
SEE? JUST LIKE WE TOLD YOU, OOBAYASHI.
HOU-TAROU-SAMA. JINKUROU-SAMA.
I AM MATSU, THE PRIN-CESS'S WET NURSE.
YOU THREE AND OO-BAYASHI-SAMA.
PLEASE TAKE HER AND RUN FAR AWAY.
I BEG YOU.

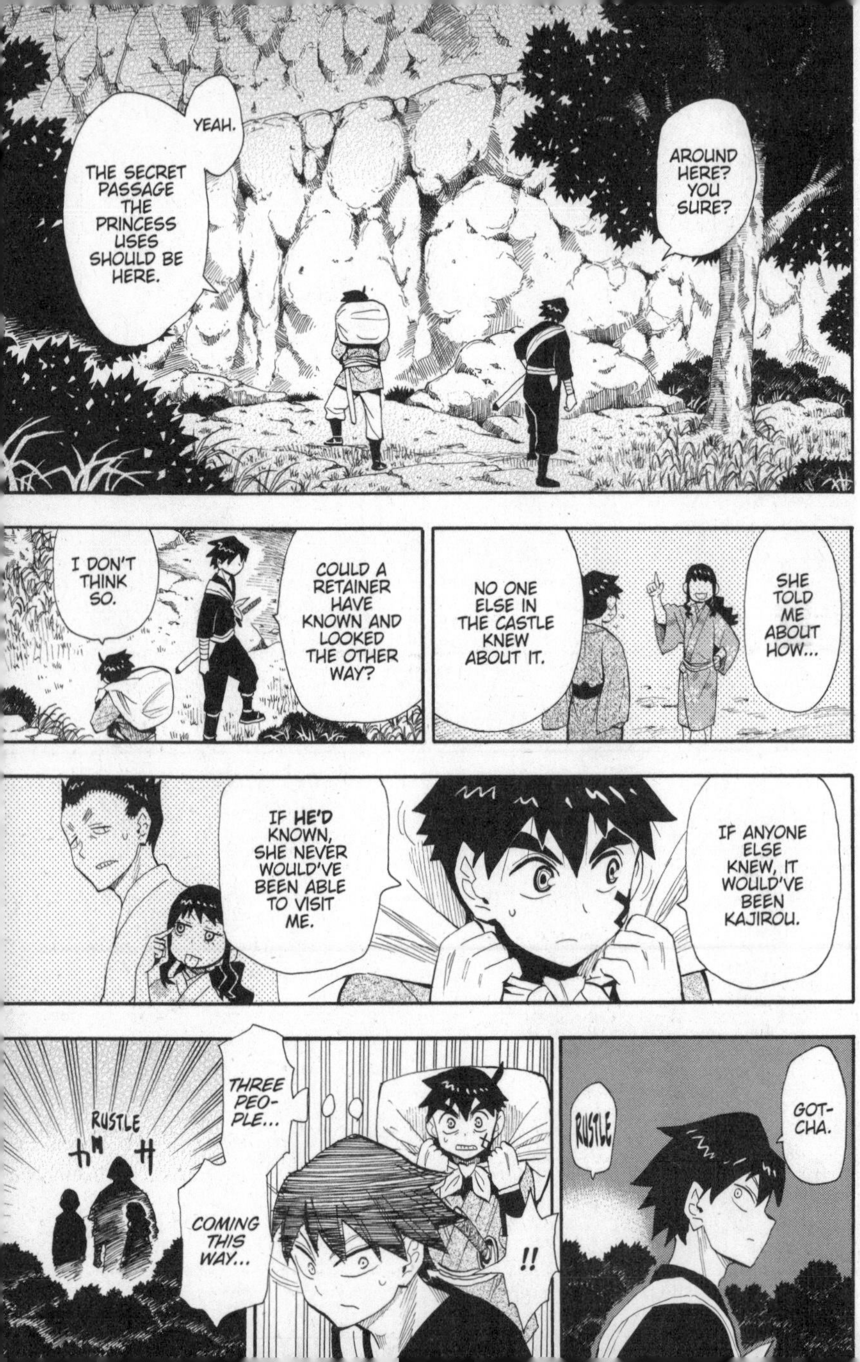
AROUND HERE? YOU SURE?
YEAH.
THE SECRET PASSAGE THE PRINCESS USES SHOULD BE HERE.
SHE TOLD ME ABOUT HOW...
NO ONE ELSE IN THE CASTLE KNEW ABOUT IT.
COULD A RETAINER HAVE KNOWN AND LOOKED THE OTHER WAY?
I DON'T THINK SO.
IF ANYONE ELSE KNEW, IT WOULD'VE BEEN KAJIROU.
IF HE'D KNOWN, SHE NEVER WOULD'VE BEEN ABLE TO VISIT ME.
GOT-CHA.
RUSTLE
THREE PEO-PLE...
!!
COMING THIS WAY...
RUSTLE

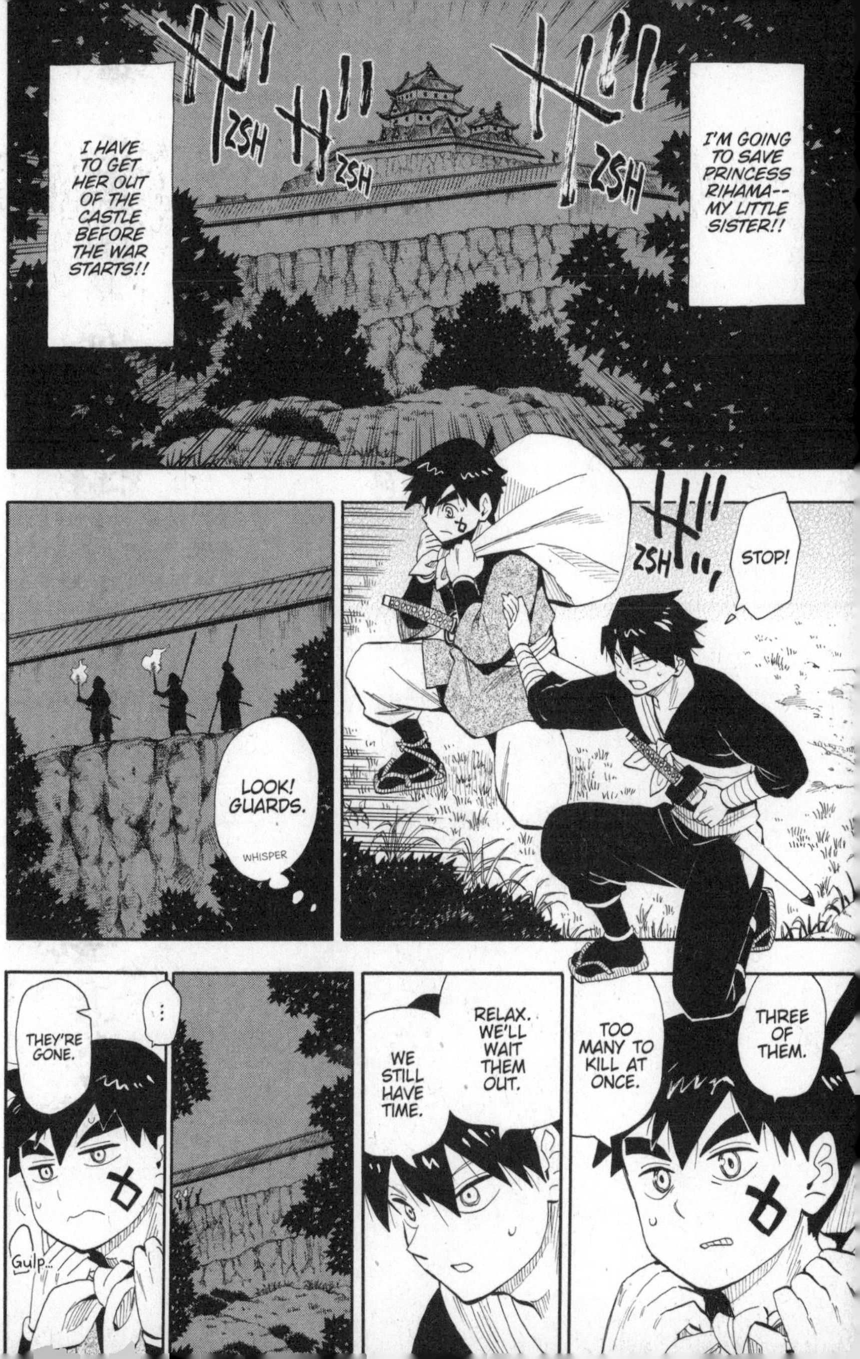
I'M GOING TO SAVE PRINCESS RIHAMA-- MY LITTLE SISTER!!
I HAVE TO GET HER OUT OF THE CASTLE BEFORE THE WAR STARTS!!
ZSH
ZSH
ZSH
ZSH
STOP!
LOOK! GUARDS.
WHISPER
THREE OF THEM.
TOO MANY TO KILL AT ONCE.
RELAX. WE'LL WAIT THEM OUT.
WE STILL HAVE TIME.
...
THEY'RE GONE.
Gulp...

Circle 18
Houtarou
4

Mom

Spirit Circle

I HAVE A BAD FEELING.

GOING TO DIE FOR MY SISTER.

I'M...

I'M PRAY-ING, LORD BUD-DHA!!

FOR THE FIRST TIME IN MY LIFE...

Circle 17/END

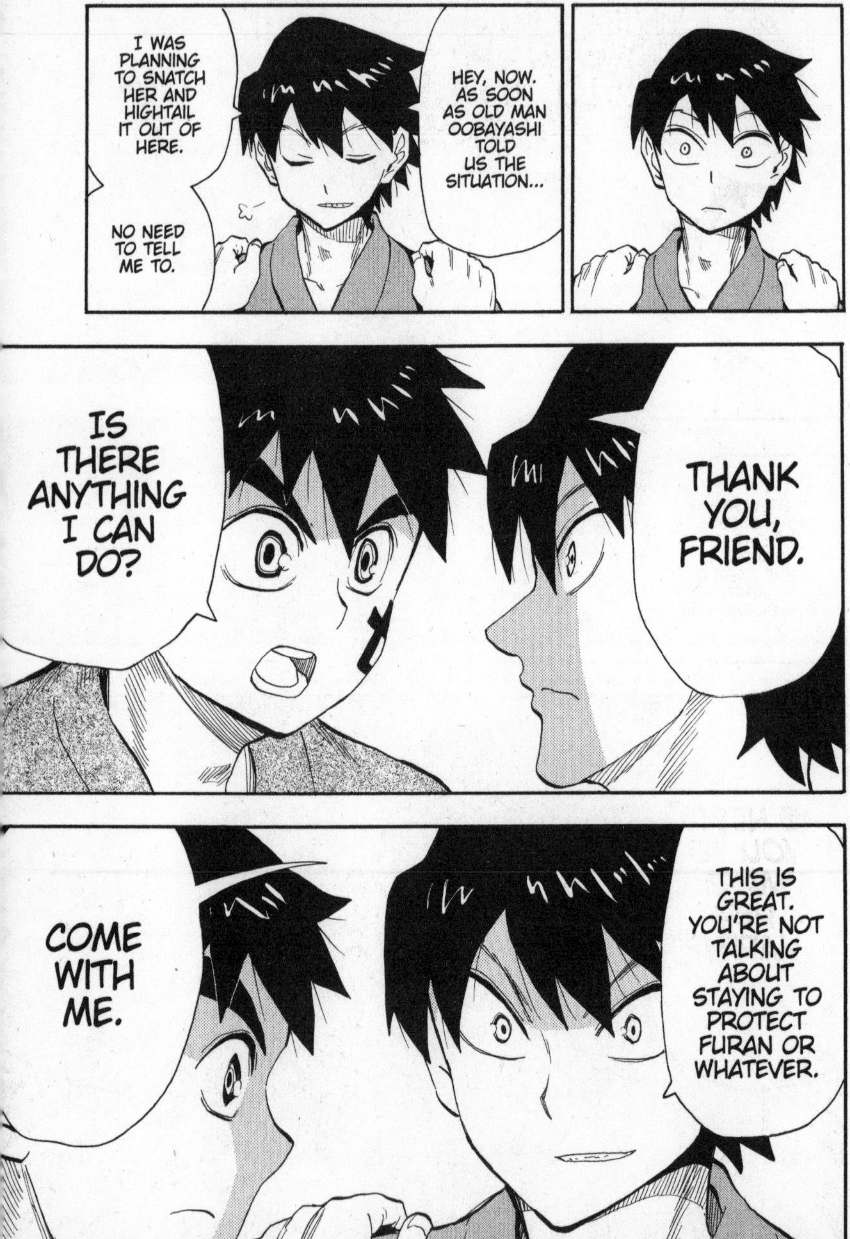
HEY, NOW. AS SOON AS OLD MAN OOBAYASHI TOLD US THE SITUATION...
I WAS PLANNING TO SNATCH HER AND HIGHTAIL IT OUT OF HERE.
NO NEED TO TELL ME TO.
THANK YOU, FRIEND.
IS THERE ANYTHING I CAN DO?
THIS IS GREAT. YOU'RE NOT TALKING ABOUT STAYING TO PROTECT FURAN OR WHATEVER.
COME WITH ME.

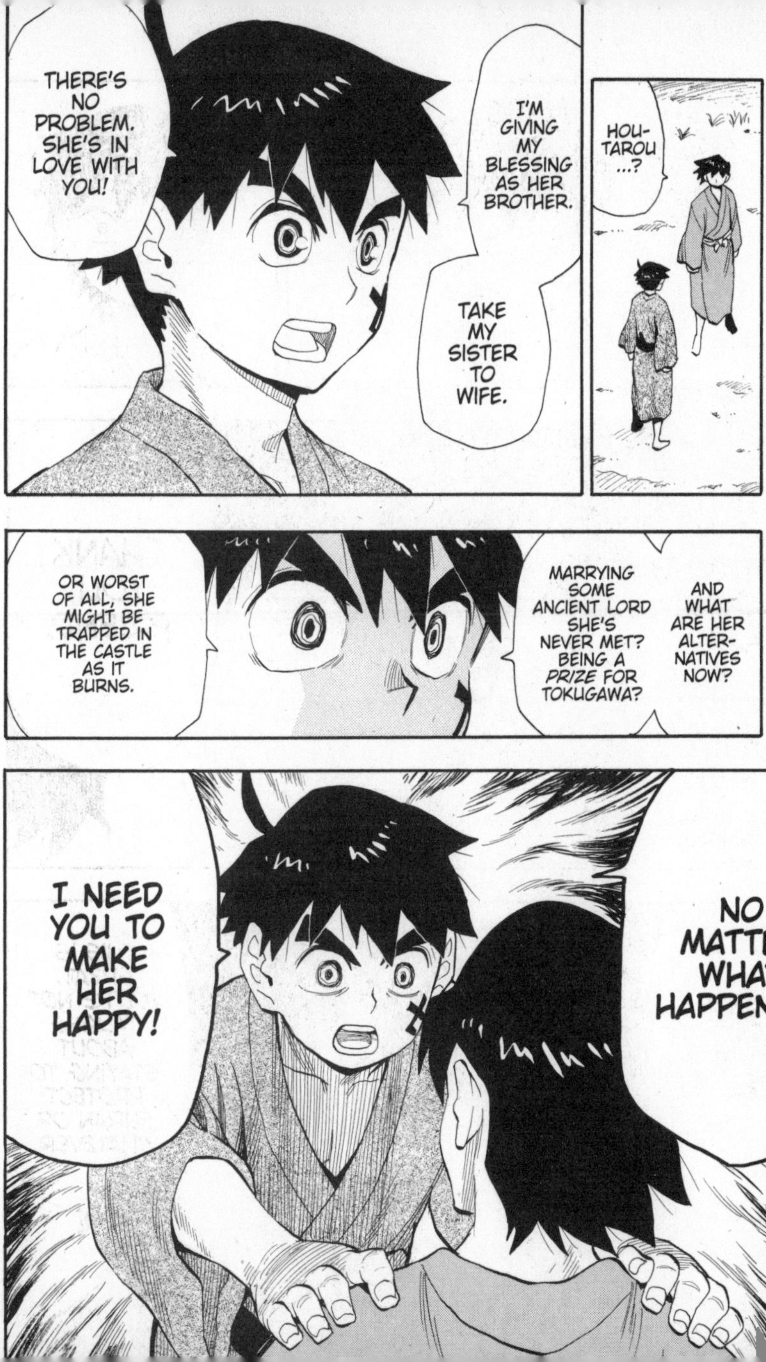
HOU-TAROU ...?
I'M GIVING MY BLESSING AS HER BROTHER.
TAKE MY SISTER TO WIFE.
THERE'S NO PROBLEM. SHE'S IN LOVE WITH YOU!
AND WHAT ARE HER ALTER-NATIVES NOW?
MARRYING SOME ANCIENT LORD SHE'S NEVER MET? BEING A *PRIZE* FOR TOKUGAWA?
OR WORST OF ALL, SHE MIGHT BE TRAPPED IN THE CASTLE AS IT BURNS.
NO MATTER WHAT HAPPENS...
I NEED YOU TO MAKE HER HAPPY!

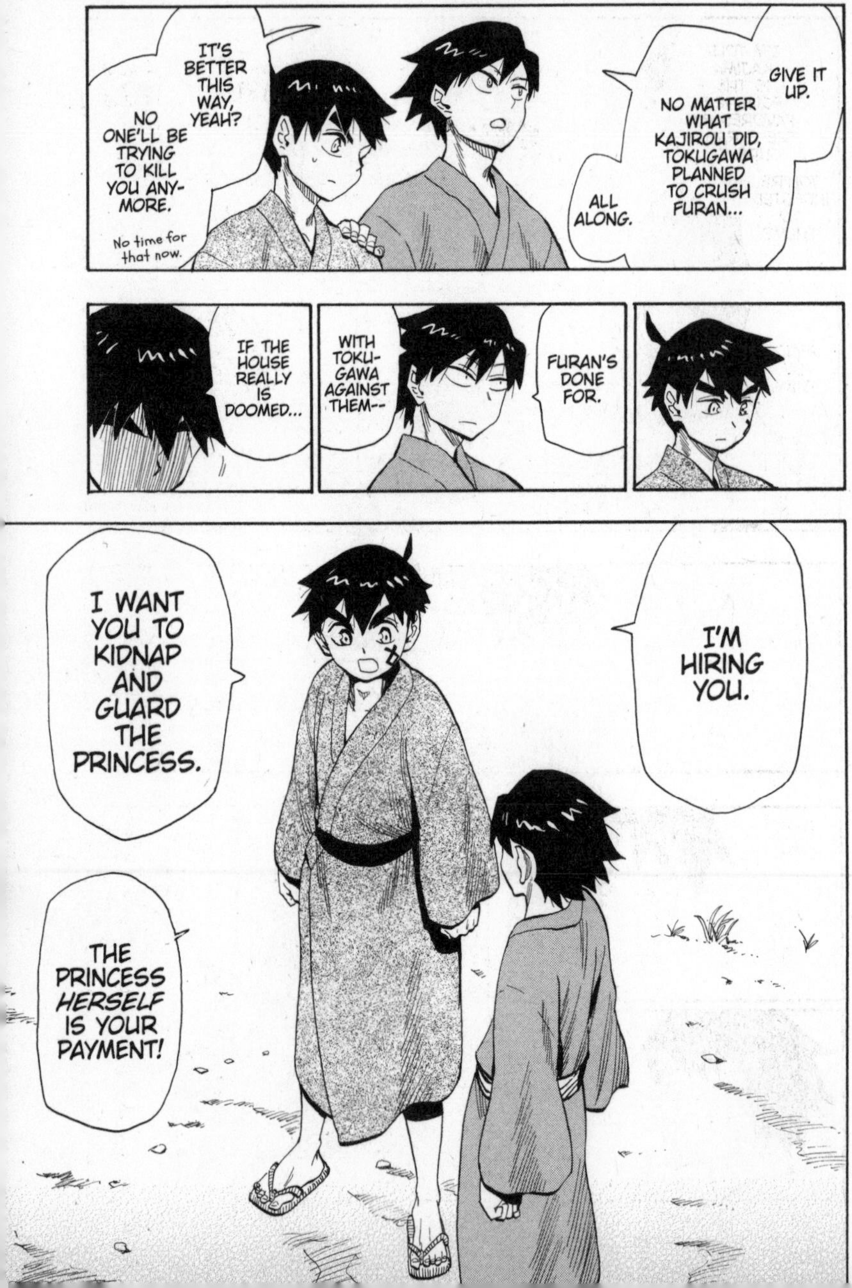
GIVE IT UP.
NO MATTER WHAT KAJIROU DID, TOKUGAWA PLANNED TO CRUSH FURAN...
ALL ALONG.
IT'S BETTER THIS WAY, YEAH?
NO ONE'LL BE TRYING TO KILL YOU ANY-MORE.
No time for that now.
FURAN'S DONE FOR.
WITH TOKU-GAWA AGAINST THEM--
IF THE HOUSE REALLY IS DOOMED...
I'M HIRING YOU.
I WANT YOU TO KIDNAP AND GUARD THE PRINCESS.
THE PRINCESS *HERSELF* IS YOUR PAYMENT!

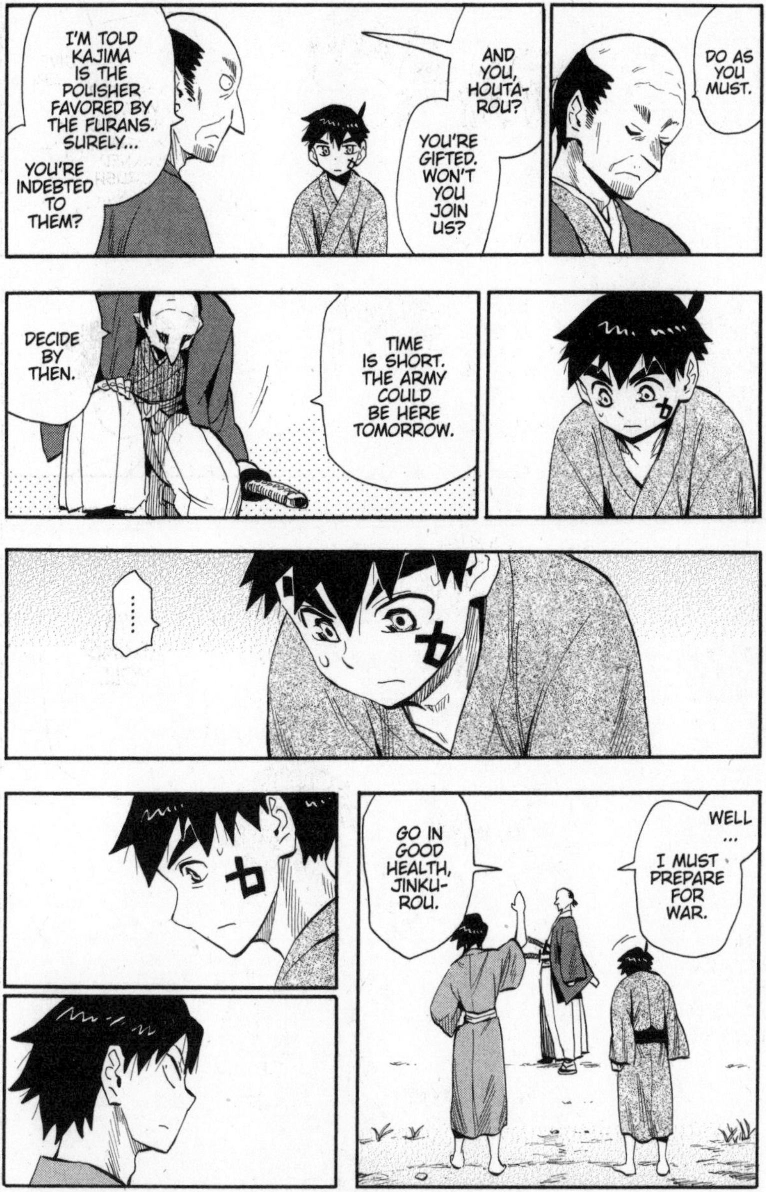
DO AS YOU MUST.
AND YOU, HOUTAROU?
YOU'RE GIFTED. WON'T YOU JOIN US?
I'M TOLD KAJIMA IS THE POLISHER FAVORED BY THE FURANS. SURELY...
YOU'RE INDEBTED TO THEM?
TIME IS SHORT. THE ARMY COULD BE HERE TOMORROW.
DECIDE BY THEN.
......
WELL ... I MUST PREPARE FOR WAR.
GO IN GOOD HEALTH, JINKUROU.

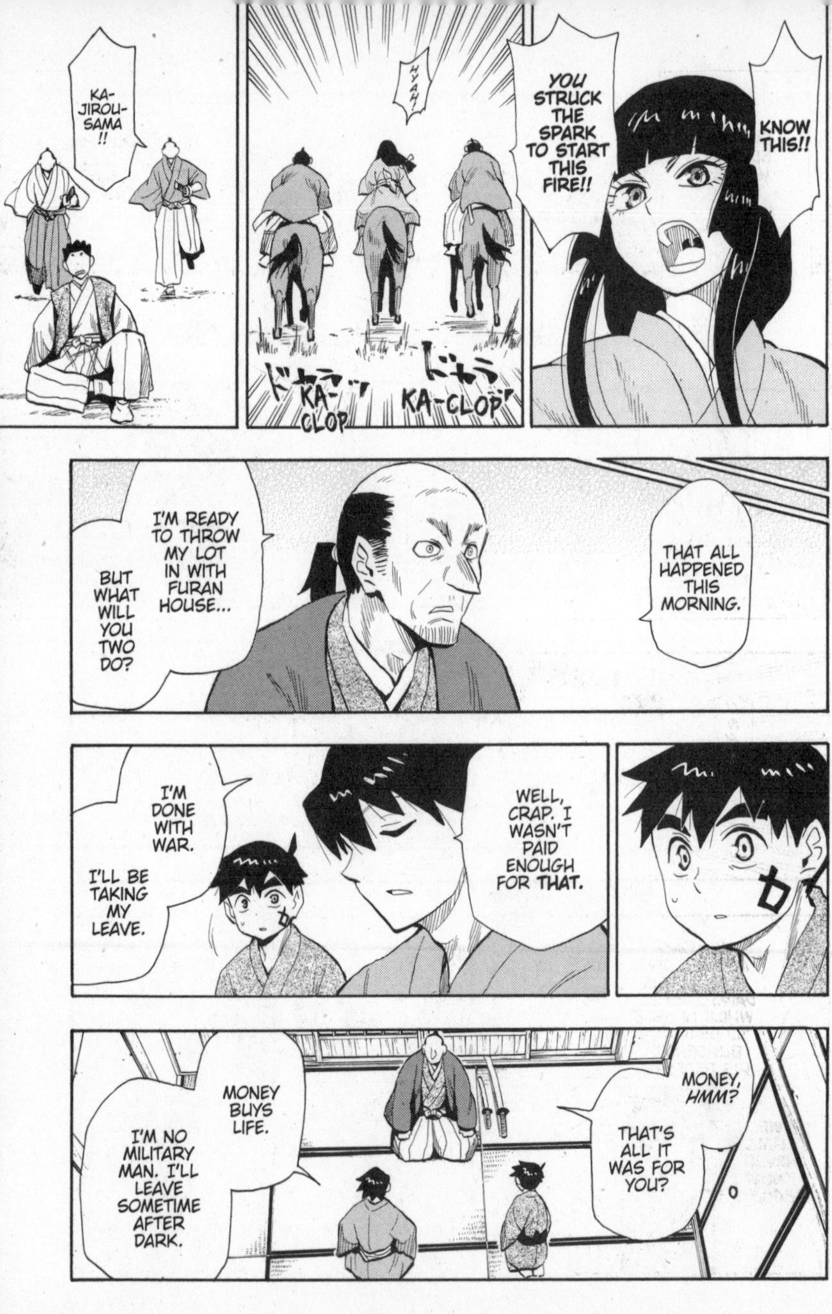
KNOW THIS!!
YOU STRUCK THE SPARK TO START THIS FIRE!!
HYAH!
KA-CLOP
KA-CLOP
KAJIROU-SAMA!!
THAT ALL HAPPENED THIS MORNING.
I'M READY TO THROW MY LOT IN WITH FURAN HOUSE...
BUT WHAT WILL YOU TWO DO?
WELL, CRAP. I WASN'T PAID ENOUGH FOR THAT.
I'M DONE WITH WAR.
I'LL BE TAKING MY LEAVE.
MONEY, HMM?
THAT'S ALL IT WAS FOR YOU?
MONEY BUYS LIFE.
I'M NO MILITARY MAN. I'LL LEAVE SOMETIME AFTER DARK.

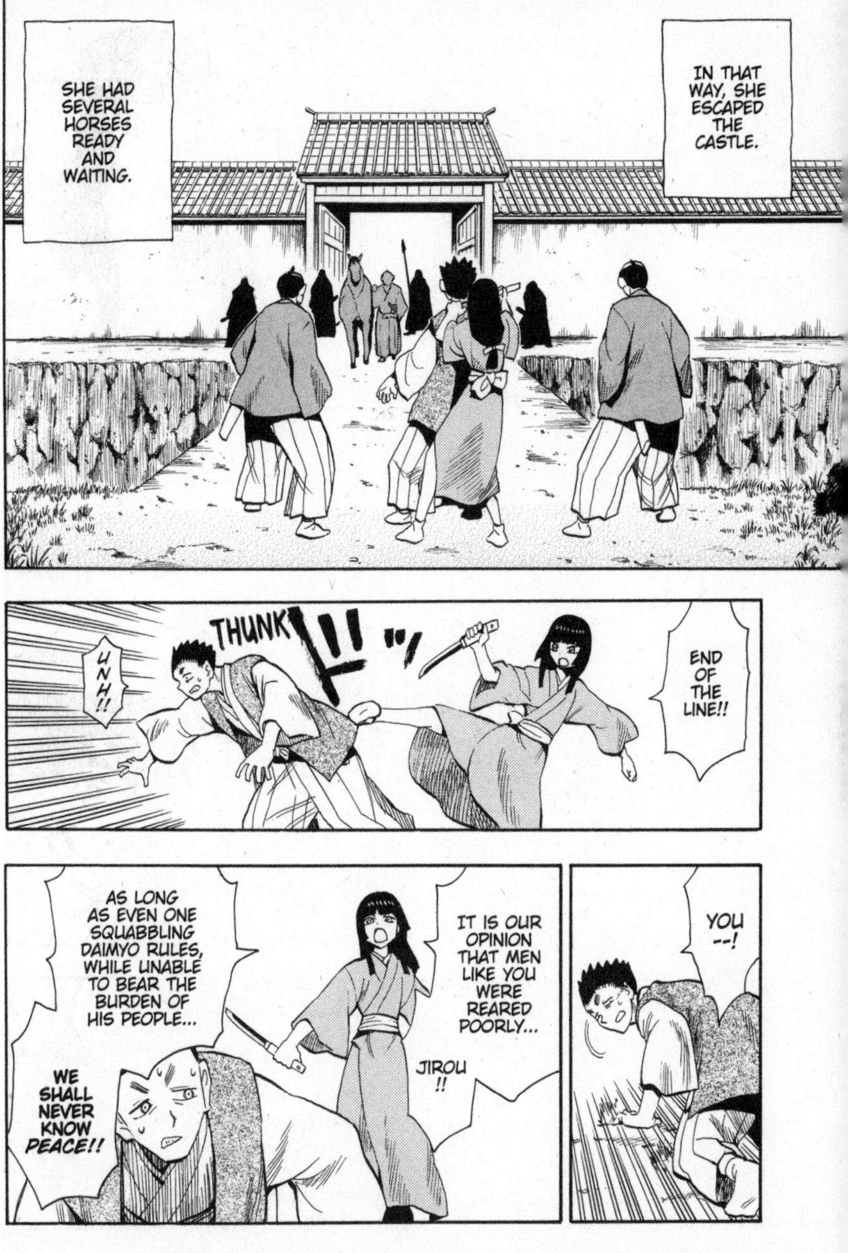
IN THAT WAY, SHE ESCAPED THE CASTLE.
SHE HAD SEVERAL HORSES READY AND WAITING.
END OF THE LINE!!
THUNK
UNH!!
YOU --!
IT IS OUR OPINION THAT MEN LIKE YOU WERE REARED POORLY...
JIROU !!
AS LONG AS EVEN ONE SQUABBLING DAIMYO RULES, WHILE UNABLE TO BEAR THE BURDEN OF HIS PEOPLE...
WE SHALL NEVER KNOW PEACE!!

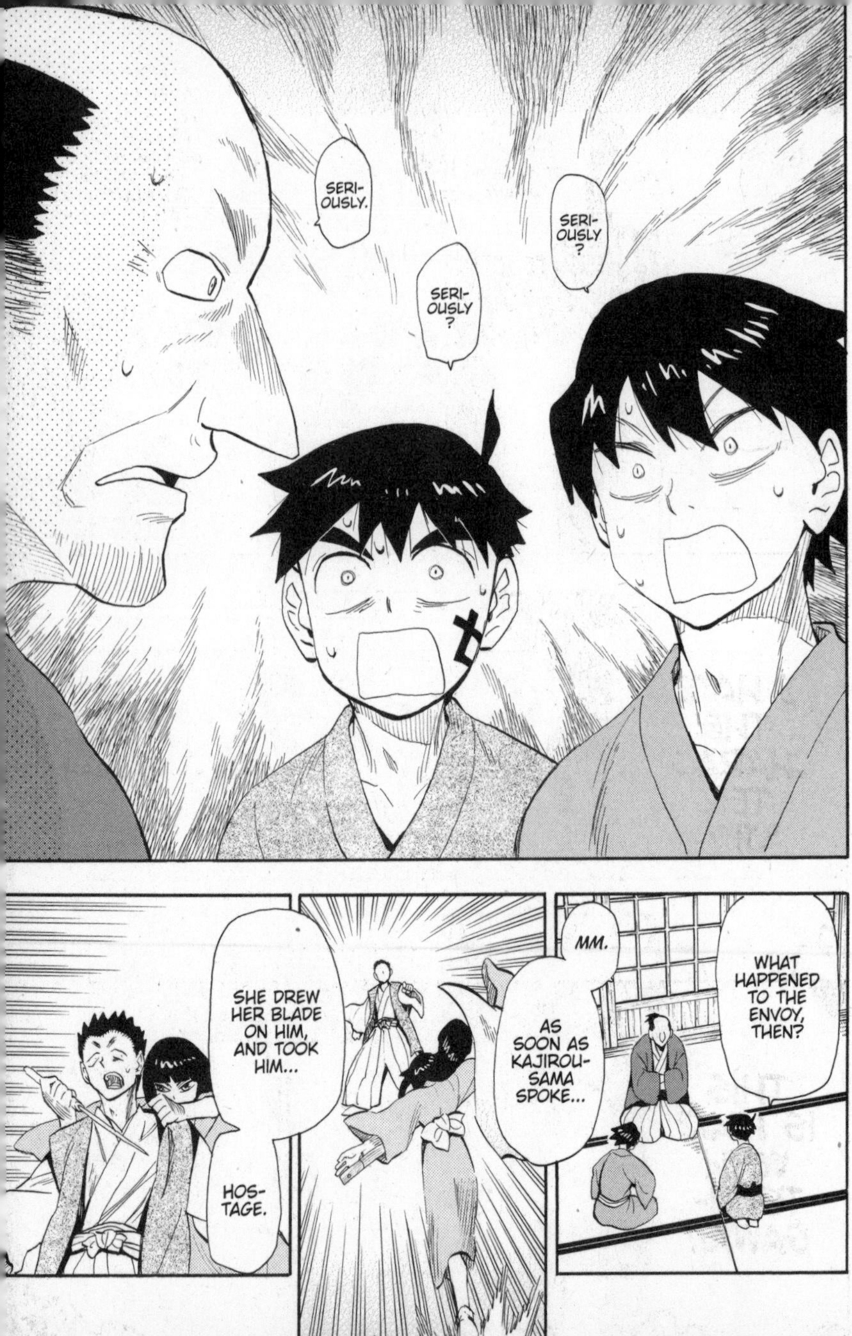
SERI-OUSLY?
SERI-OUSLY?
SERI-OUSLY.
WHAT HAPPENED TO THE ENVOY, THEN?
MM.
AS SOON AS KAJIROU-SAMA SPOKE...
SHE DREW HER BLADE ON HIM, AND TOOK HIM...
HOS-TAGE.

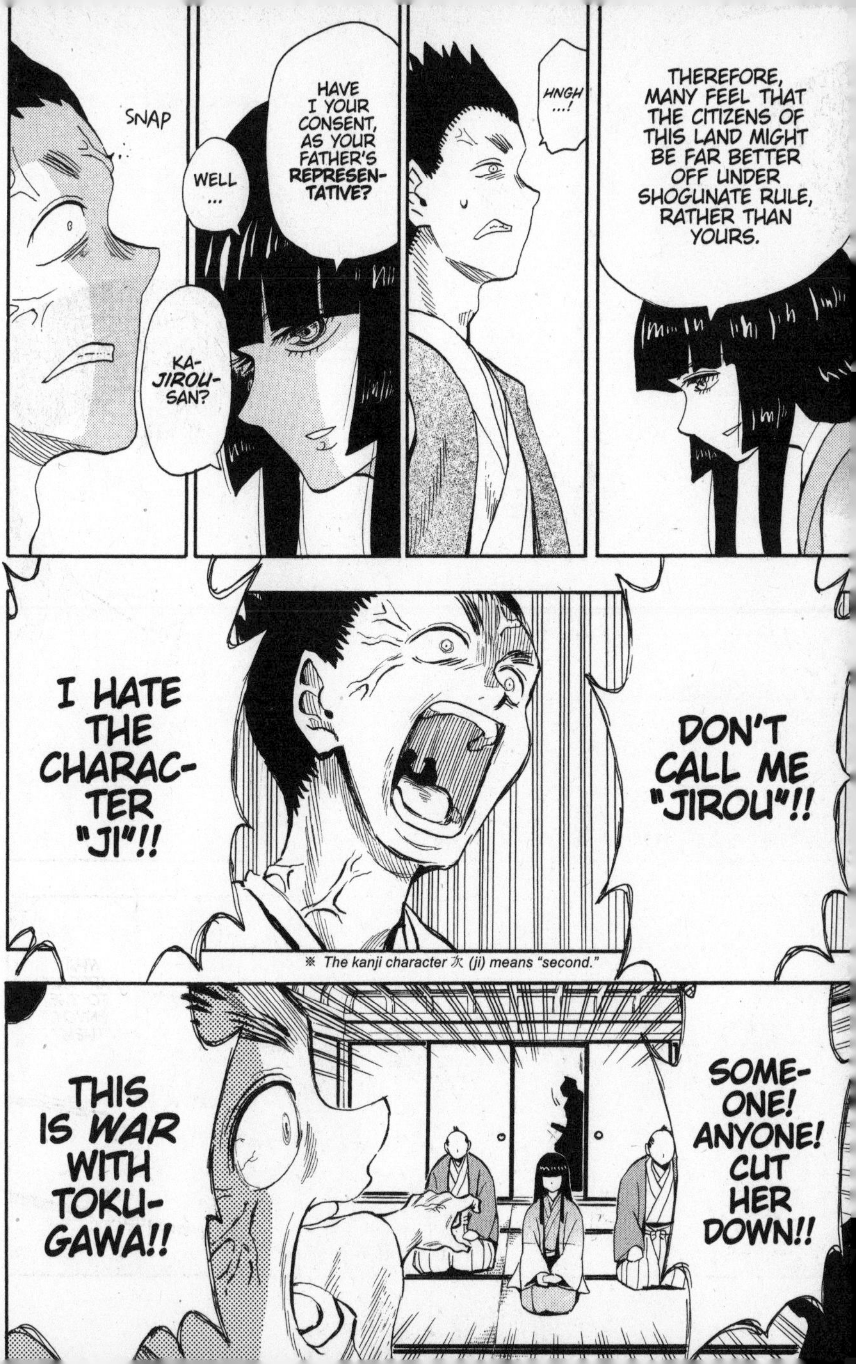
THEREFORE, MANY FEEL THAT THE CITIZENS OF THIS LAND MIGHT BE FAR BETTER OFF UNDER SHOGUNATE RULE, RATHER THAN YOURS.
HNGH ...!
HAVE I YOUR CONSENT, AS YOUR FATHER'S REPRESENTATIVE?
WELL ...
KAJIROU-SAN?
SNAP
DON'T CALL ME "JIROU"!!
I HATE THE CHARACTER "JI"!!
※ The kanji character 次 (ji) means "second."
SOMEONE! ANYONE! CUT HER DOWN!!
THIS IS WAR WITH TOKUGAWA!!

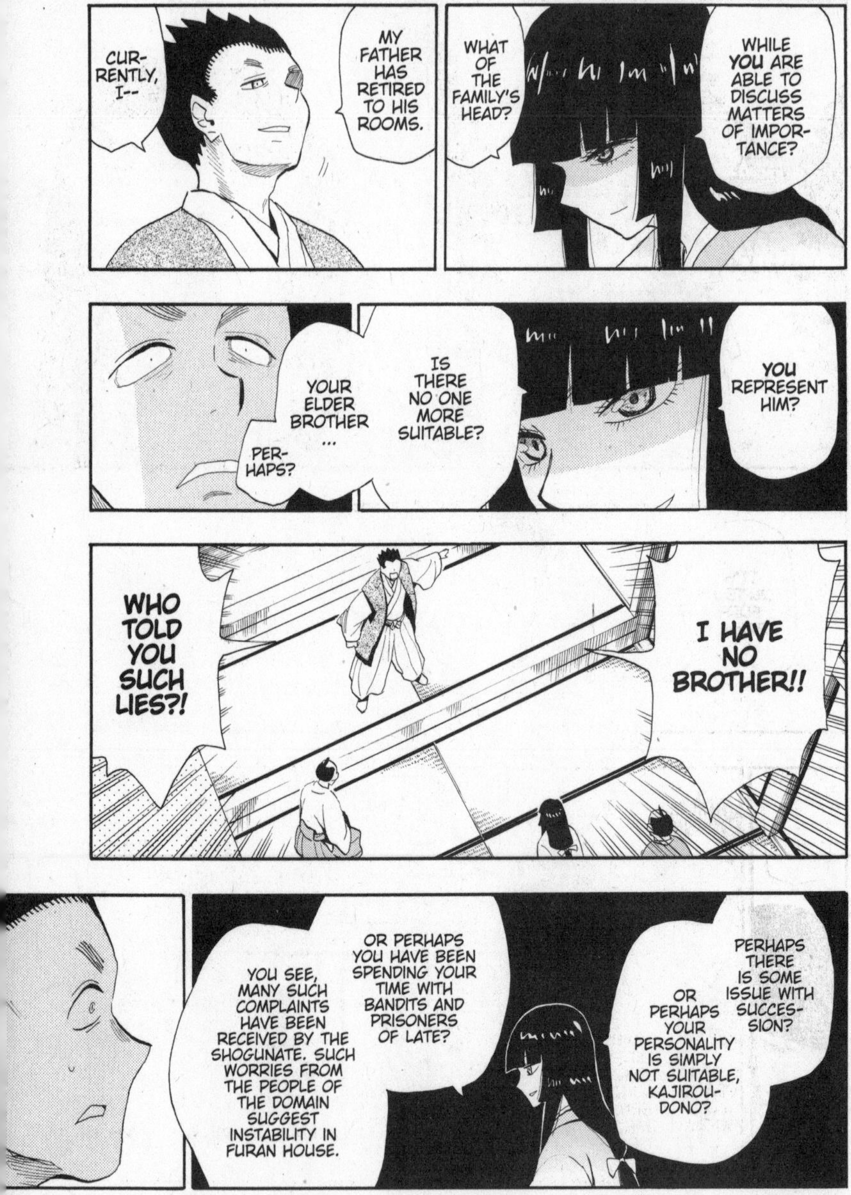
WHILE YOU ARE ABLE TO DISCUSS MATTERS OF IMPORTANCE?
WHAT OF THE FAMILY'S HEAD?
MY FATHER HAS RETIRED TO HIS ROOMS.
CURRENTLY, I--
YOU REPRESENT HIM?
IS THERE NO ONE MORE SUITABLE?
YOUR ELDER BROTHER ...
PERHAPS?
I HAVE NO BROTHER!!
WHO TOLD YOU SUCH LIES?!
PERHAPS THERE IS SOME ISSUE WITH SUCCESSION?
OR PERHAPS YOUR PERSONALITY IS SIMPLY NOT SUITABLE, KAJIROU-DONO?
OR PERHAPS YOU HAVE BEEN SPENDING YOUR TIME WITH BANDITS AND PRISONERS OF LATE?
YOU SEE, MANY SUCH COMPLAINTS HAVE BEEN RECEIVED BY THE SHOGUNATE. SUCH WORRIES FROM THE PEOPLE OF THE DOMAIN SUGGEST INSTABILITY IN FURAN HOUSE.

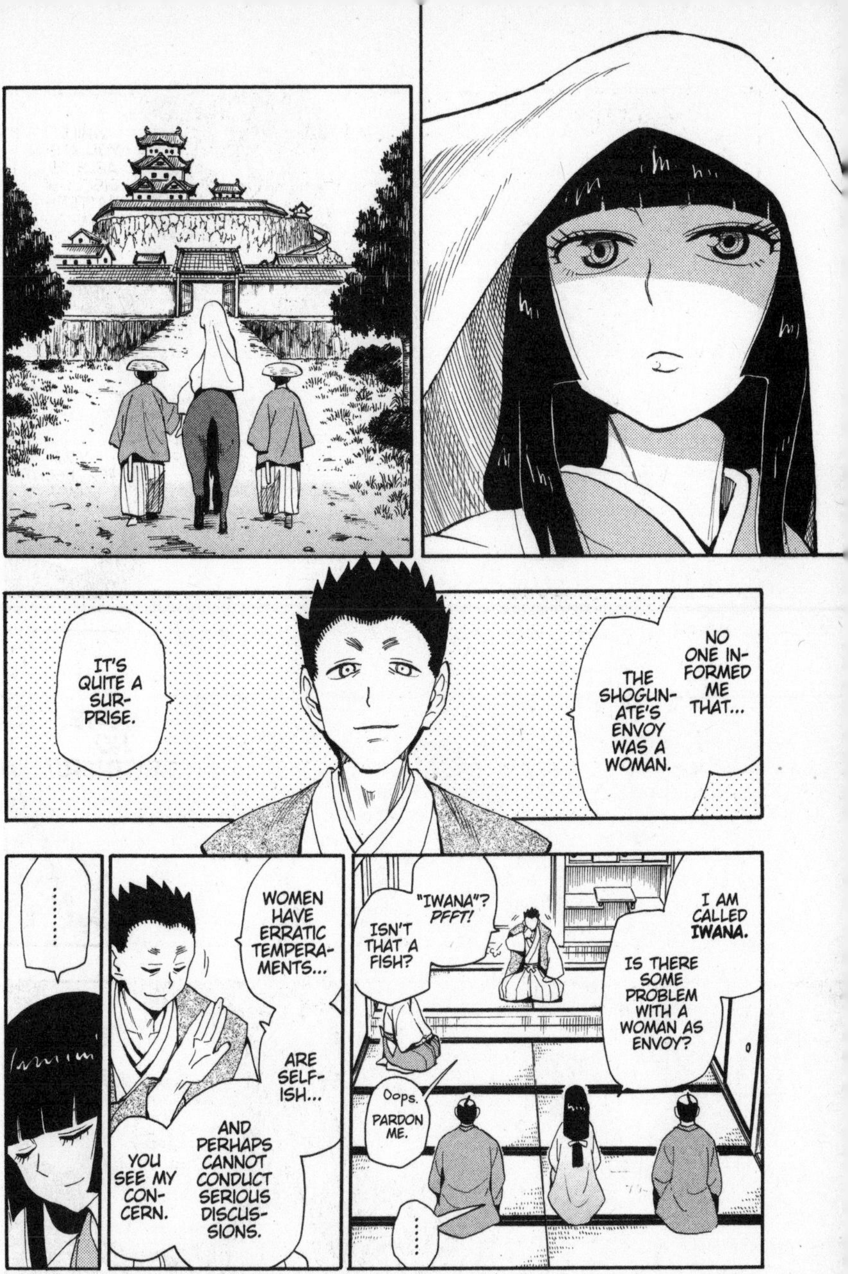
NO ONE INFORMED ME THAT... THE SHOGUNATE'S ENVOY WAS A WOMAN.
IT'S QUITE A SURPRISE.
I AM CALLED IWANA.
IS THERE SOME PROBLEM WITH A WOMAN AS ENVOY?
"IWANA"? PFFT!
ISN'T THAT A FISH?
Oops. PARDON ME.
......
WOMEN HAVE ERRATIC TEMPERAMENTS...
ARE SELFISH...
AND PERHAPS CANNOT CONDUCT SERIOUS DISCUSSIONS.
YOU SEE MY CONCERN.
......

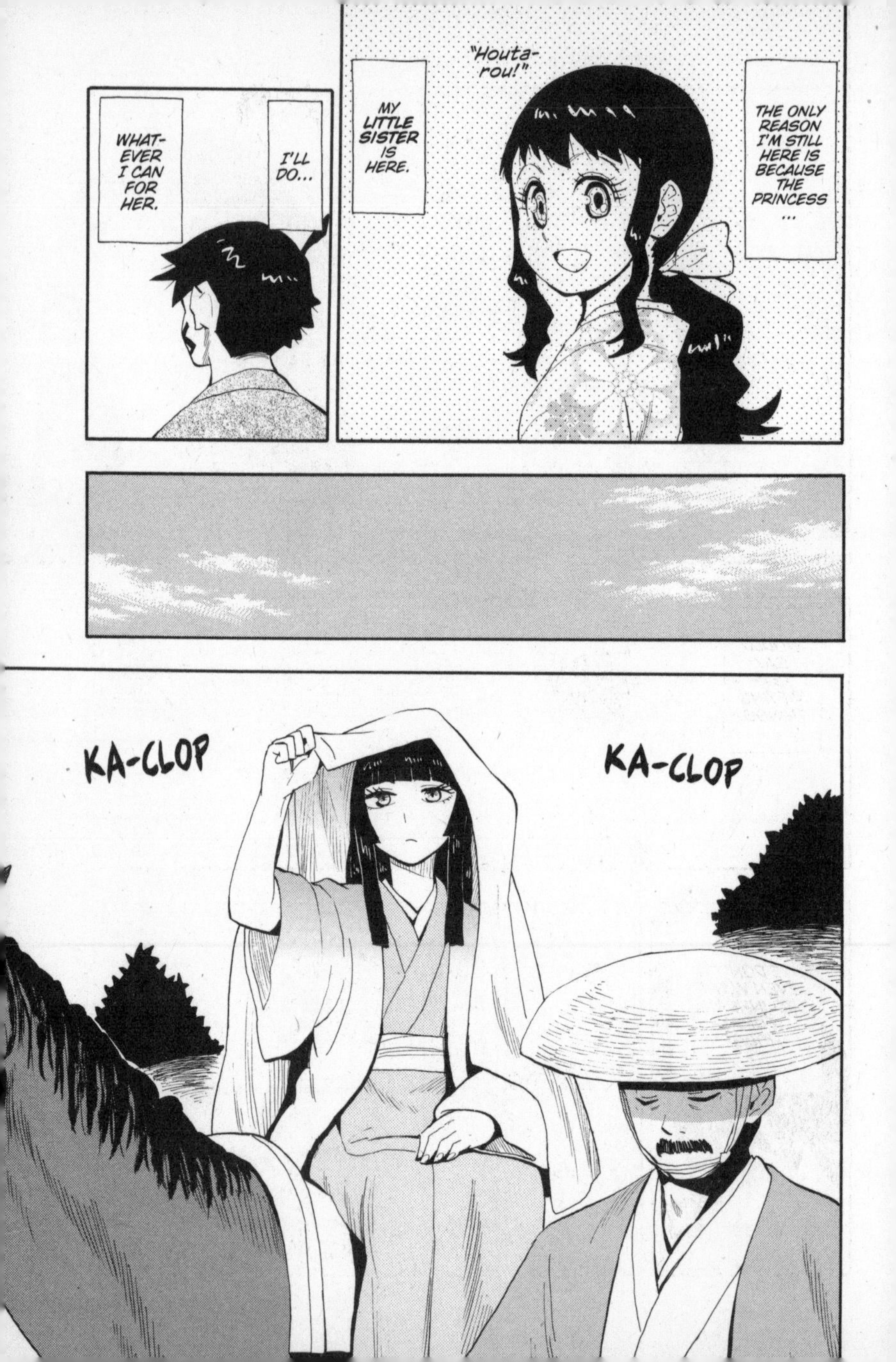
THE ONLY REASON I'M STILL HERE IS BECAUSE THE PRINCESS...
"Houta-rou!"
MY LITTLE SISTER IS HERE.
I'LL DO...
WHAT-EVER I CAN FOR HER.
KA-CLOP
KA-CLOP

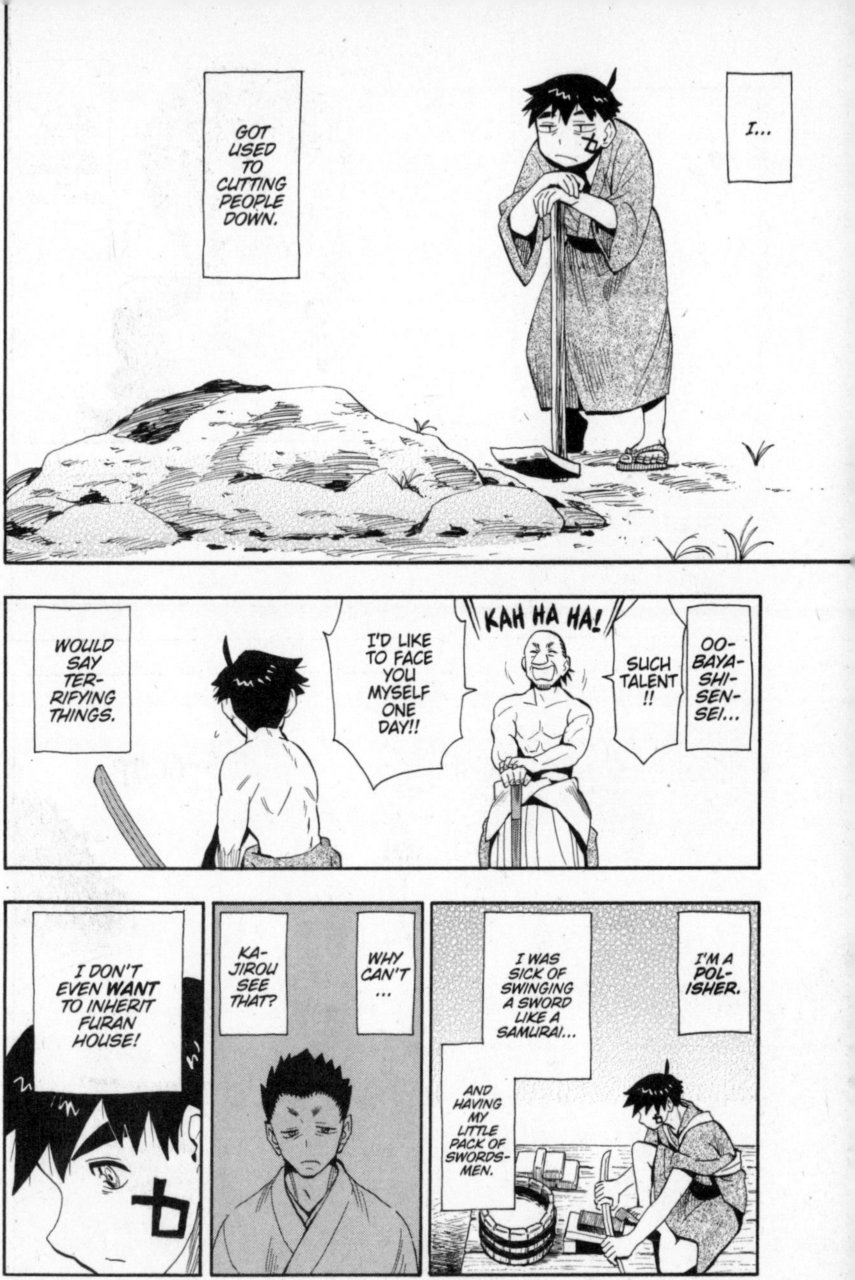
I...
GOT USED TO CUTTING PEOPLE DOWN.
OO-BAYA-SHI-SEN-SEI...
SUCH TALENT !!
KAH HA HA!
I'D LIKE TO FACE YOU MYSELF ONE DAY!!
WOULD SAY TER-RIFYING THINGS.
I'M A POL-ISHER.
I WAS SICK OF SWINGING A SWORD LIKE A SAMURAI...
AND HAVING MY LITTLE PACK OF SWORDS-MEN.
WHY CAN'T ...
KA-JIROU SEE THAT?
I DON'T EVEN WANT TO INHERIT FURAN HOUSE!

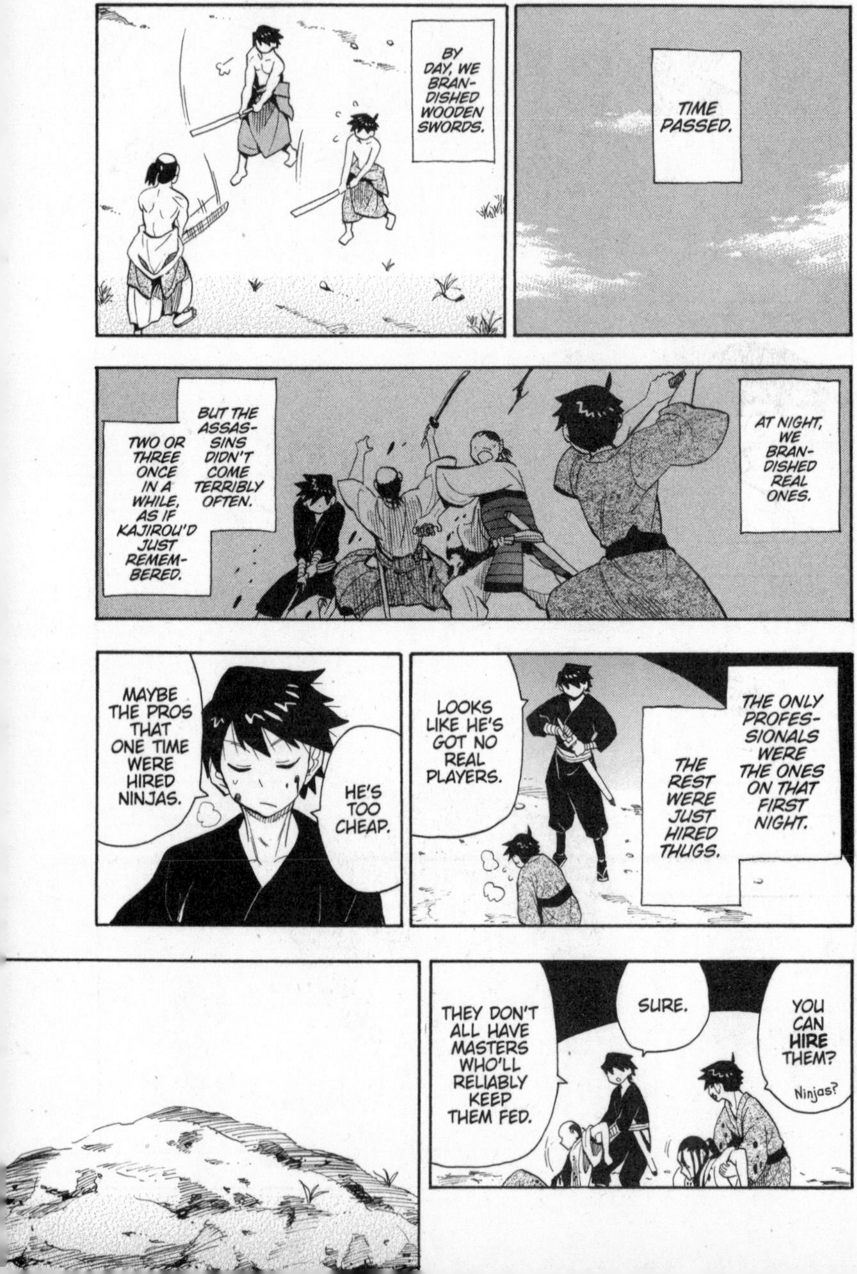
TIME PASSED.
BY DAY, WE BRANDISHED WOODEN SWORDS.
AT NIGHT, WE BRANDISHED REAL ONES.
BUT THE ASSASSINS DIDN'T COME TERRIBLY OFTEN.
TWO OR THREE ONCE IN A WHILE, AS IF KAJIROU'D JUST REMEMBERED.
THE ONLY PROFESSIONALS WERE THE ONES ON THAT FIRST NIGHT.
THE REST WERE JUST HIRED THUGS.
LOOKS LIKE HE'S GOT NO REAL PLAYERS.
HE'S TOO CHEAP.
MAYBE THE PROS THAT ONE TIME WERE HIRED NINJAS.
YOU CAN **HIRE** THEM?
Ninjas?
SURE.
THEY DON'T ALL HAVE MASTERS WHO'LL RELIABLY KEEP THEM FED.

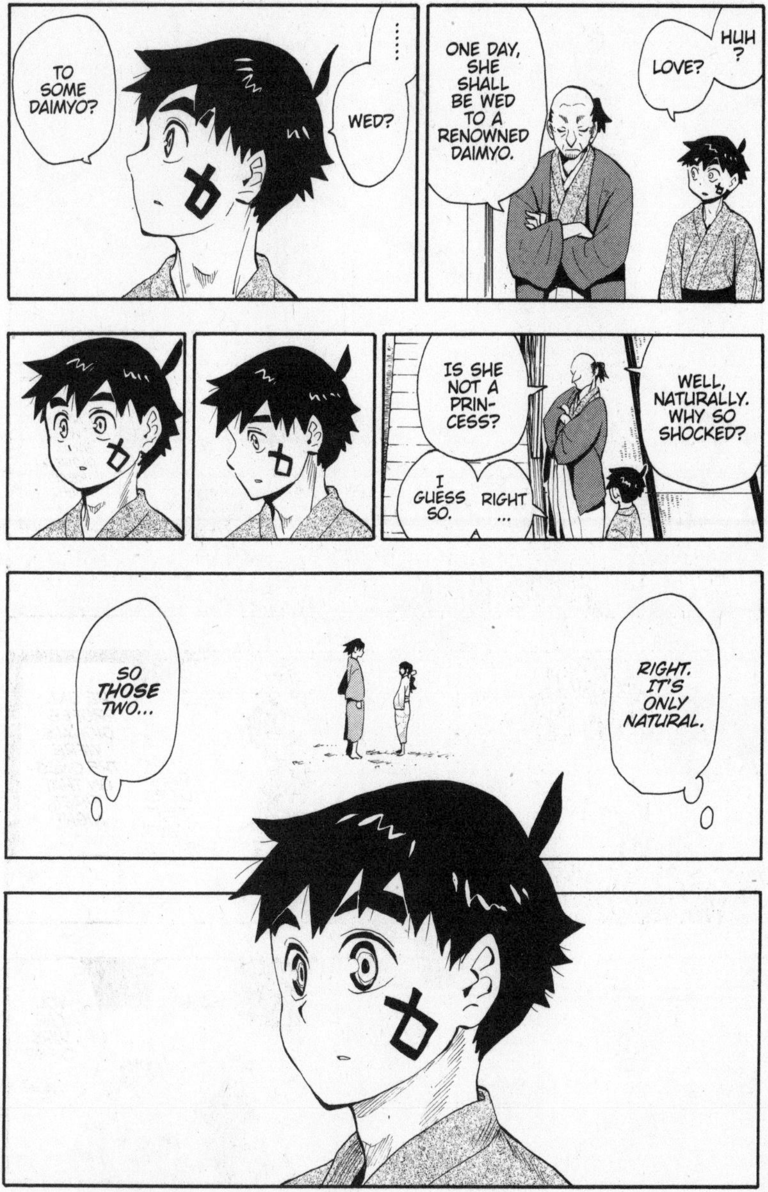
HUH?
LOVE?
ONE DAY, SHE SHALL BE WED TO A RENOWNED DAIMYO.
......
WED?
TO SOME DAIMYO?
WELL, NATURALLY. WHY SO SHOCKED?
IS SHE NOT A PRIN-CESS?
RIGHT...
I GUESS SO.
RIGHT. IT'S ONLY NATURAL.
SO THOSE TWO...

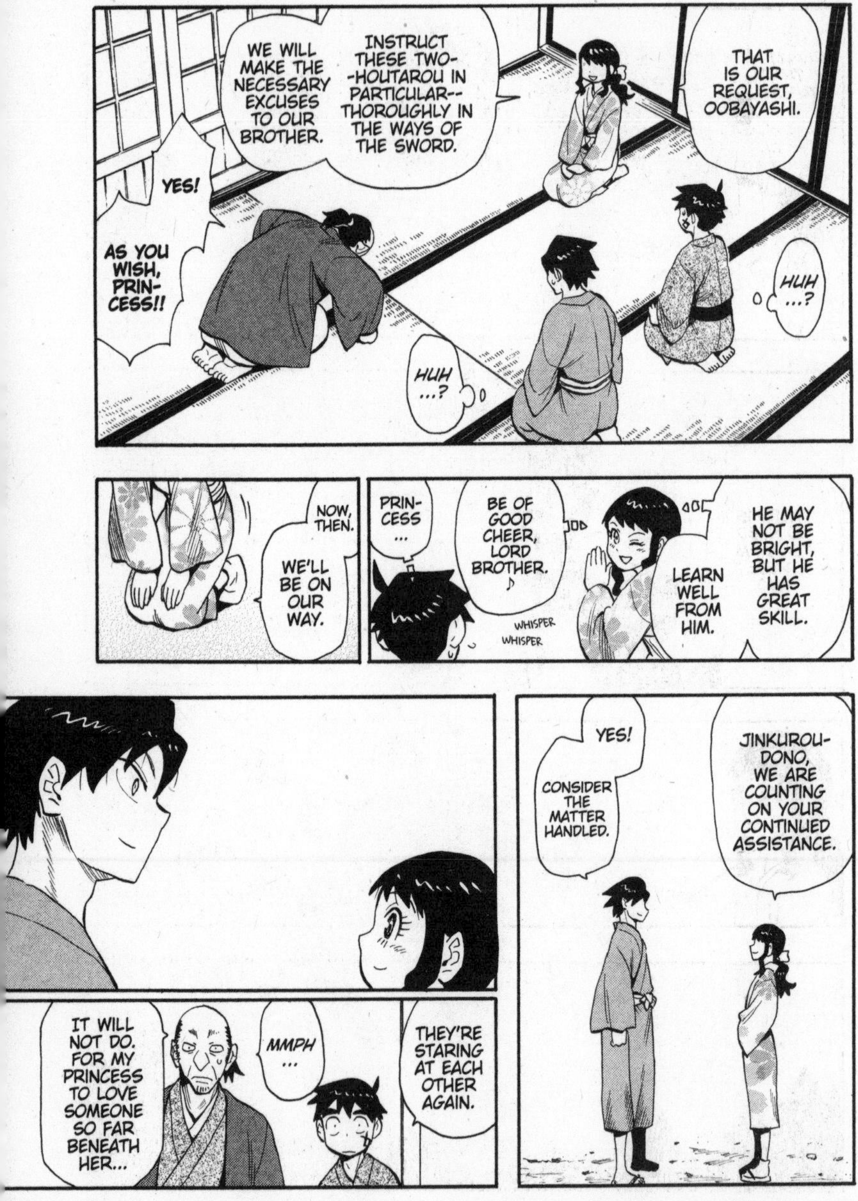
THAT IS OUR REQUEST, OOBAYASHI.
INSTRUCT THESE TWO--HOUTAROU IN PARTICULAR--THOROUGHLY IN THE WAYS OF THE SWORD.
WE WILL MAKE THE NECESSARY EXCUSES TO OUR BROTHER.
YES!
AS YOU WISH, PRINCESS!!
HUH ...?
HUH ...?
HE MAY NOT BE BRIGHT, BUT HE HAS GREAT SKILL.
LEARN WELL FROM HIM.
BE OF GOOD CHEER, LORD BROTHER. ♪
PRINCESS ...
WHISPER WHISPER
NOW, THEN.
WE'LL BE ON OUR WAY.
JINKUROU-DONO, WE ARE COUNTING ON YOUR CONTINUED ASSISTANCE.
YES!
CONSIDER THE MATTER HANDLED.
THEY'RE STARING AT EACH OTHER AGAIN.
MMPH ...
IT WILL NOT DO. FOR MY PRINCESS TO LOVE SOMEONE SO FAR BENEATH HER...

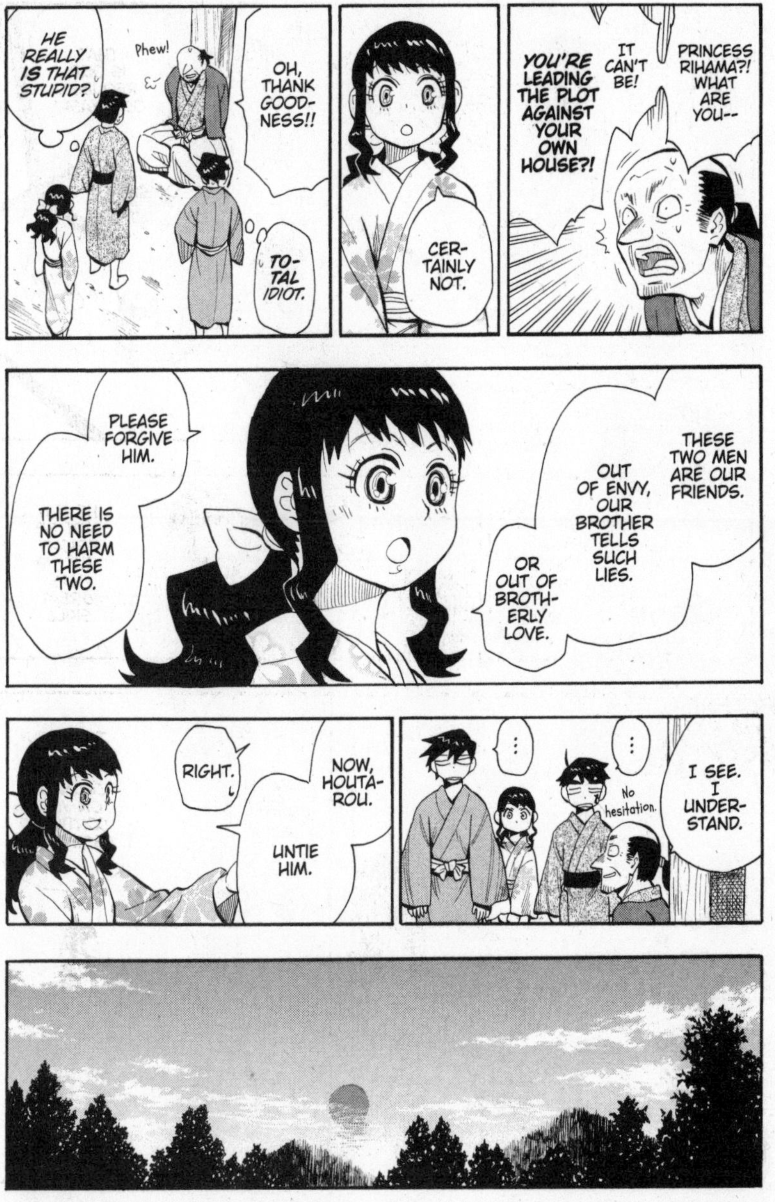
PRINCESS RIHAMA?! WHAT ARE YOU--
IT CAN'T BE!
YOU'RE LEADING THE PLOT AGAINST YOUR OWN HOUSE?!
CERTAINLY NOT.
OH, THANK GOODNESS!!
Phew!
HE REALLY IS THAT STUPID?
TOTAL IDIOT.
THESE TWO MEN ARE OUR FRIENDS.
OUT OF ENVY, OUR BROTHER TELLS SUCH LIES.
OR OUT OF BROTHERLY LOVE.
PLEASE FORGIVE HIM.
THERE IS NO NEED TO HARM THESE TWO.
I SEE. I UNDERSTAND.
...
...
No hesitation.
NOW, HOUTAROU.
RIGHT.
UNTIE HIM.

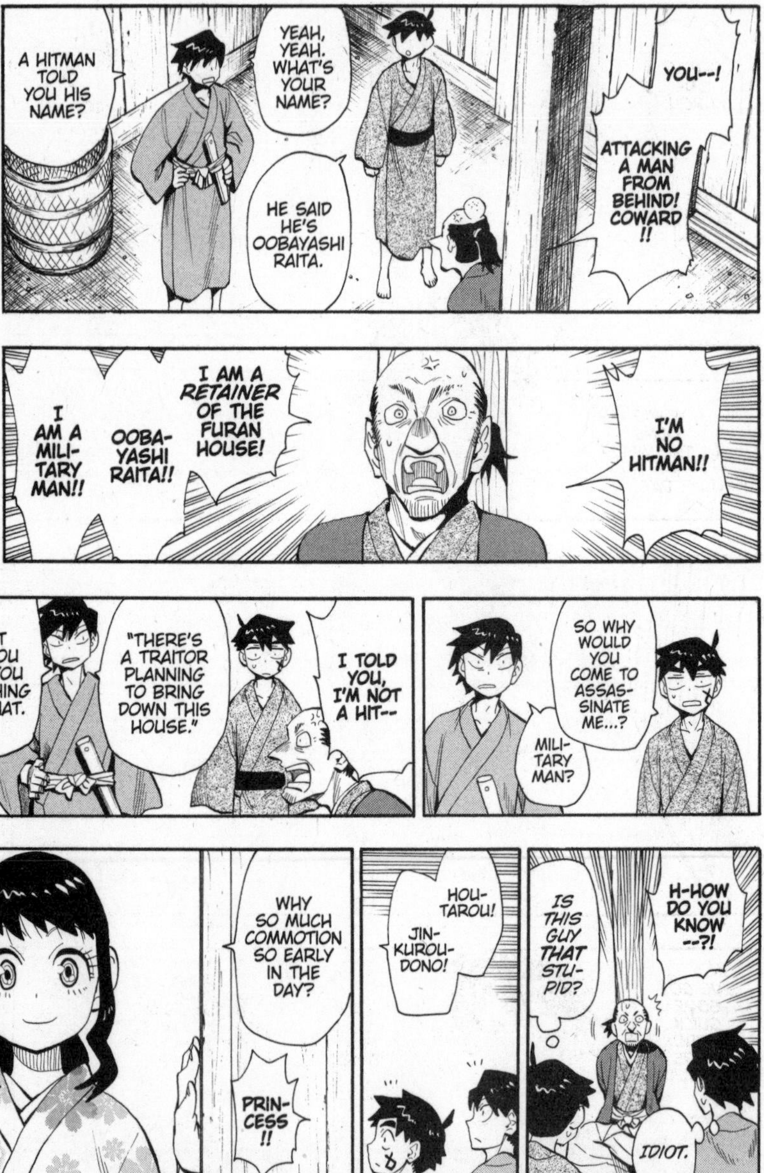
YOU--!
ATTACKING A MAN FROM BEHIND! COWARD!!
YEAH, YEAH. WHAT'S YOUR NAME?
HE SAID HE'S OOBAYASHI RAITA.
A HITMAN TOLD YOU HIS NAME?
I'M NO HITMAN!!
I AM A RETAINER OF THE FURAN HOUSE!
OOBAYASHI RAITA!!
I AM A MILITARY MAN!!
SO WHY WOULD YOU COME TO ASSASSINATE ME...?
MILITARY MAN?
I TOLD YOU, I'M NOT A HIT--
"THERE'S A TRAITOR PLANNING TO BRING DOWN THIS HOUSE."
I BET KAJIROU TOLD YOU SOMETHING LIKE THAT.
Of course.
H-HOW DO YOU KNOW--?!
IS THIS GUY THAT STUPID?
IDIOT.
HOUTAROU!
JINKUROU-DONO!
WHY SO MUCH COMMOTION SO EARLY IN THE DAY?
PRINCESS!!

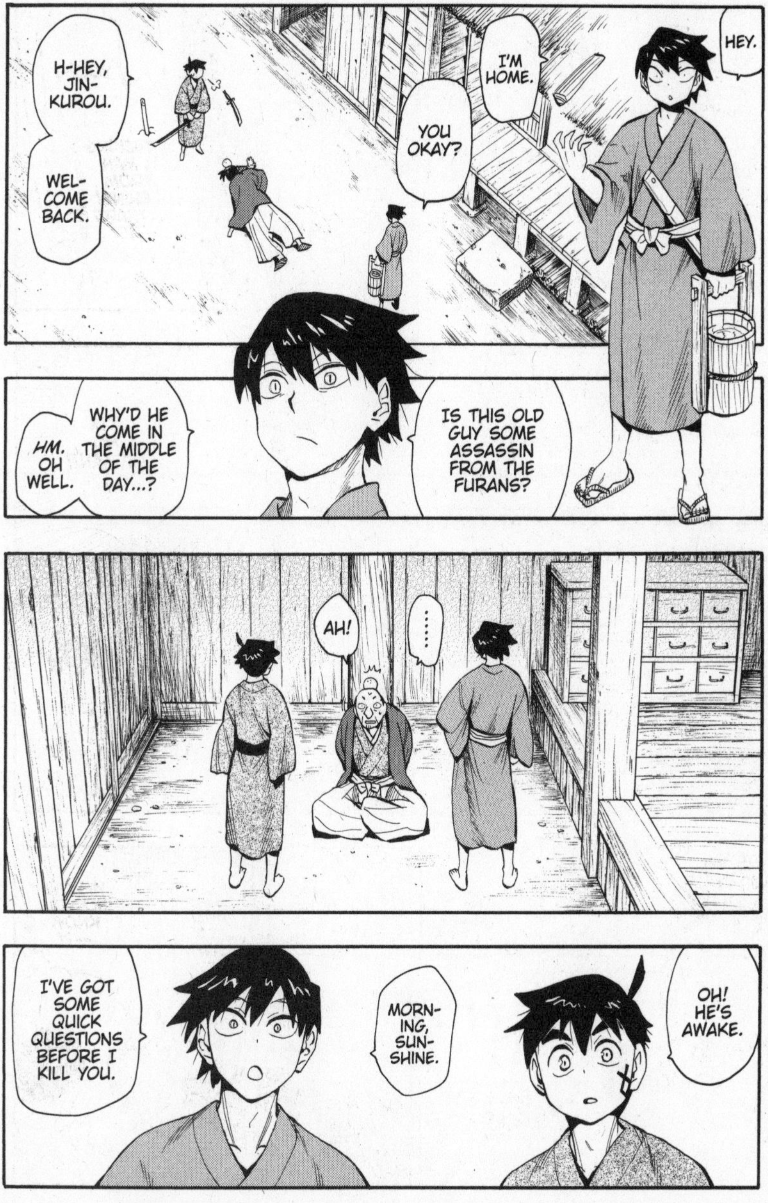
HEY.
I'M HOME.
YOU OKAY?
H-HEY, JIN-KUROU.
WEL-COME BACK.
IS THIS OLD GUY SOME ASSASSIN FROM THE FURANS?
WHY'D HE COME IN THE MIDDLE OF THE DAY...?
HM. OH WELL.
......
AH!
OH! HE'S AWAKE.
MORN-ING, SUN-SHINE.
I'VE GOT SOME QUICK QUESTIONS BEFORE I KILL YOU.

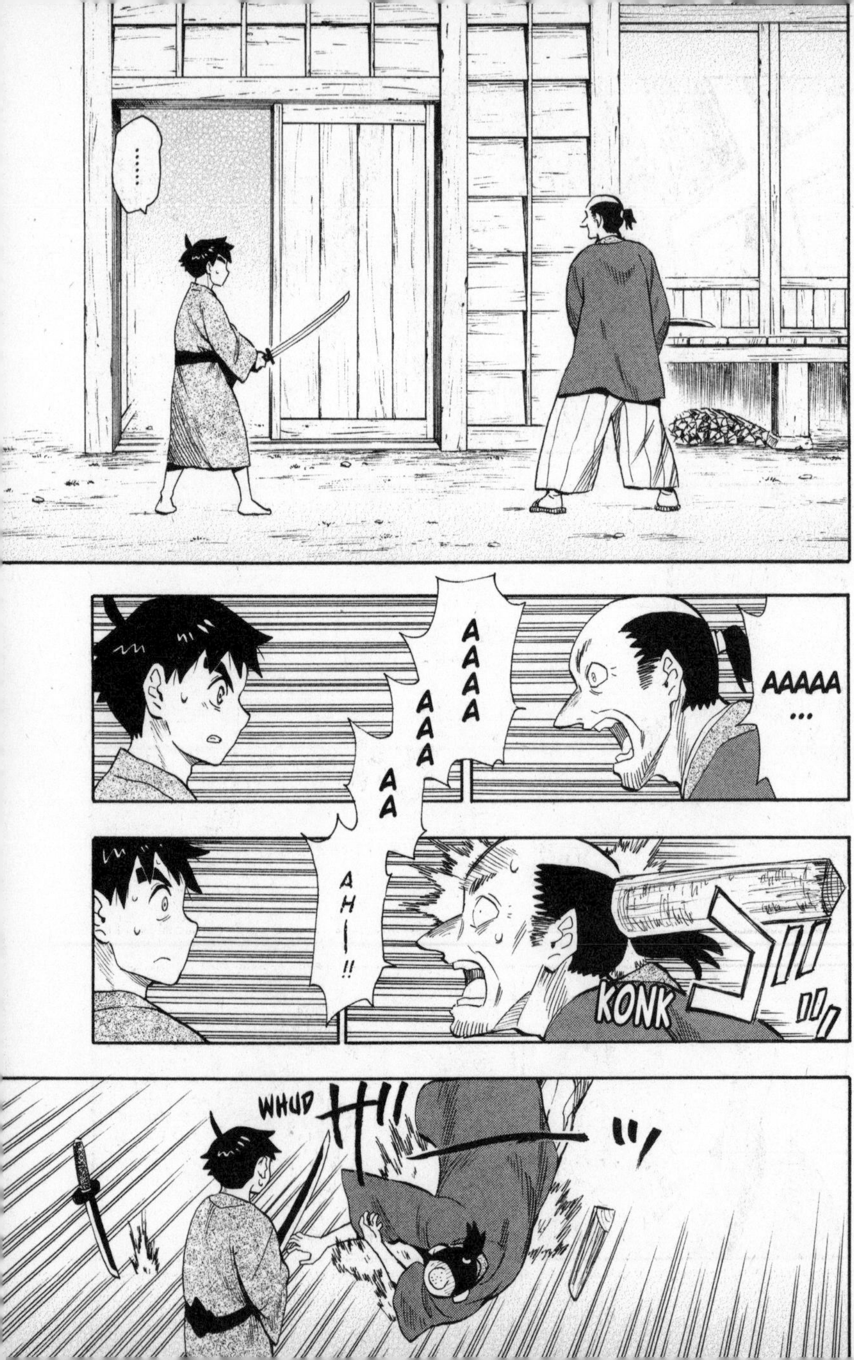

......
AAAAA...
AAAAAAAAAAAA
AH-!!
KONK
WHUD

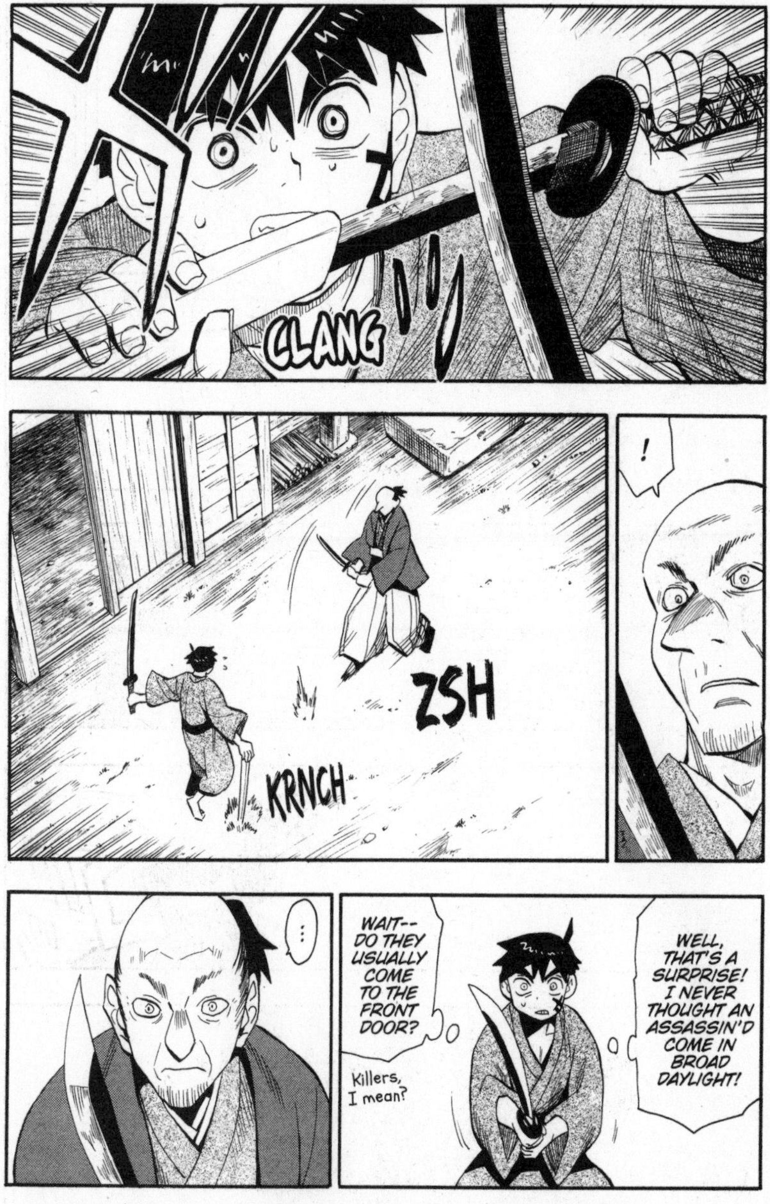
CLANG
!
ZSH
KRNCH
WELL, THAT'S A SURPRISE! I NEVER THOUGHT AN ASSASSIN'D COME IN BROAD DAYLIGHT!
WAIT-- DO THEY USUALLY COME TO THE FRONT DOOR?
Killers, I mean?
...

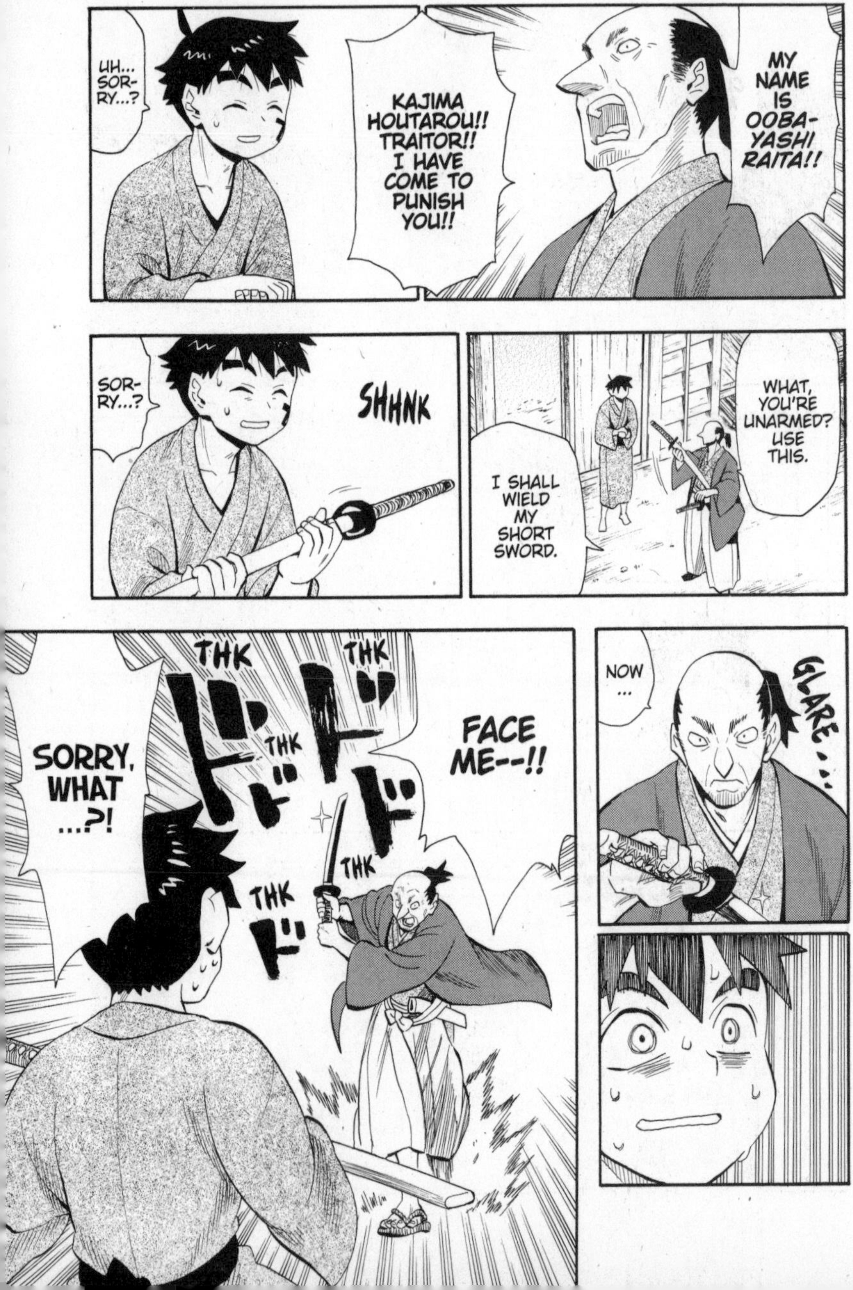
MY NAME IS OOBA-YASHI RAITA!!
KAJIMA HOUTAROU!! TRAITOR!! I HAVE COME TO PUNISH YOU!!
UH... SOR-RY...?
WHAT, YOU'RE UNARMED? USE THIS.
I SHALL WIELD MY SHORT SWORD.
SHHNK
SOR-RY...?
NOW ...
GLARE...
FACE ME--!!
THK
THK
THK
THK
THK
SORRY, WHAT ...?!

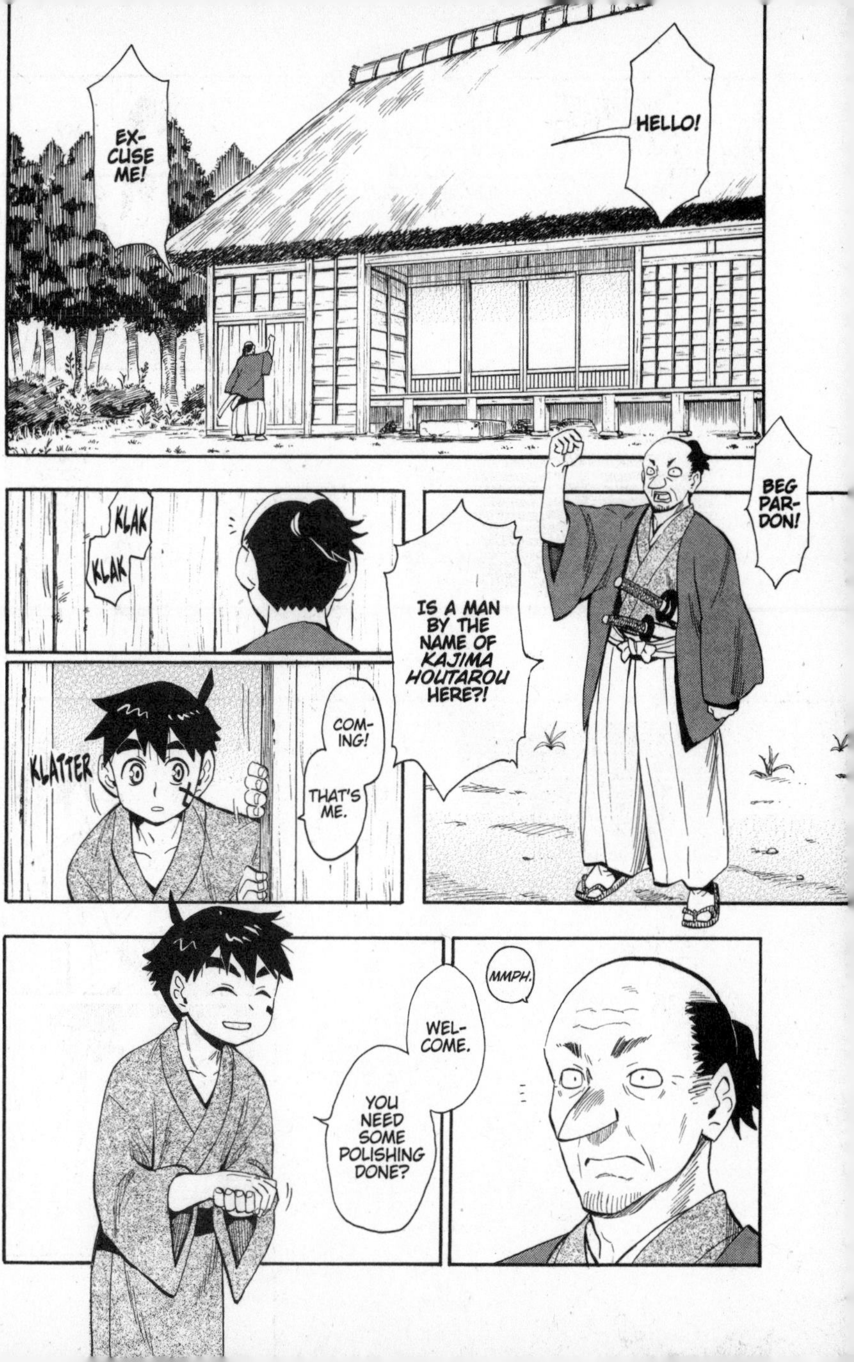
HELLO!
EX-CUSE ME!
BEG PAR-DON!
IS A MAN BY THE NAME OF KAJIMA HOUTAROU HERE?!
KLAK
KLAK
KLATTER
COM-ING!
THAT'S ME.
MMPH.
WEL-COME.
YOU NEED SOME POLISHING DONE?

Circle 17
Houtarou
3

Dad

Spirit Circle

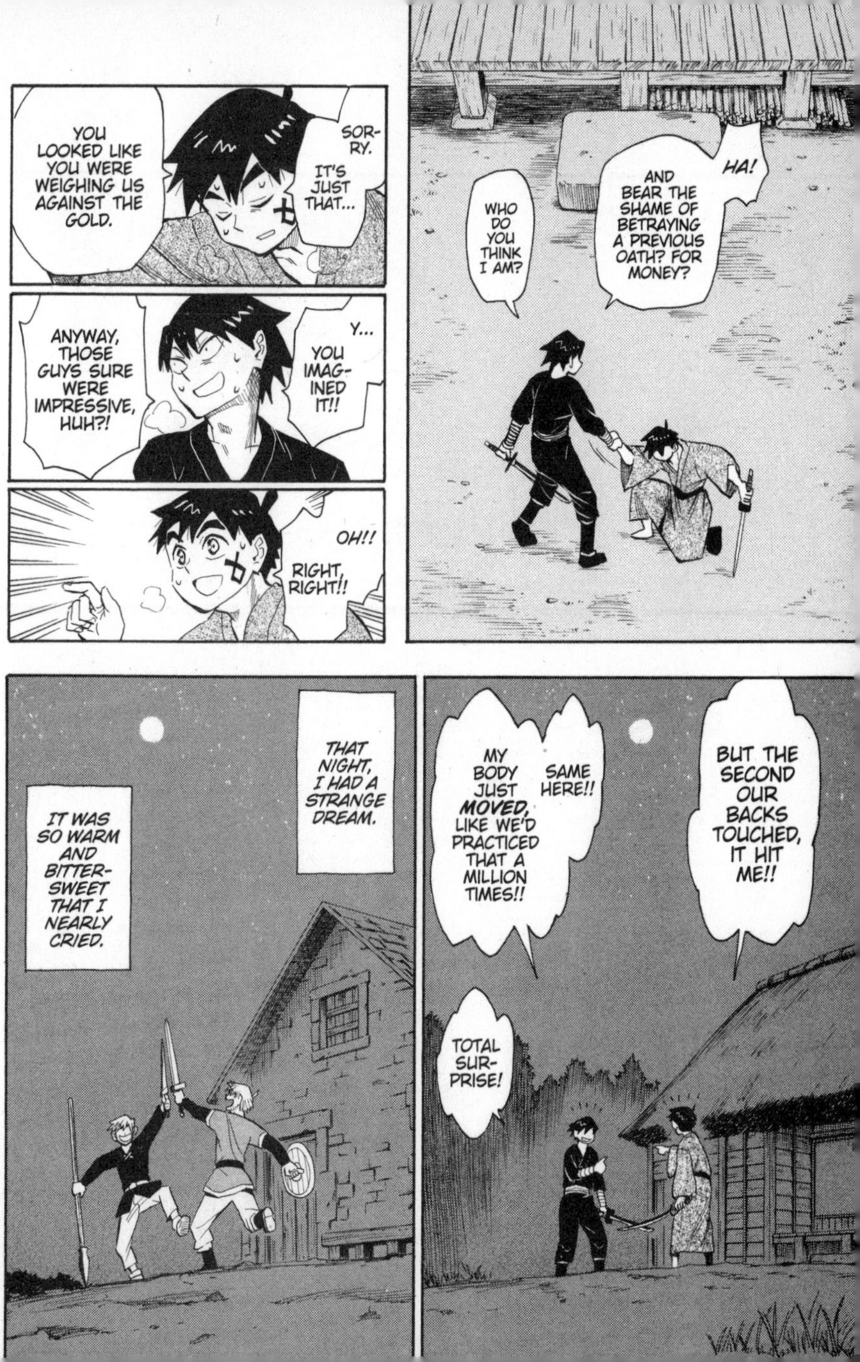
HA!
AND BEAR THE SHAME OF BETRAYING A PREVIOUS OATH? FOR MONEY?
WHO DO YOU THINK I AM?
SORRY. IT'S JUST THAT...
YOU LOOKED LIKE YOU WERE WEIGHING US AGAINST THE GOLD.
Y... YOU IMAGINED IT!!
ANYWAY, THOSE GUYS SURE WERE IMPRESSIVE, HUH?!
OH!! RIGHT, RIGHT!!
BUT THE SECOND OUR BACKS TOUCHED, IT HIT ME!!
SAME HERE!!
MY BODY JUST ***MOVED***, LIKE WE'D PRACTICED THAT A MILLION TIMES!!
TOTAL SURPRISE!
THAT NIGHT, I HAD A STRANGE DREAM.
IT WAS SO WARM AND BITTERSWEET THAT I NEARLY CRIED.

Circle 16/END

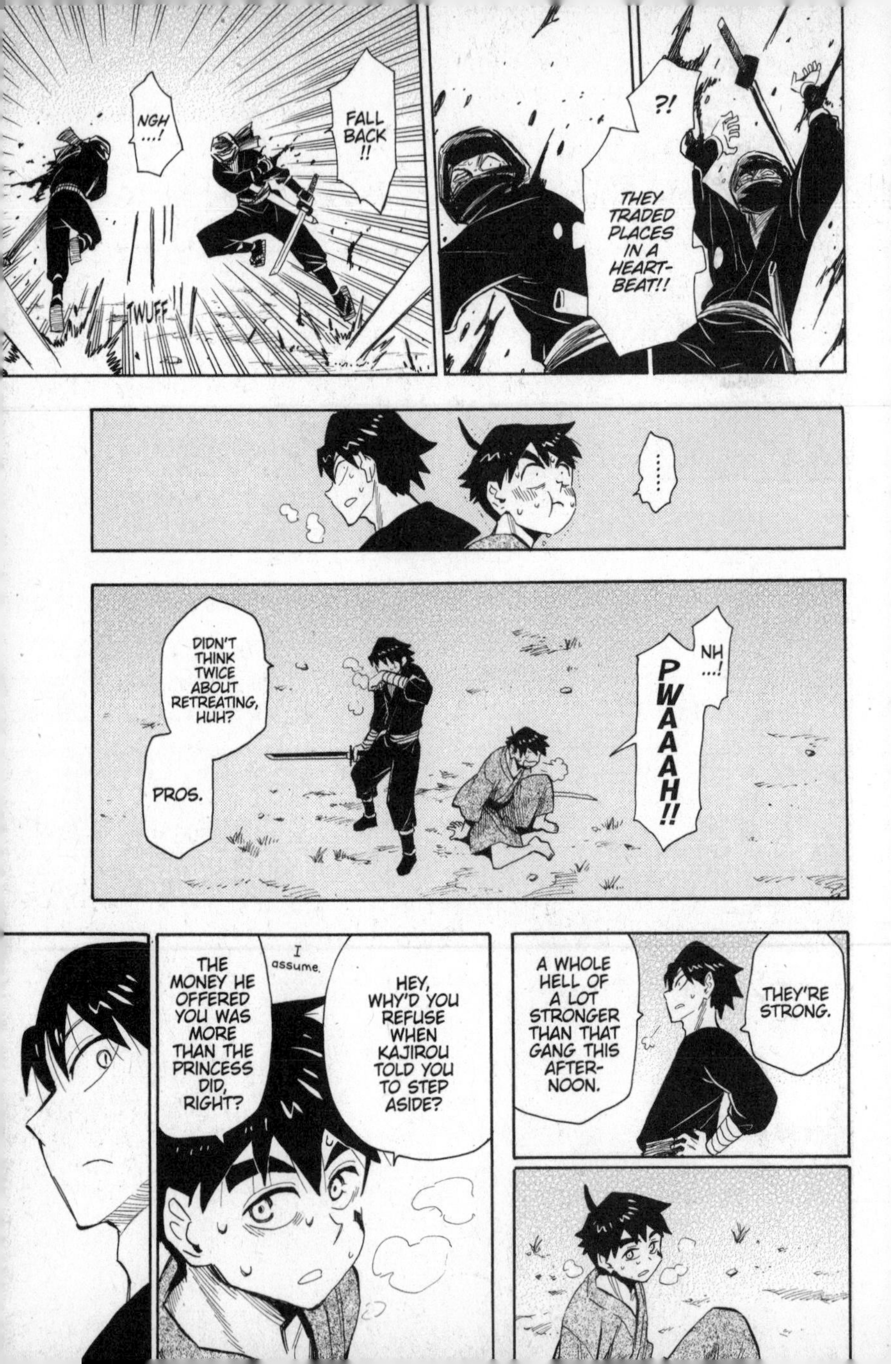
?!
THEY TRADED PLACES IN A HEART-BEAT!!
FALL BACK!!
NGH ...!
TWUFF
......
NH ...!
PWAAAAH!!
DIDN'T THINK TWICE ABOUT RETREATING, HUH?
PROS.
THEY'RE STRONG.
A WHOLE HELL OF A LOT STRONGER THAN THAT GANG THIS AFTER-NOON.
HEY, WHY'D YOU REFUSE WHEN KAJIROU TOLD YOU TO STEP ASIDE?
THE MONEY HE OFFERED YOU WAS MORE THAN THE PRINCESS DID, RIGHT?
I assume.

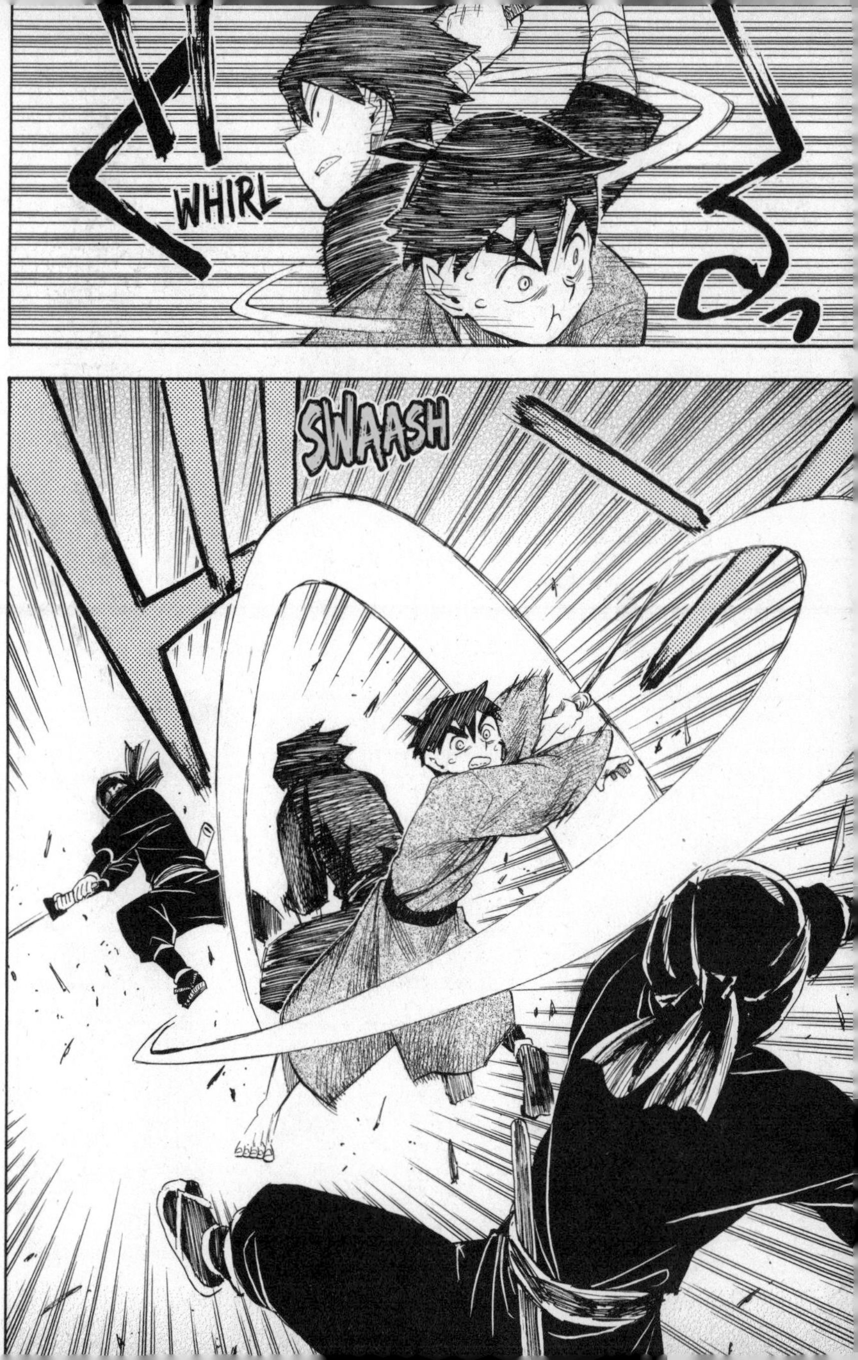
WHIRL
SWAASH

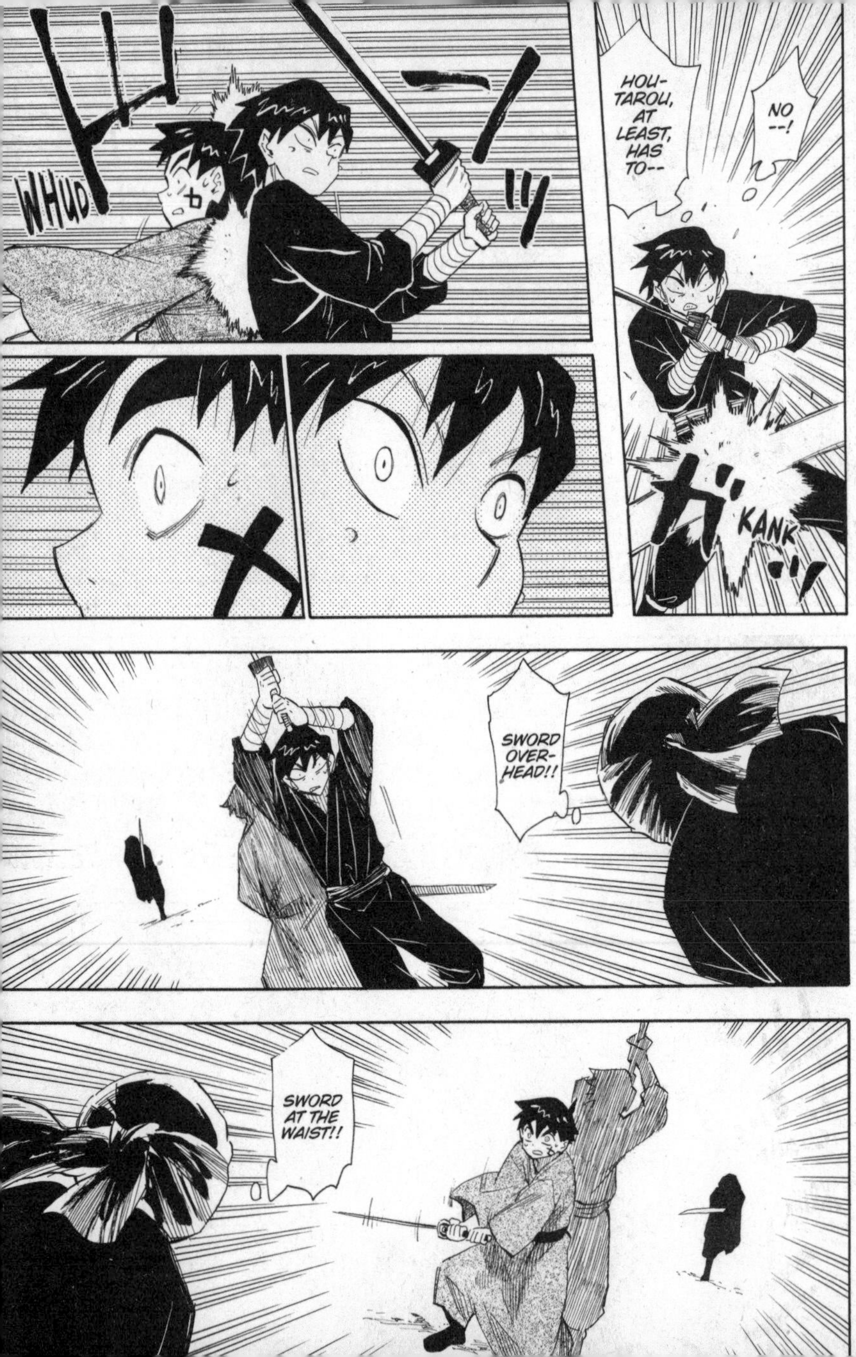
NO--!
HOUTAROU, AT LEAST, HAS TO--
ガ
KANK
WHUD
SWORD OVER-HEAD!!
SWORD AT THE WAIST!!

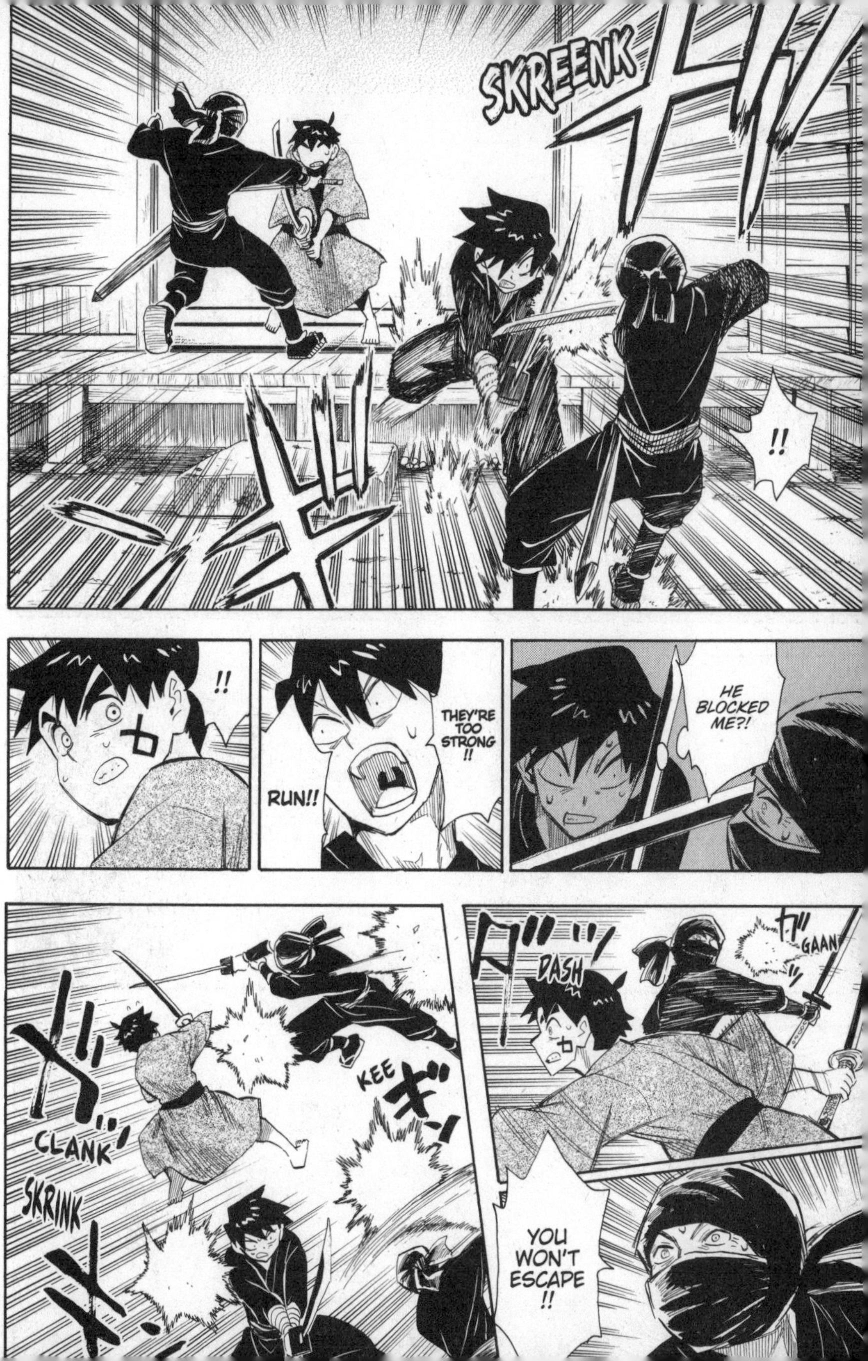
SKREENK
!!
HE BLOCKED ME?!
THEY'RE TOO STRONG!!
RUN!!
!!
GAAN
DASH
YOU WON'T ESCAPE!!
KEE
CLANK
SKRINK

SHAK

SHF...

CLANG

?!

YAAAAH!!

SHAK

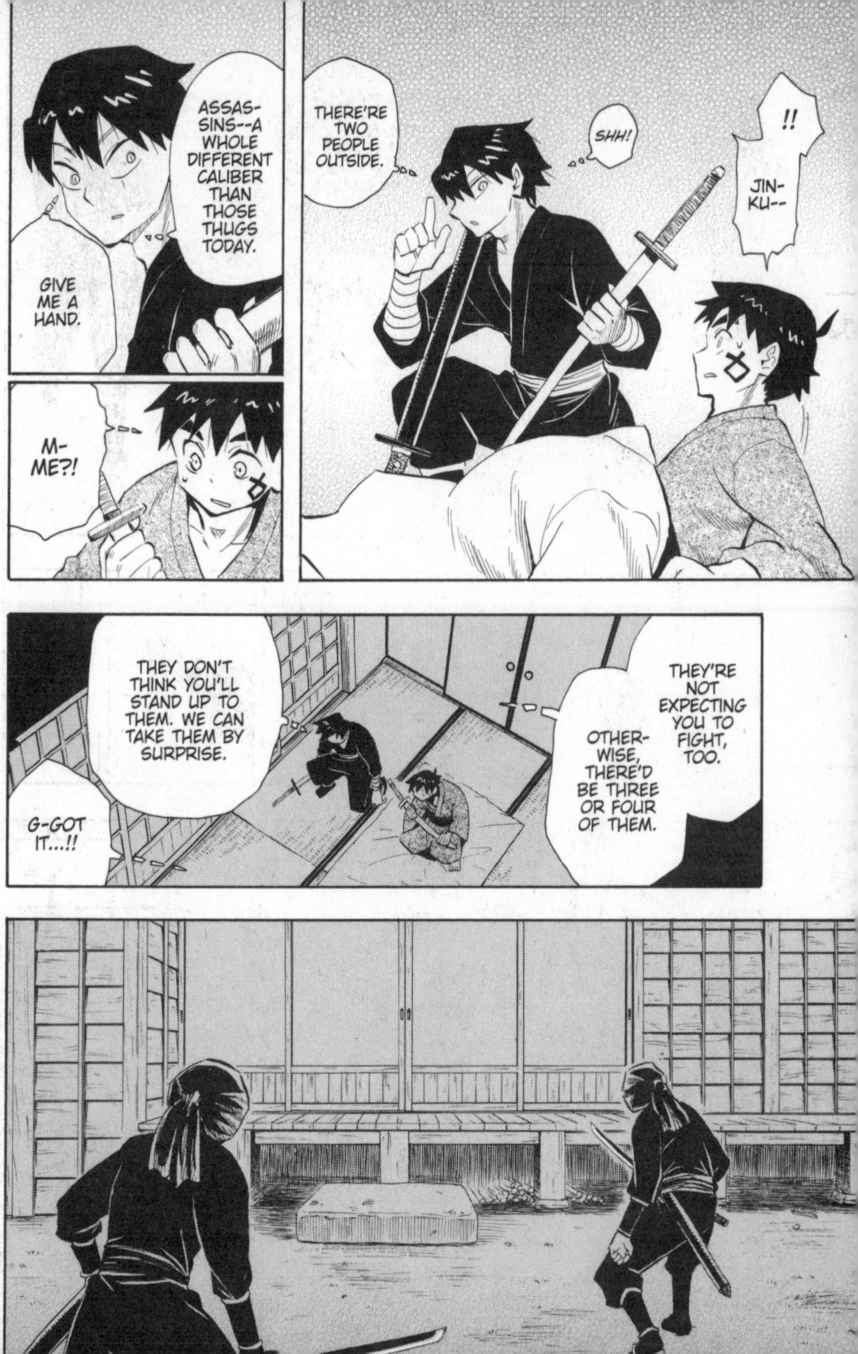
!!
JIN-KU--
SHH!
THERE'RE TWO PEOPLE OUTSIDE.
ASSAS-SINS--A WHOLE DIFFERENT CALIBER THAN THOSE THUGS TODAY.
GIVE ME A HAND.
M-ME?!
THEY'RE NOT EXPECTING YOU TO FIGHT, TOO.
OTHER-WISE, THERE'D BE THREE OR FOUR OF THEM.
THEY DON'T THINK YOU'LL STAND UP TO THEM. WE CAN TAKE THEM BY SURPRISE.
G-GOT IT...!!

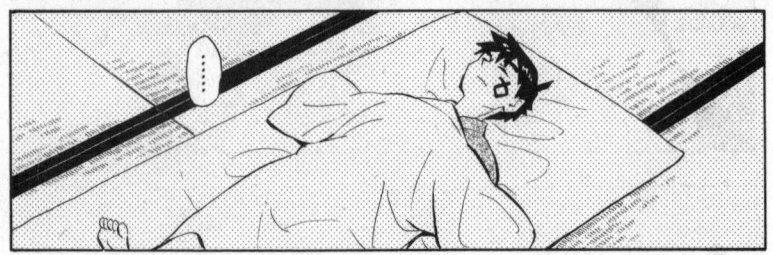

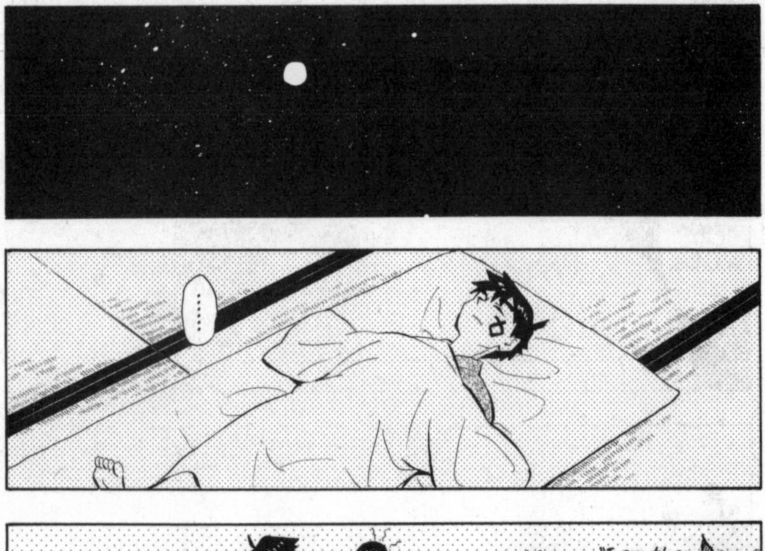

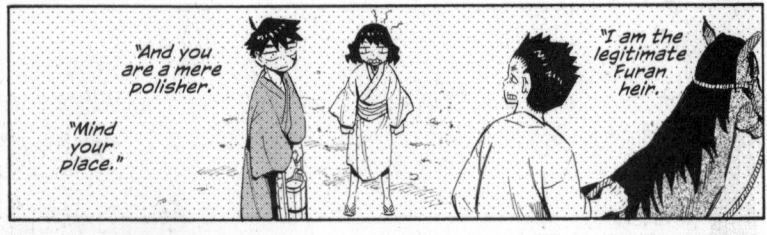

......
"I am the legitimate Furan heir.
"And you are a mere polisher.
"Mind your place."
YOU'RE THE ONE WHO DOESN'T UNDERSTAND OUR PLACES...
KAJIROU.
YOU'RE THE LEGITIMATE HEIR TO FURAN.
WHY DO YOU FEAR ME?
I ONLY WANT TO PLY MY TRADE PEACEFULLY.
KLATTER...

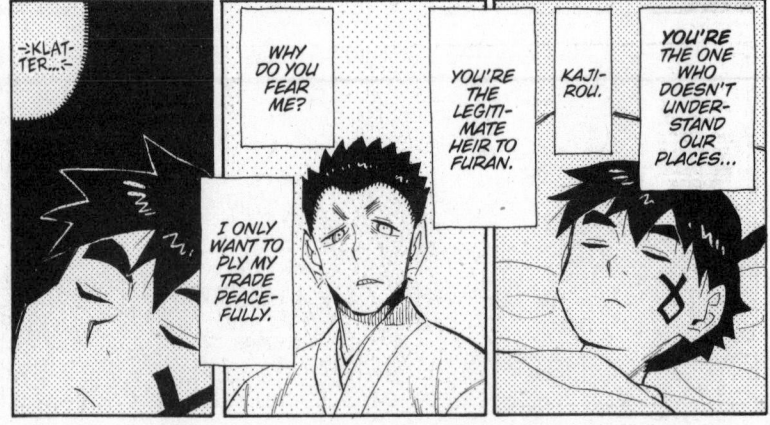

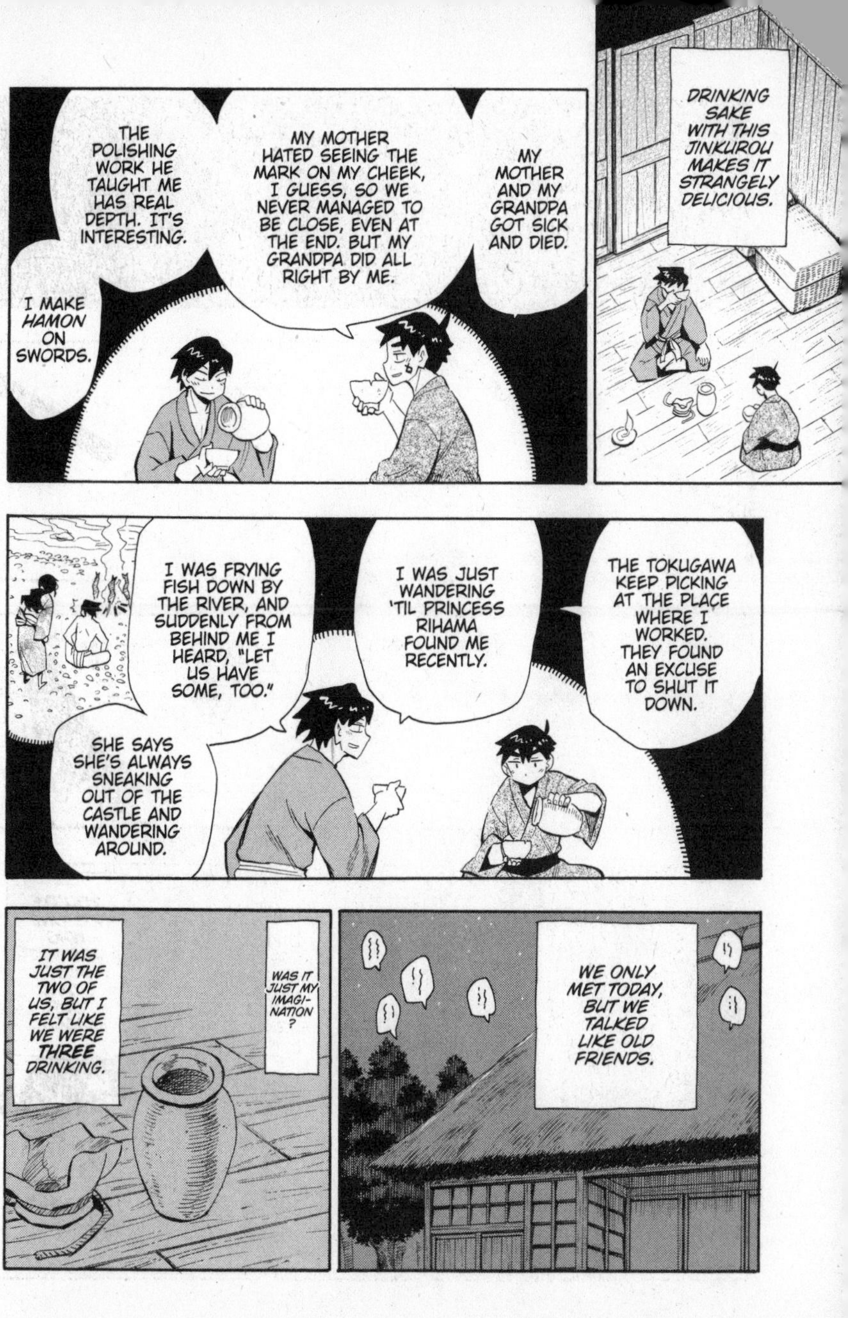
DRINKING SAKE WITH THIS JINKUROU MAKES IT STRANGELY DELICIOUS.
MY MOTHER AND MY GRANDPA GOT SICK AND DIED.
MY MOTHER HATED SEEING THE MARK ON MY CHEEK, I GUESS, SO WE NEVER MANAGED TO BE CLOSE, EVEN AT THE END. BUT MY GRANDPA DID ALL RIGHT BY ME.
THE POLISHING WORK HE TAUGHT ME HAS REAL DEPTH. IT'S INTERESTING.
I MAKE HAMON ON SWORDS.
THE TOKUGAWA KEEP PICKING AT THE PLACE WHERE I WORKED. THEY FOUND AN EXCUSE TO SHUT IT DOWN.
I WAS JUST WANDERING 'TIL PRINCESS RIHAMA FOUND ME RECENTLY.
I WAS FRYING FISH DOWN BY THE RIVER, AND SUDDENLY FROM BEHIND ME I HEARD, "LET US HAVE SOME, TOO."
SHE SAYS SHE'S ALWAYS SNEAKING OUT OF THE CASTLE AND WANDERING AROUND.
WE ONLY MET TODAY, BUT WE TALKED LIKE OLD FRIENDS.
WAS IT JUST MY IMAGINATION?
IT WAS JUST THE TWO OF US, BUT I FELT LIKE WE WERE THREE DRINKING.

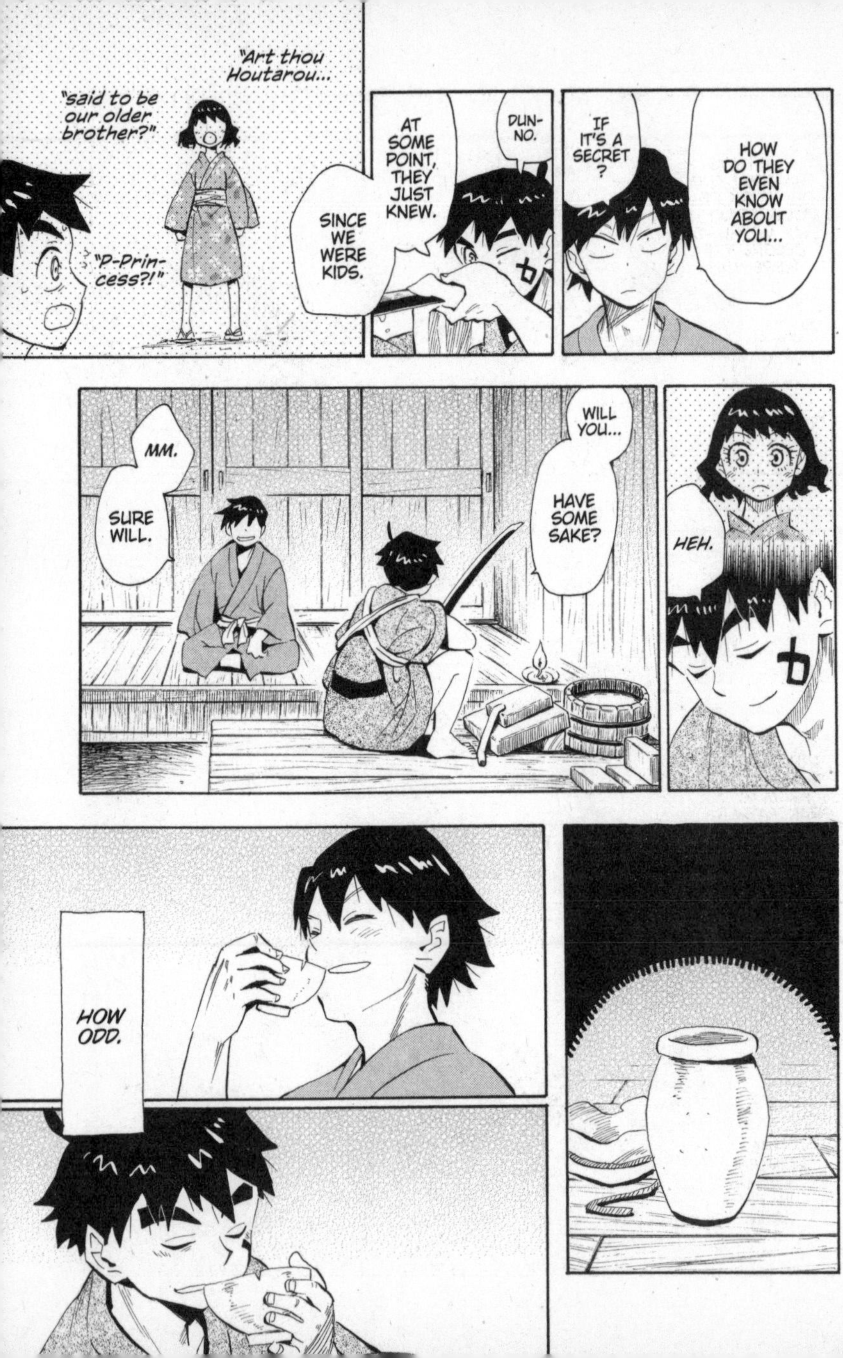
HOW DO THEY EVEN KNOW ABOUT YOU...
IF IT'S A SECRET?
DUN-NO.
AT SOME POINT, THEY JUST KNEW.
SINCE WE WERE KIDS.
"Art thou Houtarou...
"said to be our older brother?"
"P-Prin-cess?!"
HEH.
WILL YOU...
HAVE SOME SAKE?
MM.
SURE WILL.
HOW ODD.

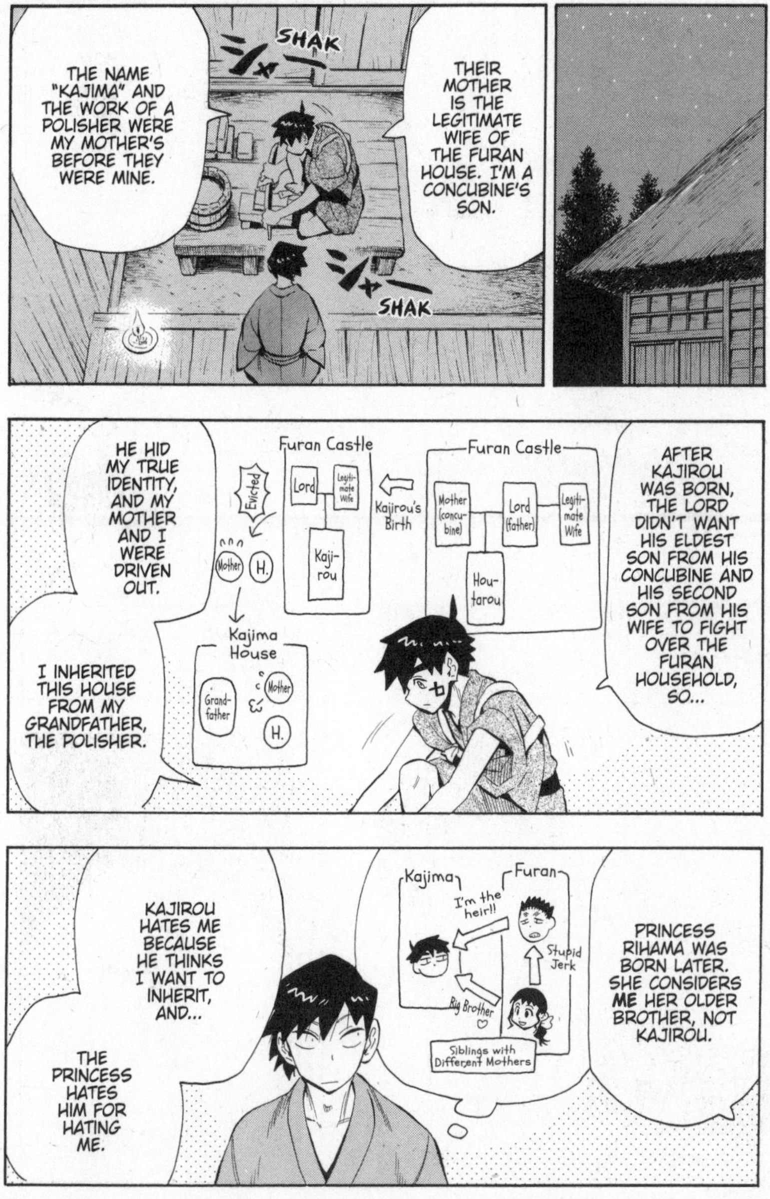
THEIR MOTHER IS THE LEGITIMATE WIFE OF THE FURAN HOUSE. I'M A CONCUBINE'S SON.
SHAK
SHAK
THE NAME "KAJIMA" AND THE WORK OF A POLISHER WERE MY MOTHER'S BEFORE THEY WERE MINE.
AFTER KAJIROU WAS BORN, THE LORD DIDN'T WANT HIS ELDEST SON FROM HIS CONCUBINE AND HIS SECOND SON FROM HIS WIFE TO FIGHT OVER THE FURAN HOUSEHOLD, SO...
Furan Castle
Mother (concubine)
Lord (father)
Legitimate Wife
Houtarou
Kajirou's Birth
Furan Castle
Lord
Legitimate Wife
Kajirou
Evicted
Mother
H.
Kajima House
Grandfather
Mother
H.
HE HID MY TRUE IDENTITY, AND MY MOTHER AND I WERE DRIVEN OUT.
I INHERITED THIS HOUSE FROM MY GRANDFATHER, THE POLISHER.
PRINCESS RIHAMA WAS BORN LATER. SHE CONSIDERS ME HER OLDER BROTHER, NOT KAJIROU.
Furan
Kajima
I'm the heir!!
Stupid Jerk
Big Brother ♡
Siblings with Different Mothers
KAJIROU HATES ME BECAUSE HE THINKS I WANT TO INHERIT, AND...
THE PRINCESS HATES HIM FOR HATING ME.

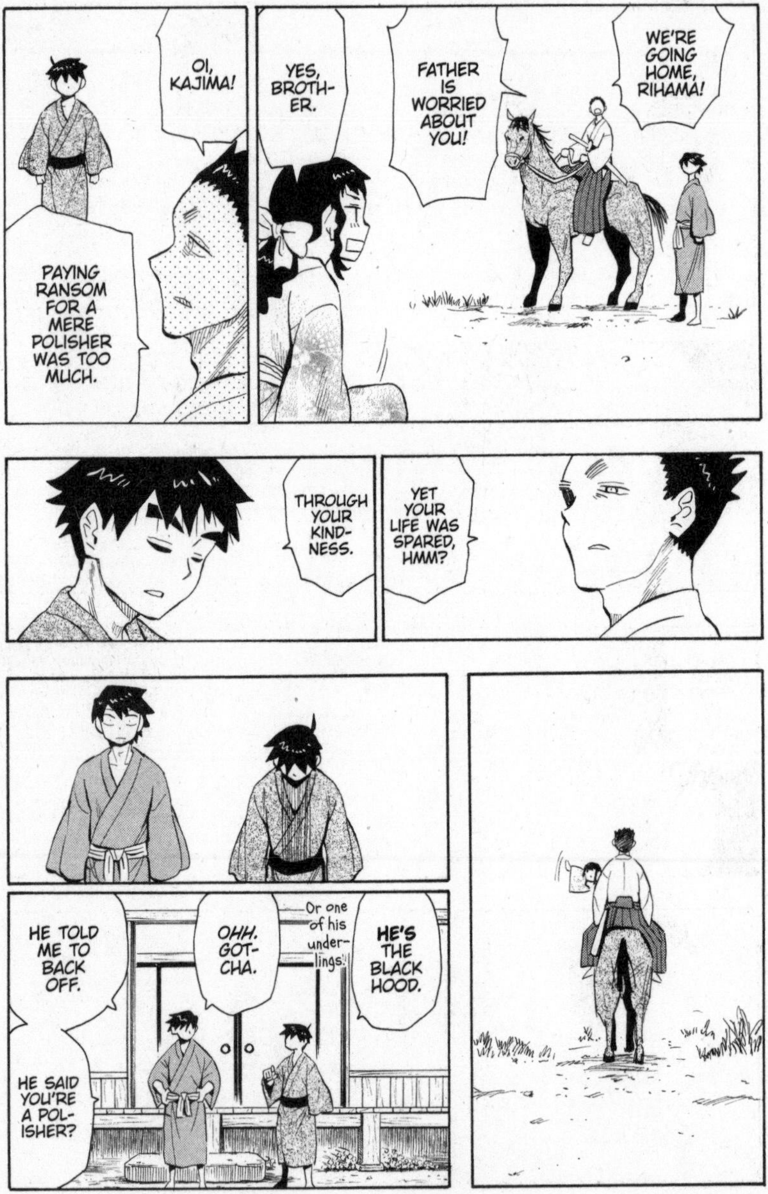
WE'RE GOING HOME, RIHAMA!
FATHER IS WORRIED ABOUT YOU!
YES, BROTH-ER.
OI, KAJIMA!
PAYING RANSOM FOR A MERE POLISHER WAS TOO MUCH.
YET YOUR LIFE WAS SPARED, HMM?
THROUGH YOUR KIND-NESS.
HE'S THE BLACK HOOD.
Or one of his under-lings!
OHH. GOT-CHA.
HE TOLD ME TO BACK OFF.
HE SAID YOU'RE A POL-ISHER?

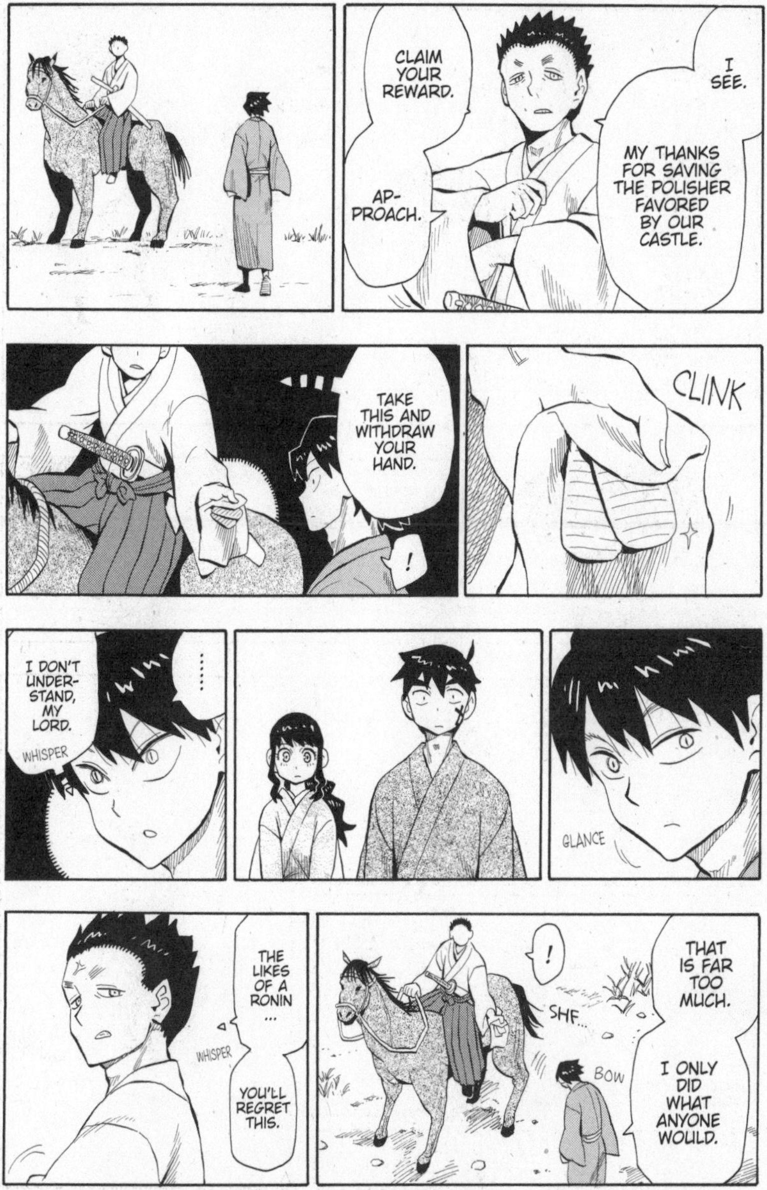
I SEE.
MY THANKS FOR SAVING THE POLISHER FAVORED BY OUR CASTLE.
CLAIM YOUR REWARD.
AP-PROACH.
CLINK
TAKE THIS AND WITHDRAW YOUR HAND.
!
GLANCE
......
I DON'T UNDER-STAND, MY LORD.
WHISPER
THAT IS FAR TOO MUCH.
!
SHF...
I ONLY DID WHAT ANYONE WOULD.
BOW
THE LIKES OF A RONIN...
WHISPER
YOU'LL REGRET THIS.

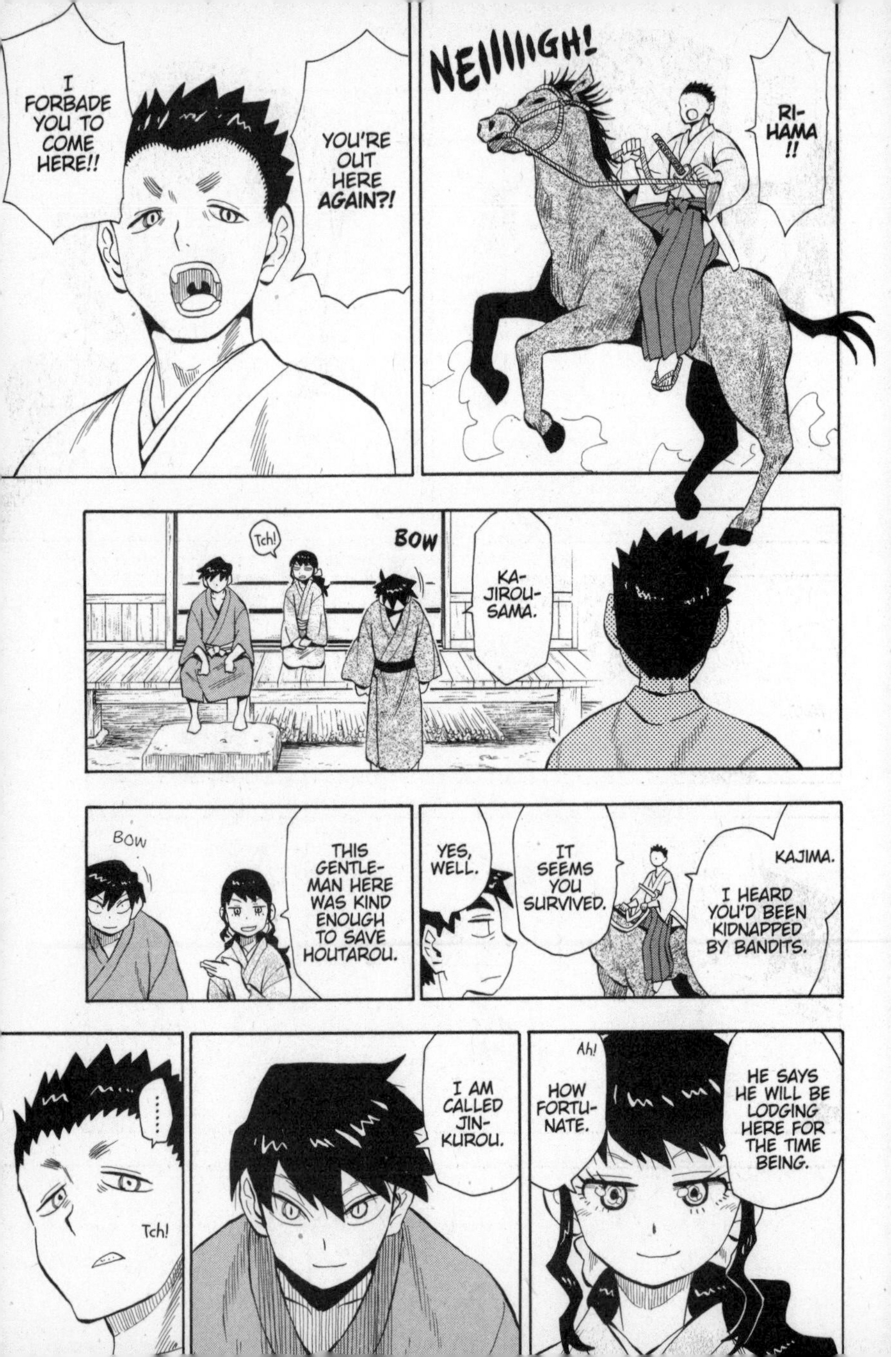
NEIIIIIGH!
RI-HAMA!!
YOU'RE OUT HERE AGAIN?!
I FORBADE YOU TO COME HERE!!
KAJIROU-SAMA.
BOW
Tch!
KAJIMA.
I HEARD YOU'D BEEN KIDNAPPED BY BANDITS.
IT SEEMS YOU SURVIVED.
YES, WELL.
THIS GENTLEMAN HERE WAS KIND ENOUGH TO SAVE HOUTAROU.
BOW
HE SAYS HE WILL BE LODGING HERE FOR THE TIME BEING.
Ah!
HOW FORTUNATE.
I AM CALLED JIN-KUROU.
......
Tch!

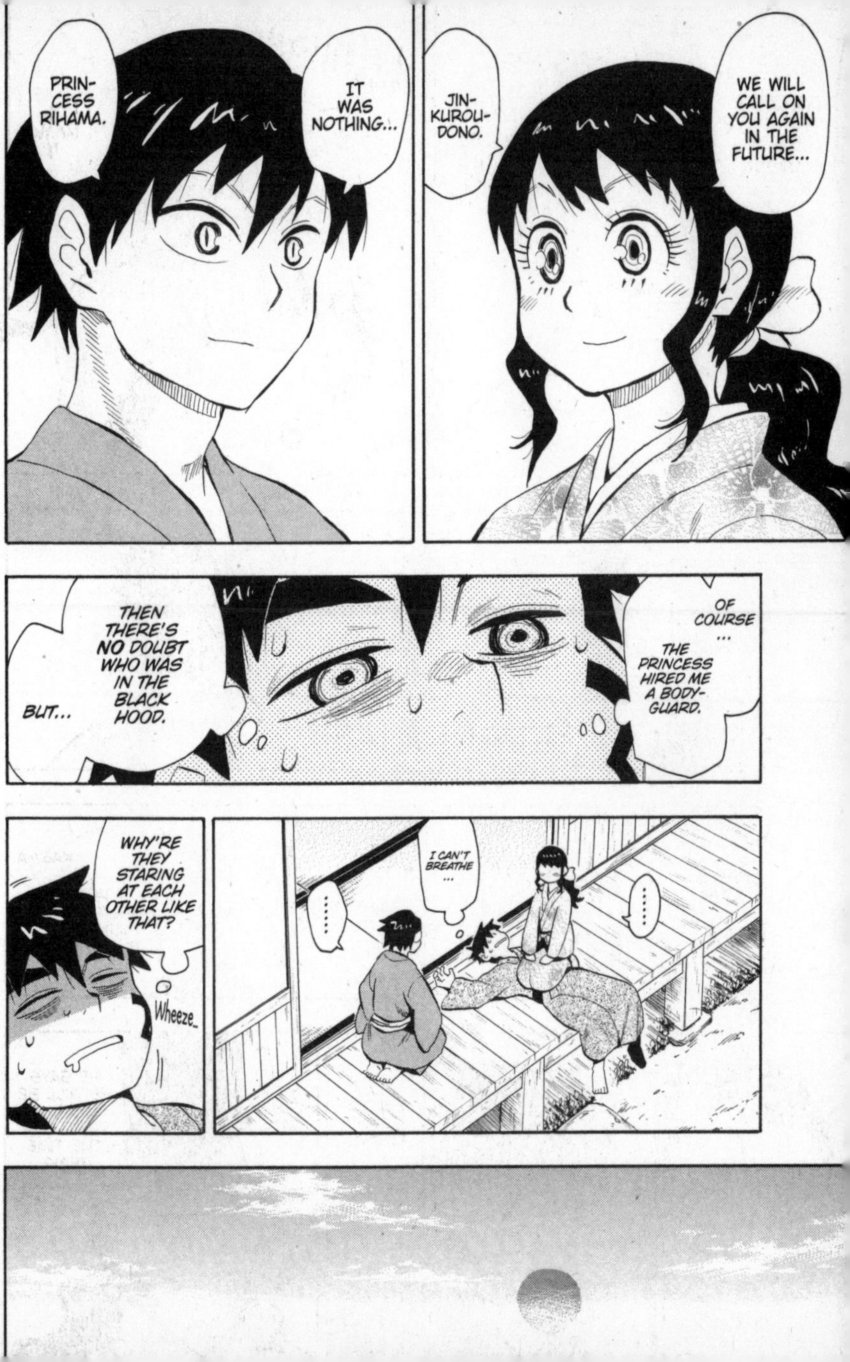
WE WILL CALL ON YOU AGAIN IN THE FUTURE...
JIN-KUROU-DONO.
IT WAS NOTHING...
PRIN-CESS RIHAMA.
OF COURSE... THE PRINCESS HIRED ME A BODY-GUARD.
THEN THERE'S NO DOUBT WHO WAS IN THE BLACK HOOD.
BUT...
......
I CAN'T BREATHE...
......
WHY'RE THEY STARING AT EACH OTHER LIKE THAT?
Wheeze_

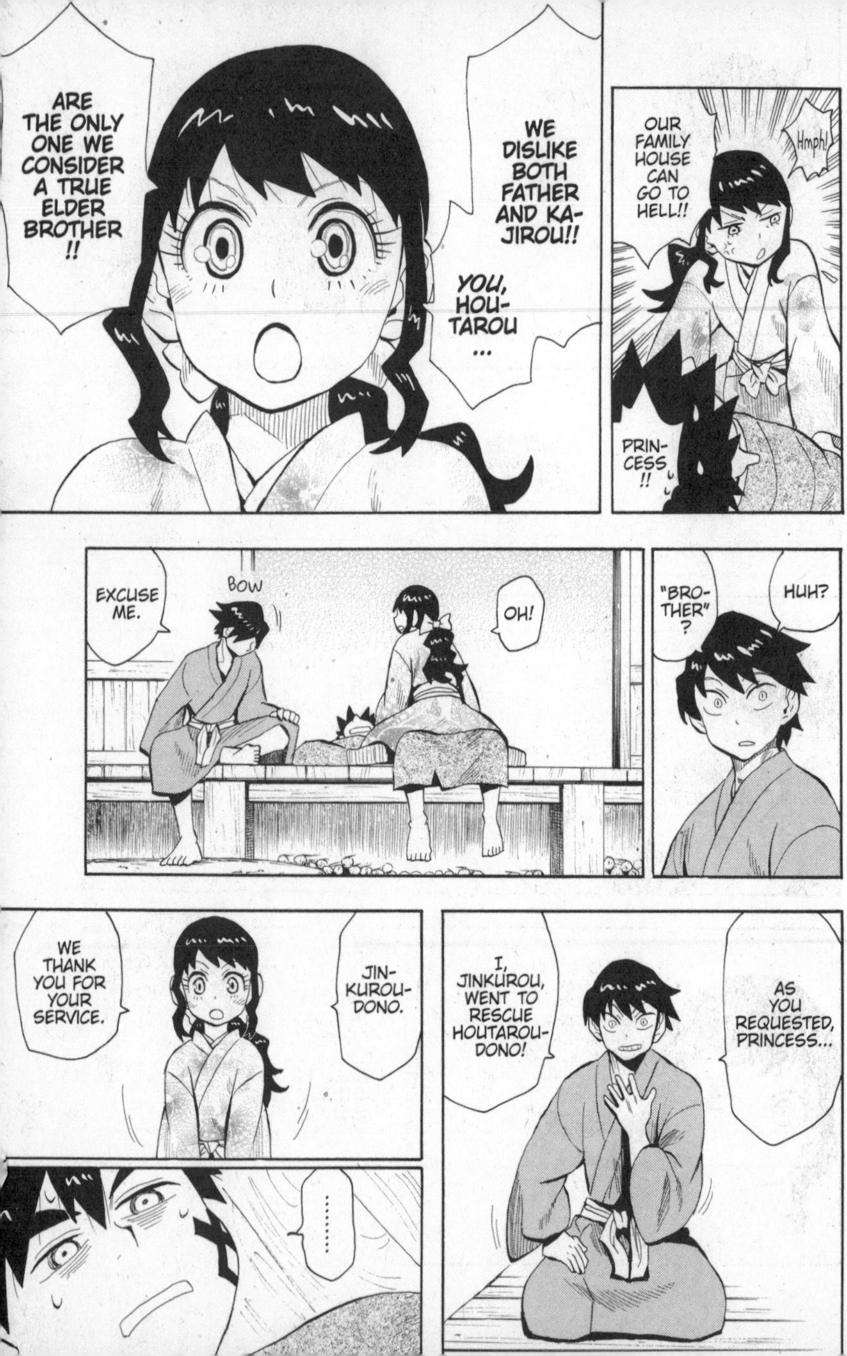
OUR FAMILY HOUSE CAN GO TO HELL!!
Hmph!
PRINCESS!!
WE DISLIKE BOTH FATHER AND KAJIROU!!
YOU, HOUTAROU...
ARE THE ONLY ONE WE CONSIDER A TRUE ELDER BROTHER!!
HUH?
"BROTHER"?
OH!
BOW
EXCUSE ME.
AS YOU REQUESTED, PRINCESS...
I, JINKUROU, WENT TO RESCUE HOUTAROU-DONO!
JINKUROU-DONO.
WE THANK YOU FOR YOUR SERVICE.
....

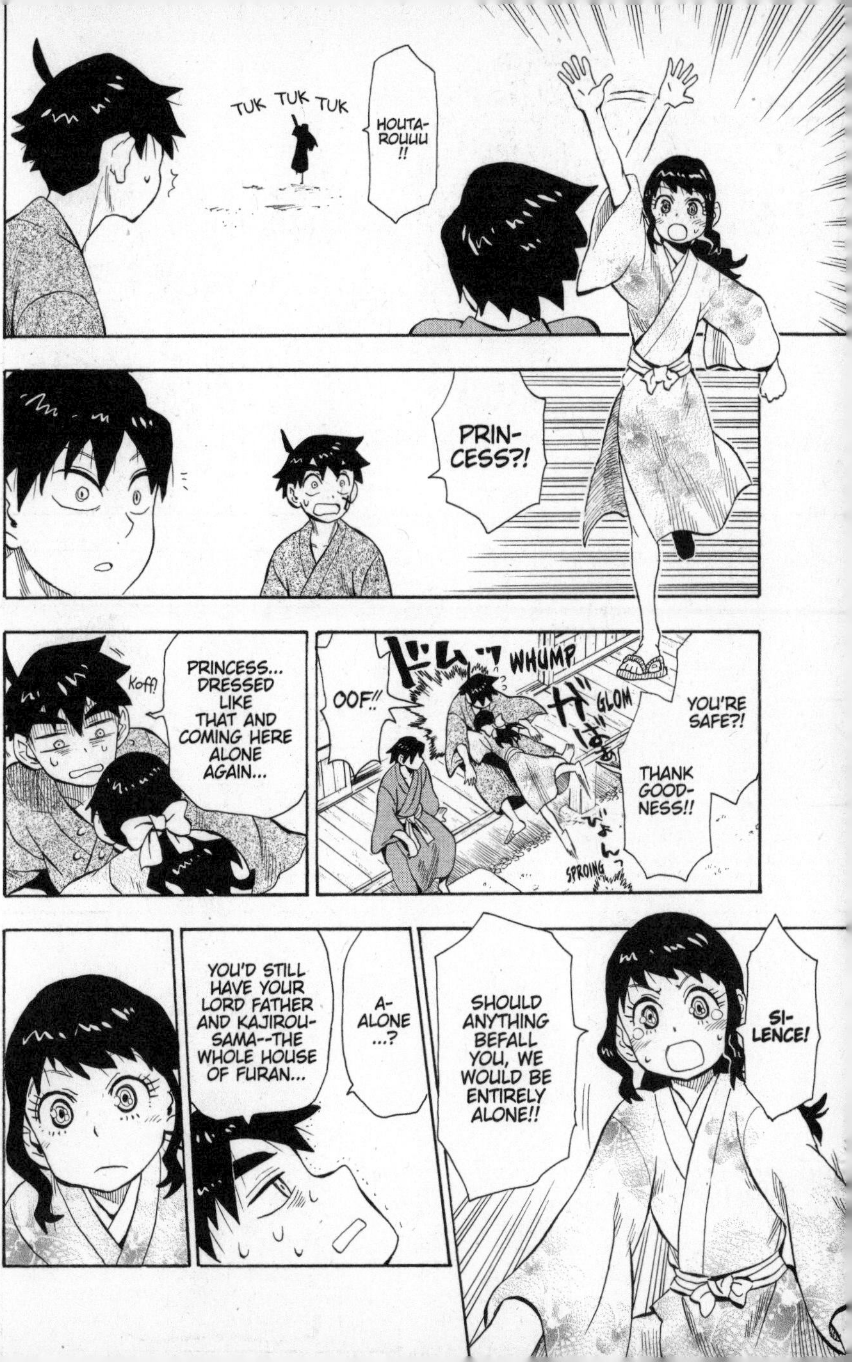
HOUTA-ROUUU!!
TUK TUK TUK
PRIN-CESS?!
YOU'RE SAFE?!
THANK GOOD-NESS!!
WHUMP
GLOM
OOF!!
SPROING
Koff!
PRINCESS... DRESSED LIKE THAT AND COMING HERE ALONE AGAIN...
SI-LENCE!
SHOULD ANYTHING BEFALL YOU, WE WOULD BE ENTIRELY ALONE!!
A-ALONE ...?
YOU'D STILL HAVE YOUR LORD FATHER AND KAJIROU-SAMA--THE WHOLE HOUSE OF FURAN...

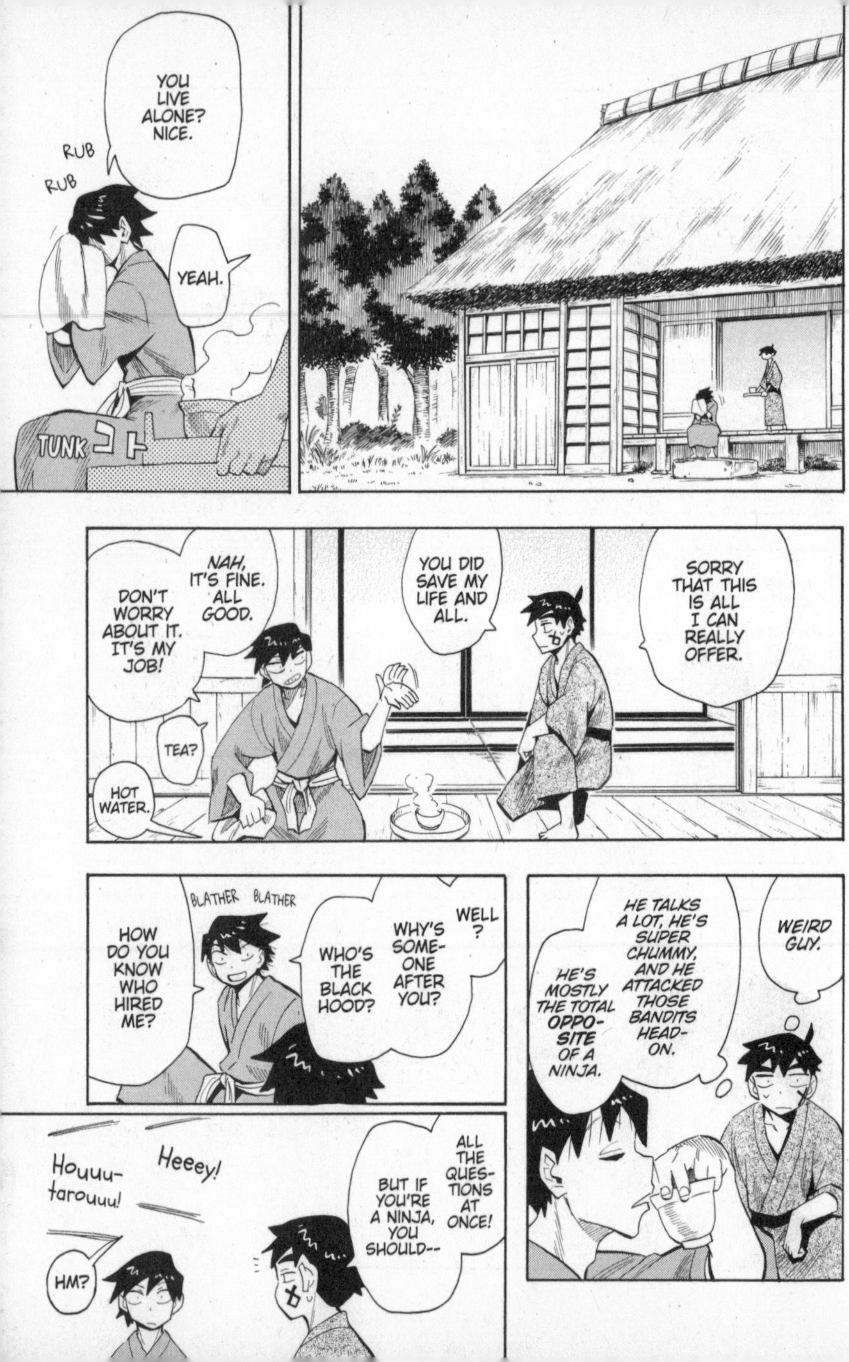
YOU LIVE ALONE? NICE.
RUB
RUB
YEAH.
TUNK
SORRY THAT THIS IS ALL I CAN REALLY OFFER.
YOU DID SAVE MY LIFE AND ALL.
NAH, IT'S FINE. ALL GOOD.
DON'T WORRY ABOUT IT. IT'S MY JOB!
TEA?
HOT WATER.
WEIRD GUY.
HE TALKS A LOT, HE'S SUPER CHUMMY, AND HE ATTACKED THOSE BANDITS HEAD-ON.
HE'S MOSTLY THE TOTAL OPPOSITE OF A NINJA.
WELL?
WHY'S SOMEONE AFTER YOU?
WHO'S THE BLACK HOOD?
BLATHER BLATHER
HOW DO YOU KNOW WHO HIRED ME?
ALL THE QUESTIONS AT ONCE!
BUT IF YOU'RE A NINJA, YOU SHOULD--
Heeey!
Houuu-tarouuu!
HM?

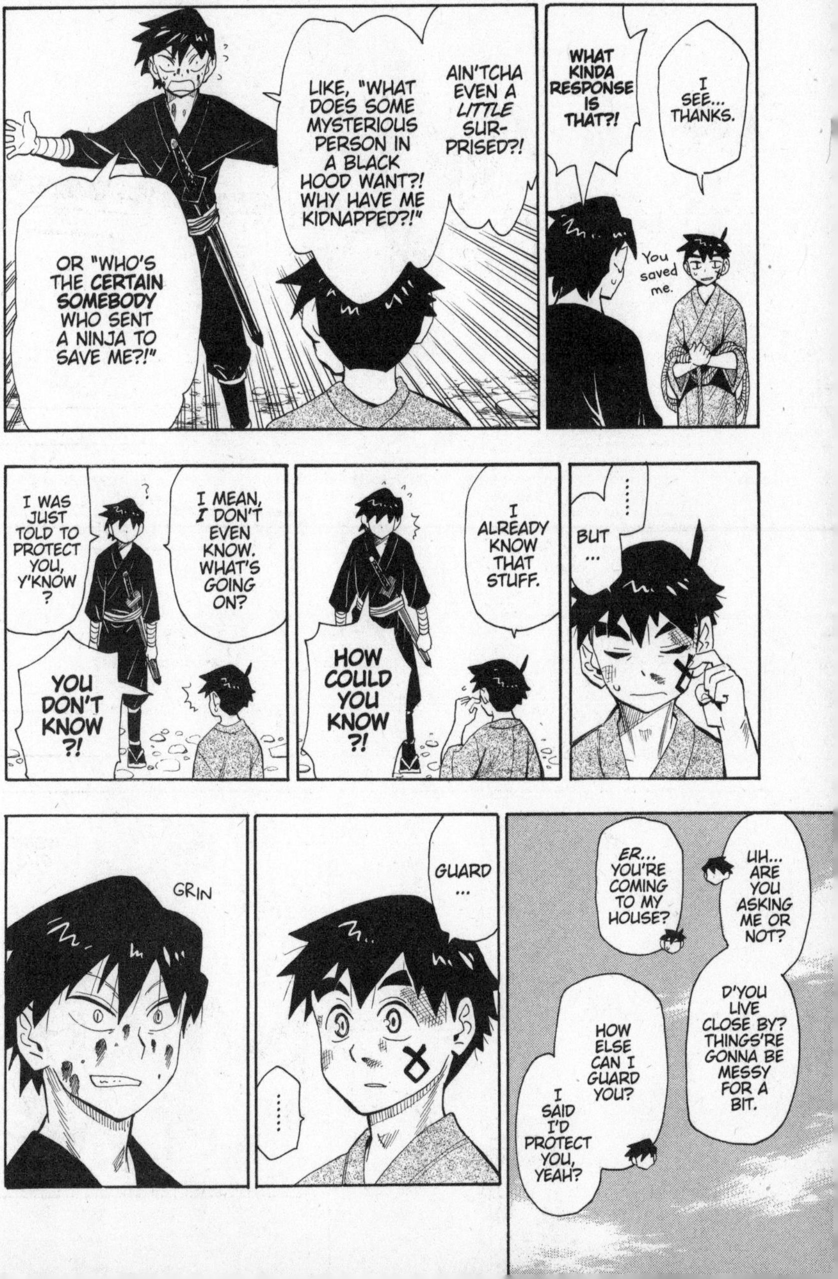
I SEE... THANKS.
WHAT KINDA RESPONSE IS THAT?!
You saved me.
AIN'TCHA EVEN A *LITTLE* SURPRISED?!
LIKE, "WHAT DOES SOME MYSTERIOUS PERSON IN A BLACK HOOD WANT?! WHY HAVE ME KIDNAPPED?!"
OR "WHO'S THE CERTAIN SOMEBODY WHO SENT A NINJA TO SAVE ME?!"
......
BUT ...
I ALREADY KNOW THAT STUFF.
HOW COULD YOU KNOW ?!
I MEAN, *I* DON'T EVEN KNOW. WHAT'S GOING ON?
I WAS JUST TOLD TO PROTECT YOU, Y'KNOW ?
YOU DON'T KNOW ?!
UH... ARE YOU ASKING ME OR NOT?
ER... YOU'RE COMING TO MY HOUSE?
D'YOU LIVE CLOSE BY? THINGS'RE GONNA BE MESSY FOR A BIT.
HOW ELSE CAN I GUARD YOU?
I SAID I'D PROTECT YOU, YEAH?
GUARD ...
......
GRIN

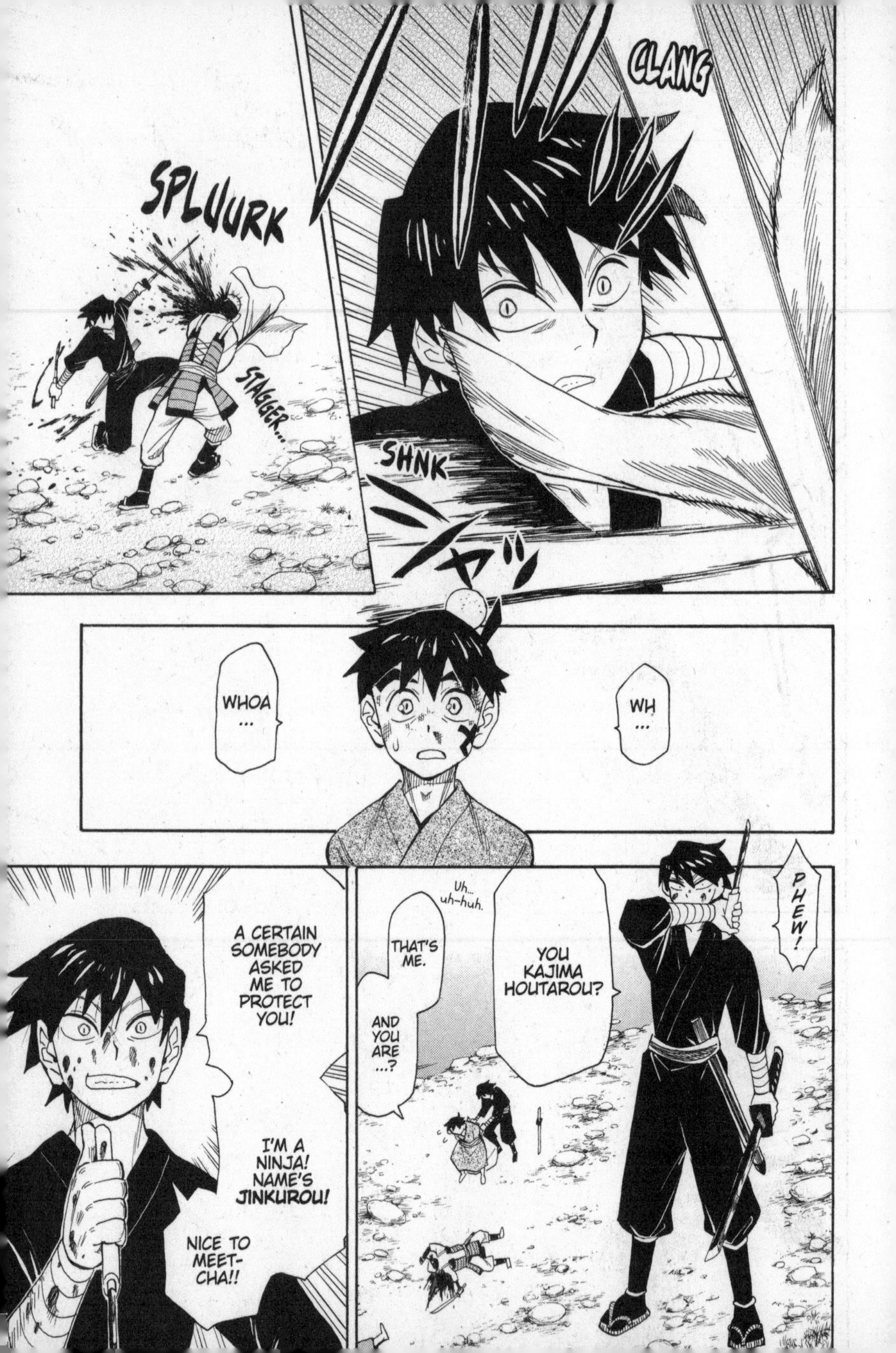
CLANG
SHNK
SPLUURK
STAGGER...
WH ...
WHOA ...
PHEW!
YOU KAJIMA HOUTAROU?
Uh... uh-huh.
THAT'S ME.
AND YOU ARE ...?
A CERTAIN SOMEBODY ASKED ME TO PROTECT YOU!
I'M A NINJA! NAME'S JINKUROU!
NICE TO MEET-CHA!!

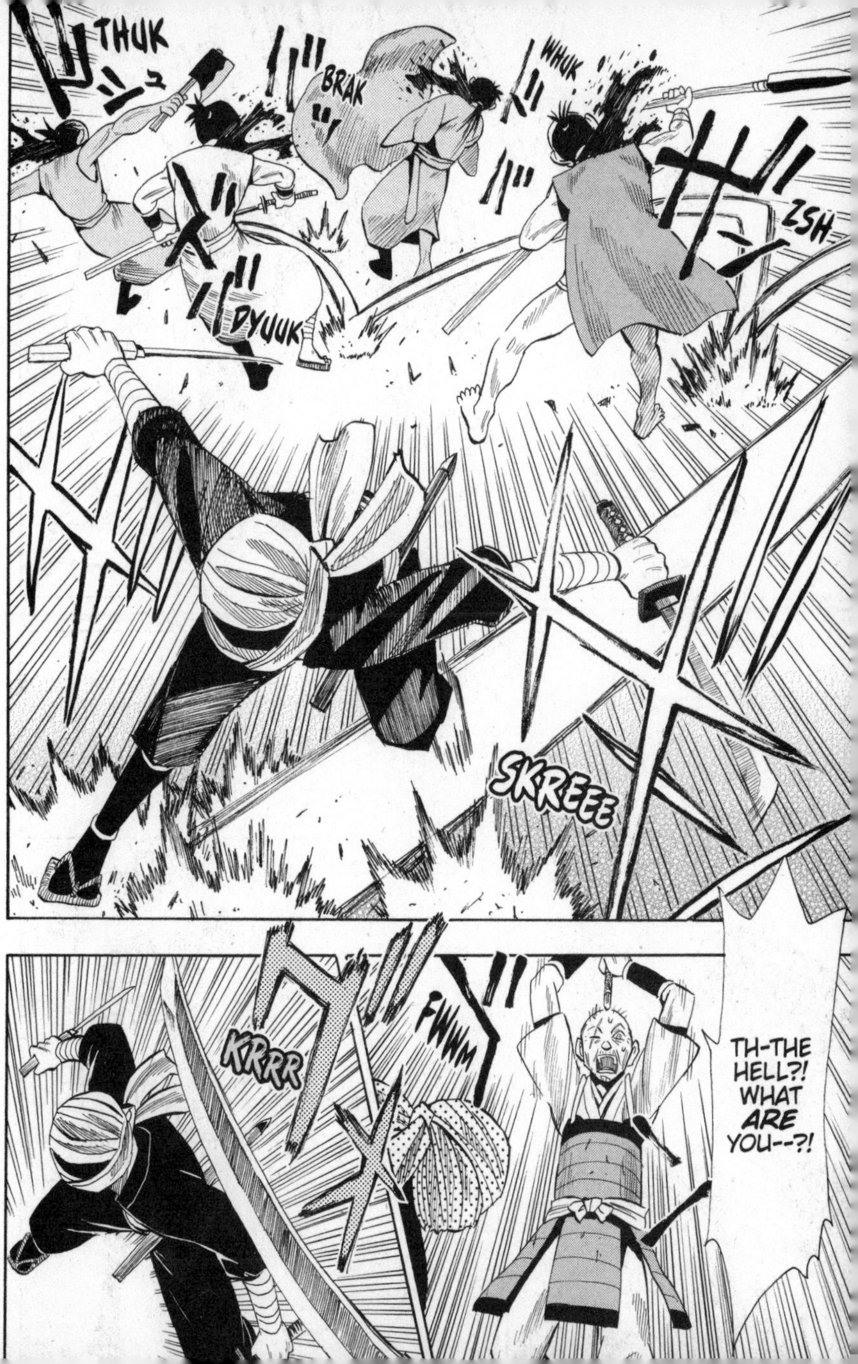
ZSH
WHUK
BRAK
THUK
DYUUK
SKREEEE
TH-THE HELL?! WHAT *ARE* YOU--?!
FWMM
KRRR

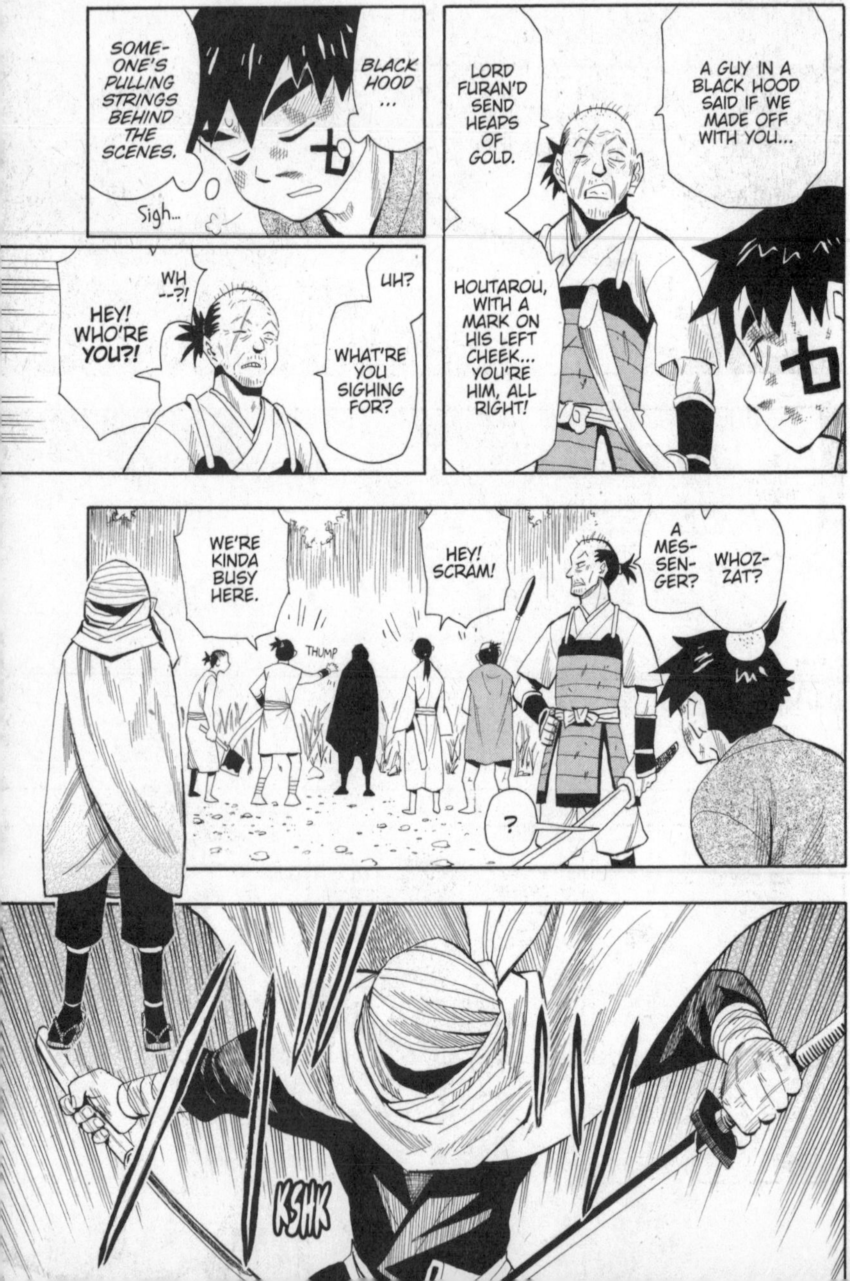
A GUY IN A BLACK HOOD SAID IF WE MADE OFF WITH YOU...
LORD FURAN'D SEND HEAPS OF GOLD.
HOUTAROU, WITH A MARK ON HIS LEFT CHEEK... YOU'RE HIM, ALL RIGHT!
BLACK HOOD ...
SOME-ONE'S PULLING STRINGS BEHIND THE SCENES.
Sigh...
UH?
WHAT'RE YOU SIGHING FOR?
WH--?!
HEY! WHO'RE YOU?!
WHOZ-ZAT?
A MES-SEN-GER?
?
HEY! SCRAM!
THUMP
WE'RE KINDA BUSY HERE.
KSHK

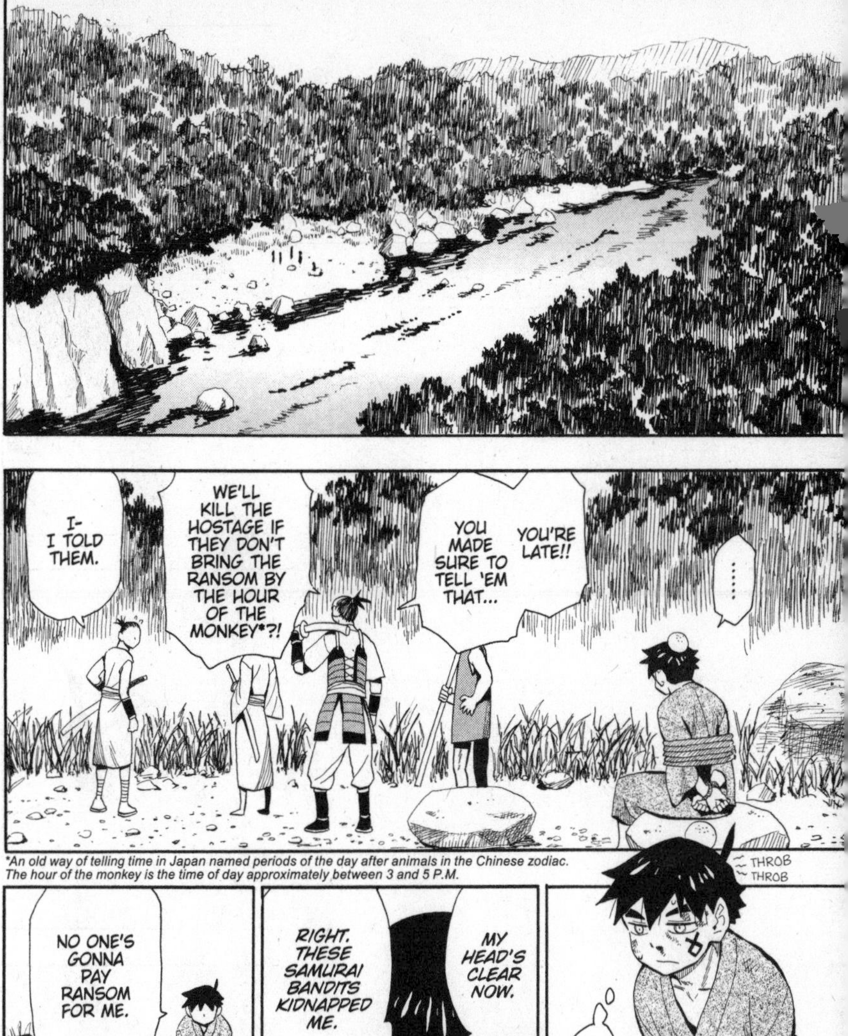
......
YOU'RE LATE!!
YOU MADE SURE TO TELL 'EM THAT...
WE'LL KILL THE HOSTAGE IF THEY DON'T BRING THE RANSOM BY THE HOUR OF THE MONKEY*?!
I- I TOLD THEM.

*An old way of telling time in Japan named periods of the day after animals in the Chinese zodiac. The hour of the monkey is the time of day approximately between 3 and 5 P.M.

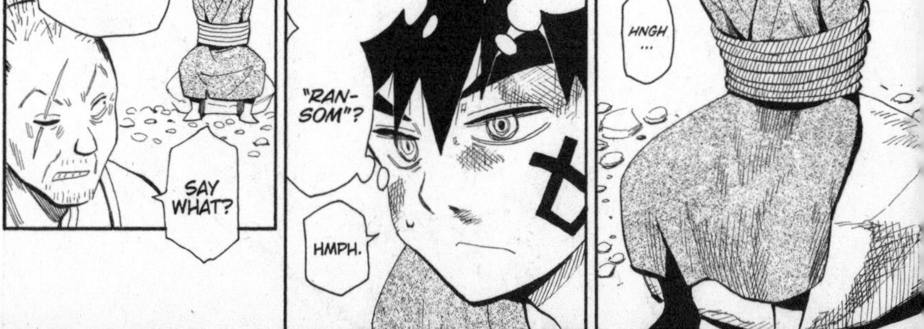
THROB
THROB
HNGH ...
MY HEAD'S CLEAR NOW.
RIGHT. THESE SAMURAI BANDITS KIDNAPPED ME.
"RAN-SOM"?
HMPH.
NO ONE'S GONNA PAY RANSOM FOR ME.
SAY WHAT?

Circle 16
Houtarou
2

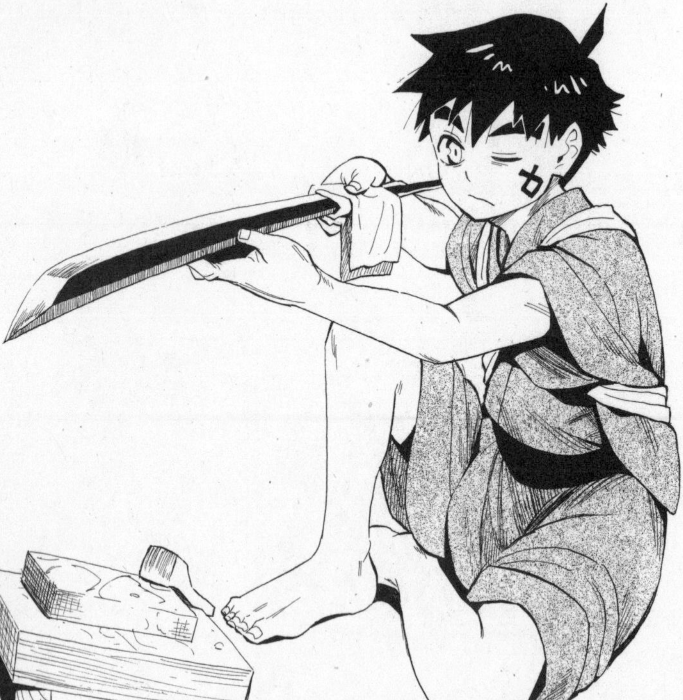

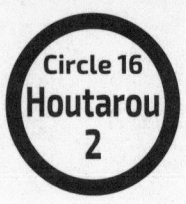

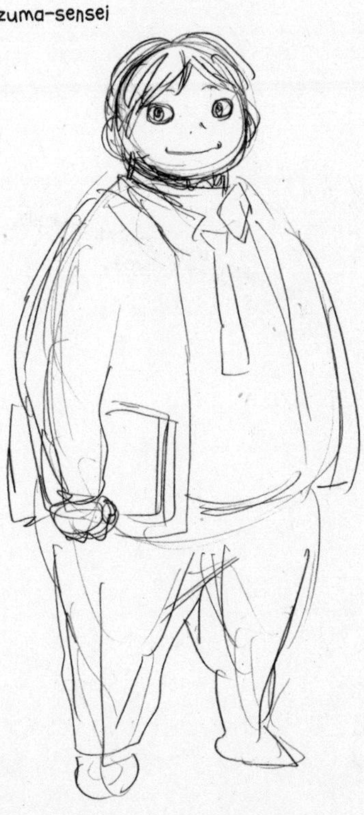
Azuma-sensei

Spirit Circle

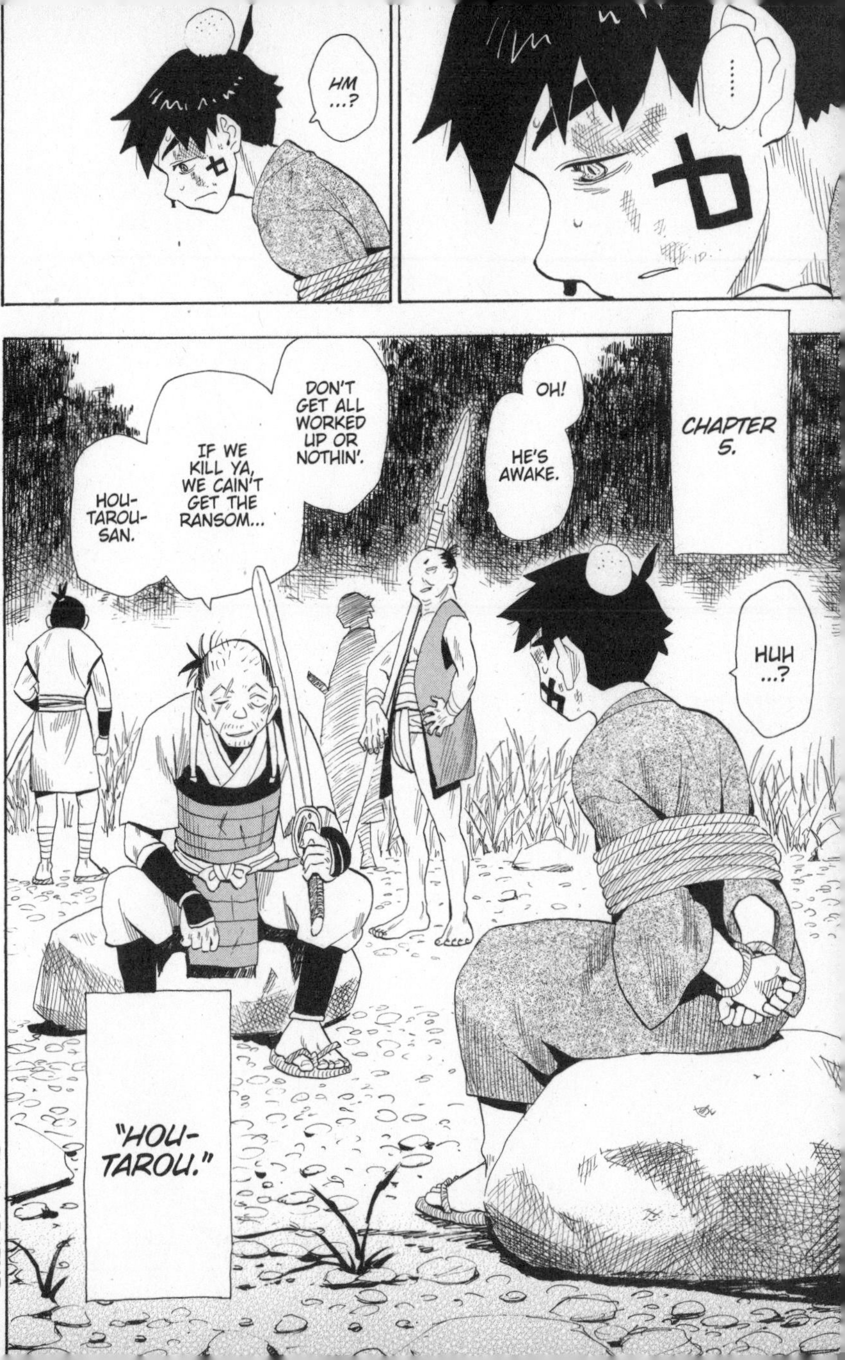
……
HM …?
CHAPTER 5.
OH!
HE'S AWAKE.
HUH …?
DON'T GET ALL WORKED UP OR NOTHIN'.
IF WE KILL YA, WE CAIN'T GET THE RANSOM…
HOU-TAROU-SAN.
"HOU-TAROU."

Circle 15/END

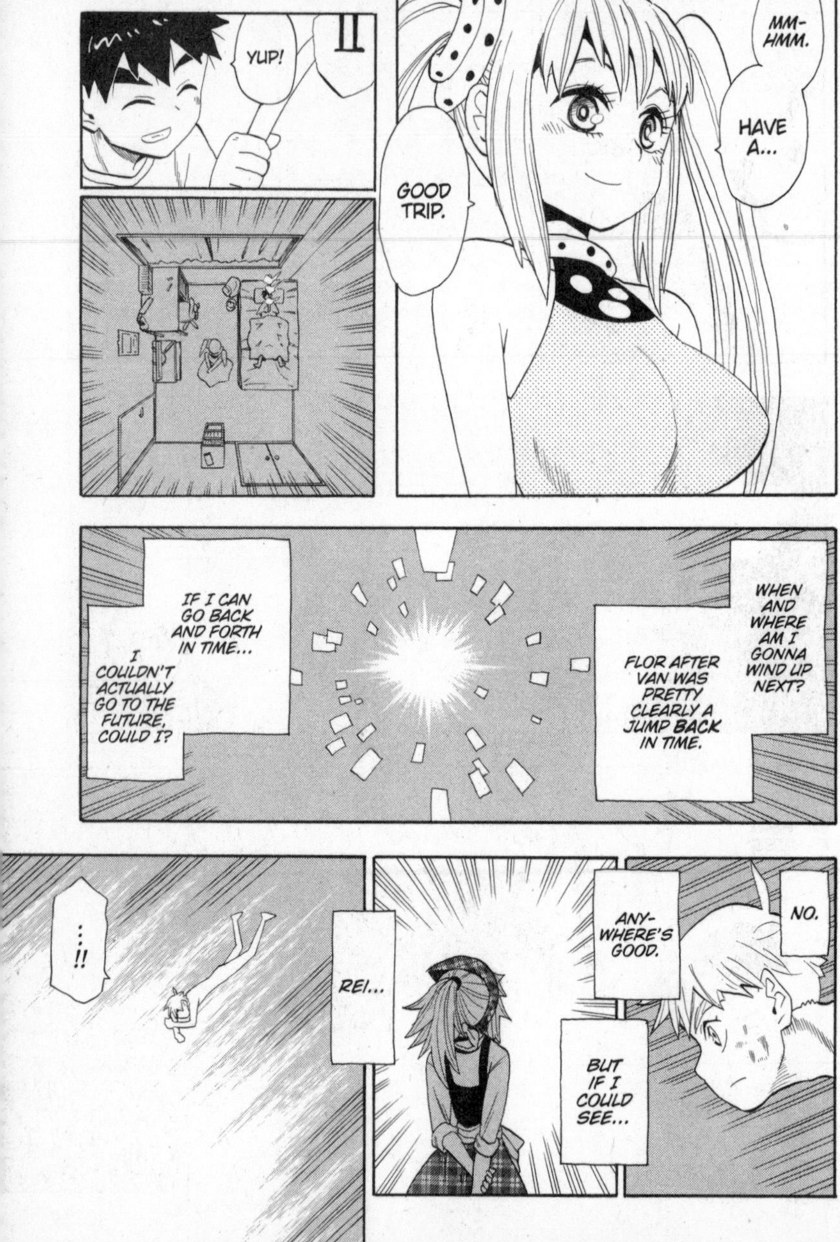
MM-HMM.
HAVE A...
GOOD TRIP.
YUP!
WHEN AND WHERE AM I GONNA WIND UP NEXT?
FLOR AFTER VAN WAS PRETTY CLEARLY A JUMP BACK IN TIME.
IF I CAN GO BACK AND FORTH IN TIME...
I COULDN'T ACTUALLY GO TO THE FUTURE, COULD I?
NO.
ANY-WHERE'S GOOD.
BUT IF I COULD SEE...
REI...
...!!

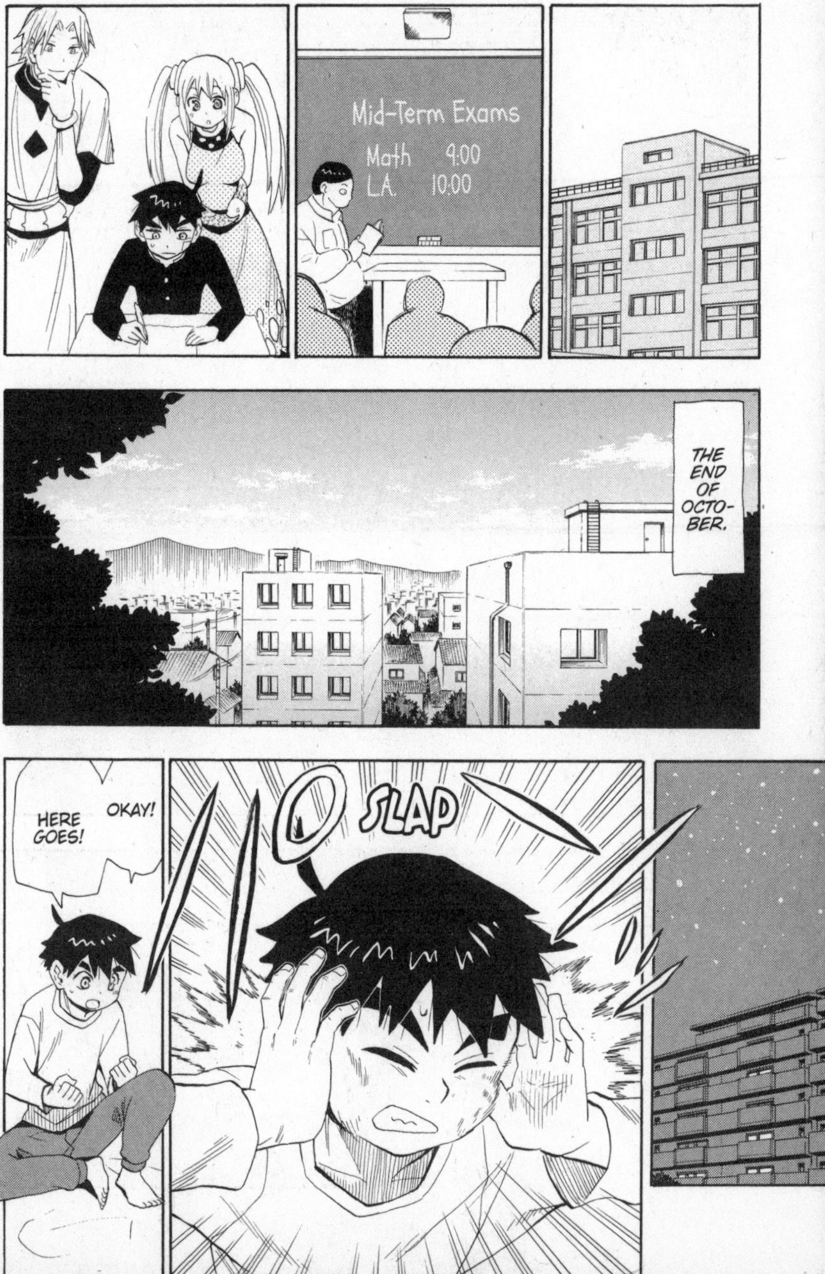
Mid-Term Exams
Math 9:00
L.A. 10:00
THE END OF OCTO-BER.
SLAP
OKAY!
HERE GOES!

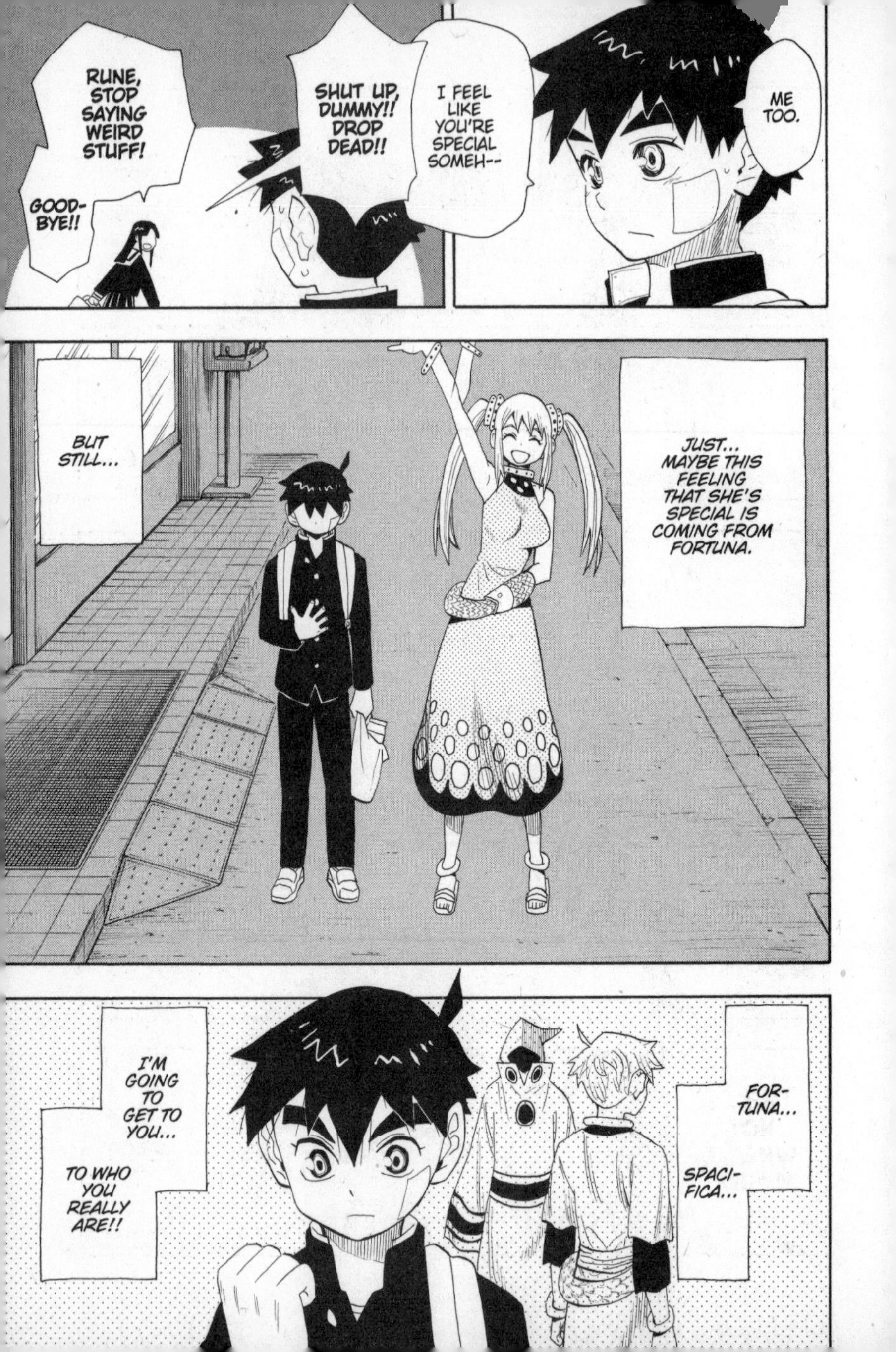
ME TOO.
I FEEL LIKE YOU'RE SPECIAL SOMEH--
SHUT UP, DUMMY!! DROP DEAD!!
RUNE, STOP SAYING WEIRD STUFF!
GOOD-BYE!!
JUST... MAYBE THIS FEELING THAT SHE'S SPECIAL IS COMING FROM FORTUNA.
BUT STILL...
FOR-TUNA...
SPACI-FICA...
I'M GOING TO GET TO YOU...
TO WHO YOU REALLY ARE!!

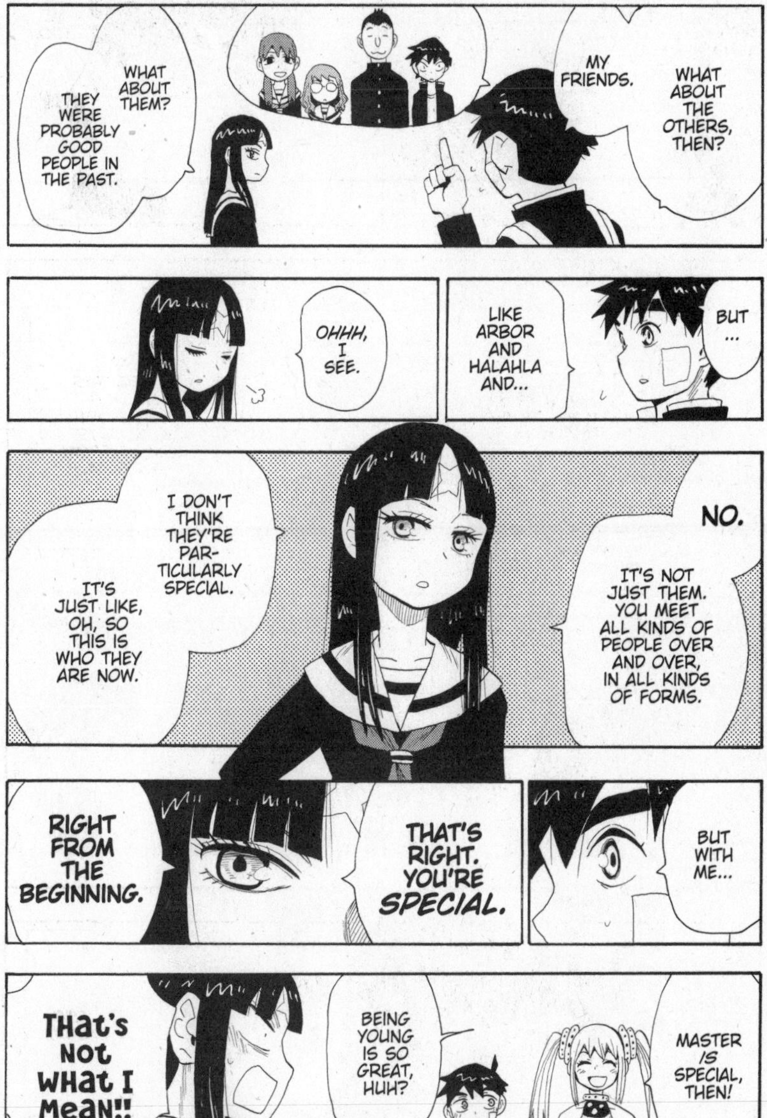

WHAT ABOUT THE OTHERS, THEN?
MY FRIENDS.
WHAT ABOUT THEM?
THEY WERE PROBABLY GOOD PEOPLE IN THE PAST.
BUT ...
LIKE ARBOR AND HALAHLA AND...
OHHH, I SEE.
NO.
IT'S NOT JUST THEM. YOU MEET ALL KINDS OF PEOPLE OVER AND OVER, IN ALL KINDS OF FORMS.
I DON'T THINK THEY'RE PAR-TICULARLY SPECIAL.
IT'S JUST LIKE, OH, SO THIS IS WHO THEY ARE NOW.
BUT WITH ME...
THAT'S RIGHT. YOU'RE *SPECIAL*.
RIGHT FROM THE BEGINNING.
MASTER *IS* SPECIAL, THEN!
BEING YOUNG IS SO GREAT, HUH?
THAT'S NOT WHAT I MEAN!!

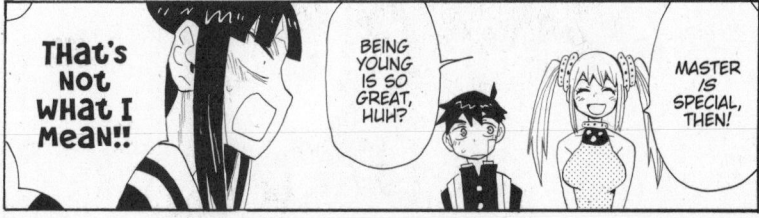

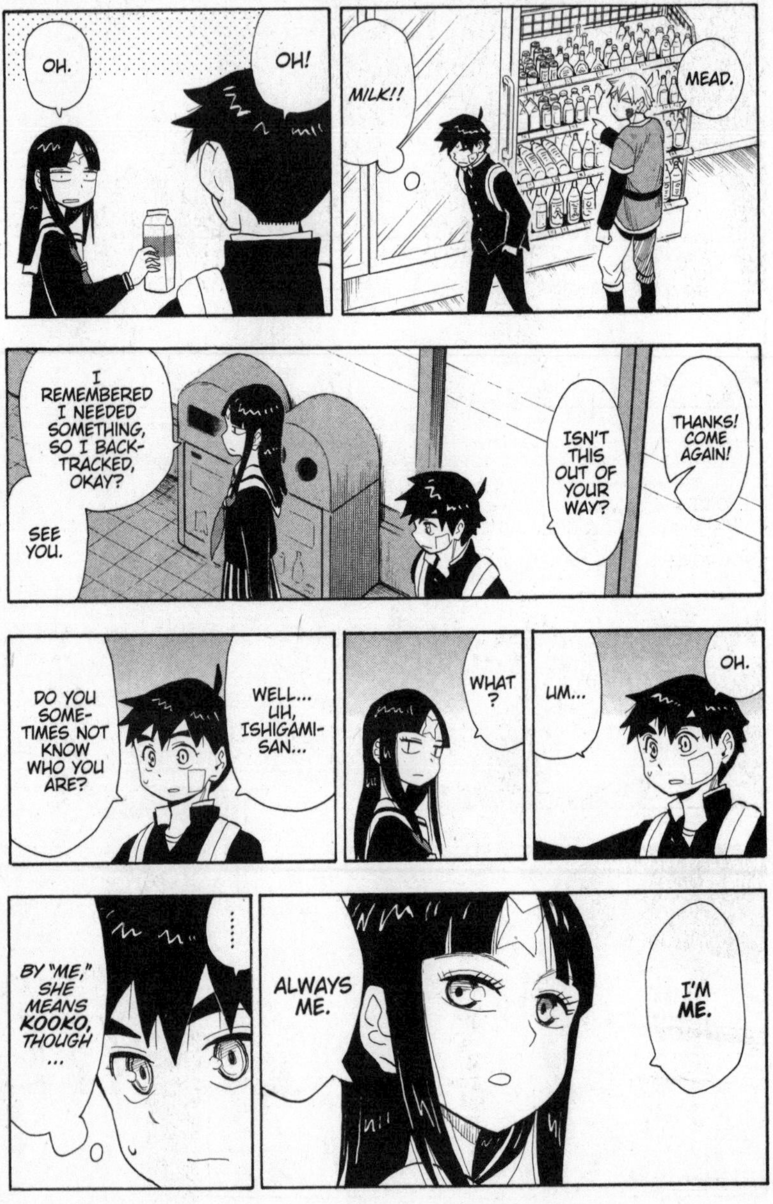
MEAD.
MILK!!
OH!
OH.
THANKS! COME AGAIN!
ISN'T THIS OUT OF YOUR WAY?
I REMEMBERED I NEEDED SOMETHING, SO I BACK-TRACKED, OKAY?
SEE YOU.
OH.
UM...
WHAT?
WELL... UH, ISHIGAMI-SAN...
DO YOU SOME-TIMES NOT KNOW WHO YOU ARE?
I'M ME.
ALWAYS ME.
......
BY "ME," SHE MEANS KOOKO, THOUGH...

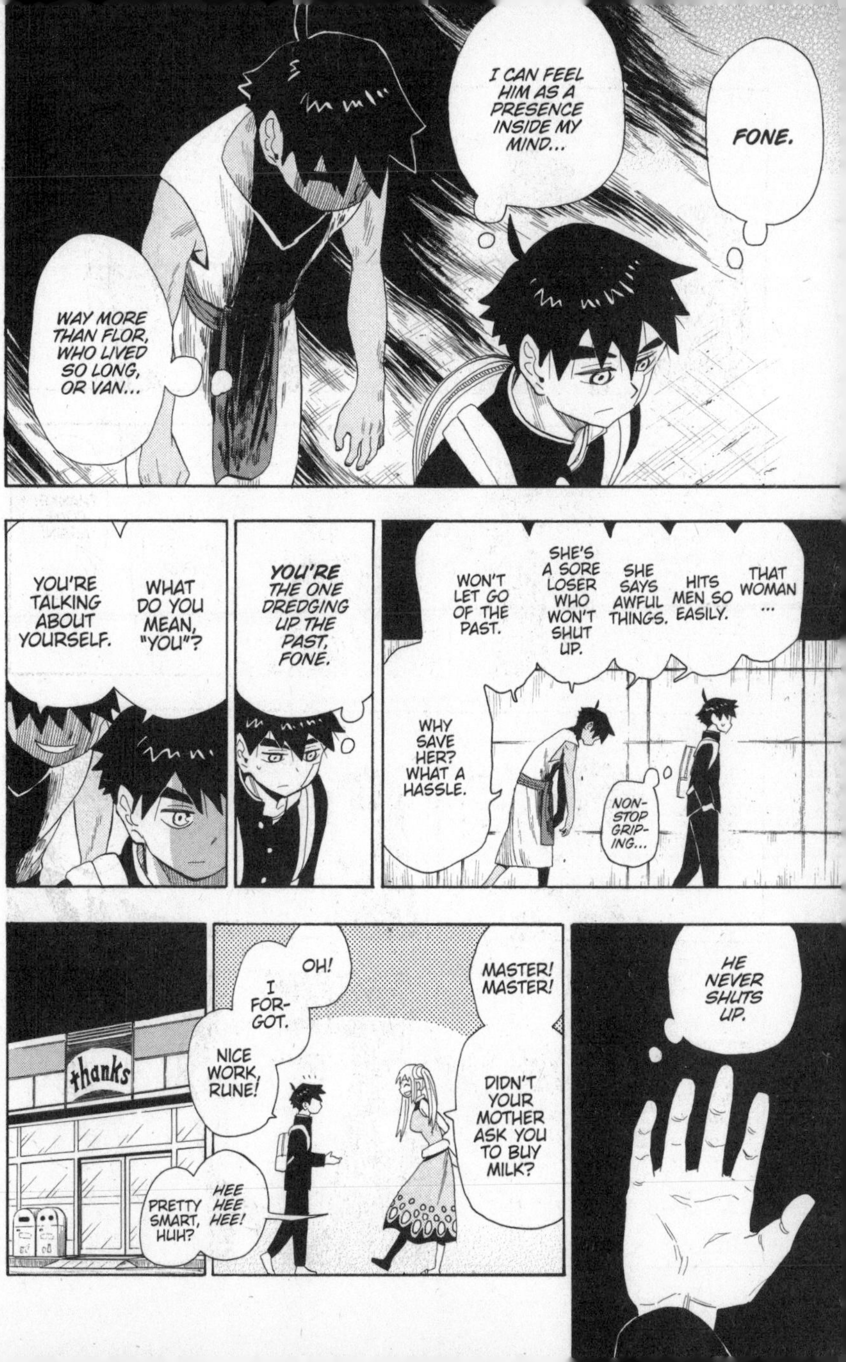
FONE.
I CAN FEEL HIM AS A PRESENCE INSIDE MY MIND...
WAY MORE THAN FLOR, WHO LIVED SO LONG, OR VAN...
THAT WOMAN ...
HITS MEN SO EASILY.
SHE SAYS AWFUL THINGS.
SHE'S A SORE LOSER WHO WON'T SHUT UP.
WON'T LET GO OF THE PAST.
WHY SAVE HER? WHAT A HASSLE.
NON-STOP GRIPING...
YOU'RE THE ONE DREDGING UP THE PAST, FONE.
WHAT DO YOU MEAN, "YOU"?
YOU'RE TALKING ABOUT YOURSELF.
HE NEVER SHUTS UP.
MASTER! MASTER!
DIDN'T YOUR MOTHER ASK YOU TO BUY MILK?
OH!
I FOR-GOT.
NICE WORK, RUNE!
HEE HEE HEE!
PRETTY SMART, HUH?
thanks

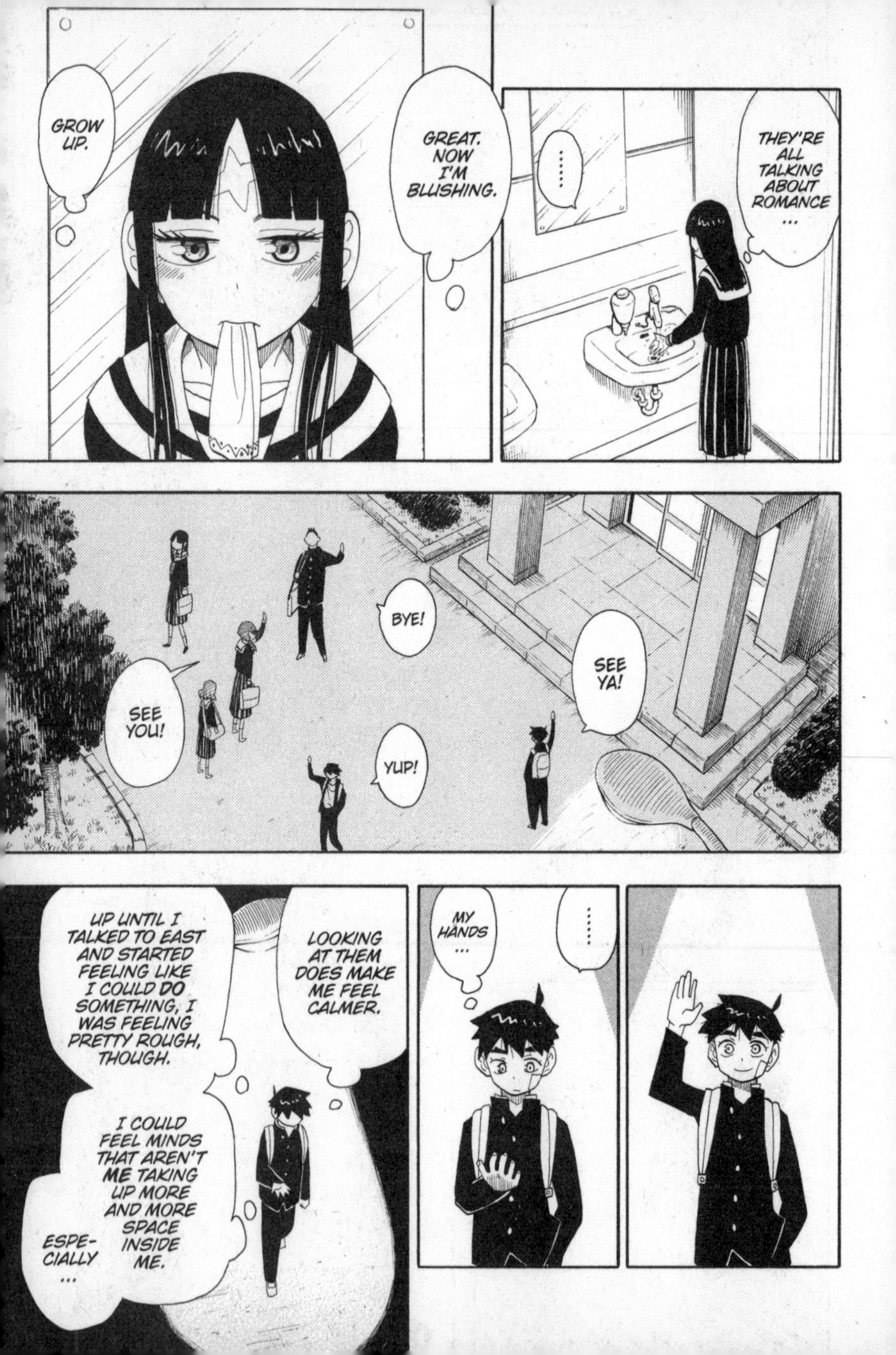
THEY'RE ALL TALKING ABOUT ROMANCE ...
......
GREAT. NOW I'M BLUSHING.
GROW UP.
SEE YA!
BYE!
YUP!
SEE YOU!
......
MY HANDS ...
LOOKING AT THEM DOES MAKE ME FEEL CALMER.
UP UNTIL I TALKED TO EAST AND STARTED FEELING LIKE I COULD DO SOMETHING, I WAS FEELING PRETTY ROUGH, THOUGH.
I COULD FEEL MINDS THAT AREN'T ME TAKING UP MORE AND MORE SPACE INSIDE ME.
ESPE-CIALLY ...

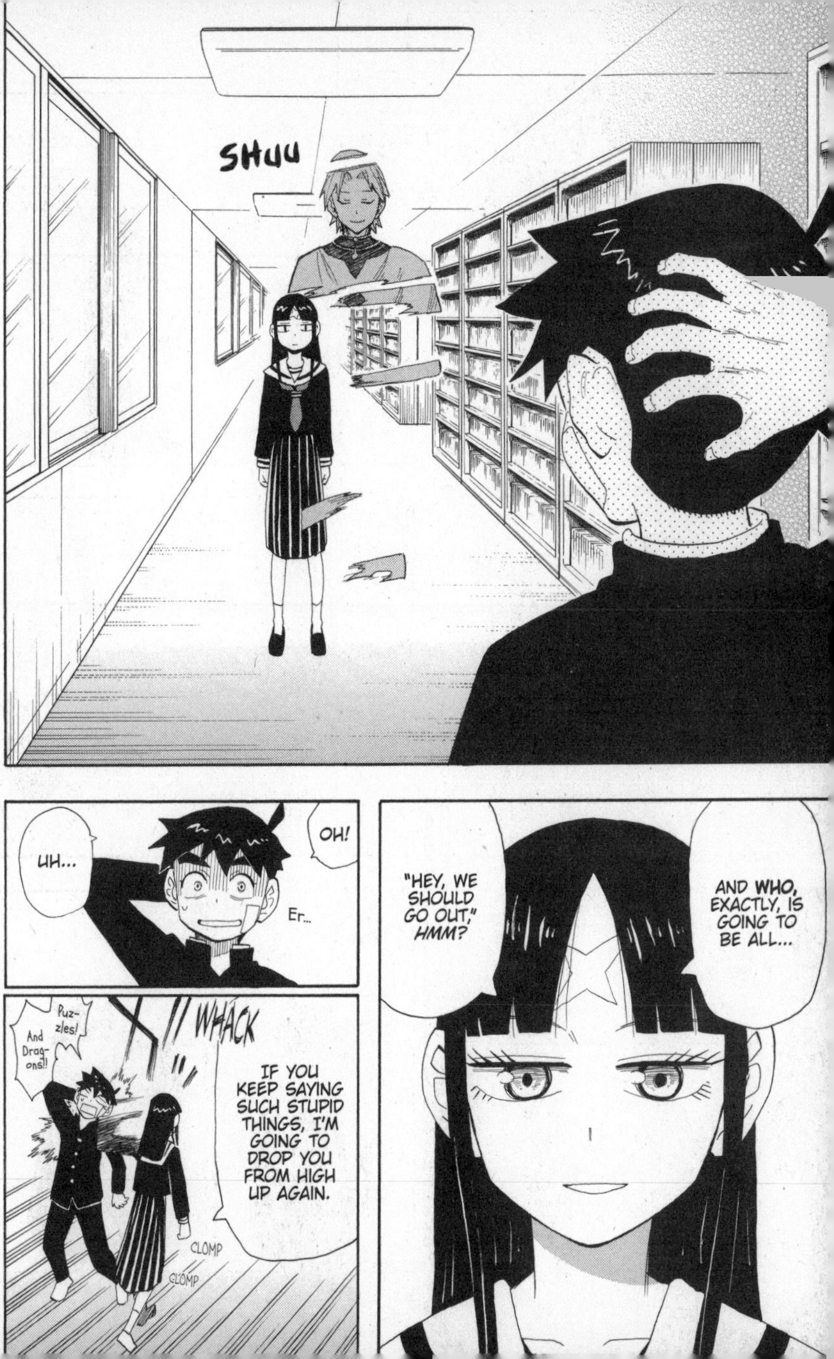
SHUU
AND WHO, EXACTLY, IS GOING TO BE ALL...
"HEY, WE SHOULD GO OUT," HMM?
OH!
UH...
Er...
WHACK
IF YOU KEEP SAYING SUCH STUPID THINGS, I'M GOING TO DROP YOU FROM HIGH UP AGAIN.
Puz-zles!
And Drag-ons!!
CLOMP
CLOMP

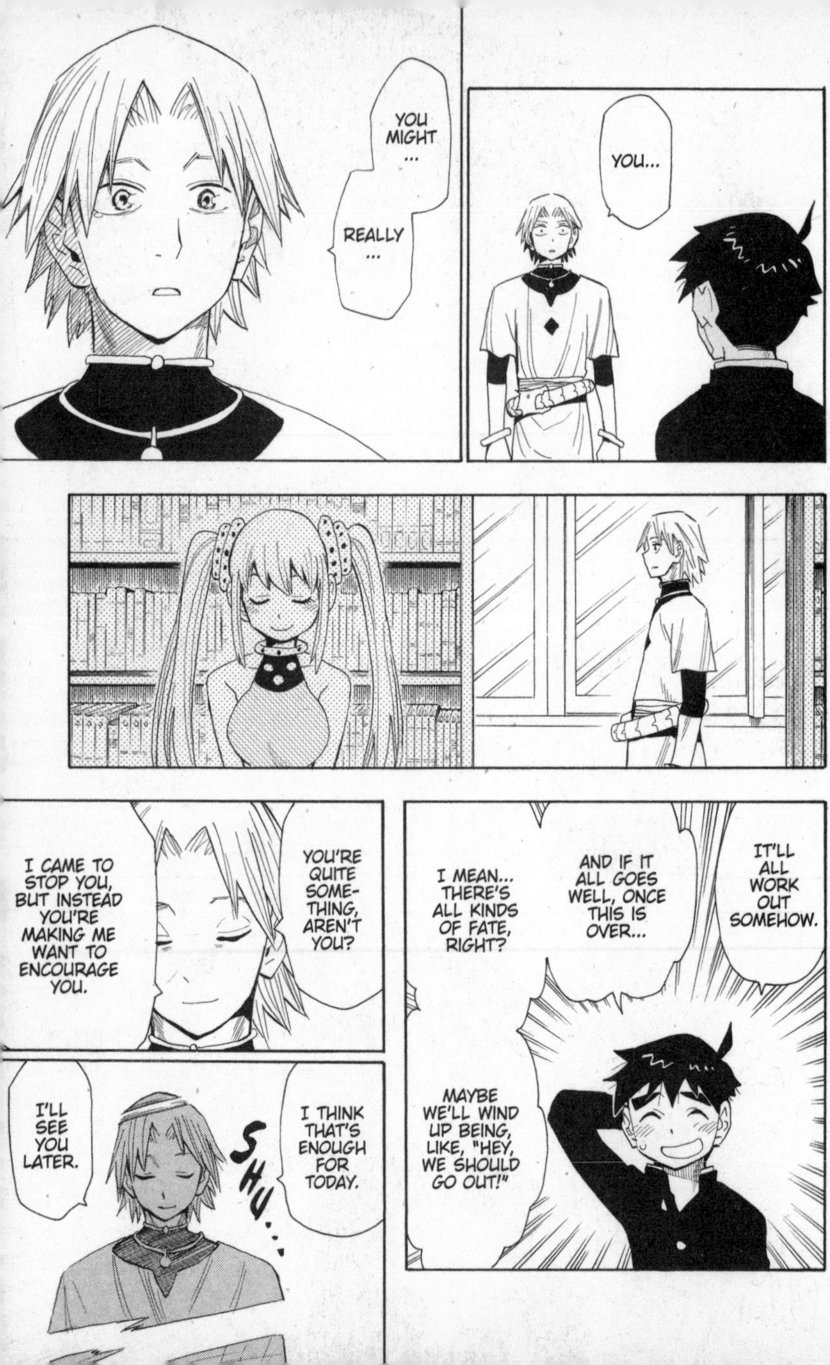
YOU...
YOU MIGHT ...
REALLY ...
IT'LL ALL WORK OUT SOMEHOW.
AND IF IT ALL GOES WELL, ONCE THIS IS OVER...
I MEAN... THERE'S ALL KINDS OF FATE, RIGHT?
MAYBE WE'LL WIND UP BEING, LIKE, "HEY, WE SHOULD GO OUT!"
YOU'RE QUITE SOME-THING, AREN'T YOU?
I CAME TO STOP YOU, BUT INSTEAD YOU'RE MAKING ME WANT TO ENCOURAGE YOU.
I THINK THAT'S ENOUGH FOR TODAY.
SHU...
I'LL SEE YOU LATER.

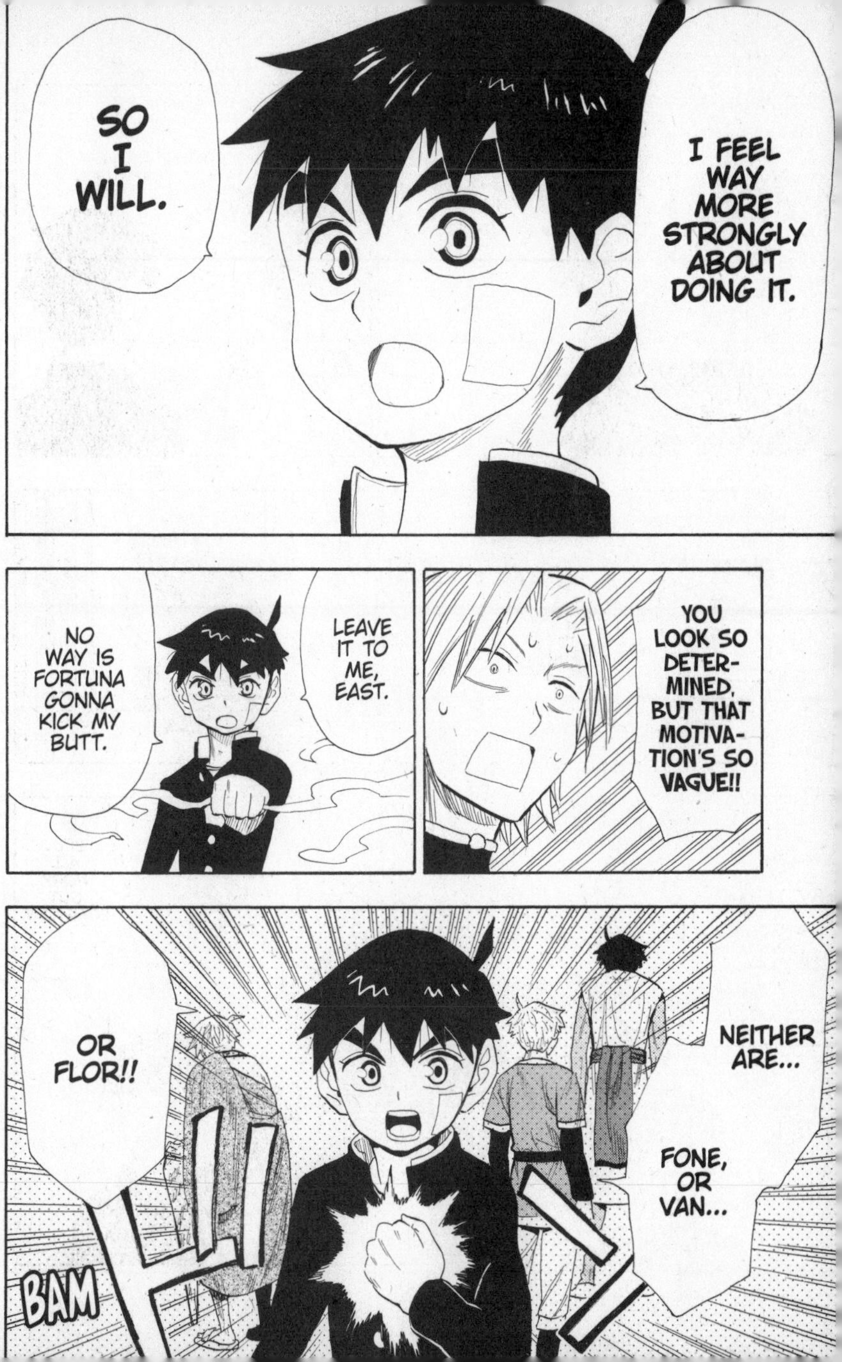
I FEEL WAY MORE STRONGLY ABOUT DOING IT.
SO I WILL.
YOU LOOK SO DETER-MINED, BUT THAT MOTIVA-TION'S SO VAGUE!!
LEAVE IT TO ME, EAST.
NO WAY IS FORTUNA GONNA KICK MY BUTT.
NEITHER ARE...
FONE, OR VAN...
OR FLOR!!
BAM

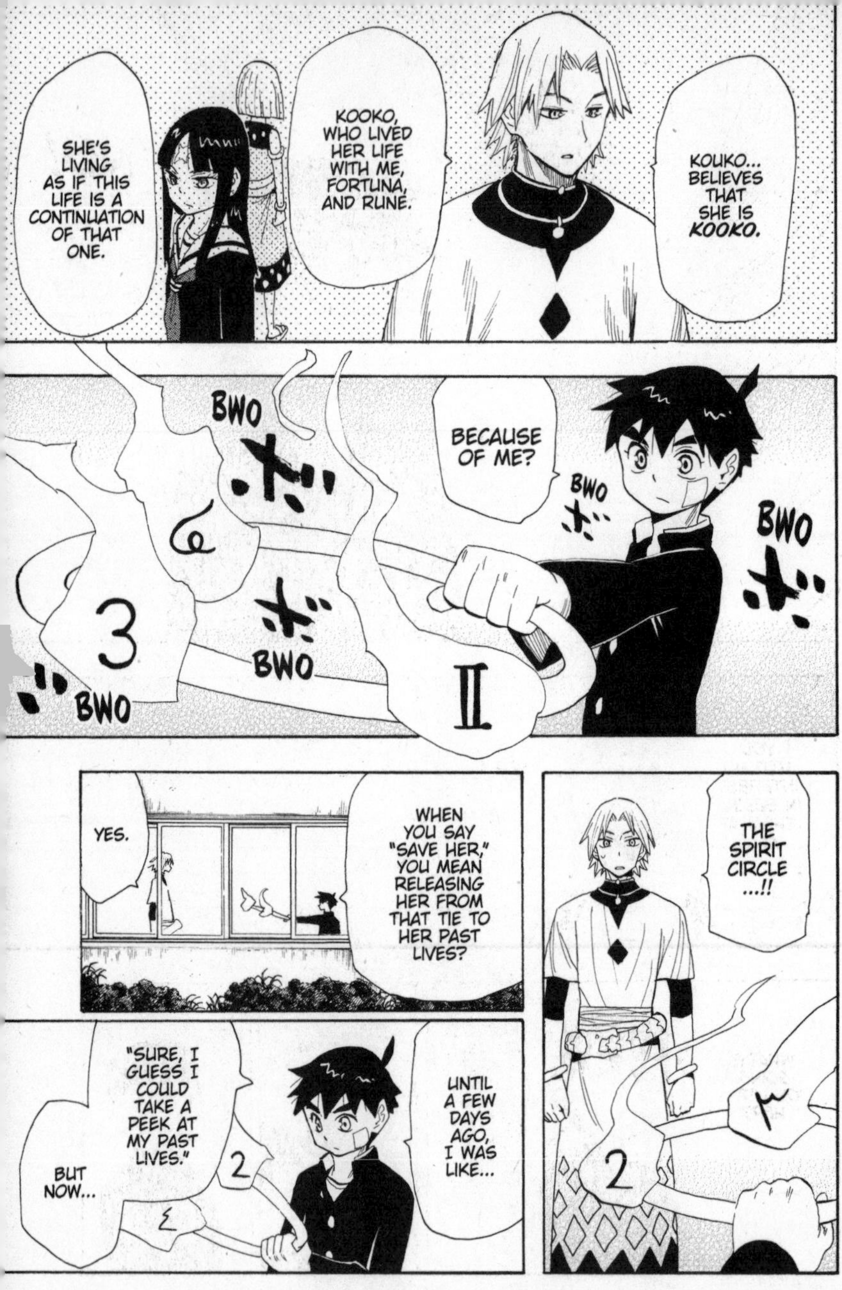
KOUKO... BELIEVES THAT SHE IS KOOKO.
KOOKO, WHO LIVED HER LIFE WITH ME, FORTUNA, AND RUNE.
SHE'S LIVING AS IF THIS LIFE IS A CONTINUATION OF THAT ONE.
BWO
BECAUSE OF ME?
BWO
BWO
BWO
BWO
THE SPIRIT CIRCLE ...!!
WHEN YOU SAY "SAVE HER," YOU MEAN RELEASING HER FROM THAT TIE TO HER PAST LIVES?
YES.
UNTIL A FEW DAYS AGO, I WAS LIKE...
"SURE, I GUESS I COULD TAKE A PEEK AT MY PAST LIVES."
BUT NOW...

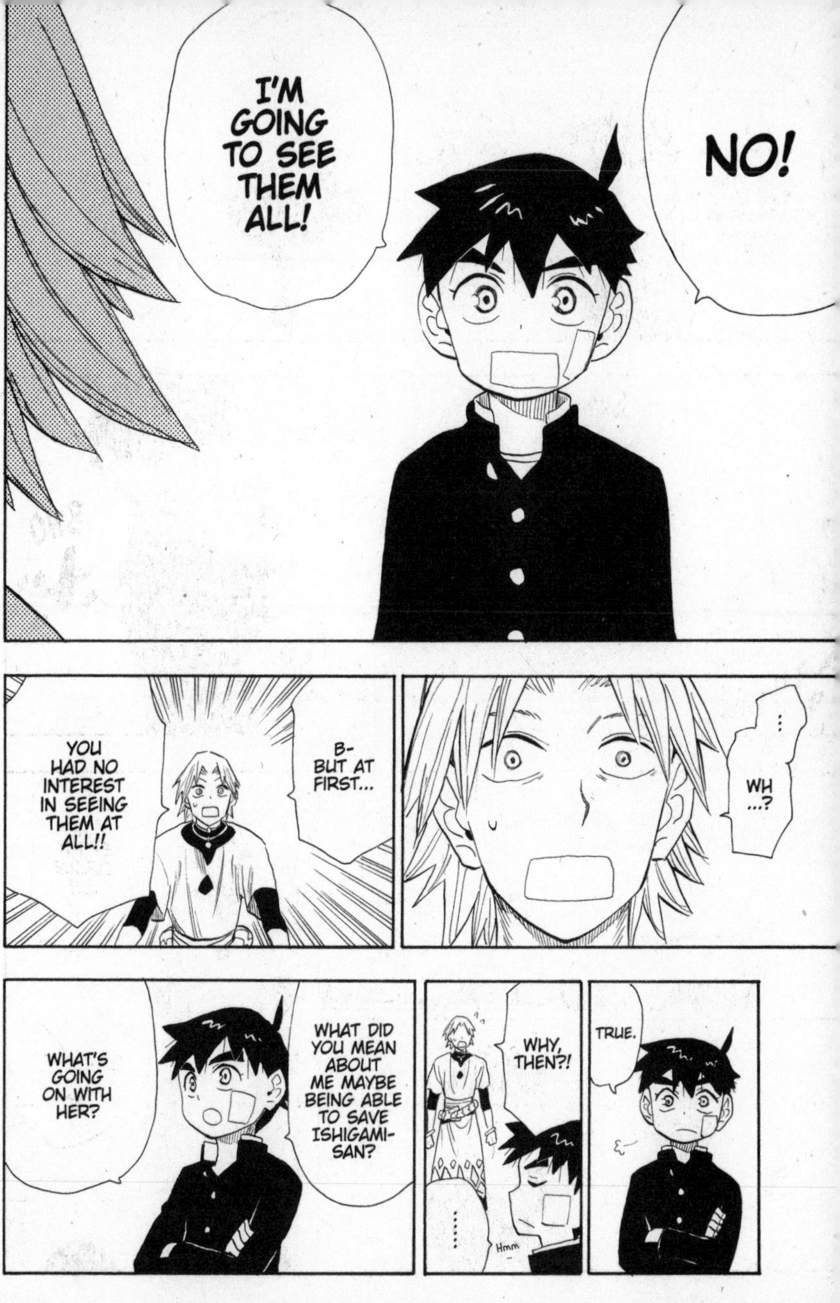
NO!
I'M GOING TO SEE THEM ALL!
...
WH ...?
B-BUT AT FIRST...
YOU HAD NO INTEREST IN SEEING THEM AT ALL!!
TRUE.
WHY, THEN?!
......
Hmm
WHAT DID YOU MEAN ABOUT ME MAYBE BEING ABLE TO SAVE ISHIGAMI-SAN?
WHAT'S GOING ON WITH HER?

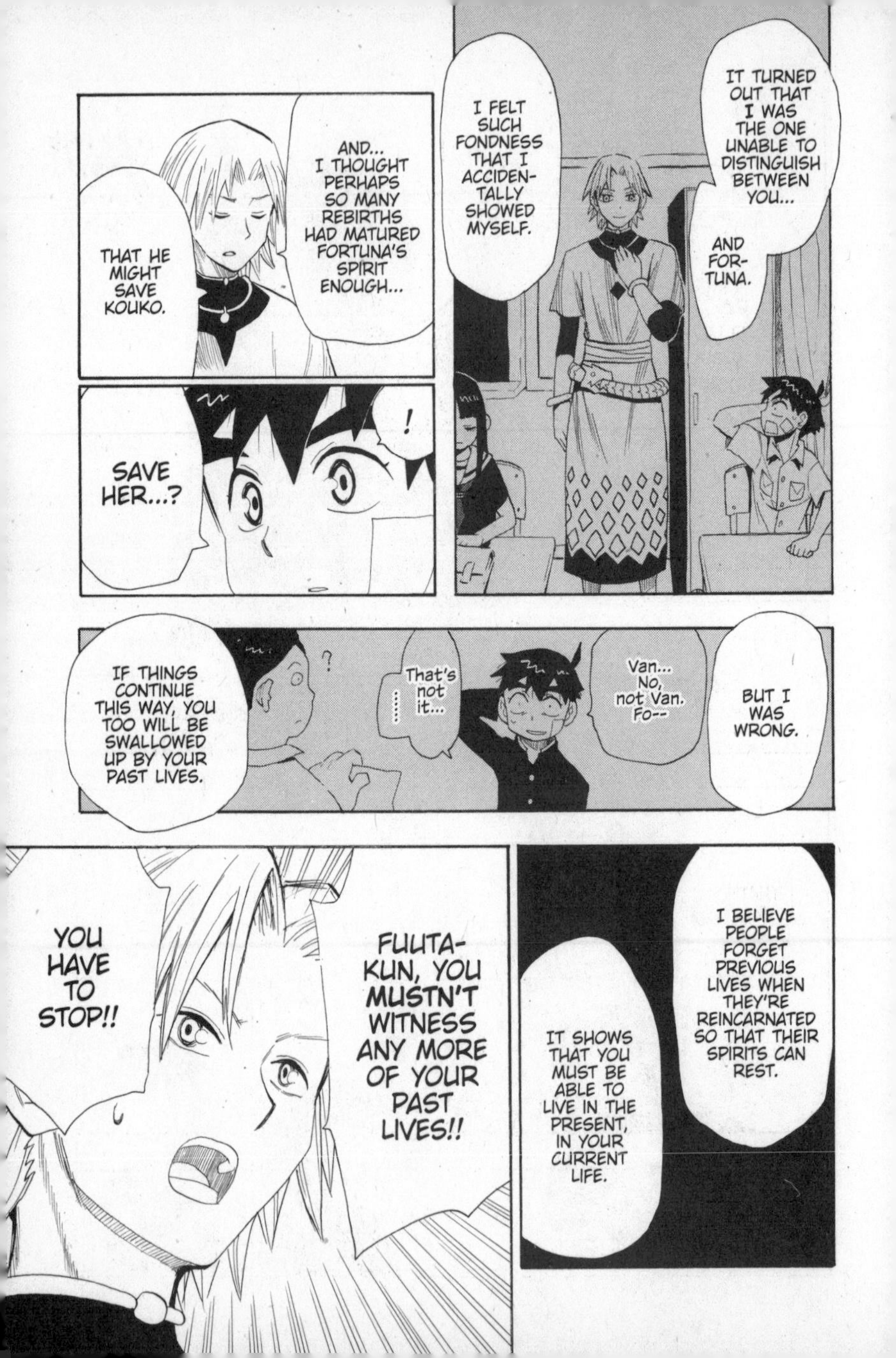
IT TURNED OUT THAT I WAS THE ONE UNABLE TO DISTINGUISH BETWEEN YOU...
AND FOR-TUNA.
I FELT SUCH FONDNESS THAT I ACCIDEN-TALLY SHOWED MYSELF.
AND... I THOUGHT PERHAPS SO MANY REBIRTHS HAD MATURED FORTUNA'S SPIRIT ENOUGH...
THAT HE MIGHT SAVE KOUKO.
!
SAVE HER...?
BUT I WAS WRONG.
Van... No, not Van. Fo--
That's not it...
......
?
IF THINGS CONTINUE THIS WAY, YOU TOO WILL BE SWALLOWED UP BY YOUR PAST LIVES.
I BELIEVE PEOPLE FORGET PREVIOUS LIVES WHEN THEY'RE REINCARNATED SO THAT THEIR SPIRITS CAN REST.
IT SHOWS THAT YOU MUST BE ABLE TO LIVE IN THE PRESENT, IN YOUR CURRENT LIFE.
FUUTA-KUN, YOU MUSTN'T WITNESS ANY MORE OF YOUR PAST LIVES!!
YOU HAVE TO STOP!!

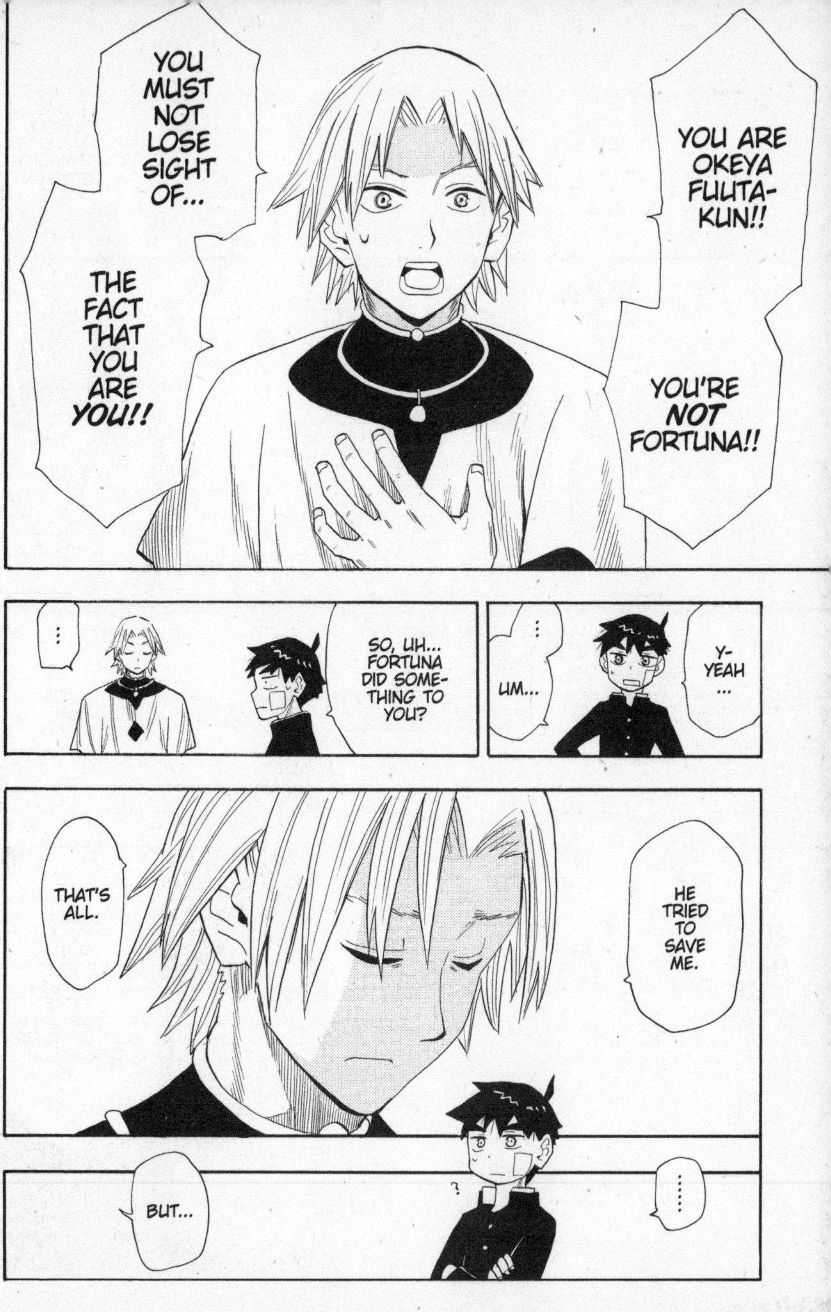
YOU ARE OKEYA FUUTA-KUN!!
YOU'RE *NOT* FORTUNA!!
YOU MUST NOT LOSE SIGHT OF...
THE FACT THAT YOU ARE *YOU!!*
Y-YEAH ...
UM...
...
SO, UH... FORTUNA DID SOME-THING TO YOU?
...
HE TRIED TO SAVE ME.
THAT'S ALL.
......
?
BUT...

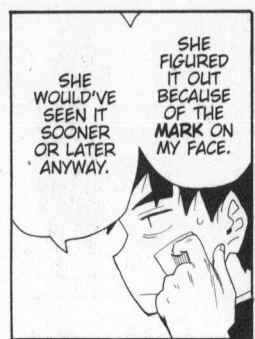

ER ...
HUH?
KOUKO REALIZED WHO YOU ARE BECAUSE OF ME.
I SHOULDN'T HAVE SHOWN MYSELF TO YOU.
SHE FIGURED IT OUT BECAUSE OF THE **MARK** ON MY FACE.
SHE WOULD'VE SEEN IT SOONER OR LATER ANYWAY.
BUT--
SERIOUSLY, IT'S FINE.
BUT I HAVE TO ASK...
"Because of you, East is...
"My **father** is--!!"
EAST ...
DID I DO SOMETHING TO YOU?
!
NO. IT WASN'T YOU.
IT WAS FORTUNA.
EXCEPT THAT WAS ME.
FUUTA-KUN!!
YOU MUSTN'T DO THIS!!

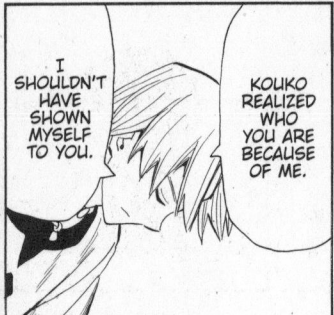

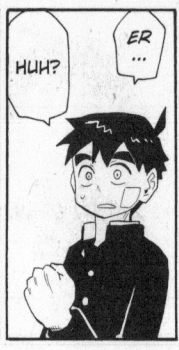

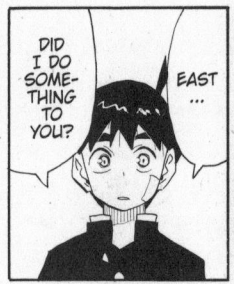

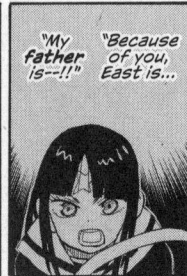

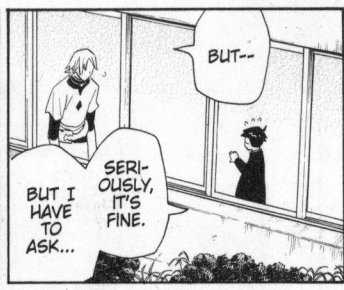

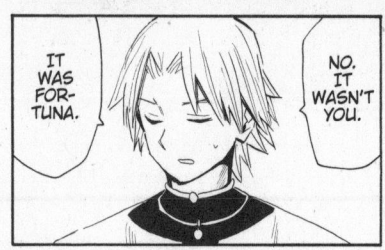

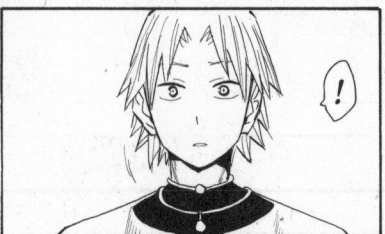

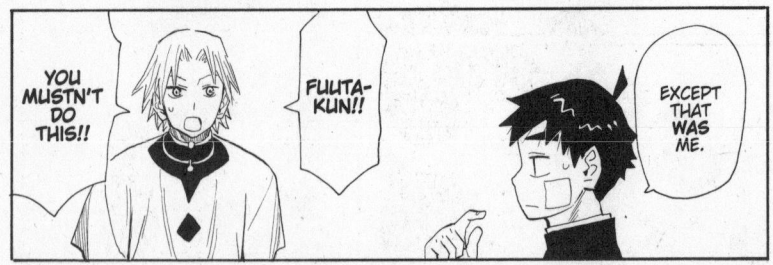

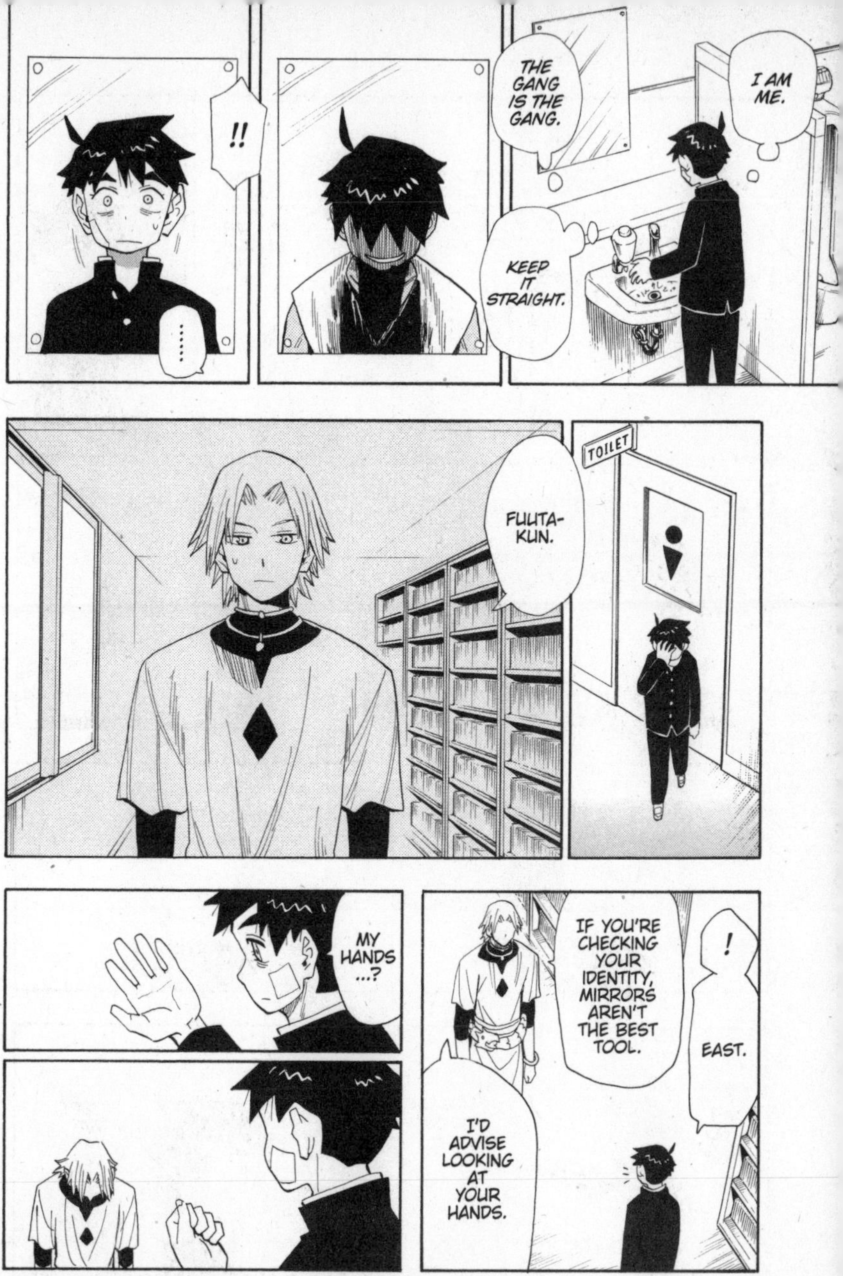
I AM ME.
THE GANG IS THE GANG.
KEEP IT STRAIGHT.
!!
......
TOILET
FUUTA-KUN.
!
EAST.
IF YOU'RE CHECKING YOUR IDENTITY, MIRRORS AREN'T THE BEST TOOL.
I'D ADVISE LOOKING AT YOUR HANDS.
MY HANDS ...?

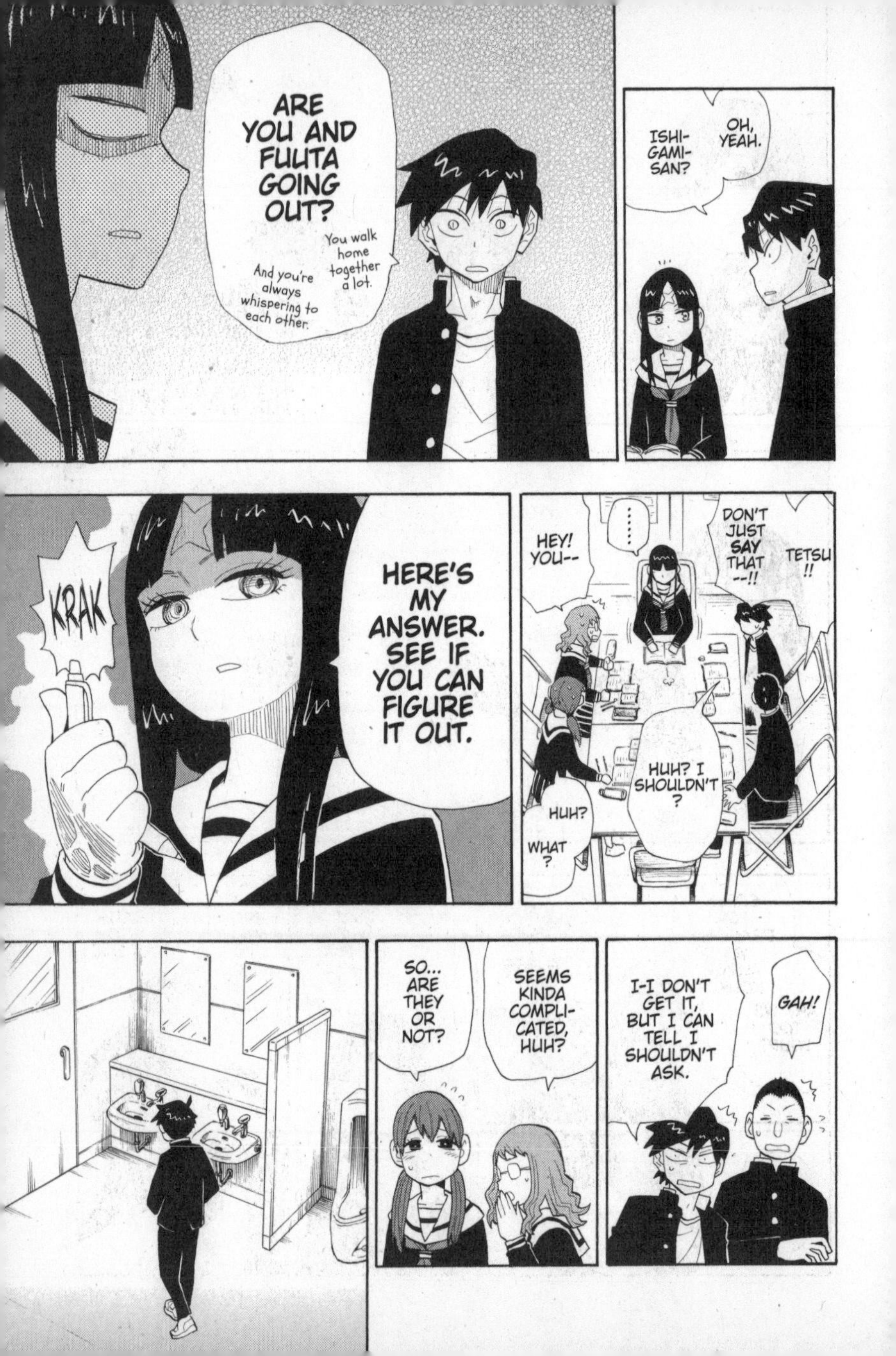
OH, YEAH.
ISHI-GAMI-SAN?
ARE YOU AND FUUTA GOING OUT?
You walk home together a lot.
And you're always whispering to each other.
TETSU!!
DON'T JUST SAY THAT--!!
......
HEY! YOU--
HUH? I SHOULDN'T?
HUH?
WHAT?
HERE'S MY ANSWER. SEE IF YOU CAN FIGURE IT OUT.
KRAK
GAH!
I-I DON'T GET IT, BUT I CAN TELL I SHOULDN'T ASK.
SEEMS KINDA COMPLICATED, HUH?
SO... ARE THEY OR NOT?

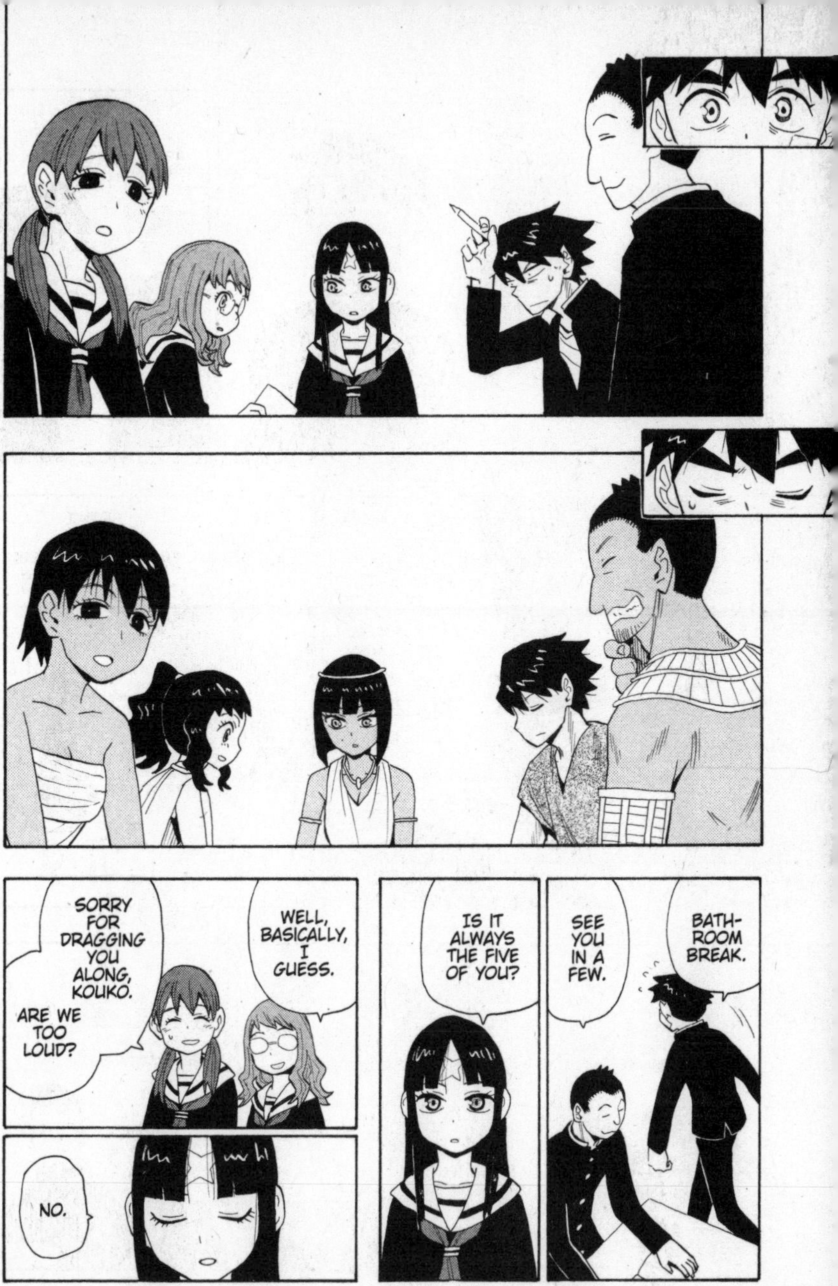
BATH-ROOM BREAK.
SEE YOU IN A FEW.
IS IT ALWAYS THE FIVE OF YOU?
WELL, BASICALLY, I GUESS.
SORRY FOR DRAGGING YOU ALONG, KOUKO.
ARE WE TOO LOUD?
NO.

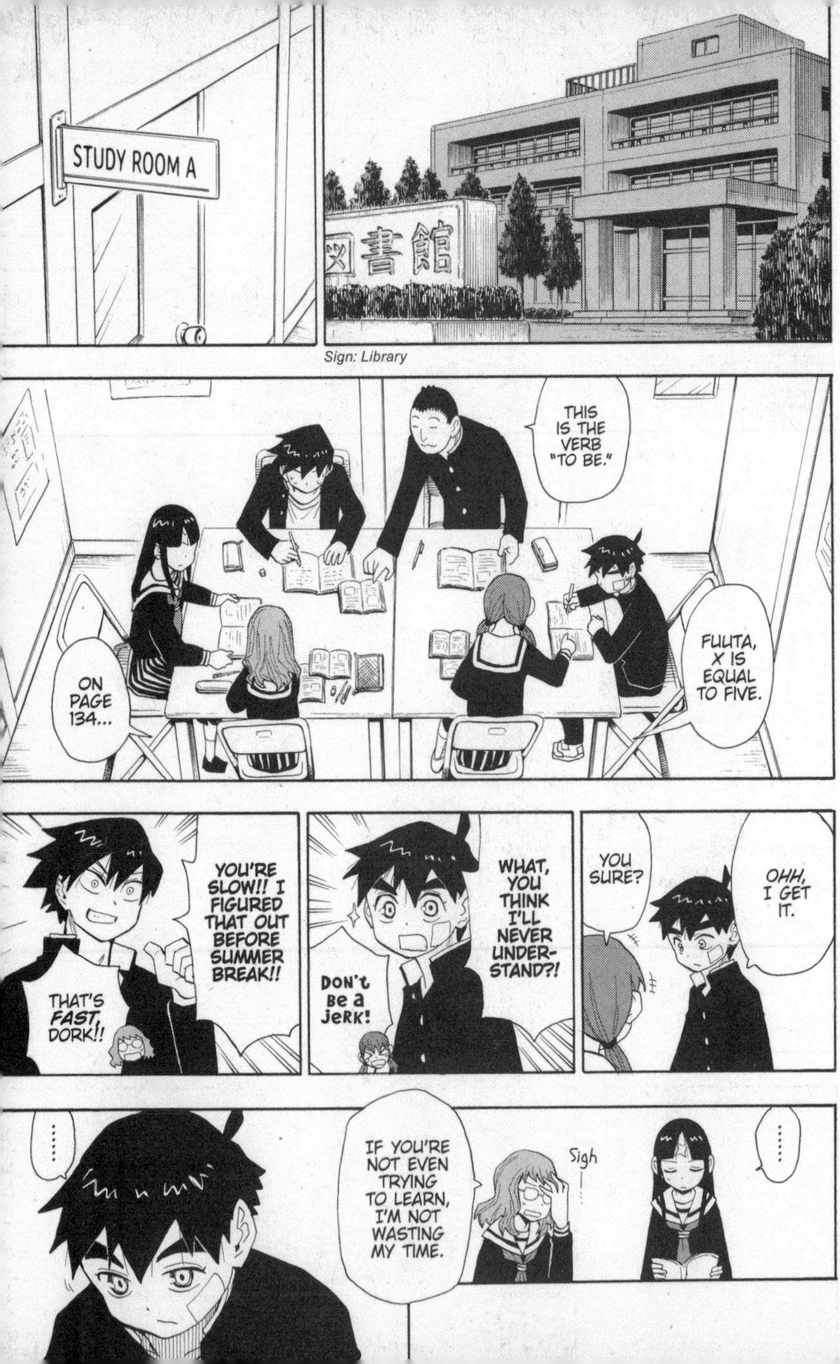
Sign: Library
STUDY ROOM A
THIS IS THE VERB "TO BE."
FUUTA, X IS EQUAL TO FIVE.
ON PAGE 134...
OHH, I GET IT.
YOU SURE?
WHAT, YOU THINK I'LL NEVER UNDER-STAND?!
Don't be a jerk!
YOU'RE SLOW!! I FIGURED THAT OUT BEFORE SUMMER BREAK!!
THAT'S FAST, DORK!!
......
Sigh
IF YOU'RE NOT EVEN TRYING TO LEARN, I'M NOT WASTING MY TIME.
......

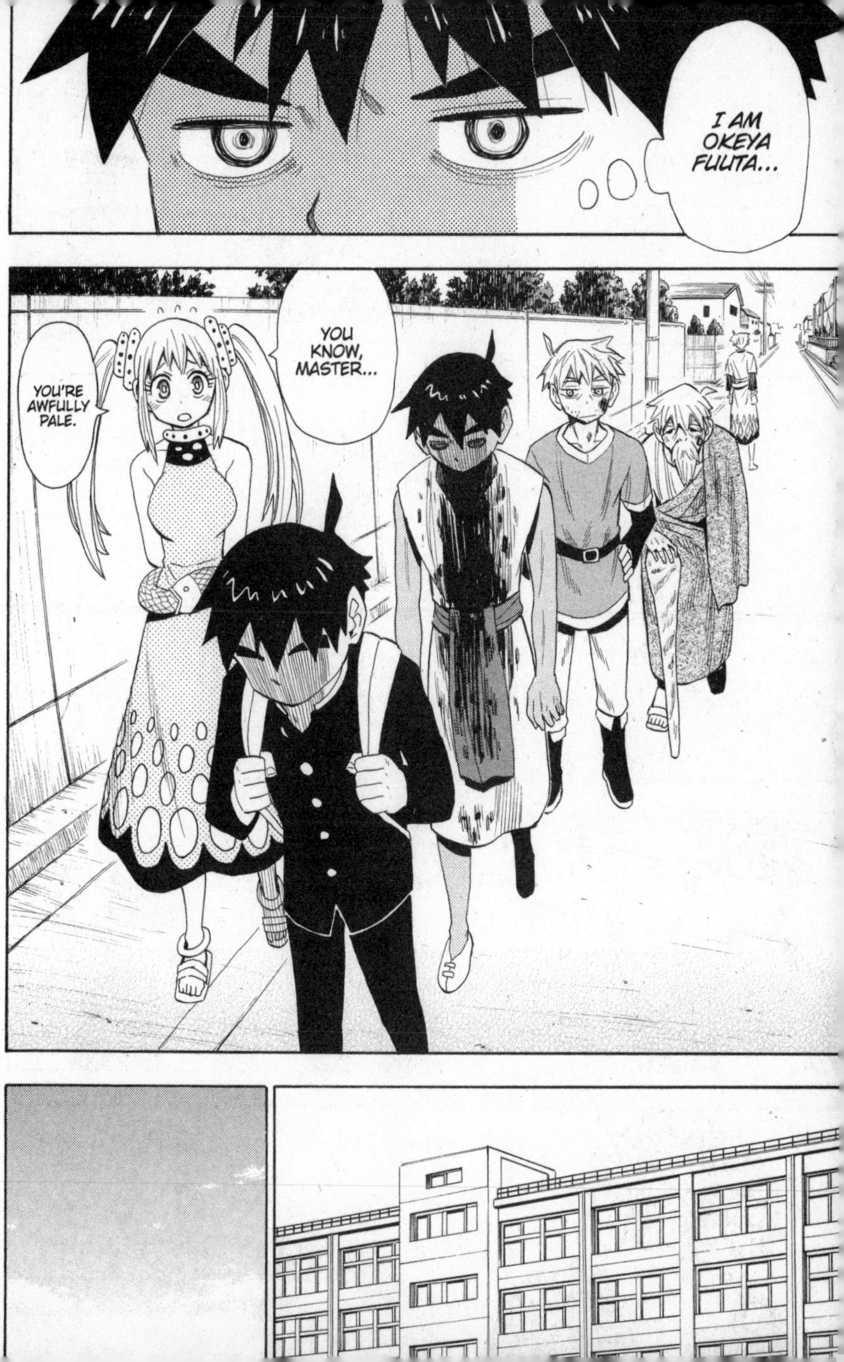
I AM OKEYA FUUTA...
YOU KNOW, MASTER...
YOU'RE AWFULLY PALE.

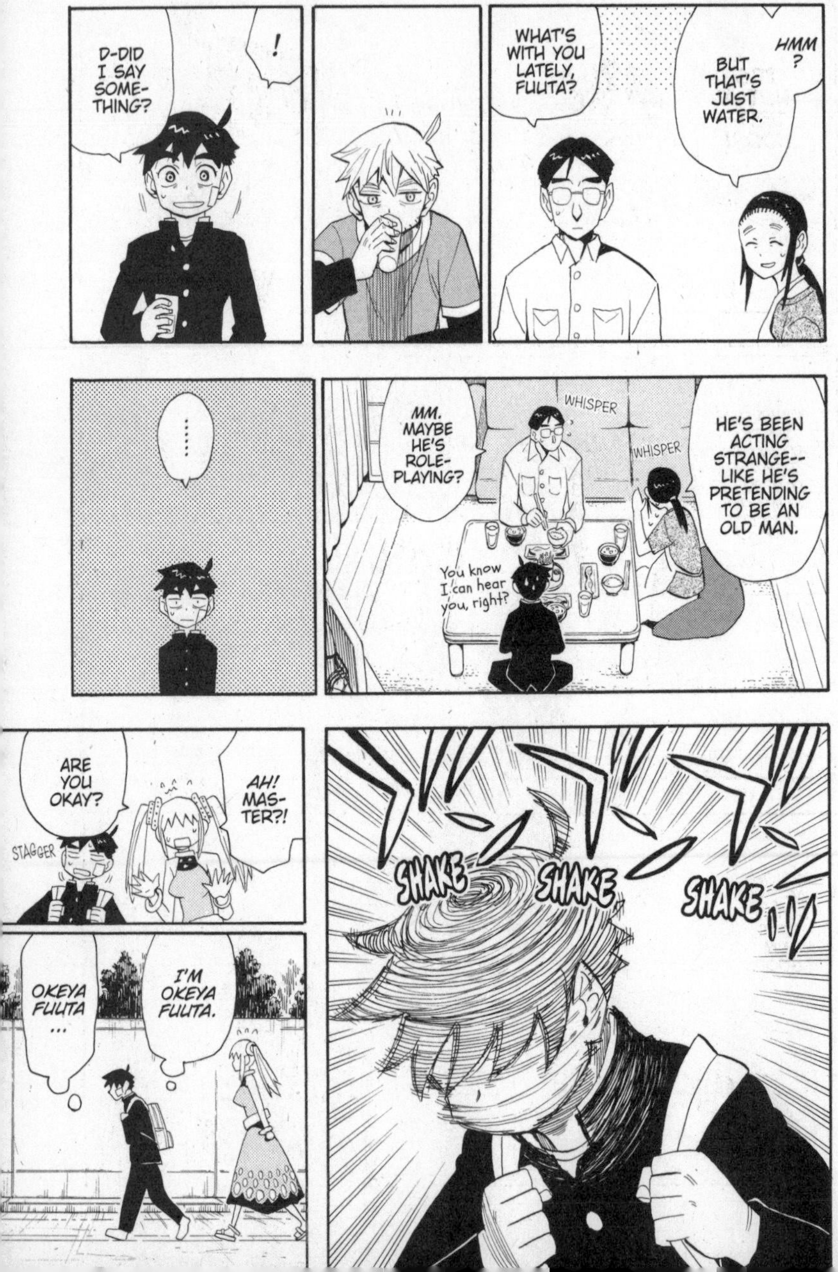
HMM?
BUT THAT'S JUST WATER.
WHAT'S WITH YOU LATELY, FUUTA?
!
D-DID I SAY SOMETHING?
HE'S BEEN ACTING STRANGE-- LIKE HE'S PRETENDING TO BE AN OLD MAN.
WHISPER
WHISPER
MM. MAYBE HE'S ROLE-PLAYING?
You know I can hear you, right?
......
SHAKE
SHAKE
SHAKE
AH! MASTER?!
ARE YOU OKAY?
STAGGER
I'M OKEYA FUUTA.
OKEYA FUUTA...

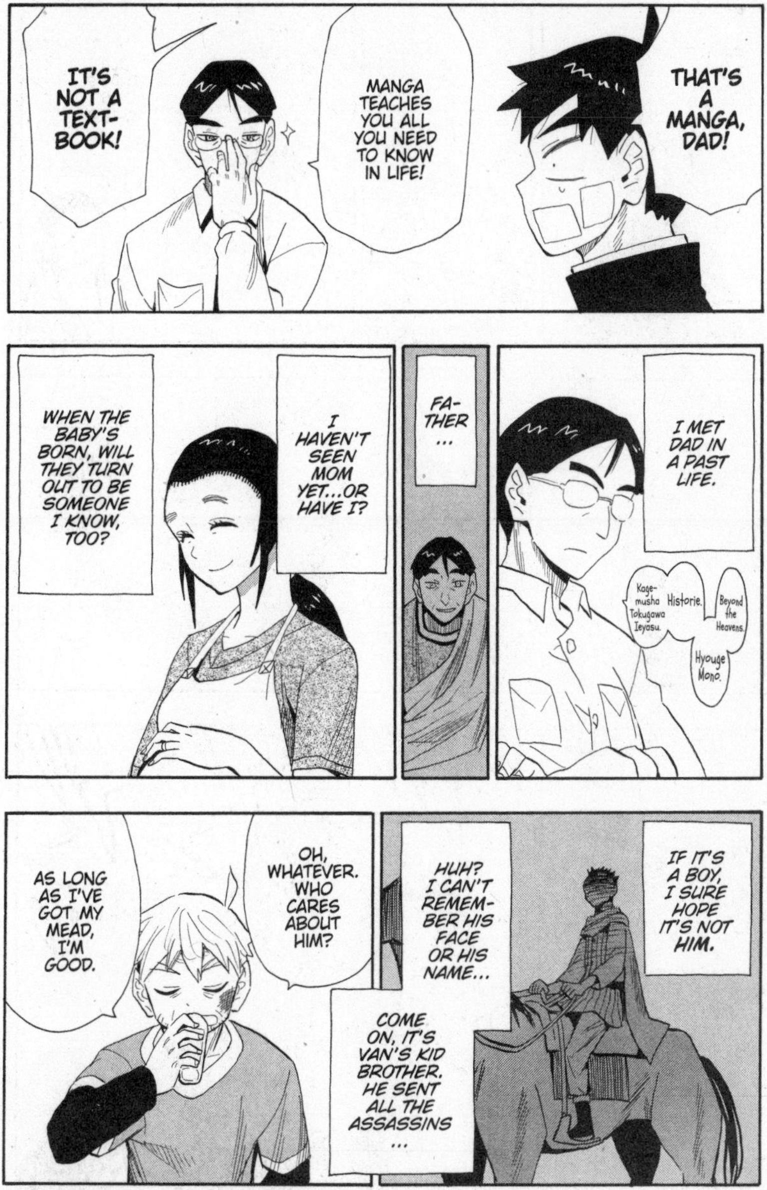
THAT'S A MANGA, DAD!
MANGA TEACHES YOU ALL YOU NEED TO KNOW IN LIFE!
IT'S NOT A TEXT-BOOK!
I MET DAD IN A PAST LIFE.
Beyond the Heavens.
Historie.
Kage-musha Tokugawa Ieyasu.
Hyouge Mono.
FA-THER...
I HAVEN'T SEEN MOM YET...OR HAVE I?
WHEN THE BABY'S BORN, WILL THEY TURN OUT TO BE SOMEONE I KNOW, TOO?
IF IT'S A BOY, I SURE HOPE IT'S NOT HIM.
HUH? I CAN'T REMEMBER HIS FACE OR HIS NAME...
COME ON, IT'S VAN'S KID BROTHER. HE SENT ALL THE ASSASSINS...
OH, WHATEVER. WHO CARES ABOUT HIM?
AS LONG AS I'VE GOT MY MEAD, I'M GOOD.

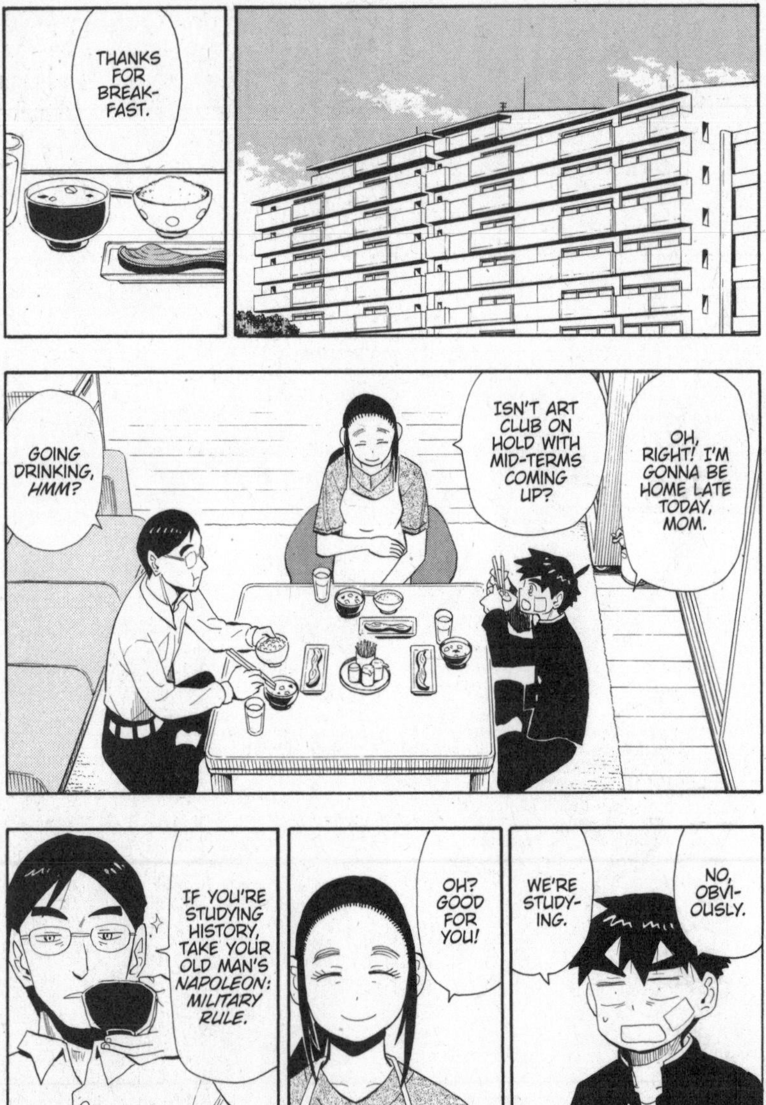
THANKS FOR BREAK-FAST.
OH, RIGHT! I'M GONNA BE HOME LATE TODAY, MOM.
ISN'T ART CLUB ON HOLD WITH MID-TERMS COMING UP?
GOING DRINKING, *HMM?*
NO, OBVI-OUSLY.
WE'RE STUDY-ING.
OKEYA FUUTA (14)
OH? GOOD FOR YOU!
OKEYA SAWA (36)
IF YOU'RE STUDYING HISTORY, TAKE YOUR OLD MAN'S *NAPOLEON: MILITARY RULE.*
OKEYA TOUKICHI (37)

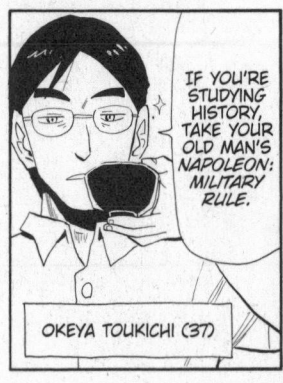

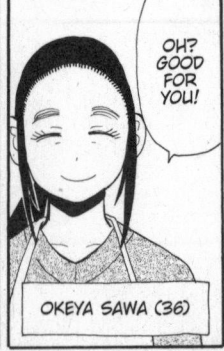

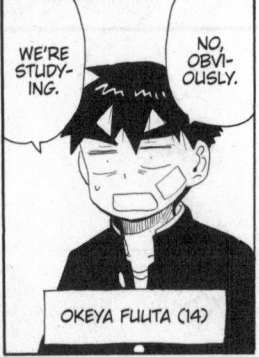

THUD

SHHP

NGAH
?!

BECAUSE
OF ME,
EAST...
EAST WHAT?
WHAT
HAPPENED
...?

A
DREAM
...

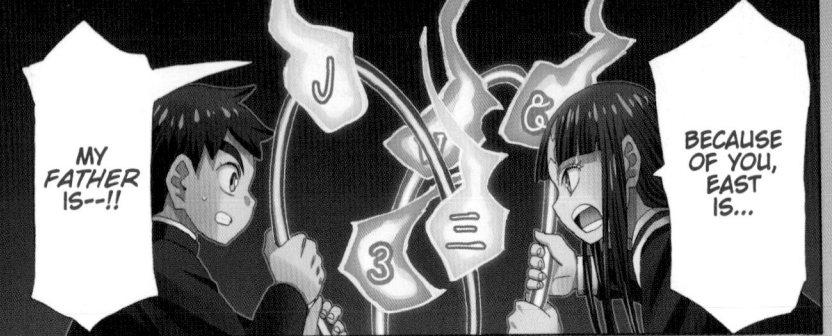

MY FATHER IS--!!

BECAUSE OF YOU, EAST IS...

EVEN IF IT TAKES A THOUSAND YEARS...

EVEN IF IT TAKES *TEN* THOUSAND YEARS...

THIS CURSE OF YOURS!!

I...

WILL DESTROY...

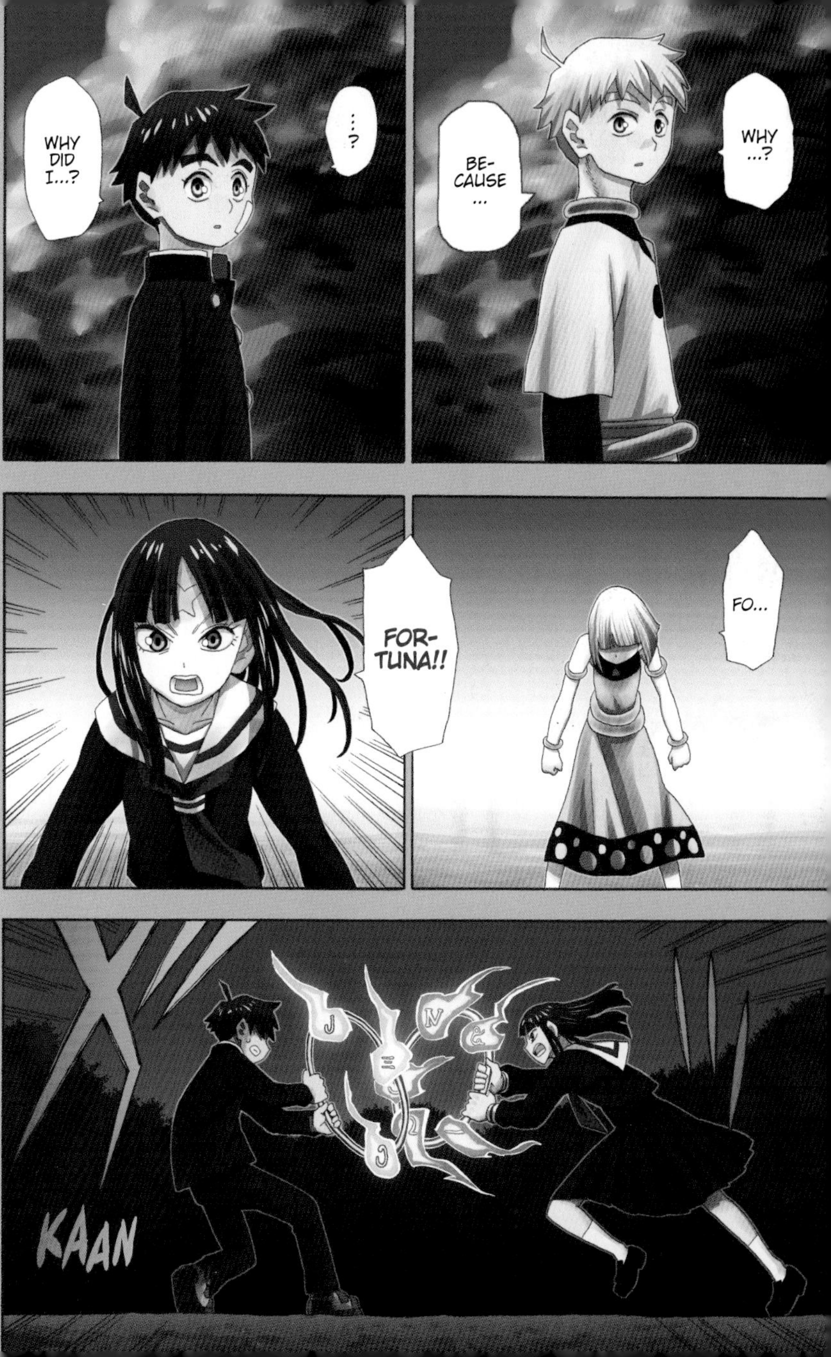
WHY ...?
BE- CAUSE ...
...?
WHY DID I...?
FO...
FOR- TUNA!!
KAAN

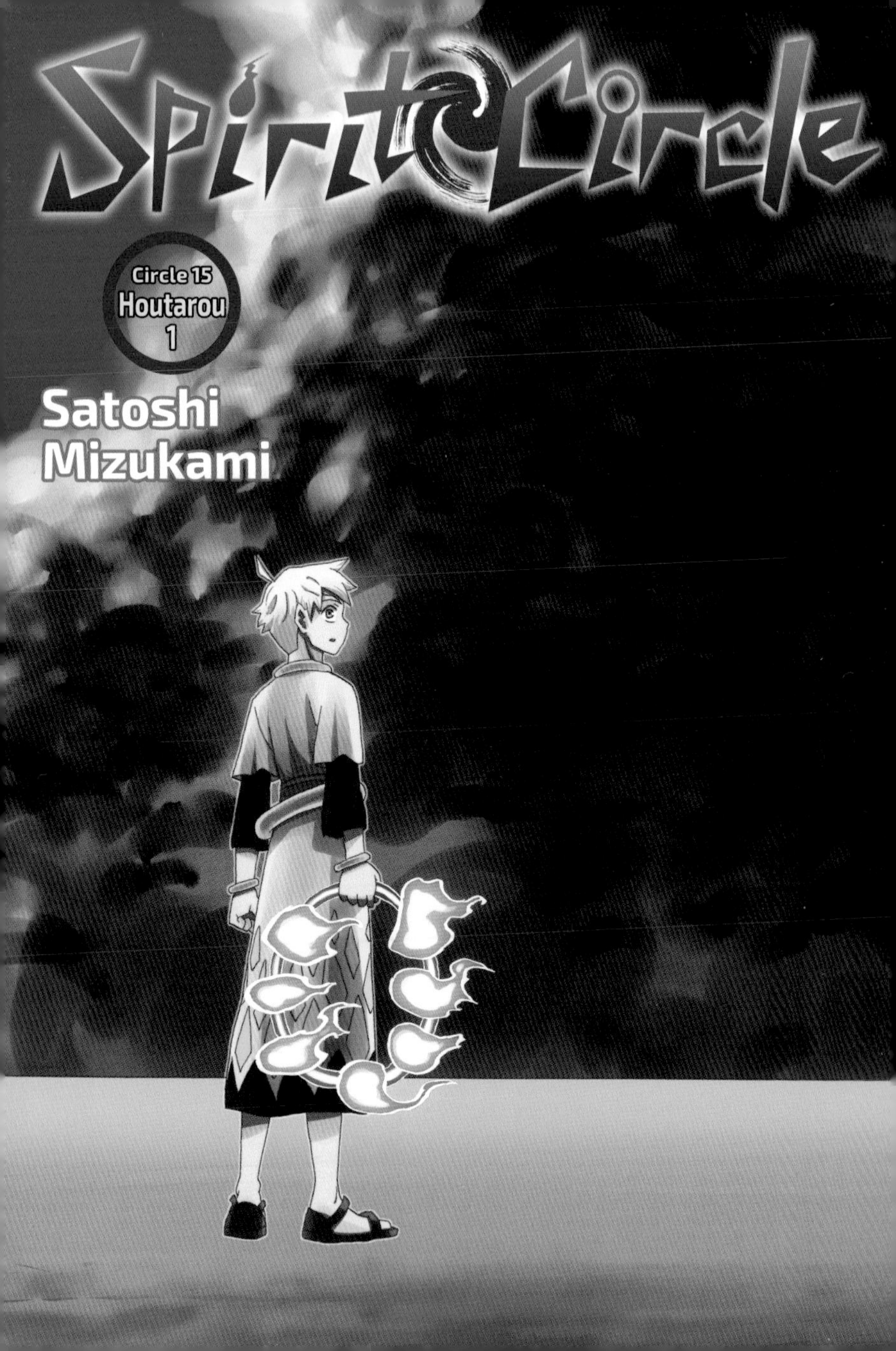
Spirit Circle
Circle 15
Houtarou
1
Satoshi
Mizukami

WHY WOULD YOU DO THIS?!

KOOKO ...

WHY ...?

FOR- TUNA ...!

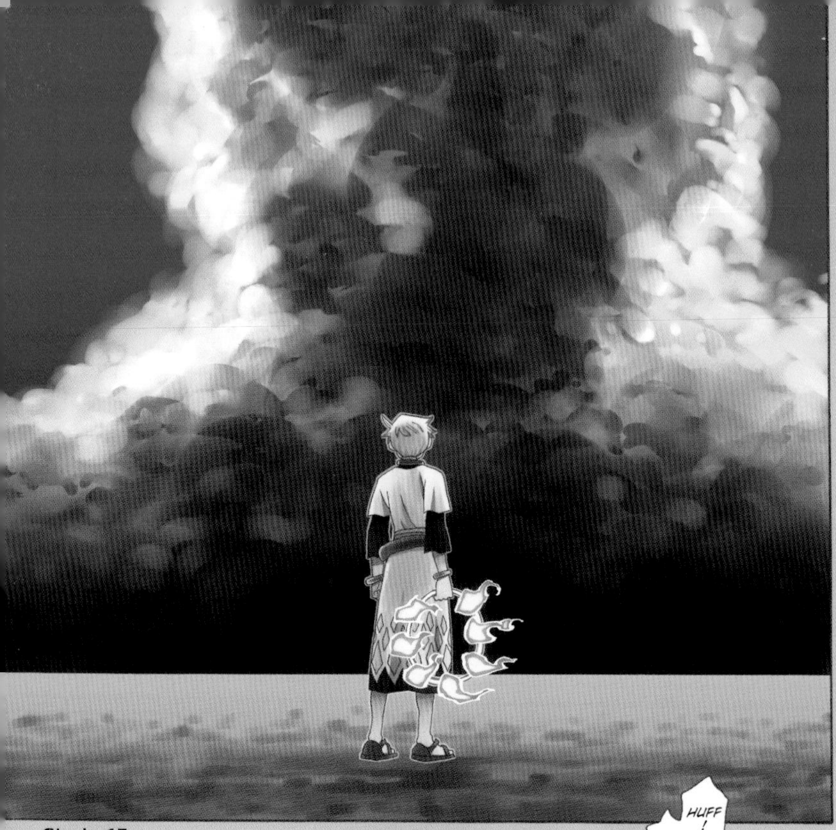

Circle 15

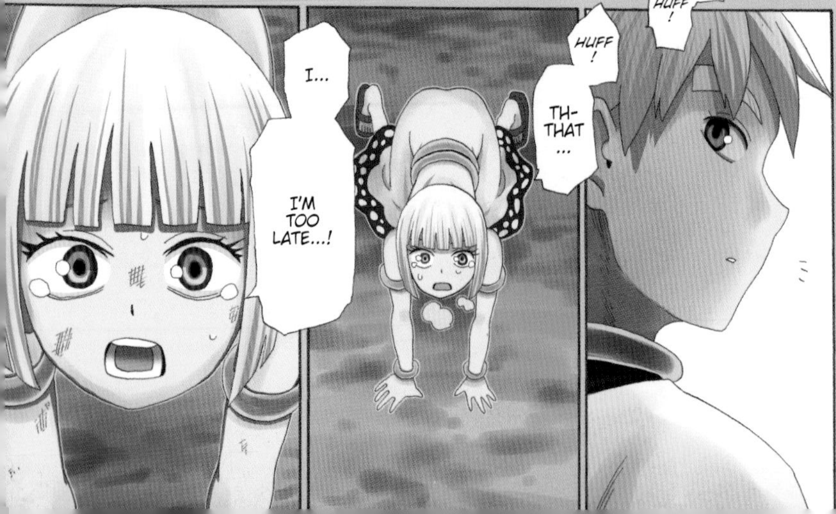
HUFF!
HUFF!
HUFF!
TH-THAT...
I...
I'M TOO LATE...!